To Glen and Millie

In memory of our UN years

with all best wishes

Jean

AFICS meeting, 15 May 1996

JOURNEYS FOR A BETTER WORLD

A Personal Adventure in War and Peace

An Inside Story of the United Nations by One of Its First Senior Officials

Jean Richardot

Foreword by
Sir Brian Urquhart

UNIVERSITY
PRESS OF
AMERICA

Lanham • New York • London

Copyright © 1994 by
University Press of America® Inc.
4720 Boston Way
Lanham, Maryland 20706

3 Henrietta Street
London WC2E 8LU England

All rights reserved
Printed in the United States of America
British Cataloging in Publication Information Available

All "famous quotations" in the title and appendix can be found in *Planethood,* by Benjamin B. Ferencz and Ken Keys, Jr. (Coos Bay, Oregon: Loveline Books, 1991).

Joan Anstee is quoted with her permission.

Enzo de Chetelat is quoted with permission from his daughter.

Richard Gardner is quoted with his permission.

Cover design: Nancy Richardot Tenney.

Library of Congress Cataloging-in-Publication Data

Richardot, Jean.
Journeys for a better world : a personal adventure in war and peace : an inside story of the United Nations by one of its first senior officials / Jean Richardot.
p.   cm.
1. United Nations—History. 2. United Nations—Officials and employees—Biography. 3. Richardot, Jean. I. Title.
JX1977.R514   1993   341.23'24'092—dc20   93–48958 CIP
[B]

ISBN 0–8191–9381–X (cloth : alk. paper)
ISBN 0–8191–9382–8 (pbk. : alk. paper)

 The paper used in this publication meets the minimum requirements of American National Standard for Information Sciences—Permanence of Paper for Printed Library Materials, ANSI Z39.48–1984.

Peace, if it ever exists, will not be based on the fear of war but on the love of peace. It will not be the abstaining from an act but the coming of a state of mind.

Julien Benda
French essayist and philosopher
1867-1936

With all my heart I believe that the world's present system of sovereign nations can lead only to barbarism, war and inhumanity.

Albert Einstein

Unless some effective supranational government can be set up and brought quickly into action, the prospects of peace and human progress are dark and doubtful.

Winston Churchill

To Amy, Andy, Ian, Sarah and Whitney

Acknowledgements

At the request of my daughters, Carole and Nancy, this book was started as the story of a UN family in the field. In the course of the writing, it turned into a work on the UN, its international civil service, and its role in the Cold War and the world of tomorrow.

I wish to thank my wife, Natalie, and my daughters for their constant support and help during the years we lived the story and as I wrote this book. I also thank Don and Elizabeth Manders for their invaluable assistance in editing and preparing the manuscript for publication.

Further, I am deeply grateful to Deborah Clifford, Jay Parini, Ron Powers, David Bain, Russel Leng, and John Clagett, all of Middlebury College and distinguished authors, who read all or parts of the manuscript and commented on it.

Finally, thanks go to Brian Urquhart, Robert Muller and Hans Janitschek of the United Nations for their most generous support.

Jean Richardot
Middlebury, Vt.
August, 1993

Contents

Dedication	*v*
Acknowledgements	*vii*
Contents	*ix*
Maps and Photos	*xi*
Foreword by Sir Brian Urquhart	*xiii*
Preface	*xv*
Part I The War to End All Wars and the Fragile Peace	*1*
Part II The Second World War: Fighting under Two Flags	*39*
Part III The UN Years at Turtle Bay	*109*
Part IV Six Missions to the Third World	*167*
Morocco: First Steps in Self-Reliance	*171*
Haiti: Mission Impossible? The Tragic Tale of a Fractured Country	*197*
Uganda: The Pearl of Africa Before and After Idi Amin	*231*
Cyprus: With the Blue Helmets	*259*
Jamaica: Out of Many, One People	*275*
Bénin: From Neo-Colonialism to Marxism-Leninism	*303*
Helping the Third World: An Overview	*327*
Part V At the Dawn of a New World Order	*333*
Epilogue	*351*
Appendix I: The UN System: United Nations Organs, Specialized Agencies and Special Programs	*357*
Appendix II: Highlights of UN History	*359*
Appendix III: Famous Quotes	*361*
Index	*363*
About the Author	*369*

Maps and Illustrations

Maps

World War I: A 400 Mile Trench Line	*after 38*
World War II: The Route of the 4th Armored Division during the Liberation of France	*before 39*
Morocco, Haiti, Uganda	*after 168*
Cyprus, Jamaica, Bénin	*before 169*

Illustrations

Assorted Photographs	*after 109*

Foreword

In his thirty years as a member of the United Nations Secretariat, Jean Richardot worked both in New York and in a number of developing countries. During this time he never lost sight, as bureaucrats sometimes do, of the basic function of the United Nations—helping human beings to live a better life. Wherever he was he made a point of remaining constantly in touch with everyday reality and with the life of the people of the country in which he was serving. This attitude illuminates his account of his experience as an international civil servant.

Experience of war was the motivation and the inspiration for Jean Richardot's international service. He was introduced to the horrors of war as a child in Eastern France in World War I. In World War II he served in the French Army in 1940, and in the U.S. Army in 1944. Experience of war has molded some of the best international servants of peace. The experience of disaster, aspiration, failure, and ultimate success is good breeding ground for the stamina and determination which are, and will be, required to make the United Nations work.

A great human experiment on a global scale can only succeed if its servants are animated by the conviction that the human race can and must overcome the perennial challenges that face it, and that it is the individual human being which really counts. In his pilgrimage through some of the world's more bewildering places, Jean Richardot never lost this conviction. His book is both a fascinating reminiscence and an inspiration for the future.

Sir Brian Urquhart
former Under Secretary-General of the United Nations
for Special Political Affairs

Preface

March 1988

Today, skiing in the Green Mountains of Vermont is pure delight for me. From January to March I enjoy the forest trails at Breadloaf, a mountain owned by Middlebury College covering many square miles of Addison County in west-central Vermont. I hear the gentle hiss of my skis in the tracks. I am alone. The woods are silent except for the occasional poof of snow falling from a ladened branch. The snow-covered pines, spruce, maple and birch lend the forest a fairyland aspect, with their trunks light grey, beige and dark umber. The firs shoot their fine conical shapes vertically toward the sky while their deciduous kin gracefully extend their naked branches in all directions to form a giant graphic before my eyes. With the foliage gone I can see the sky between the trees—today a beautiful blue. The sun shines gloriously, projecting grey shadows and lovely arabesques across the trail and the forest's white floor. There is solitude, but no feeling of loneliness. As I ski, lost in this kingdom of silence and beauty, I can dream and think at will, my mind wandering to many of the places where I once lived in the developing world.

I am struck, as I have been many times before, in contrasting my way of life in retirement in prosperous New England with the slums, the indescribable ghettos, cities, villages and rural settlements in which I worked with poverty, illness, malnutrition, hunger and death that assail millions in the Third World as they constantly struggle for survival. I ask myself, "Are these two worlds, ours and theirs, ever going to meet and make one world? Will we be able to avoid global destruction in a nuclear holocaust?" In 1988 it still is a question on the minds of so many who prayed for a dramatic reduction in nuclear weapons. The risk of annihilation, I know, is less threatening now with the fall of Communism, but there is still the danger of the proliferation of these weapons.

The second most important problem in the world today, along with environmental degradation, is what to do about the enormous gap in the standards of living between the developed and developing countries. The gap is so wide that, if not soon reduced, the world economy will be further disrupted and lead to more conflicts and wars. Can we reach a stage where better conditions for peace and a decent standard of living for most of the world's population can be attained? To do so, trust and confidence will be necessary among nations, along with a give-and-take, the willingness to reach suitable agreements, and the political will to take the necessary actions at a global level. This will take time, but I strongly believe it can be done.

* * *

I worked for thirty years as a senior member of the United Nations Secretariat, serving in New York and in several countries—Chile, Morocco, Haiti, Uganda, Jamaica, and Bénin—as advisor to the governments of those countries and as Director and Coordinator (Resident Representative, United Nations Development Program) of programs assisting their economic and social development. In 1964 I was a senior advisor to the General commanding the UN Peacekeeping Forces on Cyprus on non-military aspects of the conflict between the Greek and Turkish communities, negotiating agreements across the Nicosia "green line." I also worked for UNESCO and the International Labor Organization, and later for the U.S. Department of State in its Agency of International Development (USAID).

When I retired, my children asked me to write about my life across the world. One day, skiing at Breadloaf, I decided it might be useful to share my experiences with the younger generations. While mainly autobiographical, enabling more freedom, this book focuses on the importance of the United Nations and of the international civil service, and discusses some key aspects of UN work. It takes the readers inside the Secretariat at UN headquarters and in half a dozen Third World countries where the UN carries on important economic, social and humanitarian work, which I assess.

Books on the United Nations are often written by scholars—most of whom have not participated in the organization's inner workings—or by delegates of member states who focus on General Assembly debates, Security Council vetoes and violations of the UN Charter. Such books contribute outstandingly to the understanding of the workings and procedures of the UN, but they miss what, to me, represents the most satisfying work, the work done in the field, helping people directly. Those jobs were the most exciting and satisfying parts of my life—living day by day helping struggling nations understand and endeavor to solve their problems.

Today more than 40,000 international civil servants work for international agencies in more than 100 countries throughout the world. They are the closest to what might truly be called world citizens. All take oaths to neither seek nor follow instructions from any government—including their own. They work exclusively for the UN in the sole interest of the world community.

The work of these men and women deserves to be better known. Not only is there a high purpose for which they stand but also because now so many affairs affecting our daily lives are conducted multilaterally through such international organizations as the UN, its specialized agencies, the World Bank, the International Monetary Fund in a variety of fields—political, economic, social, environmental, scientific and technological—that we already live in a rudimentary global state. Multilateral, as opposed to bilateral, handling of international public affairs is bound to significantly expand in the future as the world becomes increasingly interdependent. This will require the services of an even greater number of men and women working not only with their national interests in mind but for the world as a whole.

This personal story, however, starts much earlier. I describe some of my early childhood experiences during World War I in a small village in Eastern France—where I first was introduced to the horrors of war—followed by stories of my education and then early professional years in Paris in the '30s during the fragile peace between the two wars and the failure of the League of Nations. I then describe my battlefield service in France in two armies during World War II.

These war experiences were indeed the prelude to and the reason for my joining the United Nations and for me they are necessarily a part of this book. History is a continuum. It explains the present, it sticks to us. We must never forget that the United Nations is the child of the Second World War, created from and shaped to abolish the scourge of war from the face of the earth, born of the realization that killing millions of people and destroying untold material wealth are senseless.

Living through this tragic period of history as a participant in and witness to some of its most crucial events affected me profoundly. It formed my character as a child and as a young adult as no other experience could have, and it shaped my resolve to devote my life to peace. It led me to the United Nations career that ultimately became the focus of my professional life.

This story also depicts some of my travels in the little-known exotic lands in which I served with the UN. They recall some of the important political events which were integral parts of my experiences and provide an accurate footnote to history.

August 1992

Four years have passed since I started to write this Preface and work on the story. Since 1988 changes in the world have been nothing short of revolutionary: we are no longer in the Cold War; except for China and Cuba, Communism is dead; the Soviet Union as such has ceased to exist; the two Germanies have reunited; Eastern European countries have rid themselves of their dictatorships. In 1988 the United States and Russia, convinced that the UN could be used in their interest, began to cooperate. In 1990, the UN in an unprecedented resolve, faced Iraq's aggression against Kuwait with a powerful coalition force from various UN member states led by the United States, drawing into full use its system of economic and military sanctions against an aggressor.

More recently, fierce ethnic battles have exploded in various parts of Eastern Europe. The UN intervention in Bosnia is fraught with difficulties and at the time of this writing its efforts have not yet been crowned with success. One can only hope that the resurgence of ethnic nationalism and fundamentalism is merely transitional and that stability will soon return to these lands. In assuming new functions in bringing humanitarian relief and restoring peace to these war-torn areas, the UN is breaking new ground. It has decided to create an international tribunal to judge dictators responsible for atrocities, genocide and other cirmes against humanity.

With the end of the Cold War, the global problems of the maintenance of peace have become more manageable. We are no longer faced with the holocaust of nuclear war. The present security problems are at present limited to local wars and internal conflicts which still endangers world peace. We must seriously envisage the creation of a permanent UN military force which would always be ready to deal with the menace of new wars any where in the world. Within the United Nations, more has changed. It has regained center stage, as Secretary-General Boutros Boutros Ghali recently stated:

> Never before has the UN seemed to be so popular with its member states; never have its services been requested with such frequency, not only in its traditional role of peacekeeping and peacemaking, but in new roles including providing assistance to democratic institutions in countries of the Third World. Although the crucial problem of adequately financing its operations has not been solved, today the UN has a clear agenda for peace. In the last two years the organization has launched 13 peacekeeping operations—as many as it had launched in the previous 47 years of its existence.

Yet, without adequate financing, an internal UN report acknowledges that it "lacks the technical, administrative and logistical tools required to implement effectively the peacekeeping agenda."[1] It is asked to do too much with too little.

---

1 Michaels, Marguerite, "Blue helmet blues." *Time* (15 November 1993) p. 66.

ERRATUM

Two sentences were omitted at the top of page xix. This error will be corrected in the second printing of the book.

> There remains also on the Agenda the frightening condition of the world's poor. We must be alarmed as we see how the gap between rich and poor has widened. In 1992, the richest 20% of the world's population, most of whom live in industrialized countries, receive at least 150 times more income than the poorest 20%, most of who live in underdeveloped countries.[2]

poorest 20%, most of whom live in underdeveloped countries.[1]

As we shall see in this book, it is crucially important to reduce this frightening gap. John E. Fobes, a former Deputy Director-General of UNESCO, pointed out that, "disparities and inequities are growing locally, regionally and within and among nations as well as between countries in this world. That and environmental degradation constitute the two most disruptive and destabilizing factors in the world today. the situation calls, among other things, for local, self-reliant remedies, not only for external measures, including assistance. The relatively poor are justified, moreover, in asking the affluent nations to reduce consumption and shift investment of their surplus to more worthy and productive development."

I have wanted, in the last part of this book, entitled "At the Dawn of a New World Order" to reflect on all these recent events, thus completing a comprehensive story of the UN from its inception to the present, explaining the role that the Organization can and should play in the world of tomorrow.

All these new developments have reinforced the *raison d'être* for this book. Perhaps my candid recounting of my path across a tumultuous world will spark desire and courage in others, particularly the young. I hope my life's adventure, as it constantly did for me, will inspire them, too, to work for peace. I dedicate it to my grandchildren, Amy, Andy, Ian, Sarah and Whitney. I will feel rewarded if, in reading it, they determine—in their own chosen ways—to further the cause of peace in the world.

* * *

In 1977, after various long-term assignments abroad, my wife, Natalie, and I returned from Haiti to the United States, seeking to divide our retirement between New Canaan, Connecticut and Middlebury, Vermont, and to live closer to our children and their families. We both found something special about Vermont, a sort of mystique, and opted to settle in Middlebury. Vermont is a beautiful state of meadows, gentle green mountains and the spectacular Lake Champlain. There is no smog. Billboards are not allowed along its highways. The population is small and, until recently, there were more cows than people. Most of all, for us, it is New England, a place where the people participate actively in community affairs: they still go to town meetings, an institution near dormant elsewhere. Vermont farmers are straight-talkers, frank and open. Many Middlebury College alumni have returned

---

1 United Nations Development Program, *Human Development Report* (New York: Oxford University Press, 1992).

to this pleasant town to retire in the shadow of their *alma mater*. Our friends number college faculty, lawyers, doctors, craftsmen, farmers, businessmen and members of the Audubon Society, a veritable cross-section of the state's population.

Natalie and I enjoy skiing in the winter and swimming in the summer. We paint. We don't mind Vermont's frigid winters, and when the "snowbirds" return to their homes in March we take off for Jamaica and Florida to enjoy the tropical Caribbean and the Gulf of Mexico. From time to time we fly to France to revisit the country in which I was raised and where all of my French relatives still live. Days pass rapidly, but I hope we still have a fair distance to run.

Our life is simple. On Sunday mornings we attend service at St. Stephen's, the stone Episcopal church on the Middlebury Green, near the Congregational Church whose gleaming steeple dominates the town landscape. At St. Stephen's one feels an extraordinary friendliness; its priest, Addison, is truly inspirational, and we have come to cherish the church and have attended faithfully for more than fifteen years.

It is tradition, according to the liturgy at St. Stephen's, to conduct one of the responsive Prayers of the People after the Nicene Creed. During one of these the priest says: *Father, we pray for your holy catholic church.* The people reply: *That we all may be one.* These last words always signify for me "the spirit of the United Nations, the One World," that preoccupied me that day a few years ago when I was cross-country skiing in the mountains at Breadloaf and decided to write this book.

My mother, who had come to live with us in Haiti, died at the age of 94 in Middlebury, barely six months after our arrival there in 1977. Her funeral at St. Stephen's was attended by the small group of friends we had then made in town. It was a touching service during which our daughter Carole, in a loving and short eulogy, explained to people who hardly knew Mother the type of person she had been and what a courageous life she had led.

As her casket left the church my thoughts focused on the distant time when she and my father had first settled in Manhattan, two years before my birth. I could picture life in their brownstone apartment and, in a flash, see the furniture and the blue drapes that my mother had often described to me. A larger image of New York in the first decade of our century passed through my mind: it was a period of relative innocence which preceded two monstrous World Wars and the Cold War which has dominated our times. For my parents, those two gentle years were followed by tragedy, but they were the beginning of my own journey, which has taken me from my French boyhood, through both World Wars, to a career in the United Nations, working for peace.

PART I

THE WAR TO END ALL WARS AND THE FRAGILE PEACE

PART I

THE WAR TO END ALL WARS AND THE FRAGILE PEACE

"The war to end all wars!" This expression was on all lips in France on November 11, 1918, the day the Armistice was signed. I was in school in Dasle, a village in the East of France near the front, when the bells of our little church started ringing jubilantly, announcing the end of World War I,[1]

Later, American General Omar N. Bradley under whom I served in World War II, observed that Armistice Day is a constant reminder that we won a war and lost a peace. It is both a tribute and an indictment. A tribute to men who died that their neighbors might live without fear of aggression. An indictment of those who lived and forfeited their chance for peace.[2] I was born on the threshold of that terrible four-year war and witnessed its impact on the people of Dasle.

New York 1910

In the year 1910, the first of December dawned dark and cold in New York City. My mother told me that just as I was born, at three in the afternoon, the sun came out. She took this for a good omen, but the following months proved it to be quite the contrary, as she was ill for some weeks and unable to feed me. When I was one year old, surgery was performed on my neck for the removal of glands that were feared to be tubercular. Eight months later, my father was rushed to hospital by horse-drawn ambulance and operated on for a duodenal ulcer. Perhaps the rough trip had shaken his body beyond endurance. Peritonitis developed, and he died on the operating table on May 26th, 1912.

The following year when my mother returned to France she took with her the box containing his ashes, intending to have these buried in the family plot. However,

---

1 In those days we called it The Great War.
2 Remarks by Omar N. Bradley, General of the United States Army, delivered in Boston, November 11, 1948.

cremation was not then practiced in France, and she was informed by a lawyer cousin that, since French law prohibited the private possession and transportation of human ashes, she might run into serious difficulties. On the return voyage to New York, she took the box to the upper deck of the ship and strew my father's ashes over the Atlantic.

At the time of my father's death, my mother's desolation had been compounded by my own absence. Two weeks earlier, my parents had asked my great-aunt Amélie, who had come to help my parents during my mother's illness, to take me with her to France; I was a delicate baby, and my parents felt that the air of eastern France would be better for me than that of New York City, particularly in the summer. My parents, who were French, had planned to follow Tante Amélie to France in order to visit their respective families and to bring me back with them to New York in the fall.

Tante Amélie and I were crossing the Atlantic on the *SS Bretagne*, a small ship of the French Line, on the day my father left us. When we arrived at Le Havre, she was given a telegram announcing his death. The shock of this terrible message must have been shattering. We went to spend a few days at my paternal grandfather's house near Paris before resuming our trip to the east of France, to the village of Dasle in the Pays de Montbéliard, in Franche Comté, a province north of Switzerland and south of Alsace, where Tante Amélie's sister lived.

My father's death completely changed my life. Had he lived, I would have gone back to the United States and been raised as an American. Instead I was reared in France. My mother had to stay in New York to earn a living, and I did not return to the United States until 1929, seventeen years later.

Both Protestants, my parents had met in New York around 1908 at the Huguenot Church of Manhattan on 16th Street. They fell in love and, after a short courtship, got married, and decided to make their life in America. Both, I am sure, had everything it takes to make their way successfully in the United States and live a happy life together.

I have often wondered by what mysterious force two perfect strangers like my father and mother, from the same country, were drawn together in a distant land at a given time and particular place, to a meeting that was to decide their fate. It is perhaps trivial to ask such a question, since millions of people meet every day for the first time, often with dramatic consequences for their futures. Are these meetings pure chance? Is there an unknown force that leads each of us from one event to another towards our destiny? Is our life predetermined? We cannot deny that chance is an enormous factor in each of our lives. This should not make us entirely fatalistic.

I, for one, believe that if you have a goal and work steadily toward it, you will likely reach it. As author Mary McCarthy put it: "Like many things in my life, it was largely a matter of will and drive that influenced me, a sense of duty to my own credo of self-reliance."

It must have been my father's love of adventure and his desire for attempting new things that drove him to the New World; like me he lacked the fear of the unknown. I suspect that, like me later, he sometimes took chances with his life. He came to America not because he needed to leave Europe, where he had started well, but because in the New World he would have the freedom of choice that he was seeking. I see that in myself.

Of course, I do not remember my father. The little I know of him was passed on to me by my mother and aunts. I still have a few photographs of him that I contemplate from time to time with pride. One, on a little stand in my bedroom, now is much faded. My father was holding me in his arms in front of a brownstone house in New York. Perhaps it was a Sunday morning after church. I had on a white woolen cap, and he, in a chesterfield overcoat and derby, looks elegant with his thin moustache. I also have a postcard-sized portrait of my parents and two others, and one of my father at age thirteen taken in the studio of a Paris photographer in front of a painted landscape. The last one shows Father with his parents earlier, in Brussels, my grandfather wearing a frock coat and a tall hat, and my grandmother, a beautiful woman, in a fur-trimmed outfit. Georges Bleyfus,[3] my father, was born in Brussels in 1883, the youngest of four children. He spent his early childhood in Brussels, where my grandfather, an avid French patriot from Alsace, was the representative of the French railroad interests. At twenty my father finished his formal education and moved to Dresden, in eastern Germany, to study singing. There a star-crossed romance disillusioned him, and he went to England where he taught French and German. I still have a brochure of St. Mary's College, an English "public school" which lists him as "Assistant Master, B. of Letters." From there he was lured to Winnipeg, Manitoba, by the promise of a free homestead from the Canadian government. In Winnipeg he contracted scarlet fever which left him too weak for the life of a farmer. Around 1908 he moved to New York City.

My mother was from the Pays de Montbéliard in Franche-Comté, part of a small pocket of Lutherans. Seeking to escape her stepfather, a stern disciplinarian, and a

---

3 As is often done in France, the name of my mother, Richardot, was added to my father's. During the war we had this legalized. My full name is therefore Jean-Georges Bleyfus-Richardot. Such a long name has created confusion and for short, especially in America, I am called simply Richardot.

broken heart, the result of being rejected by the aristocratic Catholic family of the young officer she wanted to marry, she followed a cousin to New York City.

After my father's death, she met the headmistress of the Spence School, who was looking for a French teacher. While my mother had a degree from the *École Normale de Montbéliard*, she had never taught, but she had a great deal of charm and Miss Spence hired her. It was a wonderful opportunity, as the Spence School was among the best and most select private girls' schools in New York. She taught the daughters of some of New York's wealthy and prominent families including Maude, the daughter of financier Otto Kahn, and Betty Bliss, daughter of banker and New York Metropolitan Opera Chairman Cornelius Bliss. She gave private lessons to his son Bobby, who also later headed the Metropolitan. She taught Marion Cartier, daughter of Fifth Avenue jeweler Pierre Cartier, as well as Caroline Prentice and Elizabeth and Barbara Whitmore, whom she loved dearly.

In addition to her classes at Spence, Mother gave private lessons, saving the money so she could spend the four months of summer vacation in France with me and Tante Amélie. She crossed the Atlantic many times, never hesitating during the First World War, despite the U-Boats. During the years of my childhood she endured the sacrifice of a hard separation, teaching French to support us. With great impatience she waited for June each year so we could be together again. She never remarried, although I know she had several opportunities to do so. In 1930 she retired to Paris after 16 years at the Spence School.

War and Innocence

Between 1912 and 1920, Tante Amélie and I lived in picturesque Dasle, not far from the town in which my mother had been born. The area was in the Belfort Gap, a natural passage used by both Germans and French to invade each other since the time of the Visigoths, who had come from the East. Dasle's inhabitants were mostly farmers, but, by the time we lived there, many of their sons had become factory workers employed by one of two area industrial complexes: Peugeot and Japy. Peugeot manufactured bicycles and cars and Japy an assortment of products such as household utensils and a nationally known typewriter, quite an innovation in those days.

Dasle contained only seven hundred people. Its houses, separated by orchards, were built on each side of its one road, which stretched about one mile, down a steep grade from Beaucourt, a town of 5,000 inhabitants, also in the Territory of Belfort, and to which many people from Dasle cycled or walked each day to work in the Japy factories. During the Franco-Prussian War (1866-1870), the defenders of

Belfort put up such a magnificent fight against the Germans that, despite tens of thousands of shells that bombarded its famous Château, the fortress did not surrender. The château was built on a high rock into which Frédérick-Auguste Bartholdi (1834-1904), an Alsatian and the sculptor of the Statue of Liberty, carved a colossal lion, a monumental bas-relief, his first masterpiece. Because its defenders had been so valiant, Belfort and its region, which were to have been annexed to Germany with Alsace, were retained as part of France.

Tante Amélie had a small apartment on the second floor of a three-story house owned by my mother's stepfather near the middle of the village where he was deputy mayor and the agent of the L'Abeille life insurance company. He had a Victrola, the only one in the village, with its large megaphone playing mainly patriotic marches such as *Sambre et Meuse*—his kind of music.

My recollections of the first years in Dasle are very sketchy. I slept in a big bed covered by a pink eiderdown spread. Tante Amélie warmed bricks in the kitchen stove or *bouillotes*, metal containers filled with hot water, wrapped them up in a cloth, and placed them at the foot of the bed to keep my feet warm all night. My room had a window facing the bed. When the moon shone, the branches of a pear tree reaching the second floor would project moving shadows, dancing crazily on the walls of the room, their shapes constantly changing with the wind. As a three- or four-year-old, the wind whistling in the trees convinced me that a man was climbing the wall outside, coming to strangle me.

We had only two bedrooms and a kitchen, with a large round dining room table where we took our meals. A kerosene lamp stood in the middle of the table, its two-foot pedestal throwing fairly good light. We ate supper around six o'clock. From the window my aunt would call me from my game of marbles at the side of the road with my playmates. I remember the small steaks and the thin *escalopes de veau*, veal cutlets that my aunt bought at the only butcher, M. Chevrolet, and broiled for me. They were so tasty.

Letters from my mother were written on pretty paper illustrated for children with colorful animals; nobody in France had writing paper like that. Mother also sent me long wool American knee-socks, which folded down below the knee, quite different from those of my friends. Because of that and because my mother lived in America, I felt different from my companions and was proud to be linked to that great country so far away.

In those days there was only one automobile in Dasle, a Peugeot, of course. It was owned by Émile Bourquin, one of our neighbors, a small industrialist who made spare parts for Peugeot. The day at age seven or eight when I fell from an apple tree and broke my left arm in two places—making my limb look strikingly like an "S"—Émile Bourquin drove me with my aunt to Beaucourt to see old Dr. Jung, who set the bone straight in a wooden splint well held by plaster. It was my first ride in an automobile.

When I was about four, one evening as we were having dinner, I was sure my father appeared to me. I heard a slight noise coming from the stairs in the semi-darkness, and I distinguished a human form passing. I felt it was the spirit of my father coming to greet me. His image, which slowly disappeared into complete darkness, stayed engraved in my mind for many years.

For me Dasle was a happy period in my life; I did not know what it was to live in the excitement and joy of a normal family, so I did not miss it. My great-aunt was very hard of hearing, but she was easy to live with and loved me. I do not remember an instance when I was taken to task. Tante Amélie was a good person and our neighbors loved her. If she taught me anything, it was tolerance and kindness towards others.

In the evenings during the summer, neighbors would gather on the other side of the road in front of the Ferciot's house. They would sit in a circle on a bench and chairs in front of the barn, a part of the main house. Under the eaves were several swallows' nests, and while the conversation carried on, the birds in the dim light darted swiftly above our heads, back and forth to their nests taking insects to their nestlings.

My friends and I delighted in building little *moulins* or windmills, which we set up in the middle of the current of the stream that flowed through the orchard behind the house. Made of two or three pieces of twigs tied with string and supported horizontally on a little wooden support, which was just a bigger twig, the system rested on two forked sticks, carefully selected from the branches of an apple tree nearby. The two forks were anchored between strong stones on the bed of the stream. It acted as a wheel and our little mill would start turning at a good clip. It was a small achievement, but this was enough to make the day for us. Several years later, I became quite adept at making my own kites and for a long time I had a passion for flying them.

Uncle Lucien, my father's brother, who became a noted post-impressionist landscape painter after the war, and his wife, Aunt Jeanne, came from Paris to see us twice when we lived in Dasle. They took an interest in me; they had no children and would like to have had me, but my mother kept that responsibility for herself. My uncle later bought me my first bicycle as a reward for passing, at 12 years old, the *Certificat d'Études Primaires* in Beaucourt. It was a beautiful black Peugeot with varnished wooden mudguards.

I was not yet four when, on June 28th, 1914, a young Serbian nationalist fanatic in Sarajevo, Bosnia, assassinated Archduke Ferdinand, heir to the Hapsburg throne. Shortly after the slaying, Austria-Hungary declared war on Serbia, and Russia mobilized against Austria-Hungary. Germany, which was seeking a motive to start a war, sent an ultimatum to Russia demanding that it revoke its mobilization order. Looking also to create a war with France, Germany sent the French an ultimatum demanding that France remain neutral in the conflict and hand over the strongholds of Verdun and Toul. The French rejected this outrageous demand and the same day ordered general mobilization. On August 3, Germany declared war on France. Great Britain declared war on Germany the next day when Germany invaded Belgium, violating Belgian neutrality guaranteed by the Great Powers and the Reich.

Europe was at war. Frenchmen in every town and village without hesitation responded to defend the mother country. Dasle was no exception. A group of young men, back from the *conseil de révision* (draft board) held in Audincourt, the next town, paraded the village streets with their tricolor cockades and bright ribbons on their chests inscribed *Bon pour le service*—to which some had added for fun *Bon pour les filles*. They all left for the front singing. Throughout the war, various military units passed by on the road in front of our house going east to the front in Alsace.

I remember quite a number of scenes from the war, more than a series of events. There was the incursion of a patrol of Uhlans, the German reconnaissance cavalry. They had ventured from Alsace into our no-man's land. They stayed only a few hours, but I will always remember them, riding on tall beautiful horses, wearing shining spiked helmets and carrying lances.

Later we garrisoned Italian troops who wore almond green uniforms with one metal star sewn on each side of their tunic collars. They had set up a clinic in the basement of my grandfather's house and I can still smell the chloroform they used and see the soiled bandages lying around, discarded without much care.

Several times we had various French units bivouacking in the village, each house a billet for the officers, the men sleeping in the barns. The Dasle people made friends with many of these *poilus* from various parts of France with their own regional accents so strange to us—what a change in our lives and what a pleasure to welcome them. I often watched the soldiers doing their daily chores, taking care of their weapons and horses. One time we had a whole cavalry regiment bivouacking behind the church. On another occasion there were African troops, which I found fascinating, especially the Zouaves and the Senegalese. A tall, magnificent Senegalese was billeted in a barn close to our house. I talked to him several times, and he showed me his combat knife and some pieces of his gear, which he carefully polished each morning. I had never seen black men before.

One morning he was taken away by the military police and thrown into the basement at the rear of the church, which had bars on its only little window and had been converted into a military prison. I was very sorry for him. What had he done? My pals and I could not understand why he had been jailed, but through the iron bars of the window we could look at him. He would come forward and talk to us in a jargon we could not understand. We marveled at how his brown skin shone against the deep shadows of the room. He tried to tell us he had been arrested wrongly; then he would break into tears.

There was never a battle in Dasle, but the front, at times an important one in the war, was less than thirty miles from us in the Vosges mountains. We were only a place of transit for the troops going to the front, but there was, from time to time, plenty of movement in our village. I saw 75mm guns, the war revelation—a deadly little cannon—and pieces of 155mm heavy artillery, pulled by horses, which left us in awe. By the end of the war we were seeing long convoys of trucks, as the French Army became more and more motorized.

When everything seemed calm in our sector and in Paris at the beginning of the war, I remember an incident which could have been disastrous for my great-aunt and me. At the invitation of my cousins in Enghien-les-Bains, near Paris, we left Dasle for a few week' visit, taking the train from Belfort not knowing that the situation had dramatically changed at the front. Just a few days before, a rapid German offensive had advanced the front dangerously close to Paris. Tante Amélie and I came near to being trapped in the Battle of the Marne. The train, which was passing south of Coulommiers, was abruptly stopped in the countryside for several days awaiting the outcome of the battle, one of the war's most decisive.

The compartment in which we were traveling was full of soldiers returning from leave to join their units, dressed in blue coats and red trousers, the French Army colors (the blue-grey uniform became *de rigueur* shortly after). They jumped from the train and crossed fields to reach distant farms and bring back cheese, milk, bread and fruit. We all were in the dark about how the battle was going, wondering whether we would reach our destinations or be taken prisoners by the Germans. The faces of all our civilian companions showed their anxiety, but Tante Amélie through all circumstances remained the optimist.

The Allies had suffered a number of shattering defeats in the north of France after the Germans had advanced their columns through Belgium, forcing the French

Fifth Army and the British Expeditionary Force (BEF) to retreat to the east of Paris after only one month of operations. France sat on the brink of losing the war. Then the "miracle of the Marne" occurred as our train waited; the battle was won and Paris saved.

We won thanks to the unflagging spirit of Marshal Joffre, the greatest general of the war and to General Gallieni, who saved the day in this desperate situation. This remarkable General, retired from field service because of ill health, had become the military governor of Paris—the Government had already left the capital for refuge in Bordeaux. Through his own sources of information Gallieni learned that the south flank of the German columns was open, just as the enemy was preparing to deal the fatal blow in the direction of the capital.

The retreating and discouraged BEF and the Fifth Army were in crucial positions just south of the Marne River, a short distance from our train. On September 7th Gallieni was able to convince Joffre and the British to halt their retreat and attack the Germans where the gap appeared, in the flank of the German armies of von Kluck and von Bulow. French troops poured into the battle, and a number of severe attacks and counter-attacks followed. The battle remained undecided into the next day. On September 9th, Gallieni requisitioned hundreds of taxis, buses and trucks on the streets of the capital to dispatch 6,000 troops to the threatened French positions—the taxis made the trip between Paris and the front lines twice during the night, carrying much-needed reinforcements.

This brilliant and unheard-of maneuver—"The Taxis of the Marne"—enabled the French Sixth Army of General Maunoury to win the battle. The Germans retreated to the Aisne River and by September 13th the battle had died down. The capital was saved. Our train started to move and several weeks after leaving to visit our cousins we returned safely to Dasle.

In the Shadow of the Trench War

The Trench War lasted almost the entire four years. The casualties were enormous, fighting and living conditions unbearable, and thousands of Allied and German soldiers alike died in it. Most of the troops passing through Dasle had been going east to the trenches in the south of Alsace.

Every day in Dasle, as in every village and town in the country, families were haunted by fear that a gendarme would knock at the door bearing the official announcement that a husband or son had been killed or wounded. I remember that the conversations of adults mostly centered on the trenches, talking about the last letter received from the front from which they gradually learned of the humanly degrading horrors of life and war in the trenches—the newspapers, subject to strict censorship, printed only the communiqués of the War Office, which stressed the victories rather than the hardship of the troops as the government sought to bolster national morale.

We learned the somber truth from the soldiers on leave or the flood of wounded who filled the hospitals. Winter and summer the men lived and fought in the trenches. During artillery bombardments they slept in heavily roofed primitive underground shelters they had built themselves with logs. They stayed there weeks at a time without relief. In the long rainy season of the north of France they waded knee deep in mud and water, waiting for the assault, their clothes heavily muddied. The air they breathed was foul. The food was poor, consisting of dry rations and the classic cans of dried beef that the French *poilus* had labeled *boîtes de singe* (monkey meat). Hot food from the *cuisines roulantes* or *popotes* (kitchens on wheels) often could not reach the front in time because of frequent bombardments. Lice plagued everyone who could not frequently and regularly get to the delousing stations well behind the lines.

Descriptions of the fighting by two men who came to Dasle on leave frightened me. Despite my young age, these stories left an indelible impression on me. I was considerably saddened that men had to go to war since I understood clearly, even in these early days, the horrors of war, wondering why men had to kill and maim each other so wastefully.

Later, at about age 14, I was better able to understand the monstrousness of fighting in the trenches. I spent two weeks in hospital for an appendectomy. The man in the next bed, who lived in a town not far from us, was about 40, a veteran. In the war as an infantryman, he had been gassed during the battle of Douaumont. His lungs had been seriously damaged by phosgene gas and the doctors could not promise him a long life since his condition ten years after the incident had improved little. I learned from him about the horrors of the fighting in the trenches. He talked to me at length about it, stopping from time to time to catch his breath and check his coughing. At times he panted. The nurse would come and tell him to rest, yet he felt under some strange compulsion to continue talking as soon as she had left the room.

The vision of those terrible days had never left him; he told me of the ways the *poilus* had had to fight across no-man's land. "Jean," he said, "believe me. When the order came to attack it took tremendous guts to leap over the parapets of our trenches, which often were already under heavy machine-gun fire. We had to crawl across an open field, its trees decapitated by artillery shells, all vegetation destroyed.

The landscape, full of bomb craters, looked like the face of the moon."

He said that the night before the attack a small patrol of volunteers was sent to cut the rolls of barbed wire barring the approach of the enemy opposite. He had been on several of these suicide missions and had won two *Croix de Guerre* with palms. Enemy flares would suddenly illuminate the sky, and the entire battlefield became as visible as if it were daylight. Then the German machine guns would start cracking, mowing down everything that moved.

"One night," he said, "when we were pinned down for hours in a shellhole, I thought we would never come out alive. The next combat phase," he added, "was the fiercest of all—the attack on the German trenches facing us, sometimes with a whole company or even a regiment. We had to throw grenades into the trench to kill or chase out the enemy. Sometimes the *Boches* ran to the rear, but more often we were forced to leap into the trench for hand-to-hand combat using bayonets and knives."

I could not imagine a more awful way to kill or be killed. Lying in my bed, deeply distressed, I contemplated my brave companion, his life wasted, he exhausted at the least effort. Had it been worth it? I tried to understand why this terrible war had lasted four years, why it could not have been avoided in the first place.

Two days later my companion told me about another somber episode from the Great War—the mutinies. These occurred in 1916, when the morale of some of the French troops was dangerously low. They were kept secret by the government to preserve civilian morale and to prevent the defection of a large part of the army that might have meant the defeat of France. Soldiers in both the Allied and German armies had inflicted injuries on themselves deliberately to cause their removal from the trenches. During gas attacks, the men usually had ten to twenty seconds to don their masks before the mustard cloud reached them. For some the temptation was there to take a little whiff of the gas then report sick. Some also would shoot themselves in the hand or foot, others sleep uncovered, hoping to catch pneumonia. My hospital room companion had seen men go berserk and leap over the parapet into no-man's land, running towards the enemy. Some were shell-shocked. Casualties were innumerable.

By that time various French political groups were urging an end to the carnage. Pacifist pamphlets circulated in Paris and the provinces. The mutinies had started at the front in August, the soldiers complaining about the food and the lack of medical treatment: the hospitals were coping with ten times more wounded than expected. The soldiers also complained about shirkers and goldbricks making money behind the lines while they were being killed at the front. The morale was so low that some divisions refused to go over the parapets.

By mid-summer, apparently, half of the French Army was in rebellion. The men said they were willing to continue to fight a defensive war but would no longer take part in offensives, and they wanted negotiations for an armistice. Fortunately their commander, General Pétain, was able to quickly calm the rebellion by severely punishing its leaders at the front and improving the quality and regularity of meals and transportation, making it possible for soldiers to spend their leaves at home.

The Battle of Verdun produced the greatest carnage in history. Hundreds of thousands of men died in that battle alone. The battle's furious, incessant bombardments, the heaviest of the war, wiped out entire villages. The Germans shot artillery shells containing phosgene gas, ten times more deadly than the mustard used at Ypres at the war's beginning. Even we children were deeply aware of Verdun's horror.

It all started on February 25th, 1916, when the fort of Douaumont fell; I was told that a single German Army company took it unopposed, as all the French soldiers in the fort had been killed. The fall of Douaumont was a blow to French pride and a great victory for the Germans, but the battle was not over. Pétain took command to stop the German advance. He brought in reinforcements by train and motor transport: 190,000 men fought to prevent a road, the *Voie sacrée*, from falling into enemy hands. Throughout France the message of Verdun—"*Ils ne passeront pas!*" (They shall not pass!)—was repeated lip to lip; it electrified the nation: the road was never surrendered and Verdun remained in French hands. Finally, the French prevailed after an immense sacrifice in terms of men and materials, and the battle of Verdun ended. Pétain became a great hero.[4]

By the end of that year the war had taken a new turn; all of France awaited the arrival of the Americans in 1917, spurring hope for a rapid conclusion of the hostilities. In Dasle, as in every French town and village, morale slowly improved as 1917 and 1918 brought the great Allied offensive, reinforced by American troops and equipment. The day the Armistice was signed, we were sent home from school. What marvelous rejoicing there was by everyone in Dasle and in the whole country.

Quite a number of men from Dasle had been killed in that monstrous war; several of my friends at school had lost their fathers and had become *pupilles de la nation* (wards of the state). The people of Dasle grieved deeply; never in the history of mankind had a war cost so much in human life and suffering. France was literally "blood drained." Four and a half million people became war casualties, with close

---

4 He subsequently headed the Vichy government in the Second World War and was declared a traitor to the cause of France.

to 1.4 million killed in action. Counting missing in action and prisoners of war, this accounted for nearly 75 percent of the French forces originally drafted for the war. The British incurred three million casualties—35 percent of the total mobilized—with 900,000 killed in action. American casualties totaled 350,000 men, or eight percent of the U.S. Expeditionary Corps, with 126,000 killed in action. The Germans lost two million men on all fronts.

To add to the global trauma, a great influenza epidemic killed millions in Europe in 1918, and it did not spare Dasle. All we had to protect ourselves were the prescribed little camphor balls our schoolmasters had told us to keep rolled up in our handkerchiefs, through which we were meant to breathe. Each day, some of our little friends would miss school because they had caught the often-fatal and terrible *grippe espagnole*, the Spanish flu, which a year later paid an equally devastating visit to North America. Many children and adults in fact died in Dasle that year.

I was not yet ten when we moved to Beaucourt, a few miles away. My great-aunt had friends there, Georges and Lucie Parrot, from Montbéliard. The Parrots had lived many years in Hanoi, Tonkin, now Vietnam, where Georges was an official of the customs administration. Having traveled the world, they were a source of fascinating conversations—I learned something about the Asian world from them; Madame Parrot loved my mother and me. After I left for boarding school at age 14, I liked to visit her to chat during the holidays.

After my *Certificat d'Études Primaires*, an exam which all boys and girls in France usually take at 12 years of age, at the end of grammar school, I continued for two years in Beaucourt at the *Cours complémentaire*, a vocational school which taught mathematics and industrial design and gave practical training in using simple machinery, lathes, drill presses, etc. At the workshop, we learned to make well-calibrated and -adjusted metal pieces. I was only average in that precise work. I knew right away that I was not going to become a good metal worker, expert in using my hands; too often I knocked my fingers with my hammer. I was better at reading blueprints and in industrial design. I went then to the *École Professionnelle de l'Est* (EPE) in Nancy, the lovely capital of Lorraine, with a four-year course in electrical and mechanical engineering, but I did not like it and subsequently enrolled, in 1926, in the *Lycée Victor Hugo* in Besançon, to acquire a liberal arts education.

Adolescence: a World of Discovery

Although I was a boarder at the Lycée (more than half the students lived in town with their families) and consequently had little freedom, I was much happier than at EPE. The studies were much more to my liking. We had permission to go to town on Thursdays, and enjoyed its amenities. Besançon was, and still is, a cultural city, the capital of Franche-Comté and France's watchmaking center. It had lovely terraced cafés in squares planted with chestnut trees. These cafés had their own string quartets which gave concerts before dinner and in the evenings. I liked the atmosphere of dignified relaxation and the graceful style of the many 17th- and 18th-century private dwellings. Besançon had its own university; it also had a spa with a lovely casino on the banks of the Doubs River and, as many other French provincial cities, its resident theater troupe, which performed several times a week. I became acquainted with operas and operettas, as it was easy for the Lycée students to obtain tickets. I enjoyed Besançon for three years while studying for my baccalaureate.

There are important differences between the French Baccalaureate and the U.S. Bachelor of Arts or Bachelor of Science degree. The normal age for completing studies at a French Lycée and getting the baccalaureate is eighteen years of age. Students are supposed to have completed their general education by then and are ready to enter university as graduate students in letters, languages, philosophy, sciences, etc., leading to a *licence* (master's degree) or a specialized professional school for training as lawyers, doctors, architects, engineers and so on. By contrast, American students at the same age are just completing high school and entering undergraduate college or university.

I agree with my friend and former colleague, Robert Muller, a former Assistant Secretary General of the United Nations, himself a product of French education, that the French Lycée is a marvelous institution which forms, by the age of eighteen, human beings equipped with the necessary knowledge, philosophy and mental means to face life and thus ready to begin specialization at university or in other institutions of higher learning. The Lycée in Muller's and my time produced happy and balanced individuals, but in my view perhaps with too much emphasis on knowledge and intelligence at the expense of developing a sense of service to the community as it is emphasized in American schools. Muller also points out that the great axiom of French education was a philosophy of moderation, balance and personal equilibrium with suspicion for all extremes. He concludes that the "golden rule of the middle" which made France a happy and much admired country in the world also rendered it extremely vulnerable to the Nazis in 1940 as thousands of Frenchmen refused to accept the idea of war.[5]

Grandfather's Love For Alsace
During my studies at the Lycée I had the opportunity to visit my paternal grandfather

---

[5] Robert Muller, *What War Taught Me About Peace*. (New York: Doubleday, 1985).

in Nice. He wrote me from time to time in his well-scripted handwriting, although nearing the advanced age of 90 at which he died. I always wanted to learn more about him and about Strasbourg, the city where he was born in 1840, so my aunts Jeanne and Lucie filled me in on that. My grandfather's story illustrates the mentality of the people of France when I was growing up.

Raised and educated there, he spoke French and German fluently. Conscripted into the French Army at nineteen, he won a medal for valor in the Italian campaign, when Napoleon III won the great battle of Solferino against the Austrians in 1859. My aunt gave me a beautifully hand-scripted diploma he had received on that occasion, now much yellowed by time. Other military papers showed that he had served seven years in the Army as a conscript. For men in those days this was, I think, an enormous sacrifice. On his return to Strasbourg after such extraordinarily long service in several French garrison towns, he married Fanny Fritsch and settled in the residential district of Strasbourg called La Robertsau.

In Strasbourg, according to Tante Lucie, my grandfather lived the life of a well-off gentleman. He did not have to work for a living. He was well-versed in French culture and became a poet, publishing his works under the pen name Léon Harold. I still own some of his published poems and a portfolio containing more than a hundred poems ready for publication. Truly a gifted poet, he handled verse elegantly. His style resembled that of Lamartine, whom Grandfather greatly admired for his immense talent as a romantic poet and for his role as a politician during the historic events of 1848. My grandfather's poems sang of the beauty of Alsace and the glory of France. One can imagine how he must have suffered when France lost Alsace after the stinging defeat and shameful surrender of the French Army by General MacMahon at Sedan in 1871.

Strasbourg, which had greatly suffered from the Franco-Prussian War, had offered magnificent resistance to the enemy, but it was now over. For my grandfather it was intolerable to think of living under German boots. Shortly after the defeat he left Alsace to settle in Paris, leaving behind everything he owned.

I admired my grandfather, who despite a good life in Alsace had the courage to forsake forever the country he loved. Fortunately three of his children were later born in the Paris area and my father in Brussels, sparing them the difficulties endured by those who stayed. In France he was extremely active in the newly-created *Société des Alsaciens-Lorrains de France*, as were thousands of his compatriots who had also left their homes and resettled in France. In 1901, he published a poem entitled *Retour en Alsace*, which was considered admirable by the President of the Society and was sold all over France, the proceeds going toward construction of a national monument honoring the Alsatians and the people of Lorraine who had gone to France after the defeat of 1871 rather than staying under the Germans. The poem was composed with direct and tender elegance and the heartfelt desire of a native son for an early return of Alsace to France. The first verse translates:

> *Alsace, O my country, lovely jewel of France*
> *I come to see, at last, the place where I was born*
> *In the shade of your woods, I evoke my childhood,*
> *My fortunate past.*

In 1981, I attended an international Seminar on Human Rights in Strasbourg. While there I visited the European Parliament located close to the Robertsau, where my family had lived. I would have liked to have been able to discover the house in which they resided, which probably still exists. To find it, if at all possible, would have required considerable time and research; thus I had to abandon the idea.

During that visit I could see that the mentality of the people had changed drastically. Until the end of World War II, the French hated the Germans and vice-versa. For both countries Alsace had been a key stake in both World Wars, causing the deaths of millions and untold material losses. Happily those days are over. The two nations are at peace and actively working together toward a unification of Europe, and Strasbourg is the seat of the European Parliament. They have friendly relations and their leaders discuss common problems in the most cordial manner. How I wish my grandfather had been able to visit his dear city with me, and realize the progress that has been achieved.

How things had changed since my days in grammar school in Dasle during the First World War, reading patriotic stories about lost Alsace. The problem of loyalty felt by the Alsatian people had been tragic during the period of German occupation between 1871 and the end of the First World War. Many Alsatian families were divided by opposing allegiances as the men were called to serve in the German Army. Most felt they could do no more than accept the call; others attempted to desert by escaping to France across the Vosges border.

I will always remember the novel *Les Oberlé* by René Bazin of the *Académie française*, one of the most popular French writers at the turn of the century when the country experienced an intense nationalism. Most French children knew the passage in this famous novel in which a young man, Jean Oberlé, the hero, not wanting to serve in the German Army, made a dramatic escape to France from his village across the mountains, at the risk of being shot as a deserter. Despite being pursued through the forest and wounded by a German forester's bullet, he succeeded in reaching French soil. His uncle Ulrich helped him escape by drawing his pursuers in another direction, risking his own arrest. Found by the French Guard, lying in a ditch, Jean was taken to the French village of Masevaux. Free at last, and in the country he loved, he was ready to enlist in the French Army.

Throughout Alsace, brothers grew estranged, one obeying the law of his legal country, Germany, the other answering his heart's call to France. Mothers implored that if they must separate, they do so peacefully and respectfully. Most brothers hoped not to end up in battle shooting at each other.

When my grandfather settled in Paris in 1871 the railroads were in full development. This new industry needed new energies. He was fortunate to find a position with a company called *Les Chemins de Fer de l'Est*, one of the four largest railroad networks in France, later to merge to form the *Société Nationale des Chemins de Fer* (SNCF), a government monopoly.

A hard worker who was always taking initiatives, he set up a system for the classification of freight, and soon became head of a division at national headquarters in Paris. Later he was selected as the company representative in Belgium and the Netherlands. The family lived in Brussels for a number of years. Back in France, at 55, the early age of compulsory retirement in the railroads, he was pensioned and settled in Nice on the French Riviera, where he died in 1930 at age 90. In Nice he applied his sharp analytical mind to developing *martingales*, systems to win at the Monte Carlo roulette tables. According to Tante Lucie, he never gambled, but only carefully observed the games in the casino salons.

Except for that first stop at his home near Paris on my way to Dasle in 1912, I didn't visit my grandfather until 1925. He gave me a small roulette wheel in beautifully polished mahogany, a miniature of those used in the Monte Carlo salons.

It was not an easy period for him. After the First World War the franc lost much of its purchasing power, and pensions were not indexed to the cost of living as they are today. There came a time when my grandfather had to count every *sou* as did all Frenchmen on fixed incomes. He lived in a pleasant flat opening in the rear on an inside garden in one of the first tall apartment buildings in Nice at the turn of the century. It had an elevator and was pretentiously called *Palais de France*. As the rent could not be increased, the landlords stopped making even the most elementary repairs and these had to be made at the occupant's expense. When I went to Nice, the apartment, otherwise very nicely furnished, had not been painted for years, as was the case with most apartments in France in the post-war years. Dressed in a brown gown with velvet lapels, his back curved and looking very old, my grandfather appeared to me as belonging to the preceding century. Unable to go out, he spent most of his time in bed. He was formal, calling me, at times, *Monsieur* instead of Jean, using *vous* instead of *tu*, addressing me in a friendly way, but pretty much as a member of a high bourgeois family would have addressed a distant relative during the monarchy in the 19th century. He was almost too weak to carry on much of a conversation and perhaps he was a little confused. I am sure, however, he was glad to see his only grandson, my only visit since I was a baby.

A Cruise from New York to the Mediterranean and French North Africa

In the Fall of 1929 I returned to the country of my birth for the first time since my father's death in 1912. My mother intended to spend one more year in New York and then retire to France, and asked me to join her for one year to see if I would like living with her in New York.

We boarded the elegant, small, *SS de Grasse* of the French Line at Le Havre and arrived in New York just after the stock market crashed. Traveling on my American passport, I passed through immigration before she did, as she was still French and was in the line of non-American citizens. I was asked by the authorities if I had enough funds to survive in New York or expected to find work. My English still was most hesitant, but I answered as best I could. My mother started her last year of teaching. She lost part of her savings in the Stock Market crash—the broker who had taken care of her account had lost his personal assets and committed suicide by jumping from the window of his Wall Street office—but she was tired out and decided not to continue teaching to try to recoup her losses.

I had made arrangements before leaving to take correspondence courses from a French school in Paris, to prepare for the very competitive entrance examination to the *École des Hautes Études Commerciales* (HEC) in Paris, the best graduate school of business administration in France. This was a most unusual and difficult way to prepare for such an exam, but the only one at my disposal save staying in Paris.

The best use of my time in New York was first to improve my English by taking courses at the School of General Studies at Columbia University. There, unfortunately, I met mostly foreigners. As my mother was very busy, I met few Americans through her and thus missed opportunities to acquire a thorough knowledge of the people. There was little for me to do during the day except ride the subway between Columbia and the apartment my mother had rented on East 54th Street, near Lexington Avenue, in an old building which eventually housed the glamorous El Morocco nightclub.

During that winter I also did an enormous amount of walking in the streets of Manhattan. I went to the movies many times, and often to Radio City Music Hall.

After a few months of this regimen I started to dislike New York of which, I realized, I knew only the surface. Feeling somewhat alien in the country of my birth, I was not at all convinced I should try to settle there.

The father of one of my mother's pupils at Spence wanted to brush up on his French and read *Les Miserables* in the original French. He asked me to read this long novel with him, and for this paid me the royal fee of four dollars per lesson. After a few months I had saved enough money to book myself tourist class on a cruise on the *SS France*, returning to Europe via Spain, North Africa, Gibraltar and Naples. From there I planned to visit my cousins, Émile and Angèle Richardot in Belfort and cram for my entrance exam to HEC, which was scheduled for Paris in June 1930.

This was a wonderful way to return to France before resuming my studies. It also was my first extended trip alone and, looking back, it was a memorable adventure visiting ports in Spain, Gibraltar, and French North Africa. It was the only time in my life that I kept a diary—written in French in a little leatherbound book a friend gave me before sailing. Recently I found it in a trunk. It is obvious that these notes are the reflections of a 19-year-old, written with all the enthusiasm of a young world traveler—the trip greatly enlarged my horizons since colonial North Africa was my first encounter with what we later called the Third World in which I've spent much of my adult life serving under the UN banner. Little did I know then that I would come back to North Africa's shores twenty-seven years later, 1957-58, to work for the United Nations in Morocco, and later on a short mission to Algeria and Tunisia, a part of the world which so deeply impressed me in my youth.

I finally landed in Genoa, but I had to get to Belfort as soon as possible. Arriving there by train, I had linked two cities of the world which owned Bartholdi masterpieces—the Statue of Liberty and the Lion of Belfort. I spent a month with my Richardot cousins, brushing up on my entrance examination for the HEC, to be held in Paris in June. Unfortunately, I failed by two points.

Two Summers in Spain and the Civil War

My first visit to Spain was to Burgos, the ancient capital of Castille, during the summer of 1931. I was studying Spanish with a large group of European students, mostly French, at the well-known *Instituto* of that city where the best Castilian language was being taught.

We met many of its young people. In the evenings after our day at the Institute, as we were impatiently waiting for dinner—never served before 10 p.m.—we would take part in the promenade of the people on the Espolón, a long public garden in the center of town. Crowds of young men and women, teenagers and children, strolled back and forth along the park's main footpaths, laughing and exchanging jokes. We, the foreign students, joined them. We could exchange smiles and make eye contact with beautiful señoritas, exclaiming *"que guapa"* ("what a beauty") but attempted no flirting. Girls were closely chaperoned in Spain in those days. We also went on picnics in the lovely hills surrounding Burgos with groups of Spanish students. We enjoyed their friendship and the deep interest they showed in us.

In Burgos I befriended Roger Varin, a Frenchman from the HEC in Paris who was a class ahead of me. As I began this manuscript, after fifty-seven years, he remained my closest friend; he died in 1988. As a student billeted with Spanish families, I lived in a low-cost apartment building in a popular part of town, a walk-up with five floors to climb. Roger had been assigned a room at the home of an Army colonel well known in the city. After a few days, he showed me the marks on his arms and legs left by the bites of *chinches* (bed bugs) and implored me to ask Señor Ranero, my landlord, if he could share my room. I thought it a good idea, and the Raneros agreed to put another bed in the room. Señor Ranero was a blue-collar worker, living with his wife and three children in simple but very orderly surroundings. Our room was large and spotless.

We took our meals with the Raneros. The food, mostly abundant, was the regular Spanish fare with several courses, always including fish and meat and a very strong red wine poured from a wineskin hanging from the ceiling. I still remember its special tannin taste.

We grew to like the Raneros and their children very much because of their sincerity, their friendliness and their desire to help us in so many practical aspects of our new life. Every day we learned more about the workers' hard existence in Spain and the modesty of their incomes.

In 1936 during the Civil War under the Government of the Republic, I was a summer student in Spain again, this time at the International University of Santander in the Asturias, on the Gulf of Biscayne. Santander boasted a summer castle which had belonged to King Alfonso XIII. The Spanish Civil War had just begun. The monarchy had been abolished, the king had abdicated and the new government turned his summer palace into a summer university for foreign students. The organization of courses was an experiment that I have never seen duplicated. There were several hundred young men and women from various parts of Europe, with quite a contingent from France, and Spanish students, mostly from the bourgeoisie, in law, medicine and other disciplines. In addition, the government had invited a number of young grammar- and secondary-school teachers on scholarship, who backed the new republican government, many from the working class. The desire was to facilitate exchanges among foreign students of various nationalities and backgrounds, while teaching Spanish to the foreign students.

At the palace I shared the former bedroom of the Infante with another French student, Burin des Roziers, from the *École des Sciences Politiques* of Paris, with whom I got along famously. He later became a foreign service officer and, during World War II, the aide-de-camp and, later, Chief of Cabinet for General de Gaulle when he became President.

The professors at Santander came from Spanish and European universities. While the afternoons were devoted to teaching Spanish, morning classes covered the most diverse subjects taught by the guest professors in their native language. One could attend a lecture by Professor Barthelemy of the Sorbonne on public law, followed by a German expert on medieval civilization, followed by a professor of rural sociology of the University of Madrid on the newly enacted law on land reform promulgated by the socialist government for the province of Extremadura. In originality, the course which topped all others was that of Professor Auguste Piccard, a world famous Swiss scientist. He had been first to climb into the stratosphere in a balloon he had designed himself, carrying him 55,567 feet up in 1932. Later he had invented the bathyscaphe *Triestre* that descended 10,330 feet below the sea. Professor Piccard would tell us in French, in a large drawing room of the Palace, about his famous ascent, the innovative experiments he carried out, and the properties of the stratosphere.

Afterwards, before lunch, we would walk down through the gardens to take a dip in the ocean from a wharf where King Alfonso's yacht once moored. I can still see the long-legged Piccard with his bath towel around his neck, answering our questions. I took a picture of his lanky silhouette, always recognizable among the students, ready to tell us more about his adventures.

We had been there about three weeks when the province of Santander became more directly involved in the Civil War. At the time, certain provinces were entirely in the hands of Francisco Franco's forces. So was Burgos. Santander expected an attack every day from these forces and there was much agitation in town. One day I was with students and thousands of others, lined up along the avenues awaiting the passing of a parade of the Santander militia, which wanted to show its combat spirit to the populace. As they were approaching, preceded by a group of military policemen on motorcycles, the noise of shrieking sirens filled the air. I could not stand it and clamped my hands over my ears. Two *guardia civiles* who were nearby dashed toward me, interpreting my gesture as a sign of reprobation. They grabbed me and started yelling as if they recognized me as an enemy of the regime. They took me behind the row of spectators, roughing me up a little and asking me for my identification papers. I explained I was a foreign student at the University. Fortunately, my friends came to my rescue and, after a few minutes, I was released.

The Burgos militia did not reach Santander while we were there. But every night from the Palace we could hear gunshots and, the next morning, learn about the number of rightists who had been seized by the police, some thrown into the ocean from the high cliffs bordering the city.

The situation grew more critical by the day, and the University authorities felt it unsafe to continue our courses. Since riots were breaking out in various cities on the North Shore, the French students were evacuated on the French Navy cruiser *Émile Bertin*, along with French residents of Santander and San Sebastian where serious fighting had taken place.

All in all, my Spanish odyssey left me with a deep appreciation of that country's heritage and culture and whetted a special interest in the history of Latin America. It also opened my eyes to the progress of Nazism and Fascism in Europe as Hitler, and later Mussolini, helped Franco in his struggle against the Republic.

MATURITY: RUDE AWAKENINGS TO A CHANGING WORLD

Paris: A Personal Chronicle Of The Thirties

During the '30s, while studying in Paris and later working for the French Government, life was indeed delightful. The French had recovered from the physical disaster of "the Great War" and were enjoying one of the happiest periods in their history. Paris was relaxed. The country was at peace, Art Nouveau was at its highest peak, and the *Exposition Universelle* of 1937 on the banks of the Seine showed the world that Paris was the center of elegance and innovation.

I enjoyed living in Paris despite the pressure of my studies and later my work. Just going to the Ministry of Commerce and Industry in the rue de Grenelle, from my mother's apartment in the 17th *arrondissement*, riding on the rear platform of the bus, was pure enjoyment. I preferred to stand on the outside platform rather than finding a seat inside. From my privileged station, close to the traffic, watching the flow of all the vehicles, I could at the same time appreciate daily the views of Paris I liked.

The bus route took us down the rue de Rome past the *Gare St-Lazare*, always a bustling railway station. Later we reached the Place de l'Opéra, the Madeleine and the rue Royale, before passing through the vast and magnificent Place de la Concorde. Reaching the Obélisque, in its center, I was able to contemplate the unique and sublime perspective of the Avenue of the Champs Elysées and the Arc de Triomphe on one side and the entrance to the Jardin des Tuileries on the other. I never tired of it.

After crossing the Seine the bus turned left in front of the pseudo-Greek *Palais Bourbon* and the *Chambre des Députés*—a constant reminder of the instability of French politics with its imminent ministerial crises, the fall of Cabinets and the scandals in the government of the Third Republic. For a short distance we would follow the left bank of the Seine to reach the aristocratic Boulevard St-Germain. Five minutes later I alighted from the bus at the rue de Bellechasse and the rue de Grenelle, where many ministries were located.

In those days, more than today, one had to dress well for work. I wore a navy blue double-breasted suit and a homburg, the fashion for men, imitating the style of British statesman Anthony Eden. Young executives at one time also wore bowlers as in London, but in Paris this fad did not last very long. My clothes were made by a tailor, customary in France at that time as department stores selling apparel called *prêt à porter* offered neither the choice or style one could find in New York and London. I bought my ties at the *Carnaval de Venise*, an elegant haberdasher on the Boulevard des Capucines.

In Paris, everyone felt the need to be chic, and the women were always elegant and a pleasure to watch. I found it exhilarating. Walking on the sidewalks one felt free, elated, one's mind and spirit alert to the beauty and charm of the surrounding city. William Shirer described in his memoirs that one felt part of a tolerant and civilized world, and at the time I desired no more. I even felt that if one day my destiny would drag me down to the level of a *clochard*, a bum, I would rather be in Paris than New York or London as it seemed more romantic to roam the city of light and sleep *sous les ponts de Paris*, (under the bridges of the Seine) rather than on Broadway or in Trafalgar Square.

This period of elation in Paris, sad to say, lasted only until about 1936, when the *Front Populaire* brought the first sign of the real troubles that were to engulf the country. One did not feel it in the wealthy districts of Paris, but driving through districts such as the 10th, 19th and 20th *arrondissements* and outside the peripheral boulevards north and south of the capital, in the *zone rouge*, one could perceive that France was becoming clearly divided into two irreconcilable factions: the blue-collar workers and the bourgeoisie, signaling the grave political crises which preceded World War II.

When I settled in Paris in the fall of 1930 I knew practically no one except our cousins in Enghien-les-Bains, a charming little spa only twelve minutes north of Paris, a commuter town. Mother and I shared an apartment close to the *École des Hautes Études Commerciales*. Since I had not been admitted the year before, I had to spend one more year preparing for its very competitive entrance examination. HEC was, and still is, the finest graduate school of business administration in France. It has an international reputation that nowadays enables exchanges between it and the Harvard School of Business, along with similar top schools in the United States. It was what the French called one of *les Grandes Écoles*, of which there were about ten in all. These were special graduate schools, not part of the University of Paris, under a restricted system of admission criticized today as too elitist for the interests of the country at large, and the most difficult to gain entrance to in France. (There is no doubt that the French educational system at the graduate level is in some ways antiquated—in some aspects it has not changed since the First Empire. In France there is exaggerated importance attributed to the acquisition of diplomas.) In a number of Parisian Lycées there were special HEC preparatory study programs for students who had already passed the Baccalaureate.

I registered at the *Lycée Carnot*. The HEC admission exam, which I took in June 1931, included a series of three-hour compositions covering general subjects, history, geography, French, mathematics, physics, chemistry and foreign languages. Having failed it once, I had studied very hard to pass it the second time, and my results were considered brilliant. Of 230 candidates accepted that year, I ranked fifth in the written part and seventh in the oral. More than a thousand had applied.

My two years at HEC meant hard study with little time for play. It was a city institution with no campus. Today HEC has a beautiful campus outside Paris, as have most of France's *Grandes Écoles*, which have adopted American methods and have up-to-date installations. In my day, few students even had time for sports. Our distractions were few as we had to prepare for weekly exams. The marks affected one's average and determined where one stood in the class, that rank appearing on a monthly posted list. Life was a rat race indeed.

There was little time to enjoy Parisian life, but one does find ways! Saturday afternoons I used to go to a *thé-dansant* at a little *boîte* on rue Caumartin where students, boys and girls, and also young women, often married, would come for tea and dancing after their shopping at the *Galeries Lafayette* or the *Printemps*. I also used to go skating at the *Palais de Glace* or go to *Molitor*, both well known Paris spots where I would meet friends. I went to the movies, mostly to see foreign films and to the theater as often as I could.

The HEC, as a school of business administration, naturally offered many courses on management, financial studies, economics, technology, languages and so on, but we also studied commercial and maritime law and took introductions to civil and international law taught by eminent professors from the University of Paris Law School. Because of this, quite a number of HEC students thought that they could try to graduate from the University of Paris Law School while studying at HEC, a very ambitious endeavor since the HEC program already was such a heavy one. I decided to try this myself and registered at the Law School when I was in my second HEC year, knowing, as my classmates did, that we would never be able to attend the classes.

Holding a *Baccalaureat* diploma enabled one to register in law school and never show up for the courses. It was accepted that you could study alone. The only requirement for the *Licence en Droit* degree, equivalent to the American LLB, was to pass a very tough written and oral exam at the end of each year of three years of study. The program covered three years with eliminating exams. The exams were given each summer with a second chance in the fall. The lawyer's degree was granted if one successfully passed the three examinations. To become a practicing lawyer one had to work in a lawyer's office for one year under a practical program called the *Stage* and pass the bar examination, but the difficult thing was to get the degree of *licencié*. My aim, and that of my classmates, was not to become lawyers, but to hold a law degree in addition to the HEC diploma (which is equivalent to an MBA) to help us qualify for better positions in the corporate world.

But when to find the time to study law? Since I could not possibly attend the courses, there was only one way: subscribe to the *Cours polycopiés*, a firm which would send specialists to various courses, take down the lectures verbatim, and reproduce them each week together with a summary. In principle this was adequate preparation. But even in cramming at night before exams, I was unable to cover the whole program. There was, therefore, a serious chance factor involved, and the hope that the questions asked for the written exam would deal with areas to which I had given particular attention. I must confess that my intuition was rewarded several times.

I was lucky enough to pass my first-year exam while still at HEC, my second one when I was in the French Army and the third one after I had completed my military service. I wanted to be able to earn money as soon as possible. This called for perseverance and dedication on my part, particularly when I was in officer candidates' school at the *Fort de Vincennes* in Paris' east end. This school trained second lieutenants in the management of Army hospitals. While I was doing rifle and bayonet drills and the like in the Bois de Vincennes, I rehearsed in my head the law lessons I had studied the night before in the lounge. Instead of playing bridge at night, as the others did, I sat in a corner reading law. This appeared at times a type of perversion to some of my friends, who made good-natured fun of me.

I was authorized to sit for the exam that year and, dressed in my soldier's uniform, I passed certain subjects with honors. This did not prejudice my military training as, at the end of the Vincennes course, I was appointed a second lieutenant in the French Reserve. I graduated with the LLB the following year.

Later, while working at the Ministry of Commerce, I continued my studies in law and economics and obtained two doctoral certificates in these subjects; but I left France and never found the time afterward to write the doctoral thesis that would have led to the title of *Docteur en droit*.

After HEC I worked briefly in the promotion department of Aspro, a well-known pharmaceutical firm in Paris, but I was attracted by the French Foreign Service. I needed first to get into the government and I had to pass another competitive civil service examination to enter the Ministry of Commerce and Industry as *rédacteur*, i.e. a tenured junior officer in the French civil service.

I would arrive at the Ministry at nine o'clock each morning, the beginning of a long work day that rarely saw me leave the office before seven or seven-thirty at night, most of the directors staying at their desks even longer. Passing the massive entrance gate and the graveled front courtyard, I would find myself in the hall leading to the office of the Director-General, Henri Chaumet, to whom I was the personal assistant, a lucky assignment that placed me right at the center of Ministry activities. I would be greeted by the *huissiers* or ushers with their black frock coats decorated with brass buttons and chains, who introduced visitors to my boss' office through soundproofed, well padded leather double doors. His office had elegant period furniture, a massive ornate mahogany table serving as desk and a ceiling-high mirror behind it, a large rug with grey and blue designs covering the floor. The wall facing the entrance had French doors and windows that opened onto a lovely interior French garden, the presence of which would never have been guessed from the rue de Grenelle. This was the garden of the Minister and his personal staff, which we could use, but never had time to step into!

In this first job I learned a lot about tact, discretion, deference towards superiors—all in the climate of the French bureaucracy, whose tradition goes back to the monarchy and the Napoleonic Empire. This training was good for me as I was meeting many senior civil servants making their way up the career ladder.

My boss had been a *Prefect* before becoming head of his department at the

Ministry and, as such, had held key functions as head of one of the 83 *Départements* (administrative districts) that made up the much centralized Government of France. At the Ministry of Commerce and Industry he was in charge of general administration including personnel and the bureaus of Commercial Expansion Abroad and of Economic Information. I found my job fascinating as his personal assistant.

I was the liaison officer with the various divisions under him and the offices of the other departmental directors. I prepared some of the correspondence for his signature and the Minister's. I learned a lot working for Henri Chaumet for more than two years and our relations were cordial.

Two of our divisions interested me particularly: one was handling relations with all the Commercial Counselors and Attachés assigned by the Ministry to French embassies around the world. I was in a position to read the reports of these officials dealing with French trade, call the attention of my boss to the important problems they raised and arrange meetings concerning them. The other division was relatively small, dealing with the participation of France in World Fairs and other exhibitions taking place from time to time in different countries.

There were also in the Ministry, much as in the U.S. Commerce Department in Washington, other departments, one for domestic commerce and one for trade agreements, the latter headed by Hervé Alphand of the renowned corps of *Inspecteurs des Finances*. At thirty years old he was the youngest and most brilliant senior level civil servant in France. I did not know it at the time, but later in New York, in 1940-41, I would work for him as his personal assistant at the French Embassy when he occupied the function of Financial Counsellor. He later became French Ambassador to the United States during the Kennedy and Johnson administrations in the 1960s.

In 1938, Alphand headed the Bureau of Trade Agreements, in Paris. International trade was difficult and its volume had declined substantially; it was anything but free trade, a period of severe protectionism. Our Ministry drastically controlled trade. To protect French industries, imports were subject to quotas and obtaining a license from the Government was required for most imports. French exports also were subject to similar restrictions by countries to which French products were sent. As a result, trade agreements reflected a tight situation and negotiations with other countries represented a complicated compromise of quotas and barters, which was the responsibility of our Ministry. These arrangements, originally devised by Dr. Hjalmar Schacht, a world known financier and czar of the German economy, had come to dominate European trade during World War I and its economic and financial aftermath. In fact it was a system which unfortunately prevented European recovery until after World War II.

A Talented French Family: Sundays In The Country

On Sundays during the '30s my mother and I were often invited by my distant cousins, the Labarthes,[6] to Enghien-les-Bains. They were the only family we had besides Tante Amélie, who was still in Beaucourt, as we only saw my aunts in Nice and Grasse and my uncle and his wife on certain occasions. These visits to Enghien did much for our morale; there was such warmth, gaiety, heartiness, spirit and animation at the Labarthes. We always came back at the end of the day fulfilled and encouraged.

Despite urbanization which now has spread all around Paris destroying old sites, Enghien remains an elegant small spa where people from the capital still gather to take its sulfurous waters. Its style and architecture have preserved its nineteenth-century charm. It boasts a hot springs and baths, a lovely casino and even a racetrack. What makes the town distinctive is a man-made lake. Its jetty features a long wrought-iron fence and a row of well designed lamp standards. Strolling along it one can admire a truly romantic landscape reminiscent of some impressionist paintings, with gardens and pretty villas half hidden behind trees, the white silhouette of the casino and a few sails and rowboats enlivening the water.

The lives my cousins and their friends led in this charming little place remain in my memory as a nostalgic example of the pleasant and comfortable existence people enjoyed in the twenties in the towns of Ile de France surrounding Paris, where everything seemed to go well for almost everybody.

The Labarthes owned a pretty house called *Les Hortensias* (The Hydrangeas), about ten minutes' walk from the railroad station from which trains carried them to Paris-Nord in twelve minutes, at ten-minute intervals. The villa was on Boulevard Cotte, a typical residential street lined with rows of plane trees. The property was hidden behind a black grilled fence and well-trimmed bushes. From the iron door one could see the garden, its flower beds and well-designed walkways. The house, a classic suburban villa, had three stories, tall windows, a handsome entrance door and a gabled slate roof. It looked elegant.

The person I admired most in this family of accomplished artists and musicians and was most grateful to was cousin Émile, whom we all called "Daddou", for Daddy. He took an interest in my studies and, after I had entered the Ministry of Commerce and Industry, strongly influenced the direction of my career. Born in

---

6   Cousin Eugenie, her husband Émile, and their three children Lilly, Madéleine and Jean-Pierre. The children, whom I loved dearly, were slightly older than I.

Bearn in the Pyrenées, he had many of the characteristics of the Bearnais, including the display of bravado and panache. He studied law at the University of Bordeaux, inheriting from that famous city the art of telling stories with a flourish and much charm, perhaps sometimes with a touch of exaggeration. In his youth Émile had frequented the inner circles of Bordeaux. He had come to Paris to be a lawyer, following some of his friends from law school who had made their way into French politics. He could have done likewise, but did not, he told me, because of the scrutiny and harassment to which political figures are always subjected. He preferred activities which bordered on politics without its pressures.

His real achievement was the creation of the widely-known *Comité Parlementaire du Commerce*, a private think tank and study group whose members included industrialists and personalities from the business and financial worlds as well as interested deputies and senators of the Third Republic. The *Comité's* purpose, perhaps comparable to that of the Foreign Policy Association in the U.S., was to bring to the fore international and domestic economic problems the nation faced, have them discussed with experts and prominent *rapporteurs* and publish the results widely. The *Comité* met monthly in rooms graciously lent by the French Parliament either in the *Palais Bourbon* or the *Palais de Luxembourg*. Émile was its Secretary-General. He was outstanding as a conference organizer and negotiator; thus he knew a host of prominent people in politics.

In the '30s Émile invited members of various European parliaments to create similar committees in their own countries. Many times, as we took walks on Sunday afternoons to such historic places as nearby Montmorency, he would explain his projects to me. Committees were established in many Western European nations and in the countries of the *Petite Entente* in Eastern Europe, the new nations created by the Treaty of Versailles such as Poland, Czechoslovakia, Rumania and Yugoslavia, all of which were openly francophile. This led to the setting up of bi-annual international conferences held in the various European capitals, of which he was the coordinator. In 1933 when I was studying English with a family near London during the summer, Émile invited me to attend the conference he had organized at the House of Commons. Harold MacMillan, not yet Prime Minister, was the chairman. I helped in the small secretariat and I remember sorting documents. This was my first international meeting.

On Sundays at Enghien luncheon was always lively and the food excellent. It was taken in a dining room, a former porch that had been completely glass-enclosed and which opened on the villa's rear garden. Émile always had the most entertaining tales in which he was the hero. A world traveler, he would describe his trips, the incidents which happened and how he handled them, all told with laughter and gestures and an acute sense of humor. He hated to be gouged, as so often happens when one travels abroad, but he never hesitated for the sake of fairness as well as his own personal interest to make a protest at the highest possible level. He told of one incident in Italy when he had lodged a complaint against a hotel in Rome and the Italian railroads for some reason I can't recall in detail. He directed his complaints to the *Duce* himself, who wanted tourists to visit Italy in droves and the trains to run on time. He received a letter of apology signed by Mussolini and appropriate excuses and full restitution from the Italian railroads.

At the luncheon table conversations often concerned art. As an art lover, Émile had visited literally all the museums of Europe. With his tremendous memory he could name any of the masterpieces displayed in each museum. He knew all the well-known painters and could describe the scenes on the canvases and even explain where they were located in the museum. His knowledge of history and music was also stupendous. His hobby was landscape painting. In his presence there was never a dull moment.

Clouds Over Europe: The League Of Nations Fails

From 1934 on, while I was able to enjoy my close relationship with my French family and my work in Paris, the French political situation began to deteriorate. The cleavage separating the workers and the bourgeoisie was widening. The economic situation was worsening. Prices were rising sharply with the devaluations of the franc. Wages remained low and the workers had difficulty making ends meet. They became restless under the influence of the powerful Communist party, demonstrating and loudly claiming that the upper classes were not contributing their fair share to public expenses. The tax system was shocking, soaking the poor with high indirect taxes while sparing the rich. Tax evasion was blatant. All attempts to reform the system had failed in Parliament.

The Government was led then by the Radical Socialists, a centrist formation. Despairing of democracy to improve conditions in the country, the parties of the extreme right started waging war against the government. Ernest Mercier, an electricity executive and François Coty, the perfumer, subsidized right-wing movements. One of them, *Solidarité Française*, was a full-fledged fascist organization which the Government banned. Others declared illegal were *Action Française*, headed by Charles Maurras, and two of its student organizations. I believe several of my HEC classmates were members.

The fatal day during this terrible period was February 6, 1934. I was then in the

French Army as a draftee. On that day there was a huge demonstration in the Place de la Concorde, across the Seine from the *Chambre des Députés*. The shock troops of *Action Française, Jeunesse Patriotes, Solidarité Française*, also including the *Croix de Feu* of Colonel de la Rocque, another reactionary organization, were dispersed by Government Mobile Guards. At some point the latter panicked, charged the threatening crowd and opened fire with their automatic pistols. Sixteen rioters were killed.[7]

In 1936 the *Front Populaire* acceded to power, an alliance of democratic, left-wing and revolutionary political parties having a common interest in the struggle against reactionism and fascism. It was headed by Léon Blum, the head of the French Socialist party and the architect of the coalition. He became Prime Minister. This panicked the French stock market and brought further flights of capital. The upper classes thought that France was on the brink of a Red revolution. There were a few general strikes that paralyzed transportation, occupations of industrial plants by the workers, all this orchestrated by the Communist Party and their union, the *Confédération Générale du Travail* (CGT). I remember in 1937 the demonstration at the door of the Ministry of Postal, Telegraph, Telephone and Telecommunications with which my own Ministry had a common entrance, where rioters shouted obscenities at Georges Mandel, the minister, when he tried to enter. A conservative who had been Prefect of Police of Paris and Minister of the Interior in preceding cabinets, he was famous for restoring order, but was not a particular friend of the working class. All this was going on in France while no adequate preparation (except for the construction of the Maginot Line) was being made to oppose the ever-growing threat taking shape across the Rhine.

As a student during the '30s and later as a French civil servant, I became deeply interested in the League of Nations and never failed to read the articles and news coverage in the French press on the debates in Geneva on the resolution of conflicts which endangered peace. I marveled at the brilliance of Aristide Briand and Paul Boncour's speeches—the great French tenors of the League. In 1931, when Manchuria was invaded by Japan, although both Japan and China (which held Manchuria) were League members, the organization could do nothing to stop the aggression. The most glaring aggressive acts violating the League Covenant which outraged us came later, with the invasion and occupation of Abyssinia (Ethiopia)

---

7 Harold Roditi of New York, a friend and former HEC classmate, was there as a curious bystander when he was struck by a stray bullet in the back that paralyzed him from the trunk down. This was particularly unfortunate, since he was not even French. Despite his disability, he became a patent lawyer in New York. I met him one day, twenty years later, and invited him for lunch in the UN Restaurant; he still had to be pushed in a wheelchair.

by the fascist legions of Benito Mussolini in 1935. The League, by its charter powerless to act in any meaningful way, could do nothing. The League, and France and Britain individually, were able to do nothing to prevent Hitler from seizing practically all of Europe; I was devastated when Germany withdrew from the League.

In 1936 German troops marched into the Rhineland; in 1938, into the Sudetenland; in March 1939, into Bohemia, which brought the partition of Czechoslovakia. All this amounted to a total surrender of the French and British to Nazi aggression. With millions of other people in the Western world, I listened anxiously to the radio for reports on Neville Chamberlain's three meetings with Hitler on the question of Czechoslovakia. The Czech government was not even allowed to attend the third meeting. After Munich, all hope of preserving the peace disappeared, and the world was about to plunge into a Second World War.

The 1939 New York World's Fair: A Love Story

I enjoyed my work at the Ministry, but I wanted to travel and was thinking of serving the Ministry overseas in the Foreign Service. I was in a good place to find out when and where suitable work vacancies would occur. On rainy days, so numerous, I dreamt of countries with sunny climates. In 1938 a post of Assistant Commercial Attaché came open in Sydney, Australia, but my mother and cousin Émile, each with different logic, convinced me not to go.

In the meantime, another possibility for a foreign posting came up. The World's Fair in Flushing Meadows Park, New York, in 1939, was to be the biggest and most glamorous ever and a unique opportunity to reinforce cooperation between nations. The French Government planned to have a scintillating representation in a beautiful pavilion to be designed by France's best architects. It would show all that France had to offer the world in terms of art and manufactured luxury products, wines, cultural activities, new technologies and the like.

The Commissioner General in charge of the planning, preparation and execution of the French participation in New York was appointed in 1938. He was Marcel Olivier, who had been Governor General of Madagascar and of French West Africa. A small staff was to be recruited with me as First Secretary of the Commissariat. The prestige of working in New York for the French Government at the World's Fair, and the opportunity to return to the city of my birth were very attractive, even though no tenure was associated with the New York assignment. This assignment completely changed the rest of my life.

I left Paris for New York on the *SS Normandie* in October 1938. Being on the staff of Commissioner-General Olivier, who was also President of the French Line, I was given a first class cabin.

I was dazzled by the luxury of the ship, which with its 80,000 tons was the biggest, fastest and most sophisticated vessel afloat. The meals were taken in the *Grande Salle à Manger*, 60 feet larger than the Hall of Mirrors at Versailles. The Grand Salon glittered with gold and crystal and the theater rivaled those of London and Broadway. I was invited to the Captain's table and told that anytime the *Normandie* was in port in New York I was welcome to have dinner aboard and to bring a guest, a most welcome invitation.

The Fair was to open in the spring of 1939 so there was to be much planning and preparation in the few months ahead. The gigantic symbol of the Fair, the Sphere and Trylon, was under construction at Flushing Meadows Park, which I visited a few days after landing. We had to build two French pavilions, one for Metropolitan France and the other for the French Colonial Empire. Two outstanding French architects, Expert and Patout, who had designed the Trocadero Palace in Paris, had been selected by the government; their model for the main pavilion was much acclaimed. The Pavilion was a curved amphitheater, its front all glass, very open, looking to the lagoon situated in the middle of the Foreign Governments section of the Fair, in one of the most desirable locations.

Soon great difficulties arose with the large U.S. labor unions. Commissioner-General Olivier had to threaten at one point to withdraw French participation if interference from the unions continued. They wanted American workers to be used and refused to give the Frenchmen permission to work. The French equipment for the pavilion, including the most up-to-date kitchens for the restaurant—which turned out to be one of the Fair's greatest attractions—needed to be installed by French specialists. We had also sent over from Paris a number of artisans and decorators to work on the interior of the Pavilion, a job requiring artistic ability and special training. A strike ensued, delaying construction already lagging behind schedule. James Stewart and Co., the New York contractor in charge of the actual building of the pavilion, could not stop the strike. Negotiations with the unions went all the way to Grover Whalen, President of the Fair, Fiorello La Guardia, the mayor, and Dean Acheson at the State Department in Washington. In some of the meetings held at City Hall I participated in dealing with this emergency.

Finally the conflict was settled and the work started again, but the unions had won. The crates containing the equipment and some of the exhibits, which were beginning to arrive at the site, could not be unpacked by French personnel alone and, for this work and that inside the Pavilion, which had to be done by French artisans and workers, the unions would not budge and demanded that an American worker be hired for each Frenchman used. The American would stand doing absolutely nothing while the French did the work. He had to be paid by the French Government at the prevailing rate, much more than the French rate paid to the French workers. We considered this outrageous and were quite astonished that the U.S. Government had not been able to help us. There was no question of withdrawal. It cost much more than originally expected and Paris had to accept the situation, but it showed us the tremendous power of the AFL and CIO unions in the years preceding the Second World War.

The French Pavilion was beautiful and one of the most popular at the Fair. We welcomed many dignitaries—leaders from many countries, artists, sports figures, and movie stars including Tyrone Power and Annabelle, his French wife, with whom I had cocktails. I happened also to do some protocol work, even learning how to seat people by precedence at a banquet table. The French restaurant atop the Pavilion gave a view of the whole Fair, its tables lined up on terraces at several levels. At the end of the Fair, Henri Soulé, maître d'hotel, known by everyone in New York, really benefited from the Fair—he later opened the famous Pavilion Restaurant, perhaps the most luxurious restaurant in New York.

The Fair had everything one could desire in terms of spectacles and entertainment, including the Billy Rose aquacade, with Eleanor Holmes as star, the first giant nautical ballet. Further, we found it difficult to refuse to accompany the French VIPs who had dealt with us on official Fair business. They wanted to see the Fair and tour the City on evenings when they were not being entertained by the High Commissioner or his deputy, the Commercial Counselor of the French Embassy in New York. They not only wanted to take in ballets and musical comedies, but also the cabarets and night clubs. We would show them a number of these and always took them to the Savoy in Harlem, one of the most exotic spots in those days. After that regimen I was so saturated that I later had little desire for night life.

One day, about a year after arriving in New York, I was invited to the University of Pennsylvania Club, mid-town, for drinks. There I met a fellow about my age who was working at the New York office of TWA. The next Sunday was to be the dedication of North Beach Airport, later to become La Guardia Airport, on Long Island. He and a small group of friends were to meet first at the Forest Hills Tennis Club, then go to the festivities at the airport as guests of his company, ending the day with a supper at the home of his in-laws in Westbury. He paired me with a former Smith College girl.

Barbara, my date, was a very nice girl, but soon, at the Tennis Club, my eyes refused to leave a beautiful, fairly tall young woman attending the party with a Penn alumnus. She was graceful and pretty with a slightly turned up nose and strikingly for someone her age—she was twenty-two or twenty-three—she already had some grey hair. How strange and attractive, I thought. Her skin was very light, she had twinkling blue eyes, a graceful mouth and wore a simple necklace made of little red apples of painted wood, the same color as her lips.

She was laughing, engaged in animated conversation with several other members of the party. Struck by her beauty I approached the group with the purpose of making her acquaintance. Although she had not come with me, I could not resist the pleasure of talking to her, of piercing the mystery of this young American beauty, the kind of college girl that a European would like to know. We were briefly introduced.

Her name was Natalie Tucker, of South Dartmouth, Massachusetts. A few minutes later we were chit-chatting about tennis matches at Forest Hills, the Davis Cup, French and American champions, while what I really wanted to know was who she was, where she came from, and what she was doing in New York. I returned to Barbara for a while: to my shame, I had practically forgotten my own date, who fortunately had found other companions.

By that time the airport function had drawn to an end and we had gone to our friends' home for dinner. There again I had a chance to talk to Natalie. Luckily, Barbara seemed taken with another young man. She was in good hands and would be brought back safely to the city by her new acquaintance. I was then free and managed to return to New York on the same train as Natalie and her escort. We traveled in the same car, I facing her. Evidently I was quite smitten.

I had fallen in love at first sight. There seemed no doubt about it. This was October 15th, 1939, the World's Fair had started in the spring and Europe had been at war since September. When we arrived at Pennsylvania Station and were about to say goodbye I asked Natalie if I could see her again. She readily agreed. She had a job at Lord and Taylor selling in the College Shop as, for the first time, the store had hired college graduates to sell to college students.

She was born in Providence, Rhode Island, had graduated from Mount Holyoke College in June and wanted to have the experience of New York, where her sister was married to a lawyer. A few days later I called her, and we set up our first dinner date, the start of a whirlwind romance, a time in which we lived in a dream.

I realized I was not paying full attention to my work for I was in love. Toward the end of each day I would leave my office in Rockefeller Center and walk down to Lord and Taylor on 36th Street to wait for Natalie. If the store was still open I would go straight to the College Shop on the third floor and talk to her, with the other salesgirls excited by their colleague's romance with this Frenchman, who had newly landed in the United States.

On my birthday, exactly a month and a half after meeting Natalie, I took her to Cartier to meet Jean Grelet, its sales director. My old friend and classmate from Paris, Roger Varin, then deputy to the representative of the French Railroads in the United States who worked in the same building as I, had called him in advance to announce our visit: they were friends. We chose an engagement ring, a diamond with baguettes. It was at the same time extremely elegant and, thanks to Jean Grelet, affordable. All her life Natalie has received compliments on the ring.

We were then engaged, but France was at war. I could make no definite plans to marry my fiancée as I did not know what the future held in store for me. I had not yet even met Natalie's family. My mother was still in France. We enjoyed every moment of those weeks in New York. Natalie and I went to the Fair quite a number of times, to receptions organized by the High Commissioner at the French Pavilion. We dined at the Fair. I met Natalie's sister and her brother-in-law, and finally her father and mother in South Dartmouth.

By the end of the year I knew I would have to go to war in Europe. On New Year's Eve we went to the *Réveillon* at the Plaza Hotel with another couple and danced to the romantic music of Eddy Duchin's band.

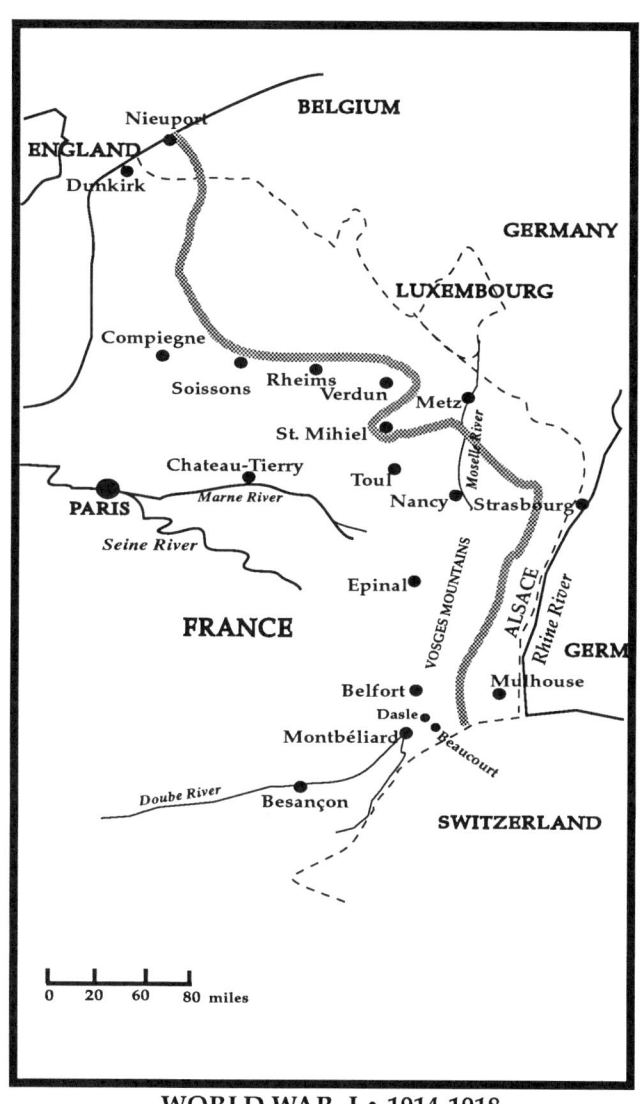

WORLD WAR I • 1914-1918
(A 400 Mile Trench Line)

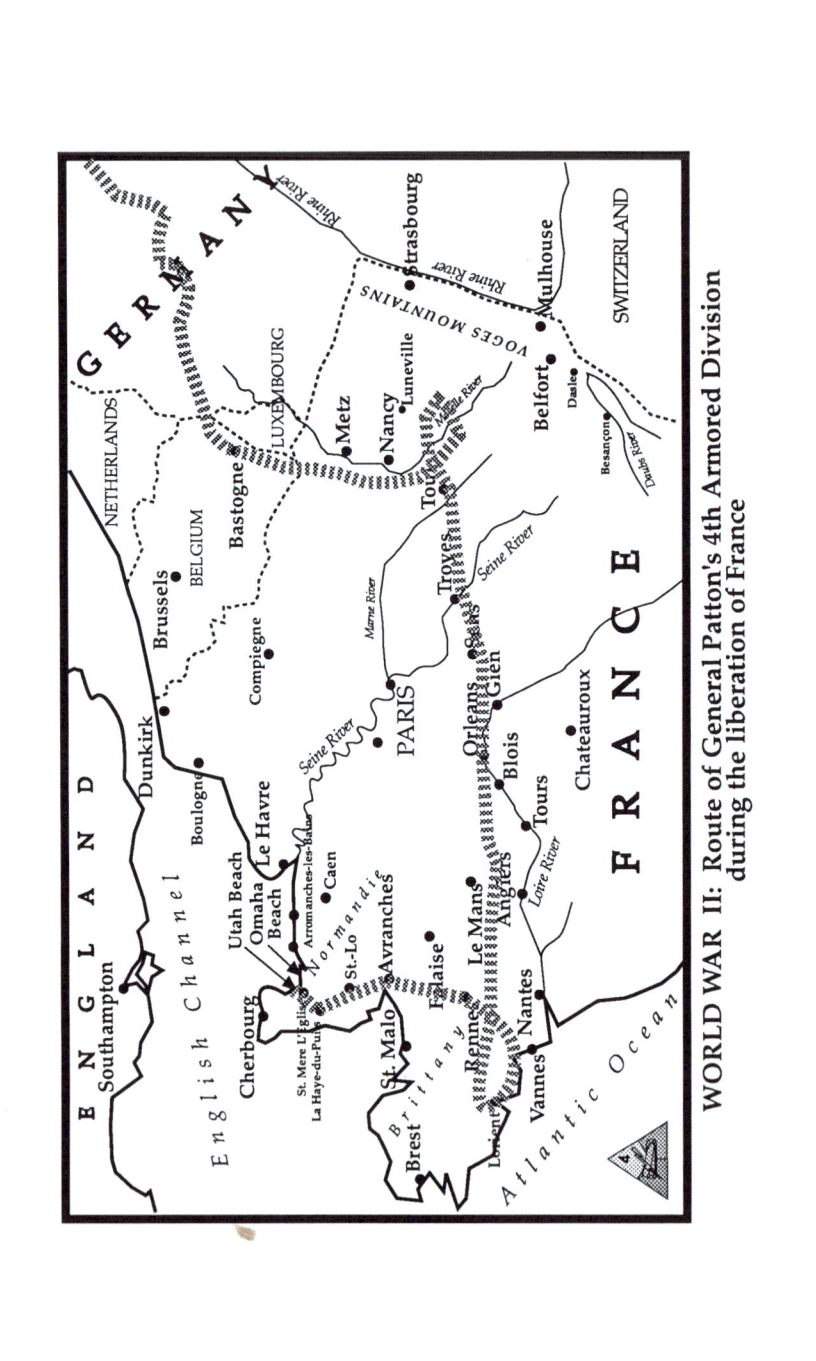

WORLD WAR II: Route of General Patton's 4th Armored Division during the liberation of France

Part II

THE SECOND WORLD WAR: FIGHTING UNDER TWO FLAGS

Part II

THE SECOND WORLD WAR: FIGHTING UNDER TWO FLAGS

Upon this battle depends the survival of Christian civilization. . . . If we fail, then the whole world, including the United States, including all we have known and cared for, will sink into the abyss of a new Dark Age.

Winston Churchill
Memoirs of World War II

The Collapse of France, June 1940

I have always hated war. I fought under two flags, not only because I was called to defend my homelands, but because I wanted to preserve democracy and protect them from tyrannies of the type perpetrated by the Third Reich. I wanted to see freedom ring again in the country in which I was brought up.

I was vacationing with two French friends in the summer of 1939 at the Domain of Baron Empain, a lovely resort in the Laurentian Mountains north of Montreal, when France declared war on Germany and armored German columns invaded Poland. While we were expecting this news, it shattered us nevertheless. We returned to New York quickly. Like everyone else in New York's international community, we wondered how events in Europe were going to affect our jobs. France's participation in the World's Fair would probably be terminated at the end of the year, and, as a tenured civil servant, I would have to return to Paris.

Although American-born, according to French nationality law (based on *jus sanguini*) because my parents were French, I was French. My mother, however, had registered me as an American citizen at the Embassy in Paris.

When I studied at the *École des Hautes Études Commerciales* in Paris from 1931 to 1933, I was required to take *préparation militaire supérieure* (equivalent to ROTC), which I had passed. Further, I was drafted into the French Army in 1934 (under the draft at that time only one year of service was required) and after twelve months on active duty I became a 2nd Lieutenant in the Reserves assigned to the Medical Corps as an administrative officer.

A few months after the war broke out, I had met Natalie and we had become engaged to be married. If I were called to war by France, what was I to do? Stay in

New York and ignore the call? I felt it my duty to return to France and fight for the French: that country had given me all my education, my culture and my upbringing. I felt I had a moral and legal obligation to return and serve France. Besides, if I had not answered my mobilization order I would have been considered a deserter by the French.

Both the British and the French governments set up various offices in New York at the end of 1939, to procure a great variety of U.S. war equipment and supplies (including clothing and other articles needed to outfit their armies). My legal training and knowledge of English, as well as some familiarity with American business, made me a useful person to help these missions. Col. Besnard, who was in charge of the French program, arranged for me to join his staff. For this he had to make an official request to the War Department in Paris. As a reserve officer, I had been assigned to a field hospital at Army Corps, to be stationed in the north of France, near Dunkirk. Col. Besnard obtained my temporary release and my departure was delayed for three months, until March of 1940.

My work involved interviewing suppliers, drafting contracts and working as a purchasing agent. The top man for all the foreign purchasing missions and coordinator for France and Britain was Jean Monnet, who later became the father of the European Community and the protagonist of the United States of Europe. He was highly respected and admired by Winston Churchill and listened to by both the British and the Americans.[1]

Three months later, my work with the Purchasing Commission completed, I left New York to rejoin my unit in France. It was a very sad occasion for me and for my fiancée. It was hard to believe that we were to be parted. We wanted to stay together, but Natalie respected my feeling about serving France, and she never reproached me.

The *SS Exochorda* was sailing at 4 p.m. from a pier of the American Export Line on the west side of New York on a rainy day in March. The "phony war" was continuing on the Maginot Line. Nothing much was happening. The Germans were broadcasting *Lily Marlene* over the front lines to discourage the French soldiers. I was late in joining the unit to which I had been assigned when the mobilization of French soldiers had been ordered. Col. Besnard had thought it unlikely that I would be sent to my Army Corps hospital on the front lines, as I would surely have been

---

1   If Monnet's ideas had been followed after the war, Europe would certainly be more closely united than it is today. He was in favor of a European supranational authority, but de Gaulle vehemently rejected the idea. Being an extreme nationalist, de Gaulle accepted a policy that went no further than *"l'Europe des Patries,"* each European country keeping its national sovereignty intact.

replaced when I did not turn up in France at the beginning of hostilities. Now I was to travel on my own from New York, possibly at my own expense, not knowing whether procedures would allow the refund of my crossing on a civilian transport such as the *Exochorda*. I was likely the only one on board returning to France to fight in the Army at that time. The ship was to go to Gibraltar and Genoa, then to the eastern ports of the Mediterranean. A number of families boarding appeared to be from the Middle East, probably returning to their countries because of the war.

The parting was a sad one. Natalie was in my cabin with her brother. Our lives—certainly mine—were entering the unknown. She did not expect to stay in New York much longer, perhaps only until the summer. She would return to Padanaram, near New Bedford, Mass. a part of the town of South Dartmouth where her parents lived. There Natalie would be safe and, she said, waiting for me. We had discussed for some time the possibility that she would join one of several groups of American women organized to help the French Red Cross and the *Foyer du Soldat*. She wanted to help the war effort, but also hoped that once abroad we would be able to see each other even if only occasionally. But her mother, wisely, was against it. It would be easier for both of us if she stayed at home.

I was so unprepared to leave her, New York and all that these two years had meant. To dispel the gloom we had champagne in the tiny cabin, and all tried to put up a good front. To avoid discussing the separation, we toured the ship and then stayed on deck. We looked at the dark waters of the East River and the Jersey shore. On the other side of the ship one could see the skyscrapers of Manhattan, ranged one behind the other, with the sky above them and its threatening, grey, fast-moving clouds. Gone was the glamorous and fascinating life I had led in this city, the many receptions and parties. Because of my contributions to the World's Fair, I had been awarded the title of Honorary Citizen of the City of New York, with an impressive parchment diploma signed by Fiorello H. LaGuardia, the mayor.

But my thoughts, sad as they were, concentrated on Natalie. What would happen to her? Would I come back to these shores? And suppose the Germans won the war? Or that I became a prisoner of war? There were so many unknowns!

The moment of separation arrived. The bell rang calling visitors ashore. We had to part. Nat was crying, and I could hardly restrain my tears. We said goodbye many times, waving, they from the pier, me from the top deck. This departure of a transatlantic liner—a small one at that—was so different from the glamorous prewar sailings of the *Normandie*, the *Queen Mary*, the Italian ships and the rest of those marvelous, luxurious floating hotels. Then, friends came to the piers to say *bon voyage*. Often the sailings were at midnight and were an occasion to celebrate in the cabins and at gatherings in the salons until the gong sounded. Each ship was a glittering party of hundreds of guests and passengers. When the visitors came down the gangway there was still the unique moment when all the multicolored streamers linking the passengers on deck with friends on the pier would tear as the massive liners, several stories high, slipped from their berths and slowly began their maneuvering down river. It was all so lively, impressive, and even moving. No, this sailing on the *SS Exochorda* was not among the departures reported in the *New York Times* society columns.

I went back to my cabin, pensive, with a heavy heart, and started unpacking my cabin trunk, which contained all my belongings. A page in my life had turned.

Instead of sailing east towards Europe, the *Exochorda* took a southeasterly bearing, as we had to report to Bermuda for the British Admiralty cargo inspection. Since the outbreak of war, all vessels crossing the Atlantic were subject to such control, staying offshore in quarantine until the inspectors came aboard. Quite a number of ships were waiting when we arrived. Anchored so far away, we could hardly distinguish the white roofs and pink walls of the houses of Hamilton, so typical of Bermuda. The weather was foul. In the distance the coast looked grey and was shrouded in mist. At no moment did we feel that we were close to a semitropical vacation island. The cargo checked, we weighed anchor during the night.

I do not remember much about that crossing, lost as I was in my thoughts and reveries about what I had left behind. The passengers in this difficult period all had personal problems preoccupying their minds. There were no parties. We landed in Genoa where I disembarked, took a train for Paris, and reported to the Ministry of War. There I found that my original assignment to a field hospital at the front, in the Dunkirk region, had been changed. It was a lucky break, since a tragic few months later thousands of British and French troops were to be taken prisoner at Dunkirk, unable to evacuate because of lack of ship to carry them. There was no doubt that, had I been assigned to my original duty station, I would have ended up a prisoner of war, since hospital units, with their wounded and their cumbersome installations, cannot easily escape capture.

A Military Hospital in Suresnes

I was told that I had to report to *Hôpital Foch* at Suresnes, perhaps one of the newest and most modern hospitals in France at that time. Originally a civilian hospital, it had been requisitioned by the Army. Located in Suresnes in the western suburbs of Paris, on the bank of the Seine, about fifteen minutes by train from the *Gare Saint Lazare*, the hospital could take care of many patients and contained hundreds of beds. As the retreat of the French grew more pronounced each day and casualties more numerous as the front moved closer to Paris, *Hôpital Foch* soon became crowded with wounded brought by French ambulances and by volunteers of the American Friends Service and by British women volunteers.

The military personnel at the hospital was ample, and I was only one of several administrative officers, serving as an assistant to the Chief Administrator. After one or two days of intensive briefings on the operations and the procedures followed at Foch (a refresher course covering what I had learned during my year at the School of Military Administration at Vincennes in 1934), I was ready to take my place in one of the administrative sections of the hospital, in charge of receiving visitors— particularly the parents of the critically wounded, those we did not think would survive. There were many gangrene cases, mostly because transportation had not become available early enough. The rapid advance of the Germans led to utter disorganization at the front in the north. I had to explain the existing situation to these parents, with tact and compassion, and tell them what to do. I was responsible for making the necessary arrangements and helping them in any way I could. It was a delicate and moving part of my daily work.

The wounded kept coming and the news on the general situation at the front worsened. The enemy had defeated our army in the north and was approaching Paris. Here and there French troops fought well against the attacks of the German panzers. Streams of refugees from Belgium and the north of France were obstructing the roads, and now the panicked Parisians and those living in the suburbs of the capital started to leave, creating enormous bottlenecks. For this gigantic evacuation— described so many times in all its horrors, including the strafing of innocent men, women and children on the roads by German and Italian planes—all kinds of transportation were being used and it was hard to find an available vehicle anywhere.

Part of my duties involved making arrangements for burial in the local cemetery or for sending home the soldiers who had died. Summary funeral services were conducted by hospital chaplains, and attended by such families as were able to come. For burials in Suresnes, it was most difficult to find the necessary vehicles to carry the coffins. Even the horse-drawn hearses had disappeared in the evacuation.

I had been doing this work for only a few days and had barely learned to cope with the difficulties when the military situation became desperate: the Germans were about to take Paris. With Paris occupied, the military personnel and the wounded at *Hôpital Foch* would be taken prisoners of war. But the total number of officers there exceeded normal requirements, so some could be spared for use elsewhere—thus avoiding (or at least delaying) the possibility of their falling into enemy hands and finishing out the war as prisoners. The names of all officers were put into a hat; the names drawn would be those who would leave Suresnes before the Germans arrived. Soon a list was posted. Thank God, my name was on it!

As the front was broken in the north and to the east of Paris and units were disorganized and dispersed, the French High Command decided to regroup various divisions to make up a new army called the "Army of Paris." The plan was that this reorganized force would go south and offer resistance to the enemy on the Loire River. Hospital officers and personnel who were on the list were to join this new army. I was assigned to the staff of General Savornin, the Chief Medical Officer commanding the French *Service de Santé Militaire* (Military Health Service). He had already left his headquarters in Paris at the famous *Hôtel des Invalides*, built by Louis XIV, then housing the heads of the armed forces and services of the Region of Paris.

The French Defeat and the Armistice

The next day, June 6, 1940, we left Suresnes at dawn in two small trucks, and met the other officers in front of the *Hôtel des Invalides* in Paris. They and we were to be Gen. Savornin's staff. We drove along deserted streets toward the Porte d'Orléans in the south of the city, which was crowded with people fleeing the capital. As we arrived the radio reported that the first German elements were entering Paris at the Porte de Clignancourt in the north. I did not know then that this would be the last I would see of the city for several years. We were going to a point south of Paris to meet the general and be told what was expected of us. His staff consisted almost entirely of senior officers who headed the various branches of the *Service de Santé Militaire*. Most were career officers and had worked in the Paris headquarters. It would be a major task given the present chaos to find where the service field units were located and to re-establish the many controls and links with the medical and pharmaceutical officers heading the various units of this new army. After regrouping, the plan also called for a coordinated resistance and, at a later stage, an offensive.

As we drove south, our little group had orders to stop for the night at various points where we would receive instructions, have dinner and sleep. We crossed the Loire at Orléans before the bridges were blown up. We were on the road with all the civilians and were strafed a few times, each time jumping from the truck and crouching in the roadside ditches. Fortunately, no one was hit.

The French officers, a part of a service of the High Command, were not used to eating K-rations. By French Army tradition, the youngest officer on staff is designated as *popotier* (i.e. the officer in charge, with the cook, of all meal arrangements and seeing that the officers are well fed). Being the youngest, with the lowest rank (2nd Lieutenant) and, further, being an administrative officer and not a doctor, I was automatically selected for the job—not a pleasant one in normal times, as one can easily be the goat in any culinary situation which goes amiss. As we were always on the move except in the evening, and especially given the exceedingly critical military situation (the defeat at our doors, the refugees on the road surrounding us and the alerts for air attacks), it was of course impossible and unthinkable to consider planned, cooked meals most of the time. At our first lunch I passed out the French Army rations packed for us before we left Paris. Soon there were many complaints: "Lieutenant, this cannot continue like this. Why don't you go to see farmers—buy chickens, ducks, butter, jam, milk and wine with the petty cash so we can have some good meals." I heard this reproach several times, and realized I was not becoming very popular. I tried once or twice to look for these supplies, but it was extremely difficult to find anything as the refugees invariably reached the farmers first. However, there were a few times when I was able to buy eggs, milk and bread and, once, four chickens. But in looking for farmers away from the road we were traveling, I was risking losing our column.

It disgusted me to realize that the officers were thinking more of their stomachs than of the war we were losing. Particularly depressing were the conversations I overheard at the occasional dinners held at a farm or a château. A long refectory table would be set up by the orderlies so that the twenty or so officers could eat together with the General. Most of the officers, doctors with ranks from Colonel down to Captain, were either from the regular service or from the reserves. As an officer and as *popotier* I was entitled to sit at the end of the table. How many times I heard declarations that proved a wind of defeat was blowing over their heads and that most of them had already given up!

The spirit of defeatism displayed by many of the staff was incomprehensible to someone so recently arrived from the U.S. Not one officer wished to continue the fighting. As the youngest, there was little I could say; I could only listen as I supervised the service of the orderlies. I had been in France barely three months when we left Paris, and this showed me how little we had known in New York of what was really going on and what the spirit was among the French people.

A few days later, on June 18th, we were at a farm in Dordogne, waiting for instructions, when we heard on the radio in the farmer's kitchen that Marshal Pétain (now head of the government) was seeking an armistice. I was dumbfounded and profoundly saddened. In the complete absence of news about what had happened in Bordeaux, to which the government had evacuated, I wondered how Marshal

Pétain, the hero of Verdun, could have come to what seemed to me a complete surrender to the enemy. Why had the government of France, as had been discussed, not sailed into exile in North Africa and continued the fight on the side of the Allies? Premier Paul Reynaud had resigned and now another group of politicians, Pierre Laval and his acolytes, pressured old Pétain to accept defeat and sign a pact with the Germans.

In the great confusion which reigned around us, I mulled those points all day. The next evening I talked with a sympathetic young warrant officer who felt as I did. By chance that morning he had heard on a radio belonging to a refugee on the road de Gaulle's famous call on the BBC from London, to which de Gaulle had escaped a few days earlier. Taking with him, as Churchill later wrote, "the honor of France," he intended to continue the fight and to create his own government in exile. In his message de Gaulle, proclaiming that "France has lost a battle! But France has not lost the war!" called on all Frenchmen and all officers and men of the armed forces to join him and fight for the liberation of the motherland. My friend said he intended to slip out of France and rally to de Gaulle. I, too, thought I had no reason to stay in France; I was sure I could better help the Allied cause from America where I wanted to return as early as possible.

Obviously there was no way to continue the battle on French territory. We had lost on all fronts. After June 5, when the Germans reached Dunkirk, the debacle progressed quickly. The French units retreating south of the Loire River were never regrouped into a cohesive army. Some fighting took place to retard the offensive of the Germans, but the French were unable to attempt resistance on a broad front. The Army of Paris was never brought sufficiently together to function either defensively or offensively. During the retreat, many soldiers simply left their units and went home. The army and the government had totally collapsed. Yet, in certain parts of the front, French troops had fought tenaciously and offered heroic resistance to the German onslaught. The roads were still full of refugees; half of France was on the road going south. Refugees were billeted everywhere, in public buildings and private homes. There were grave shortages of food and rarely any bread or milk. Gasoline was rationed and extremely difficult to find; for civilians supplies dwindled rapidly to zero. People were stuck where they were, and many slept in the streets. The chaos was indescribable; fortunately, it was summer.

When people heard Pétain announce that France was seeking an armistice, most were immensely relieved. Few wanted the fighting to continue. After the government left Paris, many believed that a Communist takeover would occur, and rumors spread of a "Red-run commune." Most of the French people were convinced that new leader Pétain had saved them and that everyone should rally to him in the spirit of patriotism. The refugees wanted to return to their homes to find out what had happened to their households. They regarded Pétain as the best defender of their interests. They believed he would be able to protect them from too harsh a life under the occupation. Most civil servants rallied and returned to their posts.

A line of demarcation was established dividing France into more or less equal occupied and unoccupied sectors. The line passed through Châteauroux, a large city in the center of the country. Soon, our unit got orders to go there, to be demobilized at an important military hub in this key garrison city. Châteauroux had a population of close to 50,000 and there was enough billeting for a vast operation of this kind—an operation that would continue for several weeks.

It was very difficult for any man under 40 years of age to leave the country: it had been strictly forbidden by both the German occupation authorities and by Vichy. As far as I was concerned, however, my plan was clear. I received a letter from my mother just the day before I left Suresnes in which she mentioned rather vaguely that she had been offered the chance to evacuate with friends should it become necessary, and she named Tulle, a small city in the center of France known for its lace making, as a possible destination. I wanted first to find her. With the sketchy inkling that she might be in Tulle, I decided to find her among the millions of refugees now temporarily settled in farms and homes, towns and villages, pensions and hotels. While still connected with my unit I had asked permission to travel toward Tulle in one of our requisitioned vans. Driving had to be done partly at night on mountain roads, without lights; using car lights was still strictly forbidden. With little difficulty I was incredibly lucky to find Mother in a small inn in Tulle. I then immediately had to return to my unit and go to Châteauroux to be demobilized from the French Army, and I asked her to go to Vichy and wait for me. Vichy had become Pétain's government seat, with him, the ministers and their skeleton staffs installed in the old palace hotels of the world-famous spa, in the salons, bedrooms and even the bathrooms! The staffs of foreign embassies had followed the government to Vichy, and my plan for returning to America was to contact the U.S. Embassy and make suitable arrangements for my mother and me as soon as feasible.

Difficult Return to America

I did not want to return to the civil service job at the Ministry of Commerce in Paris, which was still open to me. I held nothing in common with those who had made a pact with Hitler, and I could visualize what it would be like to live under the occupying authorities, work under their control and, perhaps, report for this or that to the German *Kommandantur*. To continue the war from outside France, as de Gaulle had suggested Frenchmen do, was, it seemed, the right decision, particularly for those like me who had been abroad and could help the Allies in one way or another. I was sure they would win the war in the end and restore France's freedom.

Above all, I wanted to rejoin Natalie and take my mother back to New York where she had lived for so many years. It was obvious that our future was in America, if we could reach its shores.

There was also another painful problem: Tante Amélie. She lived in Beaucourt, Territoire de Belfort, an area labeled "forbidden" by the Germans. It was on the border of Alsace-Lorraine, a province which the occupying forces had always considered their own and had lost to France after World War I. Now Alsace had been recovered and traveling to and from that area would be difficult, if not impossible. Even if I had returned to my post in the Ministry of Commerce, I could not get to her, so what could we do? Mother and I, with heavy hearts, had no choice but to leave her behind. It was among the hardest decisions we had to make; it seemed like we were abandoning her. She was close to 80 and continued to live alone in her small apartment even though she had become very deaf. We knew good and devoted friends and neighbors would look after her and help her with her food. We also knew that our cousin, Eugénie Labarthe, would be able to return to Enghien near Paris. She would write to her and send her money, as Tante Amélie had no income of her own and was entirely dependent on our family. Later we learned that she managed for a while, but little by little she lost her mind and began neglecting herself. We felt guilty, despite knowing that there was nothing we could have done. Still later we learned that she had died, at age 82, and right to the end had been helped by her good friends.

Demobilized from Châteauroux I went to Vichy by bus, bought myself civilian clothes, and found my mother, with whom I took up temporary residence in a small hotel. At the American Embassy, we were able to see the Chargé d'Affaires of the United States, Bob Murphy, and Freeman Matthews, the First Secretary.[2] They put us in touch with a clerk who told us how to get the documents we needed to leave France. For my mother it was easy. She was still a French citizen, had lived many years as a foreign resident in the United States and had a re-entry permit regularly renewed and still valid to return to the United States at any time. Provided she could find transportation she would in theory have no trouble leaving France to return to her former residence in New York City.

For me, the situation was different. First, nothing could be done at the American Embassy in Vichy. I had to see the nearest U.S. Consul, and that was in Marseille. Mother and I took a very crowded overnight train, changed at Lyons, and arrived in Marseille the next morning. We put up at a hotel not far from the famous Cannebière and the U.S. Consulate. I expected no trouble. I explained to the Consul that I had been registered at the American Consulate in Paris as a child, I had an expired U.S. passport. I wanted to apply for a new passport on the grounds that I wanted to return to the United States to join my fiancée, get married and found an American family. But I had been raised as a Frenchman, and my studies had all been in French schools. I was a French citizen according to French law. As I had lived with my great aunt, I had no possibility of returning to the United States, particularly since my mother (the only relative I had there) had come back to France in 1930 to retire, and I had lived with her since then except for the 18 months I had spent in New York at the World's Fair.

The Consul looked at me, paused in silence for some time, then stated emphatically that I was no longer an American citizen. My passport was no longer valid and he could not renew it nor issue a new one, as I had forfeited my American citizenship by serving as an officer in the French Army.

I protested that I had dual nationality and that while living in France I had to conduct myself as a Frenchman. Before the war I did not know whether I would one day be able to return to America but I was sure there were hundreds of persons who, like me, had dual nationality. The fact that I had returned to the United States in 1938, had become engaged to an American girl, and wanted to go back to her and marry her made all the difference in the world in my view. My American citizenship was a birthright, I loved America as my second home. I saw nothing wrong in my trying to get back to New York. From there, I could further help the war effort, and

---

2 Both later became top ranking U.S. ambassadors.

perhaps this should be encouraged. I explained again that if my father had not died when I was a baby I would have been raised in the U.S. as an American child. I said that serving as an officer in the French Army resulted from the fact that I was in a graduate school in Paris where ROTC was compulsory. I recognized that I had not resisted being enrolled in ROTC and had become a French Reserve officer of my own volition after having been drafted into the Army. But, I asked the Consul, could I have done otherwise? In the end, I pleaded that he postpone his decision to deny me a passport and ask for a ruling from the State Department in Washington. I would wait in Marseille for the answer. He finally agreed and told me that a reply might take weeks to come. I filed the necessary papers and left the Consulate.

As far as my mother was concerned, he looked at her re-entry permit and told her she could return to the U.S.; she had lived there for more than 35 years.

We waited patiently for the decision which was to shape my future, and while waiting visited Marseille in some detail—its old port, the Cannebière, *Notre-Dame de la Garde*, an elegant basilica built on a high hill with a statue of the Blessed Virgin blessing the harbor and dominating the whole city.

The days passed. We continued to feel the pulse of this animated old Mediterranean city dating back to the Phoenicians, and to kill time as best we could, but we were becoming seriously discouraged, despite the Consul's caveat that the answer might take a long time. Three weeks passed and we had checked the Consulate many times. At last the reply came: Washington had authorized the Consul to issue me a passport. A major hurdle had been cleared!

The problems now were how to reach New York and, as mentioned, the fact that no Frenchman below forty years of age was allowed to leave France; I was not yet thirty. The Vichy government and the Germans feared that men able to fight would escape to London to join the Free French or the French Colonial forces in the territories of the French empire that had not rallied to Vichy. They had made one exception: all those called home to the colors at the start of the war and who returned to fight in France were authorized to return to their homes abroad. My embarkation point had been New York, where I had been in temporary residence when war was declared. My permanent home, however, had been Paris. Would I fall under the exception? Or be able to explain my situation at the border? I was confident that I would be able to do so, and decided to forget that possible problem.

The real difficulty for Mother and me would now be to gain passage on one of the four liners still crossing the Atlantic via the southern route. In fact the American Export Line was the only company maintaining such service. But there were literally thousands of people in Lisbon hoping to board one of the Line's small passenger fleet plying between Lisbon and New York. Refugees, almost all of them wealthy, waited for months in that port hoping for accommodations. Reaching Lisbon through Spain was difficult, but was nothing compared to arranging for the sea voyage. We had neither the dollars nor the francs to buy the tickets, and the agent of the shipping company in Marseille only gave us a gentle smile when we sought to make reservations. All cabins on the American Export Line ships had been reserved for months.

But Mother had many friends in New York who, hopefully, could help. We cabled Barbara and Elizabeth Whitmore, who had been students of my mother's at the Spence School and who had set up the first successful travel agency in New York run by women. They, in turn, having friendly contacts at American Export Line's head office on Broadway, managed to secure two priority reservations for us on a ship leaving Lisbon barely a week after the day we received their return cable. They had even advanced the cost of the tickets. Everything being thus miraculously settled, we had only to get to Lisbon as quickly as possible.

We took the Barcelona train at the *Gare St-Charles* in Marseille. From there the difficulties began. We were informed on reaching the French-Spanish border that the exact amount of currency we had with us had not been correctly entered into our passports. This created trouble with the Customs and Immigration authorities when we later tried to leave Spain for Portugal.

We had been advised not to take the train across Spain since it was under the control of the Gestapo. We would be thoroughly searched and interrogated, and I might even be arrested because I had been in the French Army. At that time the country was full of German officers looking for men trying to escape occupied Europe; General Franco, an ally of the Axis, had given the Germans freedom to carry on their investigations. Ending up in one of El Caudillo's prisons was not exactly a pleasant prospect. So we decided to fly from Barcelona to Lisbon and took reservations for the next day on Iberia, the Spanish civil airline.

The plane on which we were flying was a relic that carried about 25 passengers—a kind of DC-3, not very comfortable. The engine did not run smoothly; decidedly something was wrong. It would, very obviously, have been dangerous to proceed with the flight. A few seconds later the engine stopped altogether, for what must have been only a few seconds, then started up again. The pilot immediately turned around and headed for a landing on the main runway. Quite relieved, we were brought back to the airport building to wait. No other Iberia aircraft was available; passengers were left to make other plans on their own.

We were about to go back to town when we were told that a scheduled Lufthansa flight was due shortly from Germany on a run to Barcelona, Madrid and Lisbon. We could transfer to that plane. Our big question was whether it would be safe to place our fate in the hands of the Germans. Obviously, Gestapo officers would be on board and there would be a serious investigation of each passenger.

The Lufthansa plane, a beautiful, spacious craft, arrived. Our tickets and baggage were duly checked and we boarded. After takeoff we were asked to show our papers. I pulled out my U.S. passport. As the United States was still neutral at the time, there could be no objection to my traveling back to America, and I didn't even have to show my French papers or explain my situation. With my mother, the officer, elegant in a grey uniform and a Gestapo agent no doubt, was most correct, and the examination of her passport was a simple formality. For a young Frenchman my age, trying to join de Gaulle in London, the Gestapo's check of papers went badly. The Gestapo agents immediately removed him from the rest of the passengers, and when we landed in Madrid, we watched with helpless sadness as he was taken by Spanish authorities—probably to spend the rest of the war in a Spanish jail.

In Madrid we again had great difficulty at the airport because of the discrepancy between the amount of *pesetas* and other currencies we were carrying and what had been written in our passports at the French-Spanish border. My mother was taken into a cabin, completely undressed by Spanish women inspectors, searched, and finally released. We arrived in Lisbon early that afternoon, blessed to have reached what we felt was a haven.

The *SS Excalibur* had arrived in port on its way to New York. We were grateful to be able to board her after only 48 hours in Lisbon. Thousands of people, turning their backs to enslaved Europe, were trying to reach the New World at untold sacrifices, having sold jewels, houses, and other personal assets (presumably at great loss) and saying adieu to their homes forever. A large majority of them were Jews fleeing persecution and the almost inevitable concentration camps.

The boat was as crowded as we had expected. My mother shared a cabin with several other ladies and I slept in the ship's lounge, in which many cots had been placed. The crossing proved calm and uneventful, the minds of the passengers fastened on the future. We landed in New York on the Presidential Election day in which "One World" Wendell L. Wilkie lost to Franklin Delano Roosevelt.

The French Embassy Under Vichy

We soon found an apartment on East 61st Street between Lexington and Third Avenues. Natalie had come to New York from Padanaram and we had a glorious time together.

The Second World War: Fighting under Two Flags

I had been in New York only a few weeks, reacquainting myself with the traffic and the tempo of life there and registering with the draft board, when Charles Taquet, the personal secretary to Hervé Alphand, the *Financial Counselor* of the French Embassy in the United States, left his job to become an American paratrooper. In Paris, I had worked in the same Ministry in a division parallel to Alphand's. He had a high reputation in France,[3] where he was the youngest of the top French civil servants, an *Inspecteur des Finances*—one of the elite corps of the French government. *Inspecteurs des Finances* serve in the most sensitive executive positions in French ministries, besides their regular service with the Ministry of Finance. But Alphand had fallen into disfavor with the Vichy government and was shelved for the duration of the war in the post of *Financial Counselor* in Washington and New York. Alphand had nothing in common with the men of Vichy. He admired de Gaulle and bided his time. Besides, there were seriously important diplomatic and economic relations with the United States to maintain or develop. He hired me in December 1940 as his personal assistant to draft some of the office correspondence, prepare reports on the economic situation in the United States, and do some liaison work.

As an American citizen I was registered with the State Department as working for a foreign government, a situation I shared with most of the other employees, naturalized U.S. citizens of French origin with experience in both countries and a knowledge of French and English which was essential for these positions.

I had some hesitation in taking even this technical job, but I needed the work. As I was not responsible for any decisions at the policy level I could easily resign if I felt that I could no longer work there for political reasons.

I soon became immersed in rewarding work in negotiations with Dean Acheson's office in the State Department and the Morgan Bank, the financial representative of the French government in the United States. We wanted to release frozen French funds for humanitarian efforts in North Africa and the French West Indies. I also translated complicated financial and banking regulations from Vichy for distribution to banks and various financial agencies in the United States.

Above M. Alphand, the government of Vichy had appointed Robert Lacour-Gayet, one of the top financial civil servants in France, as *Senior Inspecteur des Finances* in New York to oversee the work done in our office. Although Alphand continued in charge of all Washington contacts and negotiations, it seemed obvious that Lacour-Gayet had been sent to New York to watch him, and he kept a low profile

---

3   As mentioned previously, he eventually served as France's Ambassador to the United States during the Kennedy and the Johnson administrations

in the office. I had to do some work for Lacour-Gayet on several occasions; he seemed to appreciate my services and liked me.

Lacour-Gayet was a man of high standing who thought that a civil servant must continue to serve his country without regard to the political tendencies of the government; it was France that counted. This was the common position of most civil servants in France and many French officials in the United States had, on the whole, the same reaction. M. Lacour-Gayet's reasoning was that there should be no eclipse of the State. Loyal service was needed to preserve the essential elements of national sovereignty. One should remain at one's place rather than resign and count on the Allied Forces to free France under conditions that no one could foresee. Later, Lacour-Gayet wrote me a personal note to say how much he regretted I had chosen to leave my job.

Free French and Vichyites in New York: Resignation

I decided to leave my job in the summer of 1941, realizing more strongly with each passing day how the Vichy regime was anathema to me. I was for the elite movement which had started in France's overseas empire in Africa and in the Near East, and principally in London with General de Gaulle. From the papers I learned that soon after General Catroux in Indochina had joined de Gaulle as an individual, others such as Maurice Schumann, René Cassin and Gaston Palewski had also rallied to the Free French movement. Several French personalities (such as Jean Monnet, Alexis Léger and others) stayed in the United States and were struggling against Vichy, but did not join de Gaulle.

The situation of the French in New York was both difficult and disheartening. The French colony was deeply divided.[4] There were those who wanted to remain faithful to Marshal Pétain, and they were the majority of those who continued to work in the various services of the French government in the U.S. Some of these officials, however, had left Vichy. This was the case with Robert Valeur, the Cultural Attaché at the Embassy, a friend, whose office was in New York, and of Maurice Garreau-Dombasle, the *Commercial Counselor*, who had been Deputy High Commisioner, one of my superiors at New York World's Fair. These two had taken the lead of the Free French in New York which comprised the majority of the French working in the United States, not related to the French government services. The two groups daily destroyed each other in the press, at social gatherings and the like.

---

4 The *Financial Counselor's* Office, where I worked, was housed at 20 Exchange Place, New York. Except for Lacour-Gayet, I believe everyone opposed Vichy. It was much different at the Embassy in Washington where a number of staff members, under Ambassador Gaston Henry-Hayes actively defended the pro-German Vichy policies.

I had friends on both sides: those that I knew best, still working for the government of Marshal Pétain, wanted me to side with them. I was for de Gaulle one hundred percent. The atmosphere among the French in New York, and their constant bickering, was becoming unbearable.

Had I felt completely free I would probably have joined de Gaulle immediately. Natalie was still in New York, working for a cosmetics firm in Radio City. We would meet in the evening for dinner at the Blue Room on Madison Avenue, and sometimes would go to our special rock in Central Park to dream about our future and plan our marriage and life together.

Interlude, 1941—1942: A Job on a Tropical Island
One day I learned that the Standard Fruit and Steamship Company, a large banana corporation operating in Central America and the West Indies, was looking for an administrative assistant to its Vice-President for company operations in Haiti, a French-speaking country in the Caribbean. Standard Fruit in Haiti, as in other countries of Central America and in Jamaica, had important banana plantations, and also bought bananas grown by local planters for shipment to the United States. The actual company headquarters were in New Orleans and they had sent staff from Louisiana to Haiti. Standard Fruit was the second-largest banana corporation in the Western Hemisphere, after United Fruit. The company had been in Haiti for six or seven years and had a contract with the Haitian government giving it the exclusive right to purchase and export bananas from the island. They bought the crops produced by peasant farmers all over the island, and had set up plantations of their own on five or six thousand leased acres in the Artibonite Valley, with its systems for irrigating, draining and spraying the banana trees all installed by the company.

Natalie and I thought that a job with Standard Fruit in Haiti might be attractive professionally—and provide a lovely, exotic place for a honeymoon. Because the legal system in Haiti is based on Roman law, the company was looking for someone with some legal training in France and was ready to hire me. I knew absolutely nothing about the banana industry, but because of my education (the equivalent of an MBA and a French law degree) they thought I could be useful to their Haitian lawyers when the company's contract with the government called for discussion at the level of the Minister of Agriculture.

I was still somewhat confused as to the road to follow. Something was bothering me deeply. On the one hand I thought going to Port-au-Prince and spending some time away from New York, in an entirely different environment, would be beneficial and give me the time needed to sort out various important questions for my future.

I was, however, asking myself if it was not my duty to go back to war, or participate in some other way in the fight being waged against the Nazis. Was I taking the right decision in deciding to settle on a tropical island so far from the hostilities? Should I not have enlisted in the Free French Army upon resigning my job with Vichy? I had been raised, like all French youth, on the principle that one had to serve one's country in time of war. There were practically no conscientious objectors in France in those days. I was an American citizen, it is true, but I was French also. I felt that, having been brought up French and having benefited from all the advantages of French citizenship, it was my duty to continue in the war to the finish. I had also felt, in 1940, that there had been no contradiction in my going back to France to fight in the war and at the same time remaining an American. After all, hundreds of United States citizens had volunteered for the Royal Air Force or had gone to France with the American Friends Service to join the ambulance corps. All of this was going intensely through my mind over a period of time. Finally, I decided to take the job in Haiti.

I told Mr. Blackmon, Vice President of Standard Fruit, that I intended to be married before going to Port-au-Prince and would travel with my wife. He then asked me to delay our marriage for three months, to go alone to see whether I liked the work and could adjust to the life of the tropics. He obviously also wanted to find out if I "fit the bill" well. Mr. Blackmon said that by the end of November my fiancée could travel to Haiti on a company boat at company expense and we could be married there. Although the prospect of a wedding on an exotic island was attractive, the request would deprive us of a wedding at Natalie's home with her family and friends. My mother, who had questioned the wisdom of our marriage plans, said she would not be able to go to Haiti. My future father-in-law was a superintendent of schools and could not absent himself at that time.

Having accepted the job, we also had to agree that I would go to Haiti alone in July and, if all went well, Natalie would arrive in Port-au-Prince for December 1, our tentative wedding date (and, coincidentally, my thirty-first birthday).

Just after all the arrangements with Standard Fruit had been made, something extremely important happened that could have changed our plans completely and, in fact, the orientation of my life. I had resigned from my previous job a few weeks before and was still living in my mother's apartment on East 61st Street when the telephone rang. Hervé Alphand, my former boss, was on the line. I had ceased all contact with the French Embassy office when I learned that M. Alphand had suddenly resigned from his post as *Financial Counselor*. He had told the *New York Times* and the *Washington Post* that he could no longer serve Vichy, a government which now was openly collaborating with the Germans, and he was offering his services to General de Gaulle. I had not seen him since I left my job and did not know his intentions in advance, but that morning—the eve of my departure for Haiti—he informed me that he was going to Washington the next day to talk to M. René Pleven, a former minister of the French Republic, a personality so well known in France that he became number two in the Free French movement when he joined de Gaulle in London in charge of economic affairs. He had been sent as a special envoy to discuss the status of Free France with the U.S. government.

Since Alphand knew the way I felt, he was suggesting that I accompany him on his trip to Washington. A more mature person would no doubt have asked for a few hours to reflect, as Alphand's proposal certainly required a momentous decision on my part. I felt that his question demanded an immediate reply. At once I said that I could not accept because I had signed a contract with Standard Fruit and was leaving for Haiti the next day. I felt bound to honor that contract and keep my word. I also said I was going to be married. Evidently, Alphand was giving his former assistant a chance to join the Free French. Undoubtedly he would have talked about me to Pleven. I could have been taken on board and the work I would do would have been far more important to the Allied cause than what I would be doing in Haiti. I missed a chance. There are moments in life when your future is being gambled in the space of a few seconds. This was one of those. Alphand did not try to change my mind. He simply said he was sorry I was committed and hung up. My immediate future had been sealed.

A few days later my banana boat arrived at dawn at Cape Haitian, a port on the north coast of Haiti, the second-largest town of the Republic and the former Cap-Français. There the expeditionary corps of General Leclerc, the husband of Napoleon's sister Pauline Bonaparte, had landed to quell the revolt of St-Domingue, the French colony then called the "Pearl of the Antilles."

I went on deck; the sun was rising in a rosy sky. Still far away, as we were approaching, I could distinguish the shoreline with its range of coconut trees, the city of Cape Haitian, the dome of its cathedral and beyond, far away, the high blue and mauve mountains on the horizon with the famous "Citadelle," built by King Christopher at the cost of 20,000 lives.

It was my first vision of a tropical island rising from the sea. The boat had stopped in the middle of the bay. A barge was coming to meet us, bringing customs officials aboard. I could hear from the shore a strange background noise of hundreds of different human voices, punctuated by shrieks and other sounds—including the braying of donkeys, the crowing of cocks, and the beating of drums. Was I in Africa?

The noise became clearer as we moved a bit closer to the shore and I could now clearly see under the trees a public market with hundreds of people moving back and forth or standing in front of merchants' stalls.

The customs officials came aboard and authorized the unloading of the cargo onto the barge. I watched my cabin trunk emerge from the hold, swaying back and forth at the end of a cable and threatening at any moment to come to rest not on the barge but right in the middle of the bay. It was a scary moment. Then it was the turn of my old Ford motorcar to be unloaded. I watched that with palpitations. It landed abruptly on the barge, and although the fenders had been handled somewhat roughly in the process, my fears had by then been mildly allayed.

The few passengers descended a rope ladder, some helped by the crew, into a small motor boat. Finally we all reached the wharf where a representative of Standard Fruit was waiting to welcome me and to introduce a driver who would drive me—in my car—to Port-au-Prince, two hundred miles south. This journey was to take the entire day, traveling on primitive roads through the most incredibly beautiful tropical scenery. Leaving the fertile northern plain with its fields of sugar cane, banana and citrus trees, one could at times see some fairly large plantations. But the countryside was mostly divided into very small holdings, some only a fraction of an acre.

Haiti is basically a country of *minifundia*. At the end of the revolution in 1804, the freedom fighters, all former slaves, had each received from their generals a parcel of land as a reward for winning the independence of the country. These holdings became smaller and smaller as they were divided among descendants of the original freedom fighters. This practice was to constitute a considerable obstacle to agricultural development, but was also a later guarantee that Haitians would not be attracted to Communism; they love their land dearly.

One could now distinguish, far away, the famous "Citadelle," built by King Christopher at the cost of 20,000 lives. We were driving on the flank of a barren mountain, along dangerous precipices on a narrow road full of stones, potholes and gullies caused by violent tropical rains. This, the only road between Cap Haitian and Port-au-Prince, was terribly in need of repair and the going was quite difficult. It had been built under the U.S. occupation which ended in 1934, and the funds assigned by the government since then to maintain roads and build new ones were insufficient to the need. The government, having few resources of its own, had to wait until the United States was ready to help with both road building and maintenance.

We reached Gonaïve, a town on the Gulf of La Gonave (an important historic place—there, on January 1, 1804, the independence of the country was proclaimed by General Jean-Jacques Dessalines and its name changed to Haiti, meaning "mountainous land"). All I could see was mountain after mountain: beautiful mottled colors, shades of grey, brown and beige. Few trees or bushes adorned them, and one could see patches of grass in only a few areas. It was a dramatic portrait of mass erosion, a sight one could view only with great sadness.

The driver explained that the trees had been cut by the peasants to make charcoal for cooking. Haiti had been deforested in so many places for years and years. Later, in the '60s and '70s, when I returned there, the situation had worsened to such an extent that fighting erosion had become the greatest problem the country faced—along with illiteracy.

We passed several villages with huts crowded together on both sides of the road among coconut, breadfruit and other tropical trees, including numerous poincianas (called flamboyants in Haiti). Little naked children were playing by a stream.

Then we drove through a vast plateau covered with scrubby vegetation, a very hot, dry land bordered on one side by a range of barren mountains. White, enormous cumulus clouds of all shapes were slowly moving in an impeccably blue sky. On our right lay the cobalt blue Caribbean Sea and, farther out, Gonave Island—the most primitive area of Haiti. In its colorful simplicity, this landscape had an infinite grandeur, so different from other parts of the country we had crossed.

Then again we would reach another oasis of foliage with royal palms, coconut and breadfruit trees and banana plantings—with all their variations of green—surrounding peasant huts with walls of dried mud and thatched roofs. Women were cooking outside.

The profusion of fallen leaves, coating the ground and fermenting in the hot, humid atmosphere, produced a pungency that I had never before experienced. It was a heavy scent, like a heady perfume, not unpleasant, that I would remember always.

Soon after we neared Port-au-Prince. As we approached the capital there were many bicycles on the road, and traffic became heavier, although still sparse by our standards, as there were few automobiles in Haiti at the time. What struck me most was the people walking on each side of the road—mainly women—carrying loads on their heads, their bodies and necks perfectly erect. They were a most graceful sight with their simple white dresses (more like sacks hanging from their shoulders) with or without belts. The color of most of the dresses was no longer white but greyish, despite many washings in the river, soiled by road dust and tropical downpours. These women were returning from the markets to their homes, sometimes as much as 20 to 30 miles away. They had spent most of their day in

Port-au-Prince and were taking back the small number of coins and rolled *gourdes* bills they had earned. I soon became familiar with the one-*gourde* notes ($.20 U.S.) in circulation, so dirty from being passed from hand to hand that it was almost impossible to read anything printed on them.

We entered Port-au-Prince and drove along the Grande Rue, a wide, straight street crossing the whole downtown with its one-story stores painted pink or ochre or white. There were sidewalks under arcades, the front of each store being a large opening with no doors, from which one could see all the goods displayed inside. At night iron curtains were rolled down and padlocked to close up the shops. Many passers-by and poorly dressed persons milled around and stood by the doors; street vendors camped under the arcades with their own little stands, selling fried foods or knick-knacks. Dusk was approaching and the night was about to fall—abruptly, as it always does here—and traffic was heavy; people were going home.

I noticed the famous mini-buses I had been told about (the *tap-taps* as they are called), with their multi-colored inscriptions—mostly Biblical quotations. Sometimes the backs of the *tap-taps* were painted with scenes of the life of Christ. In other cases, inscriptions with letters of white or red or even two colors were more prosaic: one said *Partou*t, meaning going everywhere. But I saw no bus stops anywhere along the way. I later found out that the vehicles stopped wherever passengers wanted to alight, the drivers thus providing a totally flexible transportation service. For one *gourde* you could go anywhere in Port-au-Prince. There were also many derelict taxicabs picking up passengers along the way, so they were always full.

Downtown left an impression of poverty on me, but I had to admit that its color and animation made it picturesque, almost carnival-like. We passed the famous iron market, painted in red and green, and soon reached the non-commercial part of the city and were driving toward the residential districts built on the flank of the Morne de l'Hôpital—the mountain which dominates the city. In the lower part of town the houses were small and close together, but each had its little garden. Many of the homes had gingerbread porches and verandahs painted in pastel shades, and often one could see a small tower with a peaked roof (like a miniature church steeple) built on a housetop.

None of the roofs were tiled. All the buildings, without exception, were covered with wavy galvanized iron sheets painted Indian red. Some showed rust from lack of maintenance. The next day, looking at them under the sun, I thought that this rusty appearance gave these modest houses some respectability and dignity. They had been there a long time and their rich, warm coloring complemented the varied green foliage. As an artist, I had been discovering all day the bright colors of the rural tropics, and now I was discovering the equally colorful aspects of the Haitian capital with its beautiful and romantic name.

We climbed a steeper street and rolled to a stop before a monumental entrance with two high white pillars and a wide-open iron gate. We were entering the gardens of the famous *Hotel Oloffson*, where a room had been reserved for me. This was a most amazing structure for a hotel. One of the best-known large gingerbread houses in Haiti, it was a Port-au-Prince landmark. When a decade later Haiti became a tourist attraction (thanks to advice and a training program started with the help of the United Nations) the *Hotel Oloffson* became well known to artists, writers, journalists and "sense-seeking" travelers of the world—the types of tourist who visited Haiti to experience its unique pulse, customs, culture and, naturally, its voodoo.

The driver slowly followed the curved alley leading to the foot of the majestic white stone steps that fronted the hotel. At least two dozen beautiful, very tall, royal palm trees—their perfectly straight trunks lofting toward the sky—graced the garden. Behind them, at the top of the hill, rose the hotel itself, all white, a perfect model of the gingerbread houses that glorified the Victorian architectural era in Port-au-Prince. These houses had been designed by Haitian architects trained at the *École des Beaux Arts* in Paris at the turn of the century, and only a few remained. These same architects later designed beautiful modern European-style villas, with luxuriant gardens, scattered on the hills, where the wealthy Port-au-Princian mulatto elite lived, dominating the city and enjoying the most beautiful view of the bay.

My car was parked in the former stables of the hotel which now served as garages, and while servants were taking care of my luggage I climbed the stairs leading to a long covered porch which served as an open-air dining room. My room was in a separate part of the hotel, a sort of long annex with a front balcony on the second floor, from which I could look at the whole city—the Presidential Palace gleaming white on my right. This annex had been built as a temporary hospital for the U.S. Marines during the American occupation, from 1915 to 1934.

All I had seen was so different from what I had known in Europe and in the United States! There was something enchanting about it despite the heavy, still atmosphere of that first evening in Haiti and the heat of the summer which was beginning to hit me—and that would become hard to bear in the months ahead. There was no air conditioning in those days. But I told myself it would only be a question of getting used to it.

Bananas and U-Boats

Shortly after I unpacked, I met John Brownson, the Vice-President in Charge of Standard Fruit in Haiti, in the lounge of the hotel. He was a bachelor with a really pleasant and welcoming smile. He may have been 60 or so years of age, was of average height, had a tanned complexion and a handsome face, with a crop of silver hair carefully parted on the side and a pair of glasses with translucent frames and heavy lenses. He gave me the impression of a serious, but affable, successful banking executive. He was from New Orleans and, I learned later, had worked up through the echelons of the Company by starting as an accountant. He spoke French well and had come to Port-au-Prince seven years before to start the operations of the company in Haiti.

This had required much complicated negotiating with the government, and also involved establishing a central office in Port-au-Prince and many centers across the Republic, called *comptoirs*, where Standard Fruit agents would buy the bananas grown by Haitian peasants. The price, by the bunch, varied in accordance with the size and quality of the fruit and the number of "fingers" in each bunch. Bananas in Haiti had never been grown for export before and the peasants had to get used to these new procedures.

Soon after these centers had been established, the Haitian farmers could regularly sell their fruit there and get immediate cash for their crop. This was something completely new in Haiti. As a result, the acceptance of the company was immediate, and its reputation grew very rapidly. As a cash crop, bananas were more satisfactory than coffee. The price paid for the purchase of the coffee crop was subject to the decisions of the "speculators," the agents of the coffee exporters, and varied from one year to the next. This left great uncertainty among the peasants and they often felt cheated.

Standard Fruit, in the few years it had been in Haiti, also had helped repair—and often entirely reconstruct—the wharves needed for the loading of the fruit. As a result, there had been a marked revitalization of many of the small coastal ports all around Haiti. It would be no exaggeration to say that Standard Fruit gave new life to the country, and soon bananas became the second largest export crop after coffee. In addition, after laborious negotiations with hundreds of small farmers in the Artibonite Valley, the company had been able to assemble and lease hundreds of parcels of land belonging to individual Haitian farmers. The company had also established large plantations, called farms, totaling several thousand acres. On these they had planted a quality banana named *Gros Michel*, which was assured of a good market abroad. All this involved a great deal of work and considerable investments to install irrigation, drainage and spraying systems, and to conduct the soil studies that would determine the kinds and quantities of fertilizer and spraying materials needed. The whole enterprise required modern equipment and machinery, great managerial talents, and the technical help of a considerable number of irrigation engineers, hydrologists, experts in tropical agriculture, entomologists and other specialists—all coming from the United States and staying on the job until the project was ready for operation. Haiti had never known anything like this.

Mr. Brownson explained some of this to me over dinner. I was fascinated by the organization required to successfully carry out such a complicated venture. As a matter of fact, in a few years Standard Fruit had become the largest corporation on the island, surpassing the sisal industry and the Hasco Sugar Company, and had the largest payroll.

Unfortunately, such a situation was to create jealousies and envy—and six years later, long after my departure, Standard Fruit had to withdraw from Haiti, a damaging blow to the economy. President Estimé did not renew Standard Fruit's contract and he let his cronies, various senators, divide among themselves the territory once covered by company activities, setting up separate operations. Not having the management training necessary, knowing little about banana cultivation, and especially having to rely on foreign shipping (often with no refrigerated equipment), the Haitian export trade fell off, dropping from five million bunches a year to no more than 200,000 in less than two years. But during the time I was there, Standard Fruit was highly successful.

Later I met Haitian planters who owned large acreages of bananas in various parts of the country and who were under contract to the company to produce and sell their fruit to us. My work was interesting; I was getting more familiar every day with company operations and procedures. I prepared all the administrative correspondence in French and attended meetings from time to time with our lawyers for occasional discussions of the company's contracts, at the Ministry of Agriculture. I continued to live in the *Hotel Oloffson* and had made friends with George Moffitt, who worked at the American Embassy and who knew quite a number of the Haitian families.

One night George and I decided to go to the movies. On our way back to the hotel, around 11 o'clock, we both felt a little hungry and decided to go to the kitchen to see what we could find to eat, as the hotel service had ceased by that hour. Turning on the lights, we could not believe our eyes. An army of most lively cockroaches was running around on the kitchen counters! Our appetites immediately abated. We retreated, turned off the lights and went to bed. The next day we changed hotels.

We went to the *Splendid*, the number one hotel in town at that time, where we made friends with Madame Frankel, the owner, Alberti, the maître d'hôtel and superintendent and her friend, and with a Vice-Consul, Bob Folsom, who, with George, was to become one of our closest lifelong friends. The hotel guests also included Mort Copeland, who claimed to be a *Liberty Magazine* writer but who, we later learned, was an FBI agent sent to Haiti to identify coves along the Haitian coast where German U-boats were at times supposed to hide. Shipping in the Caribbean and the Gulf of Mexico had been torpedoed by the Germans on several occasions; the crews of several Allied merchant vessels who had had to abandon ship had been able to reach Haiti, sometimes with the help of the Haitian Coast Guard. Standard Fruit itself was beginning to lose some of its ships and the situation was becoming critical for the company.

A Wedding in Port-au-Prince

As my work had been satisfactory, I made plans for Natalie to join me, traveling to Haiti on one of the Standard Fruit Company ships. After saying goodbye to her mother, who with friends had accompanied her to Norfolk, Virginia, Natalie arrived on November 30, 1941, at the little port of Les Cayes on the south shore of the island—just the day before our wedding! I had gone to Les Cayes to wait for her, and I was on the wharf early that morning when the ship arrived. We drove all day to get back to Port-au-Prince, enchanted to be back together. Others might have felt the strangeness of arriving in an unknown country, with the prospect of a wedding surrounded by strangers, but Natalie was not upset at all, even though this was her first trip abroad. At the time I thought her very courageous, even with her adventurous spirit, to have taken ship all alone to join me. She had met a delightful couple, Everett and Bertha Shrewsbury, during the crossing. They sent her a fake telegram telling her that unfortunately I had the mumps and that the wedding ceremony would have to be postponed. They did not know that I, too, had cabled Natalie, welcoming her to Haiti, so she was one up on them.

Natalie was to spend the night with the French-Mullens. Mrs. French-Mullen was just the right kind of person for the occasion, and both she and her husband, who was number two at Standard fruit, could not have been more welcoming. The wedding was planned for 4 p.m. the next day. I already knew many people, after three months on the island, but nowhere near enough to hold the wedding in the vast Cathedral of St. Trinity, the Anglican church of Port-au-Prince. The ceremony would be held instead in the personal chapel of Bishop Burton, who married us. He was from an old Cincinnati family, an unmarried priest, and the first American to be be ordained a bishop in the Anglican church.

The little chapel looked like a grotto, with an altar of massive stone and small stained-glass windows. Beautiful plants decorated it, and enough chairs had been arranged to seat all the guests. My new friends from the *Hôtel Splendid* all came to the wedding.

Our marriage had been officially registered at the *Hôtel-de-Ville* of Port-au-Prince and transcribed into the register of the American Embassy. Bob Folsom had signed the pertinent documents.

The ceremony was short, but moving. Natalie wore a lovely wedding dress brought from the States. Wawa Sparks, daughter of the U.S. Chargé d'Affaires, was the bridesmaid and George Moffitt the best man. I wore a white linen suit with a flower in my lapel.

After the ceremony, Bishop Burton hosted a small reception for us and presented us with a gift he had had for many years: two marble dove bookends, exquisitely carved, which we always kept with us in our various homes and on our many assignments around the world.

Before the wedding, the Chargé d'Affaires and his wife, Mr. and Mrs. Edward Sparks (who also attended the wedding) graciously offered us an elegant sit-down luncheon at the Embassy. The senior officials of Standard Fruit, their wives, and the Embassy officers I knew also were invited. This was a delightfully cordial and animated gathering that gave us the feeling that we were already a part of the American colony. Not to be outdone, Mrs. Frankel, the proprietress of the *Hôtel Splendid*, also gave a reception for us attended by more than 40 people.

After the reception at the Bishop's, we left for our honeymoon at the mountain station of Kenscoff, 5,000 feet above Port-au-Prince. We spent a full week there in a little bungalow perched above a deep, arresting gorge—an abyss between two pine-covered mountains. Clouds continually passed over us, sometimes touching our roof and bringing refreshing cool breezes onto our terrace. It was all exquisitely romantic.

Americans alive on December 7th, 1941, remember Pearl Harbor and what they were doing the fateful day the Japanese attacked our fleet. Natalie and I were no exception. We had left our solitary refuge and were coming down the mountain. Natalie was bringing flowers to Mrs. French-Mullen, with whom she had spent the first night in Haiti and who had a weekend chalet down the road. She told Natalie the shattering news. We immediately realized that something had changed our world and that, sooner or later, we would feel the impact of the United States' entry into the war. Perhaps we would not be in Haiti for long.

We rented a delightful bungalow in Petionville, ten miles above Port-au-Prince and a cooler location than in town. We furnished it with local furniture—made to order for a total of about $100. Our social life was quite lively. We were invited to many parties, and liked the life of Port-au-Prince.

For the foreigners living there, life was easy and pleasant. Each family had several servants; quite a few had swimming pools. The climate was good, although warm and humid in the summer. The political situation was calm. The President of the Republic was Élie Lescot, a benevolent mulatto dictator—at least during the first years of his mandate.

But there was much misery in the ghetto districts of the city and, traveling to the rural areas as I did, one immediately sensed that Haiti was beset with tremendous economic and social problems. To begin with, there was an almost complete cleavage between the elite in Port-au-Prince and the peasants. Haiti had a population of between 3 and 4 million (there was no census) and 85 percent of them lived in rural areas.

It was, and remains, the poorest country in the Western Hemisphere. At the time of which I write, the per capita income was less than $100 a year. The peasants were extremely poor, cultivating the soil with the most primitive methods. It was more an economy of "picking" than one of farming. The plow was unknown; the peasants used only the hoe. The hillsides were deeply eroded. Malnutrition was prevalent and there were many diseases—particularly malaria and yaws—and 20 percent of newborn babies died in their first year.

While we were there, the Rockefeller Foundation started a program to eradicate yaws, an awful disease, manifesting itself in enormous ulcers on the skin, seemingly incurable and weakening the body so other diseases cause death. The program was later successfully continued by the World Health Organization after World War II. In a few years, thanks to penicillin, the country was entirely rid of this plague.

During my trips to the rural areas, I could measure the abyss separating the Haitian peasants from the mostly mulatto elite. The rural population practiced voodoo, was 90 percent illiterate, lived in grinding poverty and spoke only Creole. The elite lived well, were well educated, spoke both French and Creole, emulated French culture, and—mostly—derived their revenues from exploiting the rural people. Corruption was a way of life in the administration.

After several delightful months in Petionville, we had to leave our dream house. Due to the war, shortages were beginning to be felt in Port-au-Prince. The tires of my old Ford were wearing out. There were no replacements so, with no practical commuting facilities, save taxis, we had to move into the city. We rented a picturesque small house left by a missionary who had gone back to the States.

By this time we had been in Haiti nearly a year. Several factors abruptly brought an end to this life in paradise, a perfect place for a young recently-married couple.

A Bout of Malaria

I was not taking the heat well. Feeling very tired, I had been to the doctor twice. He recommended that I not settle in this kind of hot climate for many years. We had a small swimming pool surrounded by trees and bushes in our garden in which we cooled off, especially when I came back from the office in late afternoon. One day we both came down with malaria. We were both quite ill and had high fevers. I started losing weight.

To make matters worse, the company was now in serious difficulty. On one hand it had lost some of its ships to submarine warfare, which meant we had fewer refrigerated vessels in operation; on the other, because of the war effort in the U.S., higher priority was given to transporting mineral ores, metals and equipment needed by our factories than to bananas. The company was, therefore, losing money and started reducing its staff. There was some uncertainty as to whether they would be able to renew my contract, despite the satisfactory service I had given them.

There was also another factor: getting back into the war. I had been approached by Colonel Young, the military attaché of the U.S. Embassy in Port-au-Prince. We knew him socially, and he wanted to propose my name to the War Department in Washington as a candidate for the new post of U.S. Assistant Military Attaché taking into account my U.S. citizenship, my military training, and the fact that I spoke French fluently. He informed me that Americans were sorely needed in Latin America during the war and that this would be a desirable way for me to serve my country. All along I had been reluctant to stay in Port-au-Prince. Again, thoughts were coming back to me that men of my age had no right to stay quietly on a lovely tropical island while other men were fighting on the front lines. I did not think it right for me to stay in Haiti, and I wanted to rejoin the war effort. After I had decided to resign from Standard Fruit, Col. Young sent a letter about me to the Military Intelligence Service in the War Department, recommending that I be considered for a direct commission in the Army.

All the reasons for leaving Haiti, important as they were, became secondary when Natalie became pregnant. There was no way we could let her have our baby in Port-au-Prince. There were no suitable hospital facilities in the country at that time, so the risks were too great.

Once we decided to leave, events moved very fast. In two days, thanks to the head of Pan American Airways in Port-au-Prince where Natalie had worked as a secretary until two months after she became pregnant, we were able to secure two seats on a Pan American Clipper which had just started serving Port-au-Prince. No regular timetable governed these flights in those days, so we rushed to the pier downtown the day the Clipper was coming, flew to Miami, and took a train to New York. We hardly had time to realize that we had left our magic island. Another page had turned; we had come back to the U.S., a country now at war.

Before doing anything about joining the military, I wanted to wait for the birth of our baby. Natalie had gone to Massachusetts and her parents, and would go to the hospital in New Bedford for the birth. This was September, and the baby was not due until mid-December.

In the meantime, I had to get my health restored. I checked with my draft board upon arrival in New York; I was then 1-A. I went to Washington and learned there that the War Department, on the basis of Col. Young's letter and my qualifications, was ready to give me a direct commission as a Captain in the Military Intelligence Service. I was elated. I came back to New York, but the next day on opening the *New York Times* I found on the front page a headline announcing that, by Presidential Order, the delivering of direct commissions in the Armed Services had been stopped. This was, of course, a blow to me. As a result, the War Department was not allowed to process my appointment, and, shortly after, I received a letter to that effect. All this was only a few weeks before the American landing in Morocco, and—had I been appointed—I likely would have been shipped to Casablanca because of my special qualifications. For me, at that stage, there was nothing to do but let things take their course and await the draft. In the meantime, I forwarded a job application as an economist to the Board of Economic Warfare in Washington, D.C., for which I thought I was qualified, but had no idea how long it might take to hear from them.

New York: Broadcasting at NBC

I needed a job and started looking for one in New York. One day, walking along Fifth Avenue near Rockefeller Center, an idea hit me. I had read that the National Broadcasting Company, located in the RCA Building, had recently created an international division, broadcasting foreign-language news on short wave to various parts of the world. I knew they were beaming programs in French to the West Indies (particularly to Martinique and Guadeloupe) which were under Vichy at the time, and to other French-speaking islands of the Caribbean. These programs were also heard in Haiti and provided the French-speaking Haitians with our version of the news and United States views on the war, to counter-effect the broadcasts from

Vichy. The NBC broadcasts, in fact, were much appreciated in Port-au-Prince.

I thought of telephoning the NBC section handling these programs and asking whether they would like to hear Haitian reactions to the broadcasts, since I had just returned from a long stay there. I called them from a public booth at the foot of the RCA Building, got in touch with a Mr. Bernier, who was the head of the French unit, explained that I was in the neighborhood and if he had a spare moment I could come up to his office. He agreed. We talked perhaps 15 minutes.

He was indeed interested in what I had to say, and then told me he had a vacancy on his staff for a broadcaster who could present the news during the day and evening and could also prepare feature news and commentaries on the progress of the war. He asked me if I would be interested and if I would like to take a voice test. Although I had no experience in radio, I agreed. Ten minutes later he told me that I'd passed with flying colors; I had a good voice for the type of work, and he gave me a job application. It was fairly complicated because of the secretive nature of the job, which fell under the supervision of the U.S. Office of War Information. I had to be cleared by the FBI, and Mr. Bernier said that would take a few weeks. He introduced me to Fred Bates, the Manager of NBC News and an officer of the company. We talked further, and I left, taking the forms. I could not believe that a small idea such as I had had could have led so easily to a job offer as—of all things—an NBC broadcaster. It was too easy! But it was a case of being in the right place at the right time. The salary, while not great, was sufficient. At that time my mother lived in Manhattan and I could have a bed there. I went to South Dartmouth, filed the papers, and patiently waited for the clearance to come.

After three weeks of happy recuperation in South Dartmouth with my wife and in-laws, I received notice of my approval for the NBC position. I went to work in New York in a most electrifying atmosphere—preparing the news and broadcasting it—all this taking place at the top of the RCA Building. I can still see the long corridors with their bright red wall-to-wall carpeting down which I would run from the newsroom with its writers and reporters (a noisy place with the chattering of typewriters) to the sterile atmosphere of the broadcast studio. I would reach the studio somewhat out of breath, holding my freshly prepared script, somewhat in awe of the microphone.

For preparing the news summary, I would distill the day's news from the *New York Times*, the *Washington Post* and other major newspapers. I also prepared features in French on such figures as Eisenhower, Darlan, General Giraud, and others. At that time, the war was extremely active in North Africa and the British Army was besting General Rommel's Africa Corps in El Alamein.

The schedule was tight. One had to be in the newsroom, near the teletype, for many hours, researching the news, making selections and writing one's piece. There was no time to leave one's desk except to go to the mike several times a day—the last broadcast being at 11 p.m. I worked Sundays and holidays, and was scheduled to be there on Christmas and New Year's days. I even had difficulty getting approval to visit the hospital in New Bedford, where my wife had given birth to our first child, a little girl we named Carole. I managed to get there only two days after the event.

Yet I liked the job and probably would have stayed if I had wanted to acquire real broadcasting experience and make a career of it, but one day in December came an urgent telegram from Washington. I had been named an economist to the Board of Economic Warfare at a salary almost double what I earned at NBC. I decided to leave the network.

Washington: A Stint at the Board of Economic Warfare

I arrived in Washington with my small family in December 1942. The Board of Economic Welfare (BEW) was waging war on the international economic front, pursuing two kinds of action. First, in neutral countries it conducted pre-emptive buying of minerals and metals needed for the Allied war effort, e.g., buying non-ferrous metals in Spain, Portugal and Turkey, all under the noses of the Germans, to prevent the Axis powers from purchasing these supplies. Second, BEW was helping to develop the production of minerals in countries siding with the Allies, such as the French colonies which had not fallen under Vichy. These were the French African and Asian colonies and territories which had rallied to General de Gaulle and which could contribute economically to the war effort. This was the program I was to join. As a French-trained economist, I knew the political and economic conditions in those territories from my work in the French Ministry of Commerce and Industry in Paris before the war.

Victory in Europe, 1944 -1945: Joining the U.S. Army

I had not been at BEW more than six months when I was drafted. I was inducted into the U.S. Army in New York on July 14, 1943—Bastille Day in France! I had been a French Army Reserve Officer in the first part of the war and now I was in the U.S. Army as a private. What a difference in status this was going to be! After a few days of orientation at Stony Brook at the eastern tip of Long Island, I was sent to Fort Custer, Michigan, for basic training in the Military Police. I could not exactly see myself spending the war as a military policeman, directing traffic on the roads of a country where our troops might have landed overseas, arresting drunken GIs or stopping brawls at night in some infamous bar somewhere in occupied territory.

At Fort Custer, reveille was at 5:30 a.m.—at the sound of the bugle. This was followed by the broadcast of a number of well-known military marches over the loudspeaker system heard throughout the camp. Not having been raised in America, except for *Stars and Stripes Forever* I was hearing them for the first time. I soon learned them and enjoyed them quite a lot. It was part of my "Americanization." More than anything else, my service in the Army gave me a feeling of being an American and of the great democracy I was part of.

We had only a few minutes to wash, dress, make our beds so squarely that dimes could roll on them, then rush downstairs with our gear for roll call in formation in front of the barracks. One of us had to be the last one downstairs, despite the fact that all of us fell in line practically at the same time, with a mere one or two seconds difference after a few weeks of practice. The last recruit downstairs, however, was always penalized. He would get KP (kitchen police) for the day or be given some menial, undesirable task such as cleaning latrines. We had a tough barracks sergeant from Nebraska who did not understand my French accent. Neither did I understand him clearly when he was yelling his orders at us. I had never set foot in an American school and was not used to the various regional accents.

One day, as we were studying the machine gun, I was asked to recite the manual on disassembling the weapon while demonstrating it in front of a group. I got into trouble: the sergeant was exasperated. I don't remember what I did wrong, but in his view it was serious. He gave me a punishment I thought was totally undeserved and I tried to explain to him my difficulty in understanding his orders. The punishment was tough, consisting—for a whole week—of "testing for gas." The sergeant had said during the exercise that we were supposed to be under a gas attack. This meant that I was supposed to protect myself and continue the disassembly of the machine gun. Since I had forgotten to do this, I was to carry my gas mask with me at all times for a whole week. I alone was to test for gas each time we were starting a new drill, and even before we would sit down at the refectory. It was something ridiculous to see a man of my age—I was then 34 years old—subjected to this kind of embarrassment. It created laughs all around. I took it as best I could and made a joke of the whole thing myself.

Nevertheless, I went to see the Major in charge of our training to protest, and I explained the circumstances in detail. Although sympathetic, he did not budge, and said that for the sake of discipline he could not countermand the sergeant's orders or change the penalty—although he admitted that the sergeant's decision had been too stringent and a poor choice. The week went by without further incident, and the whole thing was soon forgotten. Aside from this incident, basic training did more than anything to quickly make me a real American in language, habits and in picking up Army slang. This little incident, of course, left not the least trace of rancor in my mind. I was getting along well with my buddies and my superiors. I think the sergeant liked me in the end, and in the fifth week of training I became the "Soldier of the Week" on the post, with a profile in the camp newspaper entitled "The Last Time I Saw Paris"—the day the Germans entered the French capital—another personal turning point.

At Fort Custer I met three buddies who were to stay excellent friends for many years. Two had foreign backgrounds, and the other was originally from Chicago but lived in New York. Of course, our selection for the Military Police had been dictated by the consideration that we later could be assigned to military government duties in occupied territories.

First was Andrew Szper, a Pole, who was soon to become an American citizen at a ceremony on the post as a result of his being in the U.S. Army. He spoke French and German, had a doctorate in law from the University of Warsaw and one from the Law School of the *Université de Lille* in France.

Second came Karel Pusta from Washington, D.C., who had lost his country, Estonia, to the Soviets. He was the son of the Minister of Estonia to the United States. Karel's father stayed at his post during the entire war, as the United States continued to recognize the Baltic States as independent from Russia. Karel also spoke several languages. Later he became an officer of the Voice of America in Munich, broadcasting to his former compatriots.

Third was Ed Block, a dilettante Harvard graduate who had traveled in many parts of Europe and who spoke excellent French. The four of us were selected for a course at the School of Military Government at Fort Custer at the end of our basic training. At the start of the war this school had given officer's commissions to its graduates. But because the President had ordered limiting the number of officer appointments, all the training gave us was the rank of Private First Class (PFC). We all graduated but the possibilities for using the knowledge we had acquired had to be postponed to the end of the war when the U.S. would occupy territories of the Axis powers.

From time to time, recruiting officers visited the basic training camps to select soldiers to be used in special ways by the Army. The four of us were selected to go to Camp Ritchie, the training camp of the U.S. Military Intelligence Service, hidden somewhere in the Blue Ridge Mountains near Hagerstown, Maryland. We were transferred to Ritchie toward the end of the year, and I had a few days' leave to relax in New England, see my wife in South Dartmouth, and to call on my mother in New York.

There was a good deal of mystery about Camp Ritchie. Few knew what went on there except that, since the war had started, it was used to train Combat Intelligence Officers. We had been told that, despite the rigorous training at Ritchie—which until then guaranteed a commission as an officer—nothing of the kind could happen for us for the same reasons we were given at Fort Custer. However, we would be promoted from PFC to Master Sergeant, the highest non-commissioned officer rank that we could receive under the circumstances. This was better than Fort Custer at least.

Camp Ritchie was indeed fascinating. There were three training sections: one for interpreting aerial photography, one for interrogating prisoners of war, and the last one—newly created—for training personnel in getting information on the enemy, under combat conditions, through friendly civilians of the invaded countries or from the intelligence agencies of the Allies operating on the front. In the case of France, for instance, these agencies were the *Deuxième Bureau*, the *Bureau Central des Renseignements de l'Armée* (BCRA) and the *Forces Françaises de l'Intérieur* (FFI)—the French Resistance. It was to this third section that my friends and I were assigned. We got into the program easily since we knew so much about Europe already. We learned a lot about cartography, topography, military procedure, organization of the U.S. Army, communications and other information needed for a campaign.

At Ritchie we had to learn the order of battle of the German Army and recognize German military formations. There was a company of American soldiers at the camp, dressed in German uniforms, who manned German equipment, vehicles and guns captured from the German Army. These would pass on the horizon in various formations and we, the students, had to recognize the units they represented and name the kind of equipment and guns they were displaying. There was also an exercise in communications and signals among the various echelons of a U.S. Army division. A number of tents had been set up representing the various battle command posts: platoon, company, battalion, division, Army Corps, Division Headquarters. While a fictitious battle was going on, we were—in turn—to help these command posts and learn how to transmit messages from one to another by telephone or telegraph. This was a good introduction to battle conditions but obviously was very sketchy.

There also were the night problems. We were taken by truck to a certain wooded area of the Blue Ridge Mountains. Two by two we were dropped on the road. We had been given a little map of the area, in German or Japanese, which showed that somewhere in the Mountains there was a clearly marked point which was the target of the exercise. There, in a forest glen, a tent was pitched where two non-commissioned officers were waiting for us. They checked the men who were able to reach the place with the help of their cryptic maps, a compass and their own sense of direction.

This was a difficult problem which could last for hours, sometimes until daybreak, and many abandoned the effort. It was basically always the same problem. The path to follow would seldom be changed, even though it was very easy to get lost and the trails very difficult to follow. The year before, in the winter, two men had drowned when a little bridge gave way and they fell into a river. Fortunately, the farmers who lived near the trail knew the general direction to follow, and I was told that by knocking at the door of one of these houses at around 11 p.m. one could get useful information for proceeding further, together with a cup of hot coffee. The farmers apparently got a real kick out of the problem. After three months of intensive work we were shipped overseas.

Going Overseas

There was no publicity about our going abroad and no leaves were granted. Natalie came from Massachusetts to say good-bye; a friend was taking care of our tiny daughter. This was a very sad moment. No destination was announced.

The *SS Queen Mary* zigzagged us across the Atlantic for 10 days to avoid German submarines. There were 14,000 men aboard, including an entire infantry division and a number of special units like ours. We carried duffel bags containing all our effects, our battle gear, our carbines and I don't know how many rounds of ammunition. This was a terrific load to carry from the end of the railroad platform to the gangway. I did not think I could do it. How I did not get a hernia in the process I don't know, but some soldiers threw rounds of ammunition overboard to lighten their load. With so many people aboard, it was impossible to serve three meals a day: we had one meal only. Sections of the infantry division, way down on the lower decks of this giant ship, were allowed to take turns sleeping on the deck as it was suffocating in the hold.

Fortunately, our unit had been billeted to the upper levels. We were in a large, reconditioned lounge which had many bunks six rows high. One man fell one night from his high bunk and broke his arm. When we were on deck, milling around, much time was spent trying to see German U-boats lying in wait to torpedo us, or eyeing the 200 nurses billeted on a restricted deck. They were, as could be expected, the object of much shouting, whistling, and other friendly cajoling by the GIs on the main deck.

One morning at dawn I went up on deck, and looking out saw that we were slowly sailing up a wide estuary with hills and green fields on each side. We had safely reached Scotland, and were to land at Glasgow. Later that day a train took our group to Broadway, a lovely little village in Worcestershire, near Evesham. It was the relocation center of the U.S. Military Intelligence in England. We stayed there several weeks and enjoyed a welcome respite in this most lovely English village, where we were lodged on a farm and drank ale at the famous Leghorn Arms pub. We also went to a few USO dances and made the acquaintance of English lasses who wanted to welcome the Yanks. We had passes to go to Evesham, with its interesting cathedral, but we were mainly drawn by the city of Bath, 50 miles away, with its famous Roman baths and elegant crescent of beautiful residences designed by Christopher Wren.

The weeks flew by quickly. It was spring and the flowers began to bloom; it was still cool, but the English countryside was in all its glory, with its hedges bordering the fields, its narrow little roads still beautifully maintained despite the war.

Operation Overlord

The U.S. Fourth Armored Division to which I was assigned did not take part in the D-Day landings on the beaches of Normandy. It did, however, play a vital part in the subsequent liberation of Normandy and of France. The landings, under the code name Operation Overlord, were a principal initiative to wind up the war in Europe. The following months saw increased involvement of various Armored Corps to advance the Allied cause through the largest air-sea-land assault ever undertaken.

Months before the landings, the Allied air forces had undertaken a systematic destruction of rail centers and marshaling yards in France and Germany, efficiently assisted by the French underground, which sabotaged German communication depots and railroads. The Germans, under Marshall von Rundstedt, had been preparing for an Allied invasion of the French coast and had built the Atlantic Wall consisting of strong coastal defenses designed to make Europe an impregnable fortress.

In early 1944 the Allies led the Germans to believe that the landing would take place in the North of France, in the Pas de Calais. Consequently, on the first days of the Normandy invasion, only one Panzer division saw action on the coast where the Allies landed. In the months preceding the invasion the Germans had only begun to strengthen their defenses on the Normandy coast, but this was in part hampered by Allied bombings and these fortifications were far from complete by D-Day. Nevertheless, they still constituted a formidable obstacle to the landing of the Allied forces.

We were briefed that they included rows of steel or timber stakes covered by the sea at high tide. Mines were attached to them to blow up craft trying to breach the fortifications. Troops reaching the beach would face rolls of barbed wire, minefields and other obstacles, and would be fired at from concrete gun emplacements built on the line of dunes along the coast. In the months preceding the invasion, however, our planes, submarines and special commandos had photographed the obstacles, while underwater demolition teams had been trained to destroy as many as possible before the Allied landing barges arrived transporting the invasion force.

By June 1 we knew the invasion could not be delayed much longer. The paramount choices for D-Day was June 5, 6, or 7. They promised the best moonlight for landing airborne troops behind the Normandy beaches and the best darkness for crossing the English Channel. June 5 offered a low tide for the work of the underwater demolition teams and for landing assault troops, but because of high winds and stormy overcast weather predicted by the Allies' meteorologists, Eisenhower postponed the operation until the 6th. Operation Overlord got into gear just before midnight, June 5.

As is well known, the beaches invaded, east to west, were code-named Sword, Juno, Gold, Omaha and Utah. The first three were assigned to the British in the area of Caen and the Orne River, the latter two to the Americans on the western part of the coast, Omaha being directly west of the British sector with Utah (on which I landed) at the bottom of the East coast of the Cotentin Peninsula, separated from Omaha by a marshy lowland. Behind Utah was a lagoon passable by causeways which, if controlled by the enemy, would constitute a formidable obstacle for the landing force. This beach had been selected because it was essential to quickly capture the port of Cherbourg at the North of the Contentin Peninsula so that it could be used immediately to land the mass of equipment and supplies needed to carry out the campaign. Two U.S. airborne divisions were dropped inland, behind the beach at Ste-Mère-1'Église to seize the beach exits and the roads leading to the interior. Then our turn came.

With Patton's Fourth Armored Division

In the weeks preceding the invasion, in the Broadway field headquarters of the U.S. Military Intelligence Service, my friends and I hardly felt the world was at war during the day. But every night around eight o'clock we would hear the roars of bombers taking off from a nearby base on their way to raid the continent. After our year of intense training and preparation, this reminded us that we, too, would soon be on our way. My friends—Andy, Karel, Ed—and I wondered every day to which unit we would be assigned before going to the Continent. Then came the announcement, with the list of Military Intelligence Teams (MITs) to be attached to the divisions earmarked to land in Normandy. Andy was to be at a higher echelon, at Corps Headquarters of the 1st Army; Karel with the MIT of the 83rd Infantry Division; Ed to another infantry division, the name of which I do not remember; and I to the 4th Armored Division to assist its G-2 in the Division Intelligence Operations.

With regrets, we parted the next day to join our respective formations somewhere in England. The 4th Armored was training in the Downs, an ideal terrain for tanks, about 100 miles north of Southampton. Our team included a Lieutenant with a Russian name, Oleg Nedzelnedsky, and two Sergeants, Bill Sheans and Vince Vincent. There I met Colonel Brown, the G-2, as well as Lieutenant Colonel Creighton Abrams, who was commanding Combat Command A, a tank battalion to which our team was to be attached. Lt. Col. Abrams, for whom we were working, was to become famous as the best tank commander in the European Theater of War and later as Commander-in-Chief of all U.S. forces in Vietnam.

D-Day was approaching, but armored divisions were not scheduled to participate in the first landings. They would, however, play a crucial role in the battle for Normandy a few weeks later.

When D-Day arrived, we were still in the Downs. We followed the landings on the radio and heard Gen. Eisenhower's broadcast to the forces which were to make the assault on the Atlantic Wall. When this attack started, we marveled at the pounding of the German positions by hundred of bombers which we heard passing over our heads. Then came the news of the daring parachute drops on Ste-Mère-l'Église by the 101st Airborne Division. We heard about the assault of the beaches at Omaha and Utah and the capture of the bunkers and the dunes at the cost of heavy casualties. We listened gravely and wondered when our turn would come to cross the Channel.

It came on D+36. In early July the U.S. armored divisions stationed in our area started rolling toward Southampton, where we were to embark. The tanks filled the narrow roads and created massive traffic bottlenecks. All along the roads leading south were endless ammunition depots set on each side, with shells neatly piled up and ready for pick-up and transport across the Channel. England looked like an immense entrenched camp.

Under the protection of the British Navy and combat planes, we crossed in a fairly large vessel, relatively without incident, and landed on Utah Beach. For four days landing craft disgorged the tanks, halftracks, jeeps and guns of the 4th Armored Division. Tanks labored up the beach trails, past what remained of the famous defenses of the Atlantic Wall, close to the village of Ste-Mère-l'Église.

We drove through Ste-Mère, half destroyed, where one could still see bits of parachutes hanging from the local church steeple, near the cemetery. Near La Haye-du-Puits and St-Lo, where a savage battle had been fought, we found the destruction appalling. Most houses had been blasted out by bombshells, and the streets were covered with stones, pieces of broken walls and debris. One could see broken furniture covered with dust in the second-story bedrooms of some of the houses, through gaping holes in crumbling walls and broken partitions. The church steeple was still standing in the middle of this upheaval. The square was completely deserted except for a few dogs. It was like a nightmare. Our column of vehicles passed through the little town which had made world history after one of the fiercest battles of the war. We bivouacked north of La-Haye-du-Puits in the meadows a few miles north of the village.

Fighting In The Hedgerows

> *"By mere chance of fate they wound up with guns in their hands. They were good boys and even though they weren't warriors born to kill, they won their battles."*[5]

Normandy was "hedgerow country," hardly a terrain where tanks could maneuver easily, The countryside comprised numerous small meadows separated by hedges, which served to delimit the fields and keep cows where they belonged. This was a country of small dairy farms. Milk and butter were the main products of the region, along with apples, from which was made a potent high quality liqueur called Calvados. When I wrote to Natalie, I could not tell her where we were. It was strictly forbidden to name any geographical locations in our correspondence; but I was able to say I had drunk Calvados and thus she knew that I had landed in France and exactly where I was located—without my breaking any regulations.

This area was to be our theater of operations for almost two weeks. The tanks had difficulty maneuvering among the hedgerows. They were parked between rows of apple trees. One or two would be called at a time for a clearing operation forward. Obviously, they could not be used in formation in such terrain. We were waiting for a time when they could try to break through German lines. In the meantime, we

---

5   Ernie Pyle, *Brave Men* (New York: Grosset and Dunlap, 1944), 39.

were fighting as foot soldiers, not as tankmen.

Our first night near La Haye-du-Puits, I was sent forward to an intersection at the edge of a no-man's land on guard duty. An M-1 rifle was my weapon. My watch was from 1 to 4 a.m. Nothing apparently separated us from the enemy except a wide empty space resembling a moor. I was to watch and signal any patrol infiltration into our territory. Other guards had been placed at other points, forming an advance cordon of surveillance to the front of our encampment.

It was so dark we could not see each other. I had not much of a view to the front of me—perhaps 50 yards. As it was the first time that I had been on guard on a battlefield, I must admit that I was scared, and from time to time I thought I heard a noise somewhere in the brush nearby, or in the tall grass farther away. The stars were invisible that night as I carefully scanned my surroundings. All was calm except for occasional shots or a detonation far away. A noise from behind startled me, but it was only the relief for my watch. Nothing had happened on my first watch, and I gladly slid into my tent until reveille.

Gradually, after the first few nights, we became more expert in identifying the night noises, including the peculiar sound of cows munching grass. Occasionally a soldier, thinking that Germans had infiltrated our encampment, would shoot blindly in the dark and kill a cow. It was dangerous simply to get up and leave one's tent, as a shadow could be mistaken for that of an enemy. One of our men was in fact shot in this way. We were still quite green, but we got used to the cows as our night and day companions.

The usefulness of our intelligence team in combat was soon recognized by the tank battalion and the Division artillery commanders. We were getting information on enemy positions mostly through the French farmers. I would leave camp by jeep with Staff Sergeant Bill Sheehan, a school teacher from Cohoes, New York, and Vince Vincent, a very young Technical Sergeant of French-Canadian descent from Lynn, Massachusetts. Both spoke French well. We were armed with our carbines, sometimes with a mounted machine gun. We would first try to obtain information on the position of the enemy by stopping at the tent of the G-3, the Operations Officer, but often he knew little about the German movements since the front was too mobile and the situation changed too rapidly. Not surprisingly this lack of information on the position of the Germans proved to be more critical for us later, when we left the Normandy hedgerows and entered the realm of moving battle. The intelligence team, operating at Combat Command level, i.e., right up front, then had to find its own sources, starting its reconnaissance from scratch.

At that time the Division was spread in depth, sometimes more than one hundred kilometers, its headquarters quite to the rear. Often there were German elements between near elements of the Division and our combat commands in front. This was a tricky situation for us and we never really knew what we could expect to meet when we set out on our forays. Andrew Szper, who was with Army Corps and should therefore have been fairly safe—since he was supposedly behind the battle lines—one morning had left Corps in his jeep with two others. Shortly after, they were shot at by the machine gun of a German tank which appeared at the corner of a wood. His leg was riddled with bullets, and today, even after 40 years, he still requires treatment at veterans' hospital and survives on drugs, his life half ruined.

But in the hedgerow country it was different: asking Normandy farmers questions about the whereabouts of the enemy almost always worked for us. Most of the older men had been soldiers and they knew a great deal about military life. They usually had good judgment. While doing routine work around the farm they could watch the horizon and observe troop movements. Usually, and sometimes precisely, they knew where the Germans were hiding. They could tell us about gun emplacements firing on our positions.

One farmer, for instance, described exactly the back and forth movements of a well-camouflaged 88mm battery which had been firing on us for several days and preventing our advance. We were able to accurately plot this information on our maps, give the coordinates showing the position of the German guns, and return to the G-2. He contacted the Artillery Commander of the Division and, minutes later, the fire-power of the Division was successfully directed to these points. After about two weeks of this type of result, we had proved ourselves as a reliable source of intelligence for the progress of Combat Command A, and the safer advance of the whole Division.

The fighting in the hedgerows of Normandy (called the *bocage* by the French) was among the fiercest and perhaps the weirdest of the whole European campaign because of the configuration of the terrain and the tenacious resistance of the enemy. It could only be carried out by the infantry, using only small fighting groups—perhaps a company at a time, but mostly just a squad.

The small meadows, bordered by the hedgerows, also served as cow pastures. . The hedgerows were thick growths of small trees (frequently apple trees) and bushes on earthen banks could be up to twenty feet high, but usually were no higher than a man. The Germans knew well how to use them. They either dug into them or placed snipers behind them. The hedges were perfect emplacements for machine guns and even for small artillery. They could also camouflage light tanks of the type that accompany infantry, always ready to open fire.

To dislodge the Germans from these fortified positions was very difficult: the battle in the hedgerows amounted to much bloody skirmishing lasting all day, killing or wounding many and exhausting everyone. Often the visibility was limited to 100 to 200 yards, and progress was measured in terms of hundreds of yards a day. I had great admiration and respect for the GIs' courage in picking out snipers and destroying machine gun nests. Sneaking along individual hedgerows they had to draw close to throw grenades, with luck, into the holes from which the Germans were fighting, much like Marine combat in the Pacific islands against the Japanese. Both sides lobbed mortar shells at the other. The "fronts" were so close together that when the Air Force was called in to support our infantry there was always danger of strafing the American positions.

In the wetlands, also part of the terrain in which we were operating, our tanks could not maneuver, often having to restrict their movements to the narrow roads lined by the hedgerows. Rarely could the infantry benefit fully from tank support when attacking German positions across the marshes.

Adding to all of this in the battle for Normandy, was that many of our men were new to combat. Reports I saw showed only 37 percent of the replacements had been trained behind the lines before being rushed forward. This was a great test for them. In the first month after the landing the attrition rate from battle fatigue was high among the rifle companies.

Behind the front, endless heavy traffic of jeeps, armored cars and tanks filled the narrow little roads well camouflaged by their bordering hedges. Traveling back and forth in our jeeps on assignments, we would pass men belonging to formations other than our own, identifying them by their shoulder flashes. One day we crossed a battalion of the 26th Infantry Division (New York) and from our jeep I recognized Capt. Maurice Hahn, who had been an instructor at Camp Ritchie and was now a combat intelligence officer with the 26th. It was a great moment, but we only had a few minutes to say hello and talk about our respective assignments.

Another day I bumped into my friend Karel Pusta in the town of Carentan. One of the "musketeers" of our little group of friends who had met at boot camp at Fort Custer we had gone together to Camp Ritchie and, recently, to Broadway, England. He was at rest for a few days with the 83rd Infantry Division, and was riding a motorcycle which, he said, he had captured along with a German. I enjoyed seeing him immensely. In combat he was still the same Pusta, always finding ways to have a good time and beat the regulations. Not surprisingly he told us, beaming, that he had already met a lovely young French girl in Carentan. He did not have to sleep in a tent as she had found a "perfect" room for him in town.

I did not see Karel again until 1953. Natalie and I met him—on the Place de la Concorde in Paris—still dashing, his smile radiant, the handsome broad-boned features of his face stood out more than ever. He had married a lovely Hungarian woman and was working for the Voice of America, broadcasting daily to Estonia following that country's takeover by the Soviet Union. He invited us to go and visit him in Munich.

A Dish To Remember

Then came Bastille Day, July 14th, when I told my friends I had a surprise for them. Instead of K-rations, I wanted them to taste a "roast of rabbit," cooked French style, one of France's finest rural dishes. It would initiate them to a real French meal and a celebration of the French national holiday. They laughed about eating rabbit, as this was practically unknown in the States, but they were game. I was talking, of course, not of wild rabbit but of domestic rabbit (*lapin de choux*) raised on almost any farm in France and by non-farming families.

But now I had to find the rabbit and someone to cook it for us! On that day, everything was calm in the area, so I took one of our jeeps and drove west on a road bordered by thick hedgerows leading to Barneville, a few miles away—a lovely, small fishing port on the coast of Cotentin. Entering the town, I saw a French housewife, perhaps forty years of age, walking on the sidewalk, obviously shopping. The town had been free of Germans for some weeks, but I might have been one of the first American soldiers she had seen, as Barneville was not in the area of immediate combat. Very politely, I told her who I was and that I wanted to ask her a favor. She was surprised and pleased that despite my American uniform I could speak French so well. The Americans I was with, I said, had never tasted rabbit. We wanted to celebrate our arrival in Normandy and Bastille Day with a typical French meal. Could I buy a rabbit, would she kindly cook it for us—in the name of French-American amity—and could I come back to get it in a few hours? She agreed and we set a price.

When I came back three hours later the rabbit was ready. But the problem was how to carry it. She had roasted it in a beautiful large brown oval earthen platter to which she evidently attached great value. No wrapping paper was available in France, and she did not want to wrap it in old newspaper. At the same time, she hesitated to lend me her plate for fear it would not be returned. I solemnly promised I would bring it back. She could count on the word of an American soldier, I said, as we were not like the Germans, whom I knew had pilfered the French right and left.

With my promise to bring it back in the afternoon, she let me have the dish. I returned to the bivouac and we feasted. All the men agreed that it was not only the best meal they had enjoyed since leaving the States, but possibly one of the best they had ever tasted. It was like chicken with a more delicate flavor. We drank old Calvados.

But, as we were cleaning our gear our major rushed up to us. He was sorry to break up our party, but we had to pack up right away, as we were moving forward in 20 minutes. There was no question in my mind that I must return the dish to the French lady in Barneville. If I did not bring it back, not only would she lose a valuable household item, but she would trust American soldiers no more than the Germans. I could see only one solution: hide the dish and return it as soon as I could on a calm day when I could drive to Barneville from wherever we happened to be. I selected a spot to hide the dish in one of the hedgerows. I noted where I had placed it in relation to the meadow entrance, as well as all the details of the terrain, thinking that I would easily recognize the dish's exact location.

A week later an occasion offered itself. I had time off and I took the chance of leaving our bivouac. I drove back to where we had been—absolutely sure of my ability to recognize our meadow. But one hedgerow looks just like another. And with our jeeps and tanks gone, one empty meadow with its rows of apple trees and its peacefully-grazing cows looks very much like any other. I tried several locations, without luck; either the dish had been stolen or I was at the wrong spot. What would the French lady think of me? I hoped she would consider the dish simply another casualty of the war.

A Vow in a Foxhole

During the battle in the hedgerows we were frequently shelled by several German 88mm guns that had zeroed in on our positions, causing many casualties. The shells had a high vertical trajectory and fell on us from heights—more like mortar fire—as if from nowhere. It was quite frightening. Our only option was to get into a foxhole as quickly as possible, even if we had to dig it on the spot, and wait for the shelling to end. That morning it was raining and a nasty wind had kicked up. I was in my foxhole, waiting for the end of the shelling, when a piece of *Stars and Stripes*, the U.S. Army newspaper, blew slowly in my direction.

It was torn, muddy and yellowed by the sun. I caught it and had begun to read when my attention was caught by a short front page article reporting on some meetings taking place at Dumbarton Oaks in Washington, DC. Experts from the U.S. and other allied countries were drafting the principles of a new peace organization to replace the defunct League of Nations and establishing the base for a future United Nations organization. Its aim would be to banish war forever from the face of the globe and help member countries to live in peace, respect human rights and improve living conditions all over the world.

I was perhaps skeptical, at first, being too much of a disciple of Montaigne and knowing what had happened to the League of Nations in the 25 years before. This announcement, however, revealed to me while I sat in danger of being shelled at any moment, had a tremendous impact on me—like a message sent by God. Right then and there I prayed for peace and the success of this great enterprise and, solemnly, in my foxhole, promised myself that I would do everything in my power to join this new organization if I came through the war alive.

Breakthrough at Avranches

A few days later, at dawn, we looked up at the sky to see the most incredible spectacle that one could ever expect on a battlefield. In the previous few minutes we had heard a continuous rumble coming from the north, light in the beginning but increasing in intensity with every second. We looked in that direction but at first saw nothing. Then the rumble grew deafening. Filling the sky across the horizon from east to west came hundreds of planes, an incredible and indescribable aerial armada in massive formation. More than a thousand planes were taking part in the mammoth "Operation Cobra."

As planned, Cobra was to start on July 24th with a spectacular aerial attack. It was canceled because of poor weather. But the Air Forces were already in the air and failed to receive word of the cancellation. Fighter planes strafed the prescribed area and the heavy bombers dropped hundreds of tons of bombs four miles in front of us. The ground beneath us trembled. Visibility was poor and, as the wind shifted the smoke markers, many bombs fell on U.S. troops occupying our most advanced positions to the south, killing many of them. On July 25th came a second attack and again, because of inaccurate bombing, hundreds of American troops were killed. Among them was Lieutenant General Leslie McNair, an observer not in command of troops, who was trapped in the raid.

The Fourth Armored was a part of "Operation Cobra." Supported by the overpowering air bombardment, we were called upon to break through on a narrow front in the direction of Coutances, then on to Avranches, in the south of the Cotentin Peninsula. Avranches was a major road junction on the way to Brittany. The plan was that once this gap was opened a mass of armored and infantry troops—including the Sixth Armored—would pour in, take the whole of Brittany, turn east and chase the Germans out of Normandy.

Until then we had held the front formerly occupied by the 4th Infantry Division, north of Carentan, and our tankmen had become temporary doughboys in the trenches again. At last we were climbing from our foxholes in the hedgerows into our vehicles to fulfill our real role. General Patton had taken over that day as Commander of the Third Army. For him the purpose of a battle was to destroy the enemy. At Avranches we did just that.

We sprang forward on the roads going south and, in a fantastic thrust, the Fourth Armored and Sixth Armored together routed the enemy and opened the way to Rennes, the capital of Brittany. The breakthrough at Avranches was a sensational victory. Few parts of the Wehrmacht at Avranches escaped the tanks, cavalry and armored infantry. We were shooting the hell out of the Krauts and taking prisoners all over the place. Column upon column of disarmed prisoners marched back unguarded to the prisoner-of-war enclosures. By July 31st the POW count surpassed 3,000. We had wiped out in our smashing of the German forces the 77th, 91st and 243rd Infantry Divisions, and the 6th Paratroop Regiment, and had dealt severe losses to three other regiments.

The bloodiness was a spectacle to contemplate. I was pained to see the grim results of our action. Along the route we could see many Germans who had been blown up by direct hits to their vehicles. I saw officers in a jeep who had been burned beyond recognition, still erect in their seats but very much shriveled. Cattle killed by shells lay bloating in the fields. Our shells had hit German halftracks and the men, surprised by the attack, lay dead, crouched under them. It was the first massive penetration into the interior of Europe, after weeks of stalemate and heavy losses in the Normandy *bocage*. The Fourth Armored had done brilliantly. For this, and for its exploits in the rest of the European campaign, it received the first Presidential citation given to an entire American division in the European Theater.

From there on, we were called "Georgie's Boys." If you belonged to the Fourth Armored you did not have to say more. The name was enough. In the *Stars and Stripes* and all the American papers the Fourth Armored became famous. It was the most talked about tank outfit of the whole Third Army in the reconquest of Europe—all the way across France to the Siegfried Line, at Bastogne, through Germany and Czechoslovakia until it joined with the Russians on the Eastern Front. From there on, too, the Krauts were terrified when being pursued by the Fourth Armored Division; they had learned to fear its daring, fast-shooting style of armored warfare.

On that day we wasted no time mopping up. We moved forward. At times we had Germans on our flanks and in the rear as well as to the front of us. When this happened, our intelligence work became extremely risky as we had to venture far from our column to find information needed by the Command.

After the Avranches breakthrough, the tanks of the Fourth rolled south. We passed east of Mont St-Michel. We were covered with dust, our faces hardly recognizable. There was little resistance on the part of the retreating Germans. We were heading for the center of Brittany and our objective was to liberate the city of Rennes, the capital of the province, which was still occupied by the enemy. We plunged toward the city, 54 miles away. The 2nd Cavalry Group encircled this ancient Breton capital. Roads and communications were cut. Emplacements of heavy anti-tank and flak guns north of the city were knocked out and the Germans were thrown into a panic.

I was sent in advance with two officers from the staff of the Division commander to contact two French military officers of the *Deuxième Bureau*. We met with them on a farm to learn the places the Germans might still try to defend in and around the city. The tank battalion sent to enter Rennes met little resistance, as the Germans were surrendering. The *Kommandantur* building was seized and all that remained was to silence snipers in various parts of the city. Rennes had been occupied by our units in a few hours.

We slept in a school. The next day one of our combat commands headed for the fortified port of Lorient, which the Germans had transformed into their most powerful submarine base on that part of the Atlantic coast. The place was so well defended that it appeared to our command that many men would have to be kept there fighting a long time if we wanted to recapture Lorient—probably at a heavy cost in lives. Anti-tank ditches and mine fields protected the city and were well manned by German Army and Navy forces. Lorient had been a U-boat haven throughout the war and surrendered only after the capitulation of the Reich. It was decided to turn our back on this formidable stronghold and to take instead the port of Vannes, toward Le Mans to the east, as well as Nantes and St-Nazaire—two key ports at the estuary of the Loire River.

Vannes

We liberated the region of Vannes and Auray on the south coast of Brittany the day after taking Rennes. Meanwhile the Sixth Armored was rushing to free the important French military port at Brest, at the tip of the Brittany peninsula. To our great surprise, near Vannes we met one of the finest Free French units fighting with the Allies. The *Deuxième Régiment de Chasseurs Parachutistes* (Second Airborne

Regiment) had jumped into Brittany before D-Day. In fact they were the first unit to be dropped into France, days before the U.S. 101th and 82nd Airborne landed in Ste-Mère L'Église. Half of the regiment landed on the Côtes du Nord, in the North of Brittany, the others in Morbihan, where we were. Their mission was to help the FFI prevent the Germans from sending reinforcements to the Normandy front, which could have attacked the Allied bridgeheads from the rear.

Led by a stout one-armed major, they told us they had been fighting in small bands for nearly two months and had suffered considerable casualties. When they had landed and regrouped the people greeted them with wine, cider, eggs, kisses and somewhat premature cries of *"Boche kaput."*

Word of the landing of the 2nd RCP in Brittany spread widely in short order and rallied thousands of Bretons to volunteer to help the Allies, one of the greater demonstrations of the Resistance's crucial role during that fateful period. In response to coded messages that poured from London the underground destroyed enemy communications during the decisive months preceding the invasion and during the first weeks following the Allied landings, a period appropriately called *la bataille du rail* (Battle of the Railway). On the day after D-Day it was reported that 180 German trains had been derailed, and 500 lines cut, in the northwest of France.

Soon a force of 3,500 men and women in the Brittany Resistance were clamoring for an airdrop of weapons so they could help mine the roads, set ambushes and do their utmost to keep the Germans from reaching the Normandy front.

The French Resistance in Brittany

The French Resistance in Brittany likely was among the most numerous and active in all of France. It had three missions: to sabotage the German troop transportation system, particularly the railroads; to prepare the French for the role they would play vis-a-vis the invasion troops at the crucial moment of liberation; and to shelter French residents from the Gestapo and prevent their deportation to Germany.

I had an opportunity, 44 years after the War, to meet Charles Tillon, who during the occupation was the Chief of the *Francs-Tireurs et Partisans français*, by far the largest and most daring movement in the Resistance. He was a Communist and, because of their importance in the Resistance, de Gaulle had to include some of them in his government. Tillon at the liberation became Air Minister in de Gaulle's first Cabinet. I met him in Rennes in September 1989, when I was invited officially by the Mayor of that city to receive the Medal of the City for the role I had played in the city's liberation on August 4, 1944. Tillon wore the same blue ribbon of the presidential citation given to the men of the Fourth Armored, as he had been a member of General Leclerc's 2nd French Armored Division which fought with us. More than 100 former resistants and French Forces members met at City Hall for the ceremony.

I found the people of Brittany loved Patton. The next day I was taken to the road in the north of the city that our Armored Division and other units had followed. It was called *la voie triomphale* and at each kilometer there is a tall stone marker with the name of General Patton, Brittany's liberator.

An Encounter With Patton

For the men at the front to have a chance to see their field commander even once during a campaign is indeed slim—pure luck in the case of the Third Army, surely, since it comprised hundreds of thousands of men distributed in a number of Army Corps, divisions and services spread over an enormous territory.

Yet I had that chance one day. Patton was not an invisible general staying at his headquarters in some castle in the country, to the rear of the battle; in combat he lived in the action zone, changing his command post practically every night. He was always on the go, keeping control over his units, visiting his Division commanders and briefing them on the next strategic move. He was always ready for an offensive—the word "defensive" was not in his vocabulary. He traveled up and down the front by light plane and jeep. When he passed columns on the road he liked to talk to the men, always speaking of "goddamn Krauts" and "sons of bitches," a type of coarse language the troops seemed to like.

That afternoon in the beginning of August, when we were moving towards Le Mans, he had come to our area to visit General Wood of the 4th Armored, like Patton a cavalryman. Lt. Nedzelnedsky, our team leader, and I were in the rear on a lonely narrow road crossing a wood, after contacting French civilians who gave us information on the locations of German artillery. A fast-moving open jeep came up behind us, followed by a second as protection. We pulled to the right to let them pass. When the first reached us it stopped. We looked at the occupants, two officers and a driver, and immediately recognized the officer in front by the three bright stars—signifying the rank of Lieutenant-General—on his helmet. There could be no mistake: it was Patton, looking just like the pictures I had previously seen.

He was unmistakable: tall, commanding immediate respect, sitting erect, handsome, blue eyed and ruddy complexioned. He wore a khaki shirt, still impeccably starched at that time of day. His shirt collar on each side carried the same three stars of his rank. He certainly cut an imposing figure. By his side I could see his ivory-handled Colt .45 hanging cowboy-style in a holster, witness to his reputation as a fancier of fine firearms even in the field.

Somewhat startled, we quickly dismounted, stood at attention and saluted. He asked who we were and what we were doing there. Ned told him that, as French interpreters, we were getting information on the enemy from friendly civilians. He seemed quite interested in what we were doing and asked whether we were meeting with many FFI (*Forces Françaises de l'Intérieur*) in the area. I explained that we had met many more FFI in Brittany than here. Patton appeared greatly interested in the role of the French Resistance in the War. He was perhaps the senior American officer most fluent in French and got along well with the French officers; in his youth he had attended Saumur, the French Cavalry school. And, having recently liberated Brittany, he was venerated by the people of that province.

For us to be addressed by the field commander himself was an experience to remember. That evening at the bivouac we agreed that Patton was the personification of the warrior's spirit, absolutely dedicated to victory. He electrified the men. They liked his style of leadership. He was not only an excellent military strategist, but a great captain of men.

The next day brought tragedy. Our team leader and great friend, Oleg Nedzelnedsky, had just returned from a typical foray toward the front, where he and his two assistants had captured three prisoners. They were proud of what they returned with, including the weapons cache. Ned was excited about the guns, which had been placed not very carefully in the rear of the trailer. He wanted one as a trophy, a Sten submachine gun which was underneath, its barrel protruding in his direction. He tugged on it to pull it out. The gun was loaded and went off. Ned took the bullet in the head and died en route to the field hospital nearby.

That night I was promoted on the battlefield to Second Lieutenant and put in charge of our intelligence team, a function I filled until the decision could be ratified by Military Intelligence Headquarters in Washington a number of weeks later.

Patton and the Falaise Gap

On August 11th we had captured Le Mans, an important city halfway between Normandy and the Loire River and about 200 miles west of Paris. The Third Army had made extraordinary progress in chasing the Germans from France. In only six days after Avranches we had covered 250 kilometers and in the process half destroyed the German 7th Army. In one week we had occupied the whole of Brittany except the ports of Lorient and Nantes. By August 15th two units of the Third Army—the U.S. 90th Infantry Division, and the famous 2nd French Armored Division of General Leclerc which had so distinguished itself in North Africa, had reached the town of Argentan, in an effort to encircle the Germans.

In contrast, the 2nd British Army and Canadian troops under General Montgomery were still fighting in the north of Normandy near the coast. They had had a much tougher time in advancing than had the Americans, due to fierce resistance from the enemy in that sector. It had taken them 55 days from D-Day to take over Caen, the major city of Normandy. By August 15th they were still slowly advancing south trying to capture Falaise and to close a 12-mile gap separating the two Allied Armies between Falaise and Argentan.

Through this gap the retreating German 7th Army was escaping toward the east. It was imperative for the Allies to close that pocket, to completely surround the enemy and destroy its forces before they could further escape and regroup on the Seine River for a counteroffensive.

The U.S. 3rd Army was ready to close the gap by moving north from Argentan. Patton, with his powerful armored forces, was seeing no difficulty in accomplishing this feat and he had received the green light from General Bradley. But suddenly an order came from Supreme Allied Headquarters forcing Patton to stop. This infuriated him. He pleaded with SHAEF to no avail. Later he said "I was certain that we could have entered Falaise and I was not certain that the British would."

We wondered what was going on. Patton got two explanations from the High Command for the sudden change of order. One was that the British had sown the Falaise area with time bombs which might have caused numerous casualties among American troops. Bradley also said on reflection that, had Patton's forces gone ahead, he feared a collision of British and American forces in the narrow gap itself, and the Germans might have trampled the Third Army in their rush to escape. Patton could not stomach the explanations. In the end the gap was not closed in time to prevent the German 7th Army's escape. The order to stop us was considered one of the major errors of the War by the Third Army commanders; we resumed our chase of the Germans.

Since then historical scholars have offered another explanation for stopping Patton. They suggest that Montgomery wanted to close the gap all by himself and had insisted that his troops should go ahead alone. They felt that Eisenhower too often was inclined, for political reasons, to approve requests the British made concerning the conduct of operations. Many believe Eisenhower made a costly error in not allowing Patton to take Falaise, a step that might well have enabled the Allies to end the War in 1944. After the Falaise Gap incident the German 7th Army was still the major enemy force on the Western Front.

The Delayed Liberation of Paris

For strategic and logistical reasons, the Allied High Command (SHAEF) had decided to postpone the liberation of Paris and to bypass the capital. From Normandy the British Army could advance toward the North of France in the direction of the lower Rhine and capture Antwerp, a crucial port for the Allies. To my great personal disappointment, the U.S. Third Army was to bypass Paris in the south. We would take over Lorraine, then cross the Siegfried Line and penetrate into Germany. The main reason for not liberating Paris right away was Eisenhower's fear that the Germans would put up a strong fight and destroy the city. He did not want our armored forces to be sucked into a city battle, nor for Patton's forces to be diverted from chasing the Germans out of France. It was estimated that taking Paris and occupying it would require at least eight divisions which would not be used in the immediate pursuit of the enemy. The need for gasoline, supplies of coal and food would be enormous as there were rumors that Paris was near starvation.

The French, however, had completely different views. They believed it was imperative to take Paris immediately. These views were submitted to SHAEF by General Pierre Koenig, head of the French Forces of the Interior, and by de Gaulle himself in heated, sometimes arrogant arguments with SHAEF. De Gaulle by then was head of the provisional Government of France, recognized by the United States and Great Britain. He contended that if the Allies did not take Paris immediately there would be an insurrection in the capital. The government at Paris would be taken over by the French Communists, who had played a major role in the Resistance. This might mean the installation of "Communes" in key positions of power, which the Allies certainly did not want.

De Gaulle thought it in the interest of France and the Allies to install his provisional government in Paris and stabilize the situation in the capital. He also demanded that French troops—the 2nd French Armored Division—be the Allied unit which would liberate Paris with the 4th American Infantry Division and other units. In this way the Parisians should be able to welcome French soldiers who had fought valiantly at Bir Hakeim in the Libyan Desert, with the 8th Army, in Sicily and Italy with the Americans, and who recently had distinguished themselves at Mortain and Argentan in Normandy under Patton's command.

We all remember with thanks that General von Choltitz, the German military governor of Paris, chose not to destroy the capital, in contravention of Hitler's order, and simply withdrew. Paris was spared great bloodshed and irreparable damage, although some fighting broke out between the FFI and the Germans a few days before the liberation as the Germans started to leave. On August 24th, while our

Fourth Armored was already in Lorraine, the two designated Allied divisions ended four years of detested occupation in Paris as General de Gaulle proudly led a victory parade down the Champs Élysée to the Cathedral of Notre Dame—one of the Western World's emotional highlights of the twentieth century.

The taking of Paris was acclaimed with joy all over the free world. I would have given much to share personally in its liberation, to witness the delirious spectacle of Parisians welcoming their liberators; to embrace my cousins and friends on this occasion. Four years had passed since the terrible day when I left the Paris by the Porte d'Orléans in the south in the same hour the Germans entered it by the Porte de Clignancourt in the north. It would have been exhilarating for me had the Fourth Armored liberated Paris, but I had to live the event vicariously through the one man in our Division who went to the liberation.

His name was Gaston, and he worked in supply at Division headquarters. We sometimes spoke in French. He had a Montmartre accent you could cut with a knife. In civilian life, he said, he'd been a cook and had been drafted into the U.S. Army from Chicago. His wife and relatives, however, were still in Paris. All he wanted was for the Fourth Armored to liberate the city and give him opportunity to see his family. When we learned that we would bypass the city he was the most disappointed man in the world. When we approached Paris, somewhere between Orléans and the Fôret de Fontainebleau, he could no longer resist. A leave request at that time surely would have been turned down, so Gaston decided to go AWOL and take the risk.

He was gone for almost two weeks. Was someone covering for him? No one reported him absent. Then one day he discreetly reappeared as we were in Lorraine, *ni vu ni connu* (neither seen nor known). He came to see us and from him we learned, in his typical Parisian French slang, what had happened. He stayed several days with his family in Menilmontant near Montmartre. There he learned that the French 2nd Armored Division was at the Porte d'Orléans heading for the Place de l'Hôtel de Ville. He and his relatives were part of the crowds lining the streets. He saw the first tanks enter with the *Croix de Lorraine* painted on them, each bearing the name of a French province, tank commanders standing erect in their turrets.

Then the crowd swarmed the Place, surrounded the tanks and jeeps and command cars as they arrived. Brightly dressed women threw bouquets to the men, who waved back. Several times, he said, one could hear distant explosions and sharp detonations nearby—there were snipers in the mansards around the Place—but the crowd would not disband. With much envy I talked with him a long time about what he had seen.

All Paris wanted the soldiers' autographs. Many soldiers were embraced by the women. Sometimes the tanks were lined up near the parks, pulled over under the trees. Women and children climbed into the tanks and kissed the men, who had shaved their beards for the occasion. They sang *La Marseillaise*, the *Madelon* and other patriotic songs—these were truly two of the most beautiful days in the history of Paris.

When I return there now, I sometimes walk in the 7th *arrondissement* near the *École Militaire* and on Place de la Concorde. There, at some street corners and on buildings can be seen the marble plaques placed at eye level as reminders to passers-by that a member of the underground had been shot there by a sniper in the last days before the capital's liberation.

Chasing the Germans Out of France

The Fourth Armored's mission was to liberate all the cities along the Loire River up to Orléans, in a rapid ploy. At that time hard fighting was still going on in the center of Normandy near Mortain and the Falaise Gap, so we moved east on the south flank of Normandy, gradually encircling the enemy. We were ahead of all other American units, striking at the retreating Germans. We took Saumur, Blois, Orléans.

Then we headed northeast, taking many prisoners, turning around Paris but far away from it, taking Troyes in Champagne, 150 kilometers east of the capital, after some tough fighting. I will always remember the capture of Troyes by Combat Command A's medium tank battalion, charging with all guns blazing and followed by two armored infantry companies. When we sighted the steeples of its many churches on the horizon, and crossing a vast open moor as the battle was still raging, we saw dozens of GIs lying dead across the field.

As we crossed those cities we were greeted by the townspeople *en delire*; they came to crowd the streets to acclaim their liberators, they tossed flowers to us. From my jeep I talked to those close to me. Surprised by this French voice in the middle of this flow of American soldiers who smiled to the people, showing their joy simply by their friendly gestures, someone would shout *un français!* (there is a Frenchman among them!). Then they rushed toward my jeep. They wanted to talk to me, to ask questions. Several times I drank champagne with the mayors of towns we went through in the course of these triumphal advances through the French countryside.

What unforgettable remembrances I keep of our triumphant course in winning the war, as each day I participated in the liberation of France. Few people have had the chance to live such experiences in the personal circumstances that were mine. I never liked war. I am no nationalist, but I count these moments of World War II among the most exhilarating of my life. Of my entire war campaign it is to those images of the Liberation that my mind returns with the greatest joy and the most intense emotion.

The rains and the cool weather had come. We were then camping in the fields rather than in villages, which often still were occupied by the Germans. The roads and fields were awash in mud, hampering the jeeps, halftracks, command cars and trucks—and not easy on the tanks themselves. We captured thousands of Germans. Having surrendered, they walked in long files toward the rear, their hands behind their heads, passing us as we continued to advance in our powerful tank columns. We captured complete convoys of loot headed for Germany. Truck after truck contained merchandise stolen from the Paris department stores such as the *Printemps* and the *Galeries Lafayette*, including the delivery vans themselves. These contained furniture, bedding, objects of art, clothing—anything you could imagine—leaving France with German soldiers fleeing a war which, in that sector, they thought they had lost. It was a true debacle.

One day, I recall with a smile, we were rolling down the road in convoy, when all of a sudden we saw a non-commissioned German officer on a stolen French motorcycle, lowering his head to the handlebar in the hope of not being recognized, and passing us speeding in the opposite direction. What was he doing there? Obviously he had taken the wrong road and found himself right in the middle of an enemy column. By then he surely had realized his mistake and must have been scared to death. Any of us could have shot him. Instead we stopped him and took him prisoner. How arrogant he was, even telling us that, according to the Geneva Convention, we had no right to confiscate his pack of French cigarettes!

That same day we captured literally truckloads of French liqueurs, *Grand Crus* wines and champagnes. Our jeep trailers were full of bottles. What were we to do with all this recaptured loot? We turned the bulk of it over to the Quartermaster; but we kept too much of it for ourselves. We were camping at the edge of a wood. Night came early. It was raining. There was nothing to do but taste our treasure. Virtually everyone was dead drunk in short order. Had there been a counterattack that night we certainly were in no condition to respond.

Out of Gas

We had been in Lorraine a few days when we received the official word that Paris had been liberated. Since the capture of Troyes we could see that the Germans were in complete confusion and were fleeing. At the Fourth Armored we all believed that the end of the war was approaching. We had made headlong and lightning progress every day and there was no reason to think that we would not be able to continue our pursuit of the enemy into Germany with the same success. But something quite unexpected happened. On August 29th the Third Army failed to receive any of the 140,000 gallons of gasoline it needed each day to move forward. We were stopped in our tracks.

Patton was enraged and protested to Bradley, in vain. Our leader said he might as well have asked for the moon. The order had come from headquarters. First it was rumored that General John Lee, who commanded the truck companies which brought gasoline to the front—the famous "Red Ball Express"—was responsible for the delay. He had moved his headquarters from Cherbourg to Paris and was supplying the population with food. Speculation was that the installation of thousands of army bureaucrats had temporarily disorganized the Red Ball or that they were distracted in Paris enjoying wine, women and song. The rumors made us angry.

But the reason for depriving us of gasoline was quite different. A temporary shortage had been caused by high consumption by the Allies during the entire offensive, and the high command had decided that for this reason, instead of the initial strategy of two major thrusts to penetrate Germany (Montgomery's army in the North and Patton's in the East), there would be only a single thrust. Simply, Eisenhower had given preference to Montgomery and was putting the Third Army on hold at the very moment when Patton's advances were so spectacular that he seemed to be winning the war all by himself? Why?

Montgomery had submitted his own plan for advancing to the Rhineland and insisted that he needed all the available gasoline. On September 2nd, when the Third Army had been deprived of gasoline for five days, Eisenhower called his chief commanders to a meeting at his headquarters in Normandy, 800 kilometers from the front. He explained that Montgomery's plan had been approved and had priority over all others.

In a few days Operation Market Garden under Montgomery was to be launched, in which 20,000 airborne troops were to land in the Netherlands with the mission of seizing crucial bridges over the Meuse and the lower Rhine rivers and linking up with the British Corps driving from the south. Unfortunately the Operation, on which various military experts had expressed their doubts, was a complete disaster. At Arnhem on the lower Rhine the British 1st Airborne, including 8,000 men called the "Red Devils," had the misfortune to land face to face with two strong German Panzer divisions. Three quarters of its men were lost. Only after fierce fighting and very high casualties were the Allies, which included the British, Canadians and the

American First Army of General Hodges, able to press forward toward the industrial Ruhr, and that only in November. Hodges captured Remagen on the Rhine, the first German city the Allies took, on March 7th, 1945.

What had happened on our Lorraine front during that time? The Third Army was without fuel for five days. Patton had expected to reach the Siegfried Line, which was unmanned, in a few days and get into Germany, foreseeing no difficulty as the situation of the Germans was indeed desperate. Over all we enjoyed a superiority of 20 to one in tanks, and even greater in the air, according to Generals Speidel and Blumentrill, the Chief of Staff of the German Army. After five days without a drop of gasoline Bradley gave us a small supply, just enough to secure the crossings of the Moselle River. But the five days had been enough to enable the German Army to reorganize and start an offensive.

Hitler had once more reappointed Rundstedt as commander in chief in the west and later, when we reached the Moselle River, the Germans offered strong resistance to us. They even were able to stage a tank battle at Arracourt against our Combat-Command A tank battalion on the edge of the Forest of Parroy. More than 200 German tanks had been hidden—information which, under heavy shelling, our team collected from the FFI and relayed to our commander, Lt.Col. Creighton Abrams. We had detected, thanks to the *maquis*, that two German divisions were ready to attack. Two days later one of the greatest tank battles of the campaign took place; the Fourth Armored stopped the Germans cold and destroyed 60 Panzers. The Germans retired, completely defeated.

Later, the weather got worse. It rained constantly. Fighting was at intervals only, combat concentrated in the northeast of Lorraine, in the area of Metz, and the Third Army finally entered this well-fortified, key city after several weeks of hard fighting.

During a lull, we got a pass and went into Nancy, which had been liberated for several weeks, to the famous Place Stanislas, an architectural jewel of a square framed by the elegant palaces built by the Polish princes who once governed Lorraine.[6] There we saw a large USO company which had come to entertain our troops. Among them was Marlene Dietrich, in an impeccably tailored khaki uniform. We were able to exchange a few words with her. As an American, but a former German, she was happy to have come to meet and entertain the fighting men of the Third Army, thus doing her part in our struggle to destroy the Nazis.

In Luneville I saw the mother of my very close friend from Paris, Roger Varin, now a naturalized U.S. citizen living in the States. He had fought the first part of

---

6 This was a stone's throw from the school I attended in 1926, but I had no time to visit it.

the war with the French and was an escaped prisoner of war. I brought his mother, whom I had not seen since the war, my rations and those of my friends; the people of Luneville had very little to eat in those days. How wonderful it was to see her again.

She was worried about her other son, René, who was working in the French railroads as an inspector some twenty miles away at a railroad station still occupied by German troops. She could not correspond with him. From the office of the stationmaster at Luneville, I called René on the special railroad telephone. We, too, were close friends and I had not seen him for many years. The Germans had forbidden the use of the telephone except for the service. But I used it nevertheless. René and his colleagues were stunned to hear my voice and to realize that I, now an American soldier, was only a few miles from where he was surrounded by German soldiers. He had had no idea the Americans were so close. I told him I had seen his mother, and gave him news from his brother, Roger, from whom he had not heard directly in several years. My telephone call was the first communication that he had had from Luneville for a long time. René later told me that after the call he and his colleagues opened their last bottle of champagne and celebrated. The next day our troops freed them.

Reconnoitering a Ford on the Moselle River

The Third Army had reached the west bank of the Moselle River with the Fourth Armored as its forward element. We were now on the hills overlooking Pagny-sur-Moselle, a town in a narrow valley by the river. Pagny harbored a small group of FFI which had its network of secret command posts in many parts of France. The Germans were entrenched on the hills along the river's east bank, and we wanted to cross. The river was a forbidding barrier to our troops, hard to cross since it was under German fire. The bridges had been destroyed, so we needed to find the best point for fording the river that at the same time promised the least danger with respect to the position and strength of the Germans on the other side.

That pitch dark night at about ten o'clock, the major who assisted Lt. Col. Abrams, to whom my team was reporting as suppliers of tactical information, stuck his head through my tent flap. We had set up a temporary camp in the evening and Combat Command A, with its tanks, halftracks and other vehicles, had assembled to our rear, hidden behind the hills. The major woke me to say we had to go to Pagny-sur-Moselle immediately to contact the French Resistance to learn whether the Moselle was fordable there. He gave us a password to use with the FFI.

It was not an easy mission. We were dead tired, and this order raised no enthusiasm in me or the two team members I took with me. But it had to be followed.

We left in our jeep and descended a long slope of open terrain, with patches of trees along the way. The road was blocked in places by heavy tree branches still covered with leaves. We could not, of course, use our headlights nor a flashlight. Pulling the branches and young trees aside to leave enough space for the jeep was wasted time. There could have been land mines, and we had to be extremely careful. There was no moon; this gave us an eerie feeling, plus the sense that in this no-man's land we could at any moment meet a German patrol, as they themselves were seeking information on the size of the enemy units which had just arrived on the west bank. We stopped from time to time to listen for any noises we might hear, and when going down hill we turned off the engine to make our presence as inconspicuous as possible.

We finally reached Pagny at close to midnight. The town was asleep, no light shone anywhere, nobody was in the streets, all shutters were closed, the iron curtains of the shops were drawn down to the ground and padlocked. How were we to discover the FFI in this tomb-like town?

Eventually we saw a thin ray of light under a door and decided to knock there. There were no longer any Germans in the town itself; they were all on the other bank. After waiting a few minutes, the door opened and a very surprised old Frenchman—perhaps a teacher—came forward. He was somewhat frightened. His wife stayed behind in the kitchen, also looking at us. We entered the room. In the light they recognized our uniforms. They welcomed us with joy. We were the first American soldiers they had met. After they recovered their emotions we explained the purpose of our mission. They told us, then showed us, where the little FFI command post was hidden in the rear of a grocery store, not far from their home.

Two young men in civilian clothes were operating a radio transmitter in a corner. We gave them the password in French and explained why we had come. Knowing of our arrival in the area, they were not unduly surprised by our visit. They gave us detailed plans of Pagny and explained where fording was possible. The German positions on the opposite hill were strong and well able to resist any troops trying to cross the river. We transposed their information onto the maps we had brought. They also gave us other maps, emphasizing that any attempt to cross the Moselle at Pagny would be most dangerous in view of the ease with which the Germans could fire on us with the machine guns and mortars installed in the hills.

We thanked them, hoped our paths would cross again, and left. We arrived safely back in camp around 3 a.m. and submitted a short report with the maps to Col. Abrams. Mission accomplished! Our negative message on the fording was immediately relayed to Division Headquarters. Col. Abrams was not going to take his battalion to Pagny and it was decided that we had to find another place to ford the river. That morning at daybreak I could hear from my tent the rumbling of our tanks. I went out to watch them in silhouette against the rosy morning sky, rolling south one behind the other.

Later that day we forded the Moselle at Dieulouard, about 40 kilometers south of Pagny—and a bad crossing at that. We were fired on from the other bank by machine guns and small shells. Our tanks and artillery returned fire on the German positions. As we began to cross I heard the characteristic whistling of a shell, coming, as it seemed, right at us, and I remember how quickly we jumped from the open jeep (except for the driver, who had to remain at the wheel) and dove into a hole full of water and pebbles—while the jeep continued slowly across. This offered little protection, if any, as there were no bushes behind which we could hide. I caught up with the jeep and for the rest of the crossing remained in it until we reached the other side. Quite a number of men were hit, but our jeep was spared.

The day after the Division crossed the Moselle and was heading for the Siegfried Line, a French officer, Captain Rateau (a *nom de guerre,* not his real name), an OSS and liaison officer with our Division, came to see me. We had had occasion to talk twice before in the course of the campaign. He was connected with the FFI and a member, I think, of the *Bureau Central de Renseignements de l'Armée* (BCRA). It might have been he who suggested the Pagny mission to our commander, as he had previously shown considerable interest in the way we were getting our intelligence from French sources. He said he had talked to our Colonel. He wanted to recommend me, as the leader of our team, to receive a *Croix de Guerre* with Palms—a higher award than the simple *Croix*—for the manner in which our difficult mission to Pagny-sur-Moselle had been accomplished, and he wanted some personal information, which I provided.

The awarding of a foreign decoration was subject to American approval. It had to be endorsed by the Colonel commanding Combat Command A, who was glad to support it and said it was most deserved. It was forwarded to Division Headquarters for submission to the French Command which would award the decoration, according to Captain Rateau. He gave me a copy of the citation for information after he had drafted it, as he was about to leave our Division for good. Our team also left the Fourth Armored a few weeks later, as we were sent back to the center of MIS near Paris.

While we were still at the front, however, a message reached Combat Command A saying that Division Headquarters had been unable to forward the proposal. The rather curious reason given was that under existing procedure the French Command had allocated a certain number of *Croix de Guerre* to each American Division, leaving to each U.S. general the responsibility for distributing the medals. All the French *Croix de Guerre* allotted to the Fourth Armored Division had already been distributed and there was, unfortunately, no way of requesting additional medals. As far as I knew, no one in our command at the front had ever received the *Croix de Guerre*. Perhaps officers at Division Headquarters considered such a foreign decoration, with its high recognition, something nice to show off back home. It was rarely awarded to junior or non-commissioned officers.

Although attributing a limited importance to decorations, I was disappointed—particularly in view of my own background—but it did not matter that much. There was no way to inquire further about it. Captain Rateau was gone. All I could do was to keep the copy of the citation as a souvenir. At any rate, I had already received the Bronze Star and I was proud to wear it.

It also may be relevant that written administrative matters in a combat zone were often slow and somewhat uncertain. For instance, it took five months from the day I was recommended for a battlefield commission by the Fourth Armored to the day I actually received my official appointment and my bars as a Second Lieutenant; the recommendation of my superior officers in the Fourth Armored Division had to be reviewed by the Military Intelligence Service (MIS) in Washington, DC, of which I was a member. We were only detailed to the Fourth Armored by MIS. Further, the appointment of Army officers required the signature of the President of the United States, even if it were a mere formality.

Other Intelligence Missions

The team left Combat Command A, the tank battalion to which it had been attached when the Third Army reached the Siegfried Line. I knew some German, but not enough to be useful in getting information for our command. We were sent to Le Vesinet, an elegant suburban residential community which was the center of MIS in the European Theater. In peacetime it likely was lovely. We were billeted in a complex of villas which had been occupied by the Germans, in the middle of a private park. There was a small lake and, in its middle, a tiny island called l'Ile des Cygnes (Swan Lake). We still ate K-rations there, but a French chef knew how to transform them into delectable dishes. All I remember of Le Vesinet is how cold it was in the houses where we were billeted. Although these had been desirable middle-class dwellings before the war, we had no coal to heat them.

Shortly after our arrival there, I was ordered, with Lt. Parks, to make a quick trip by jeep to Namur and Liège to deliver secret messages to a certain Army Command in the area. This was at the time of General von Runstedt's German passing through Liège we learned about the infiltration of German soldiers dressed in American uniforms and speaking perfect English. The German Commander, Otto Skorzeim, sent several jeeploads of bilingual men, thoroughly conversant in American slang, behind the lines to mingle with American troops, spread confusion, change signposts, cut telephone wires, give false messages to the civilian population and create panic.

The U.S. Military Police was doing what it could to stop the infiltrators, but the only way to establish after arrest whether they were truly Americans was to ask precise questions about baseball or some other typical American sport, and about the names and careers of famous players and teams. Password checks were no longer enough; nor were dog tags. But no amount of instruction could adequately cover the field of American sports.

Parks and I were driving in the rain that morning when, putting my hand to my neck under the collar of my shirt, I suddenly realized, to my horror, that I did not have my dog tags. The chain holding them had somehow come loose. Vainly I searched all my pockets. I immediately thought of the possibility of our being stopped and interrogated at a checkpoint by the Military Police or the CID. I would have been unable to correctly answer questions on American sports, having hardly had time to read a sports page since my arrival in America. With my foreign accent, I could have been taken for one of the Germans sought after by our police. Fortunately, we were not stopped, and I was sure that, had we been, Lieut. Parks likely would have been able to get me out of such a critical and embarrassing situation.

I received another interesting mission while still with MIS at Suresnes. In January 1945 I was asked to be a member of a small team of intelligence specialists from the U.S. Army dispatched to raid the offices of the Gestapo in Strasbourg when the 2nd French Armored Division of General Leclerc captured the city. Evidently, MIS wanted its own men to lay their hands on the greatest possible number of documents left by the Gestapo when they left Strasbourg. For two days we posted ourselves at Sarrebourg, which was to be on the road of the invading French column. The French Armored Division was a wild bunch of glorious and intrepid soldiers under the command of Leclerc. As mentioned, they had come all the way from the North African desert near the border of Chad and Libya, where they had successfully battled some of Rommel's units at the famous Battle of Bir Hakeim (now the name of a subway station in Paris). They had fought like lions in Italy at Monte Cassino, and their ranks included African colonial troops and Legionnaires. They were now part of the U.S. Seventh Army which had landed at St-Raphael on the French Riviera and had gone all the way up the Rhone Valley, fighting valiantly alongside the U.S. troops in the bloody battles in the south of Alsace and in the Vosges under General de Lattre de Tassigny. Strasbourg, the capital of that province, where the *Marseillaise* of Rouget de Lisle was sung for the first time, was Leclerc's final objective.

On our way to Strasbourg to join with the French division we spent the night at Sarrebourg in a manor-like dwelling in the middle of a vast garden off the main road. We saw a column of tanks, halftracks and jeeps coming at full speed past us in the direction of Strasbourg, all lights turned on. This Americans never did; we had strict orders to show no lights, but the French apparently did not observe them. They were pursuing the remnants of the German Army and perhaps thought this would scare them more than using caution. They were in a hurry to reach Strasbourg where the resistance would take place.

After they had gone, I was asked by a colleague to give up my turn guarding the estate gate from midnight to 2 a.m., so that he could get an uninterrupted night's sleep. That night, Sarrebourg was under German mortar fire. A shell fell near the gate while my replacement was on guard; he was killed. I was asleep in the house near a window when all the glass shattered. I suffered only a few insignificant cuts to my face. Again that night I thanked my lucky stars.

The Germans put up a stalwart defense before retreating from Strasbourg. We spent a week there, in the end compiling little useful information. We did, however, find a few significant documents which we sent back to Paris for analysis. We attended a brilliant parade under arms, a *prise d'armes*, on Place Kleber, with General Leclerc, the units of the Second Armored Division in battle uniforms, including some colorful colonial units, and all the dignitaries of the city. Alsace had been recovered! The liberation of Strasbourg had a tremendous significance for the French, and, in view of my own Alsatian ancestry, I was extremely proud to have witnessed this glorious event.

But Strasbourg was not yet entirely free. Many snipers were still firing on soldiers and passers-by from rooftops and apartment windows, making walking and driving perilous. It took close to one more week before the last Germans were taken prisoner, had been killed or had slipped out of the city across the Rhine.

VE Day in Paris and the Return Home

I returned to Paris. My next assignment with the Office of the General Purchasing Agent (GPA) was routine. Before I received my commission, at last, we were billeted in the *Grand Palais* on the Champs Élysée and slept in bunks three tiers high in one of the palace's vast salons. It was very cold and one needed several layers of blankets to keep warm. From our bunks we could admire the magnificently painted ceilings of angels, shepherds and shepherdesses. We ate at a restaurant off the Champs Élysée where, again, the French chef knew how to turn K-rations into savory meals.

When I got my bars I lived like a gentleman, took a nice rented room in the 17th *arrondissement*, and ate at the *Cercle Interallié*. It was altogether different. I enjoyed Paris in a U.S. officer's uniform; everyone I met remarked that I could speak French like a Frenchman. Then came VE Day, a delirious experience.

I had accumulated many battle points, having been in combat constantly between landing in Normandy and the end of 1944. As a result, I was entitled to return to the States "on points" as early as I wished. I asked my General's permission to be demobilized in Europe to go to London to ask about a job with the United Nations, which had kept open an office in Church House. The request was denied. The General said I had to be released in the U.S.

After two weeks of awaiting transport in an assembly area near Marseille, I boarded a Liberty ship headed for Boston. After two weeks at the hospital at Fort Edwards on Cape Cod for minor surgery, I was finally demobilized in Ft. Devens, Massachusetts in January 1946. I went straight to South Dartmouth, where my wife, three-year-old daughter and in-laws were impatiently waiting for me. I could not believe that I was home again, however briefly, physically unscathed by the war.

Shortly after my return I learned that, if I wanted to exercise my reinstatement rights as a veteran, a job was waiting for me in Washington. The unit of the Board of Economic Warfare where I had worked before I was drafted had, in my absence, been transferred to the State Department. I wrote, and soon after was offered an excellent job one grade higher than that I had held at BEW. I considered myself lucky, since many men released from the Army were forced to find work by themselves, not an easy task in those days.

I was assigned to the Office of Foreign Liquidation, a new State Department section entrusted with the disposal of Lend-Lease, the vast program under a special legal arrangement wherein military equipment valued at hundreds of millions of dollars had been transferred to our Allies at the onset of the war in exchange for U.S. military bases in those countries. It was time to terminate Lend-Lease.

The Office also handled the sale of U.S. surplus property left around the world by our forces in their theaters of operation, sometimes on the battlefields themselves. This job required new staff with backgrounds in economics, law and management.

I was named a deputy to the Director of the Planning Division, Dr. Joseph Taggart, a highly competent economist and a very friendly person who later was to become Dean of the Graduate School of Business Administration at New York University. My job was to help plan bulk sales of surplus property that were to be negotiated with governments in Western Europe. There I met a number of young, recently demobilized Lieutenant Commanders from the Navy. One who worked with me, still in his Navy uniform, was Scott Behoteguy, a graduate of the Wharton School of Economics, who later worked with the Marshall Plan in Europe and as a Country Director with the U.S. Agency for International Development in various parts of the world. He, too, has become a lifelong friend. The office atmosphere was agreeable and I enjoyed the company of my new friends. As a former European accustomed to more formal working arrangements, I appreciated our relaxed team spirit.

Natalie and I had rented an apartment in Georgetown, on a noisy Wisconsin Avenue street corner leading to Georgetown University. Streetcar wheels screeched each time they made the turn towards the campus. The noise was so unbearable that we kept our windows closed, resigned to the fact that the apartment was all we could find. The living room was on the second floor of an old building, just above the Little Caledonia Shop, a boutique for modern furnishing accessories. The shop owner rented us the apartment. She had done an excellent decorating job, cleverly hiding some of its imperfections. A rather stiff set of stairs led to the second floor and, on occasion, we could hear rustling below the stairs, leading us to believe that Washington's rat population visited the shop from time to time.

We received one shock when, for the first time, we entered the bedroom where our three-year-old was to sleep. When Natalie opened the second door in the room, not knowing where it led, she found that beyond its threshold, instead of a balcony or the stairs of a fire escape, there was nothing but a twenty-foot drop to the snow-covered ground below. Fortunately she did not step forward, but it set our hair on end. We put a large armoire across the door and forgot it for the rest of our stay.

The rent was exhorbitant. Almost any accommodation, no matter its condition, could rent in the capital in those days, where housing demand was at a peak. As Washington geared for an ambitious program of peaceful pursuits, new federal workers were arriving literally in droves every day, from all parts of the country.

Six months later I was offered a new position at the American Embassy in Paris to handle European sales of the surplus disposal program. I kept the offer in my pocket for a few days before making a decision. It was not expected, of course, that the Office of Liquidation would provide permanent jobs, and my wife, attracted by the romance of living in the City of Light, would have liked me to take the position; it was a great temptation.

Another opening with the State Department in Washington in the Division of Research for Europe was offered to me. Had I accepted either of these two jobs I likely would have built an excellent career in the State Department. My knowledge of Europe and special training was unusual for an American in Washington. Had I gone to Paris my experience could have been used a little later in the Marshall Plan. Instead, Scott Behoteguy took the job, using it as the springboard for a wonderful career.

But perhaps, as my father had been before, I was attracted by the unknown, which the UN at that time certainly was. I was a pioneer and I did not mind taking chances. Above all, I wanted to become part of this new peace organization with its lofty goals. A few days later I made up my mind, true to my vow in the foxhole in Normandy. I decided that I would try to join the United Nations in New York—although I had no special backing from anyone for such an attempt, except for recommendations my former superiors might be willing to forward to the UN.

*Author's Father and Mother,
New York, 1909*

*Jean with his Father,
New York, 1912*

Author's Mother, New York 1914

Jean, Beaucourt, France, 1922

Jean, Besançon, France, 1927
Lycée Victor Hugo

Jean, and the Labarthe Family,
Enghien-les Bains, France 1938

Jean and Natalie,
Jones Beach, NY 1939

Jean and Natalie,
Wedding Day
December 1, 1941 Haiti

Natalie, Haiti, 1942

Natalie (R) at
Banana Plantation Haiti, 194

Jean on leave from the Front (WWII)

U. N. Day, Port au Prince Haiti, 1962, Richardot, center, with Haitian Ministers

Jean, his mother, and daughter, Carole, Haiti 1962

Richardot family with friends, Haiti 1963

Author, left, with U.N. expert Georges Mouton, Haiti, 1963

Parliament House, Kampala, Uganda, UN Day, Oct. 1963

*Jean, left, with Prince Saddrudin
Aga Khan (talking to child),
U.N. High Commissioner for
Refugsees, Settlement in Uganda, 1964*

*Nancy and Carole Richardot
on Board RMS Queen Elizabeth
on the way to Paris to live, 1964*

Jean, Provence, 1981

PART III

THE UN YEARS AT TURTLE BAY

PART III

THE UN YEARS AT TURTLE BAY

We, the people of the United Nations, determined to save succeeding generations from the scourge of war, which twice in our lifetime has brought untold sorrow to mankind . . . .

The UN Charter

Joining the United Nations

There were many young men and women like me at the end of World War II who wanted to climb aboard the new ship for peace, the United Nations, which was expected to stop war forever. We were all fired up by the noble words in the Preamble to its Charter.

Remembering my vow in the foxhole, I was ready to work in any part of this new organization,[1] destined to become the greatest global human experiment ever. Its purposes, defined in its Charter, were to prevent war, maintain international peace and security, promote social progress and better standards of living in greater freedom, develop friendly relations among nations and achieve international cooperation.

I filled out an application form for UN Secretariat positions and wrote a covering letter to Trygve Lie, the newly-appointed Secretary-General. Then I learned that between 10,000 and 20,000 candidates had applied. My chances appeared slim. How would the UN sort out those thousands of applicants? Since I was working for the State Department I asked for an interview there with the officers of a new division called International Organizations, which had been responsible for the Dumbarton Oaks meetings where the first blueprint for the UN had been established, and for the San Francisco Conference which approved the UN Charter.

I was told I should talk to Alger Hiss, head of the Division, one of Franklin Delano Roosevelt's "fair-haired boys." A graduate of the Harvard Law School, he had served as secretary to Justice Felix Frankfurter of the Supreme Court before joining the State Department, and in 1945 had attended the Yalta Conference with

---

1 The organs and agencies of the current United Nations system are listed as Appendix I.

Roosevelt, Churchill and Stalin as the right arm of Edward Stetinius, U.S. Secretary of State.

Hiss received me. The meeting was short and cordial. I told him why I was interested in joining the UN Secretariat, explaining my background and qualifications. To my surprise, his attitude was less than encouraging. He said there would be a lot of competition and the Department had decided not to present any candidates. "Everyone will have to fend for himself," he said with a smile, wishing me good luck.

Incidentally, this rule later proved to be a very poor decision for the U.S., as a pre-screening of American candidates might have avoided the difficulties that arose later during the McCarthy "witch hunt" period, to which I refer later. After Senator McCarthy's witch hunt all Americans working at the UN or who wanted to join the Organization were investigated by the FBI.

One day, on a walk toward the Dumbarton Oaks Park up the hill from our house we met Alger Hiss; we recognized his lanky silhouette. He, too, was taking a breath of air with his young son. We stopped and talked for a while. He said he lived in the house just behind ours. I found him pleasant, and he seemed to be the hero of the day. I never saw him again after that, but, as is well known, he was later denounced by Whittaker Chambers as a spy for the Soviets, creating one of the biggest political scandals in Washington in the 1950s, when he was tried and convicted of perjury. In 1992, after the fall of the Soviet Union, Russian authorities searched their files and assured the United States that they found nothing indicating that Hiss had ever spied for the USSR.

To understand better what being recruited by the UN involved, I decided to go to New York to visit Hunter College in the Bronx, where the UN was temporarily settled, and talk to the Bureau of Personnel. This served me well as, at the precise time I visited Hunter, a session of the Economic and Social Council had just started, and they were in dire need of two additional Assistant Secretaries to serve the meeting, which was to last several weeks. I was lucky enough to meet the Director of the Economic Unit of the Secretariat, at that time Raoul Aglion, a French diplomat who needed an economist bilingual in English and French. I had never met him before, but appeared to be the person he was seeking. He was able to convince the Bureau of Personnel that they should offer me a probationary appointment.[2]

---

2 In writing this complicated story of the UN at Headquarters, I thought the simplest way was to take my readers along on my various assignments in the Secretariat as they evolved, in the hope that they can learn about the problems the organization faced and its accomplishments and failures. Although this is not a history of the UN, nor a full survey of its activities, it provides an accurate picture of the difficult and important issues dealt with at the UN during the Cold War.

A London Summer

Soon after, I was invited to join the UN Secretariat as Senior Economic Affairs Officer, to serve the newly-created UN bodies in the economic field, the Economic and Social Council and its sub-committees, and to participate in the preparation of studies requested by them. Later I was given a number of exciting assignments both at UN headquarters and in the operations field programs. Joining the UN made my life; I could hardly have chosen a more rewarding career.

I resigned from the State Department, left Washington in May 1946 to work with the Economic and Social Council until the end of its session, then was sent to London to serve a newly-created sub-committee of the Council for Reconstruction of Devastated Areas of Europe, its official name. The sub-committee was to survey war-torn areas, consult with the European governments concerned and draft recommendations for action by the UN. At that time it was hoped that the UN would have a role in the reconstruction of Europe. The Council had in mind creation of a permanent regional Commission for the whole of Europe. As will be seen, it did not turn out that way.

Our group arrived in London in June for approximately three months. It was a challenging experience for me, as it was the first time an organ of regional cooperation had been envisaged by the UN. Our group settled at Church House in Dean's Yard, Westminster, near Central Hall. Church House had been the temporary offices of the United Nations for a whole year, before the Organization was transferred to New York. The small Secretariat, now at Hunter College, was then directed by Gladwyn Jebb, a brilliant and distinguished British diplomat and the UN's first international civil servant. He was assisted by David Owen,[3] the future UN Assistant Secretary-General for Economic Affairs, with whom I was to work on my return to New York, and by Brian Urquhart, who became personal assistant to all the UN Secretary-Generals and, afterwards, a UN Under Secretary-General. Urquhart was to be among the masterminds of the UN Peacekeeping Operations and the author of Dag Hammarskjöld's biography.

In London, it rained solidly all summer long except one Sunday, but we were so busy that it did not really matter; we spent most of the days and evenings in the office or in meetings. I only remember that when we went for a walk the lawns were always wet in Hyde Park, and no young couples could be seen lying in the grass, usually a typical sight in summer.

The Sub-Committee members, each representing their governments, were soon

---

3   Not to be confused with David Owen, the former British Foreign Secretary, later responsible for peace efforts in Bosnia.

divided into three fact-finding teams, one for Western, one for Eastern and the third for Southern Europe. The teams were to confer with the governments, visit the devastated areas in the three regions, then discuss priority problems with the appropriate ministries. We would then return to London with our data and draft the sub-committee's recommendations. I was designated Secretary of the team visiting the Western European countries. We went to France, Belgium, The Netherlands and Luxembourg and took trips to the most war-torn areas of northern and northeastern France. We saw ruined port installations, particularly in Rotterdam and the region of The Netherlands which had been flooded when the enemy invaded the country; these visits were always accompanied by the inevitable official receptions.

Acting upon the report of our sub-committee, the Economic and Social Council recommended to the General Assembly the creation of a UN Economic Commission for Europe (ECE), to be installed in Geneva. Its first executive secretary was Gunnar Myrdal, the Swedish economist, a Nobel Prize laureate, well known in the U.S. for his work *The American Dilemma*, one of the first extensive sociological surveys on the conditions of blacks in the United States.

Shortly after the decision to create the UN Economic Commission, the Marshall Plan for the reconstruction of Europe was launched . It was not linked to the UN; instead it was a partnership among the Western European countries, the United States and Canada. A new organization, later called the Organization for European Cooperation and Development (OECD), was set up in Paris to implement the Plan. As is widely known, the Soviet Union was invited to join the Marshall Plan but declined. This was one of the first signals of the impending Cold War, and, soon after, the Iron Curtain fell, which divided Europe for more than four decades. Accordingly, the role of the UN Commission for Europe was less important than it would have been had Europe remained undivided.

Without the Cold War, reconstructed Europe, developing as a single continent, would have prospered faster. Instead, we were forced to wait 45 years to see a reunification of Germany, the end of Communism and the democratization of the East European countries, and the dawn of a new continent with a brighter future, on its way to greater unification of its diverse parts.

The Commission for Europe had not been planned as an operational body. It has been an outstanding research center for its Western and Eastern European member-states for more than 40 years, serving them with statistics, economic studies on the problems of Europe, giving advice to the governments on concepts and policies, doing work in many fields and providing a useful bridge between the two parts of Europe—highly appreciated by both of them. Shortly after the creation of the United

Nations Economic Commission for Europe, the Western Europeans formed their own Economic Community and elected a European Parliament which, of course are not linked to the UN, but are favored by it as the Charter encouraged regional political and economic arrangements. As a matter of fact, regional thinking and planning have become a fact of life.

During the following years, similar UN regional economic commissions were created: one for Asia and the Far East (ECAFE) in Shanghai, moved later to Bangkok; one for Latin America (ECLA), in Santiago, Chile (with which I was connected); one for Africa (ECA), in Addis Ababa, Ethiopia; and one for the Arab countries in Beirut, later moved to Baghdad, which Israel did not want to join.

The UN regional economic commissions have worked very well, promoting integrated economic and social development and regional cooperation in the areas where they have been established. They are a clear proof that many economic problems are best dealt with regionally.

Lake Success

In fall, 1946, when I returned to New York from London after the sub-commission's work had been completed, the UN Secretariat had moved from Hunter College to the vast Sperry Gyroscope plant in Lake Success, near Great Neck, Long Island, which would be its home until the permanent UN Headquarters were built on the East River in New York. Lake Success, a bedroom community, was about 45 minutes by car from New York City. While Secretariat personnel worked at the duly converted plant, the delegates to the General Assembly were meeting at a remodeled skating rink on the 1939 World's Fair grounds, a place I knew well. In those days the Secretariat still was very small, a few hundred people at most. The families of the officers who had joined the UN from their own countries lived for a while at the splendid Lido Beach Hotel on the Atlantic shore of Long Island, not far from Jones Beach. A fashionable summer resort hotel before the War, the Lido Beach had been requisitioned by the U.S. Navy until the end of the War, and was put at UN disposal because of the critical shortage of housing for our staff. Limousines shuttled us to our Lake Success offices every morning, as few owned cars in those days. At the hotel our wives had a pleasant residence and a beach. My daughter Carole was four years old and enjoyed the company of children from other countries, while the wives could play bridge and share their sometimes frightening wartime experiences. We met them at night after their comfortable day for an excellent dinner served at small linen-covered tables bearing single roses in a vase. For those who had just left the War behind them, it was pleasant to enjoy again the niceties of peacetime.

Upon leaving the Lido Beach at the end of 1946, some families moved to a new apartment complex called Parkway Village, in Queens. But we were able to rent a one-bedroom apartment in a new building on Schenk Avenue in Great Neck, where several UN Secretariat and Delegation families also lived. The housing situation continued critical and, thanks to a special arrangement made by the UN Housing office, this modern complex was among the first available to us in the area. Even though we had a child and, two years later, a second one, we could not get a larger unit. Soon we were able to buy a car. The apartment building had a garage in the basement, something new in the suburbs at that time.

Life at Schenk Avenue was pleasant. We made many good friends there, including Americans Victor and Marion Mills, and Canadians Carole and Arthur Campbell and Peter and Lee Wight, all from the UN Secretariat. There also were Lee and Jean Blanchard, Tom and Mina Powers (now dead) and the Manns, all of the American delegation, and Ecuadorians Pepe and Elba Correa. We knew also Dutch, French, Haitian and Chinese families living in the same building. We visited each other frequently and shared enjoyable parties some evenings, each family preparing a dish and the party moving from apartment to apartment as the meal progressed. The evening usually finished with dancing at the Correas to lively sambas and other Latin American music.

We also met Paul and Sophie Alpert, both French. Paul, an economic journalist, was in my office and had been in charge of Press Relations at the Quai d'Orsay. Just before joining us he had published a book in French on Franklin D. Roosevelt and the New Deal. Later he moonlighted, teaching economic history and economic development at the Graduate School of New York University after a full UN workday, an effort I greatly admired.

We all kept busy schedules during the day, and I remember spending many evenings and even nights drafting reports to meet Economic and Social Council deadlines. We were still terribly understaffed.

Once I worked so hard for several nights on an economic report related to the progress of reconstruction plans in Europe that I became overtired. The evening I wrote the last line, at 7 p.m. at my desk in Lake Success, I tried to get up from my chair but could not. The lower part of my body was paralyzed. I felt excruciating pain in my back and along my right leg. I finally stood up using both hands as a lever on the desk. No one was in the corridor to help me, as everyone had left by then. With great difficulty, practically unable to lift my feet, and under sharp pain, I made my way along the long corridors. I don't know how I reached the parking lot, dragged myself into the car, started it and was able to reach home. We could not get a doctor that evening. The next day I was taken by ambulance to a hospital in Port Washington, where I stayed a few days under strong medication. Finally, still in great pain, I was able to consult a top neurologist at New York Hospital. My trouble was a disk, but by then it was too late to operate. I gradually recovered, but for three months I had to use a wheelchair to get to the office, The sciatic nerve had been damaged, and my right foot permanently numbed.

Santiago

In 1948 the Economic and Social Council had been discussing the need to establish a UN regional Economic Commission for Latin America (ECLA). It was to assist and advise the countries of that region in the identification of their post-war problems and the establishment of regional and national policies which would help the development of the region as a whole.

The most articulate delegate favoring the proposal, Chilean Ambassador Hernan Santa Cruz, offered Chile as a host country and Santiago, its capital, as headquarters for the new Commission. This was unanimously accepted. A few staff members from the Department of Economic Affairs were to be selected to serve the first meeting of the Commission at Santiago and to staff the new organization. They needed an American in addition to Latin American economists. I spoke Spanish, a requirement for the job. The prospect of getting to Latin America and of studying the economic problems of that continent led me to apply for the new assignment. The fact that I spoke French was a plus, since some of the Caribbean countries also represented in the Commission were French-speaking. Total membership in the Commission included the twenty Latin American republics, the United States, Canada, France, The Netherlands and the UK, the latter three in view of their possessions in the Caribbean.

Invited to join ECLA,[4] I knew a new adventure was about to begin. With great expectations I would discover Latin America and meet delegates from all the countries in the area in Santiago. I would work with an almost-entirely Latin American staff on some of the region's basic international problems. The Commission's approach was to be new. The Organization of American States had been created; its main function more political than economic. We would study the post-war economic and social problems, with a view to developing policies to encourage better integration of the Latin American countries, increase their international trade and the standards of living of their people.

---

4 Later expanded to include the Caribbean, the name changed to Economic Commission for Latin America and the Caribbean (ECLAC).

Natalie was enthusiastic at the prospect of moving to Santiago. We started immediately to make the necessary arrangements for our transfer. Our apartment was easily sublet. We packed a few items of furniture and personal effects authorized to be shipped, as my assignment was for just one year. Natalie and Carole, who was then five, went by boat on the Grace Line, crossing the Panama Canal and stopping at Buenaventura in Colombia, Guyaquil in Ecuador and Lima, Peru, and landed in the beautiful port of Valparaiso several weeks after my arrival in Chile. I had flown right away to Santiago to help with the preparation for the ECLA meeting, taking an overnight Peruvian Airlines flight from Idlewild (now John F. Kennedy) Airport. The trip, still by propeller aircraft, was very long: first to Lima, where I stayed half a day, then on to Santiago. Jorge Rose, a young Peruvian statistician, who was flying with me to Santiago to join the ECLA staff, showed me Lima and its poorer districts, explaining the Peruvian political situation and the rise of a new revolutionary party which was clamoring for long overdue social reforms.

Los Cerillos Airport, at the very foot of the awesome Cordillera range of the Andes Mountains, serves Santiago. We were flying above a sea of white clouds, under glorious sun and in plain view of the sparkling peaks of the Cordilleras, still covered with snow. It was a morning in May, 1948. At ground level, our sea of white clouds was a heavy fog which forced our pilot to rely solely on his instruments for landing. Making matters worse, the airport was located on a small plain surrounded by rock peaks, several hundred feet high, raising their heads in various locations. During two hours of circling the field, the pilot made three attempts to find the runway under the clouds. Passengers could do nothing but pray. Flying into Chile is never dull.

The country's geography, called *una geografica loca* by one famous Chilean writer, is indeed mad. Chile is a quite narrow stretch of land, no more than 200 miles wide, but ten times that in length. Squeezed between the Pacific Ocean and the Andes, its northern region is desert, near Antofagasta and the country's extraordinary copper resources. Central Chile is a fertile plain, while the south boasts beautiful forests, lakes and mountains. In its extreme south is Patagonia, an area of extensive sheep raising. Later, when driving south at night on the rare roads existing in those days, I could see the long chain of volcanoes in the Cordillera all alight, spitting their fire into the dark sky.

Almost immediately after I arrived in Santiago I met an old friend, Raymond Etchats, a French Basque representing the UN Food and Agriculture Organization (FAO) at the meeting. He had been a year behind me at the HEC in Paris, and we had been evacuated from Spain on the same boat during the fighting at San Sebastian at the start of the Spanish Civil War. What a coincidence to meet again, out of the blue, on the other side of the world. For a while, until my family arrived, we lived in the same inn, run by the de la Fuente family. Señora de la Fuente came from a cultured Santiago family. Her husband was a Communist poet who knew and greatly admired Gabriella Mistral, the Nobel Prize laureate for literature who also was a Chilean Marxist. The de la Fuentes had lived in Paris for a number of years, spoke perfect French and had a beautiful raven-haired daughter, Carmen, who had been a "Bohemian" student in Paris. She had been hired temporarily as a secretary during the ECLA kickoff Conference and had recommended her parents' lodgings as a place to stay until we could find suitable housing.

Raymond fluently spoke French, Spanish and English—French because he was born in France, his father's country, Spanish because his father, a mining engineer, had moved his family to Spain for many years, and English because his mother was English and always talked to him in that language. I've seen him captivate an audience at social events as he flawlessly quoted long Bible passages in perfect King James English (an inheritance from his mother); his engaging personality and bearing and almost perfect knowledge of Shakespeare's tongue made him popular with the ranking English-speaking UN crowd.

Raymond had a dry sense of humor, and a bit of the practical joker in him. Once, after he had rented a farm on the outskirts of the city, his car broke down. He decided to get to his office in the Ministry of Agriculture in downtown Santiago on horseback. The problem was "parking" the horse, which he decided to tie in the Ministry courtyard alongside the cars belonging to officials. He knew this would draw police objections, so he very carefully attached his diplomatic license plate to the horse's tail and went to work.

The policeman assigned to the courtyard that day saw the horse. He wanted to raise an objection, but in light of the official permission implied by the license plate, he paused. After much reflection he thought it prudent to do nothing; throughout the week it took to repair Raymond's car, his horse stood in the parking lot, unbothered by the local constabulary.[5]

Santiago was then a city of close to one million people, Chile's total population being approximately eight million. Due to rural exodus, the capital's population grew later to more than two million, creating vast ghettos of jobless poor people, called *rotos*. Thousands lived literally in primitive shacks made of cardboard or

---

[5] Raymond eventually became the first appointed Resident Representative of the UN Technical Assistance Board in Latin America, and closed his career in Geneva as UN Development Program Representative for Europe.

sheet-iron or other abandoned materials and built against the retaining walls of the Mapocho River crossing the city.

We had rented a small villa in El Golf, a residential district of the city. Our street contained new houses separated by open lots. After we moved into our house, a *roto*, the father of a little family living in a shack nearby, rang our bell. He had seen the large furniture crate in front of the house and asked if he could buy it to replace the boards and corrugated iron sheets he had nailed together to house his family. Our administrative officer assured me that, although the crate belonged to the UN, I could give it to him. I never saw a man so incredibly happy in my life. Later I visited several poor *barrios* in Santiago and confirmed that the lack of housing and jobs were two of the great urban development problems of the large Latin American cities.

We hired Rosa as cook and maid. An Araucanian Indian woman of about 40 who had been recommended to us by the office, we found her to be a warm, devoted, capable woman. She had the strong character of a person who has forged her own life from tough raw materials, and it was our great blessing that she used her strength to serve as both maid and mother to Natalie throughout a difficult pregnancy with our second child.

Carole made friends with the little daughter of our Chilean neighbors. It was amazing to see the daily progress she made in speaking Spanish. In a few months she was absolutely fluent in the language. She unfortunately forgot it after we left Chile, but picked it up easily years later in college.

We enjoyed Santiago, where the climate was mild yet invigorating. We met several Chilean families and went to parties given by friends from various embassies. We danced the Cueca and learned more about the country's customs and the cordiality of the Chilean people. Many of the men in government circles and business were dynamic and spontaneous. In certain ways they resembled Americans, and perhaps that and the climate are why Chile has been called the California of Latin America.

Except for the restaurants, a few concerts and movies, Santiago offered little public entertainment. There was, however, a picturesque tavern called *La Posada del Corregidor*, an 18th-century colonial building downtown with an attractive wooden balcony, to which we would go from time to time. The place had much typically Chilean ambience. In its smoky atmosphere and subdued lighting students and other young people passed pleasant evenings drinking sangria while listening to a local string orchestra.

The first meeting of the UN Economic Commission for Latin America, which lasted two weeks, drew close to 500 delegates from governments and various organizations, and was held at the Hotel Carrera in downtown Santiago. As an officer of the Conference, I was kept busy all day by meetings of the various committees and the plenary sessions, assisting the delegates in the many ways customary at these types of international conferences. At night we worked long hours to correct the precis of the day's proceedings and see that everything was ready for the next day. I was Assistant to the Executive Secretary of the Commission, a Cuban, Eugenio Castillo, while the President was the Chilean Foreign Minister, ably assisted by Hernan Santa Cruz, who had come from New York for this purpose.

One of the purposes of the UN Conference was to approve a program of work for the Secretariat. When it ended we began to plan our daily tasks, fix our targets, start collecting data, set up a reference center and hold useful workshops. Castillo did not have the breadth of experience and training needed for such an important task. During the War, he had been the head of censorship in Havana for dictator Fulgencio Batista, and he retained the detestable habit of scrutinizing our personal mail. Fortunately, he was replaced, first by a high-level Mexican Government official, Gustavo Martinez-Cabanas, and later by the top economist in Latin America, Raul Prebisch, an Argentinian who had been Governor of the Central Bank of his country. He reorganized the Commission's work: soon after ECLA became the first economic "think tank" of Latin America.

Prebisch was known as a superb technician and a great economist. He had studied Latin American trade and development problems for years. His basic view was that Latin American economies suffered from negative terms of trade. The types of commodities they exported to industrialized countries—agricultural products and minerals—brought in too little, while manufactured products exported to Latin American countries were too expensive. This created a perpetual deficit.

The Commission conducted many studies of this problem, hoping to prove that the terms of trade needed to change. Other studies, reaching the same conclusions worldwide, were being conducted by Hans Singer, a British economist working at UN headquarters in the very Division in which I was to work on my return to the United States.

Dr. Prebisch added great prestige to the Economic Commission for Latin America, but certain U.S. economists were unconvinced by his theories; he ran into some opposition in Washington, the UN Commission being considered too radical. There is no doubt Prebisch had a point. His influence as a doctrinaire economist became world-wide. He became the champion of the underdeveloped countries.

In 1964 he was elected the first Secretary-General of the United Nations

Conference on Trade and Development (UNCTAD), which came to represent the views of the Third World regarding the kind of world economic policies which should prevail. Today again these views are far from being fully accepted by the industrialized nations, and the discussions of a "New International Economic Order" (NIEO) have been placed on a back burner, particularly since the question of the debts of Third World countries has completely changed the climate of international economic relations and must be solved before NIEO can be seriously open for negotiation. Prebisch died in 1986 after an extraordinary career.

When winter came, Natalie and I took advantage of an official holiday to go skiing in the south of Chile at a place called Volcan Ilaima, close to the famous Lake District. To get there we spent a night on the train from Santiago to Temuco then five or six hours crossing the foothills of the Andes in an old bus, jerked up and down by the most fantastic potholes I ever felt. Finally, we reached a *refugio* away up in the mountains, with the volcano in the distance. The volcano was a perfect cone covered with snow, which at sunset looked exactly like pink ice cream. The land was covered with tall Araucanian pines heavy with snow. Silhouetted against the rosy sunset, they looked like palm trees, giving the whole landscape a mysterious quality.

The *refugio* was a large log cabin, rather primitive, heated by oil drums that functioned as wood stoves; the heat was insufficient and we slept in our clothes. Our traveling companions were members of the British Ski Club of Santiago, including English and Chilean couples and a few bachelors. There was no ski lift so we used skins on our skis to climb the slopes of the Montón de Trigo, the breadloaf-shaped mountain close to the *refugio*. We were only average skiers, but we enjoyed the exercise.

Sharing the lodge with us was a group of much more intrepid skiers from Valdivia in the South of Chile, a German-speaking area. Most of its inhabitants had been born in Chile but still cherished the *vaterland* and its customs. Newspapers there were still published in German and, during the War, had favored a Nazi victory.

Our two groups ignored each other. The Germans, men and women, were excellent skiers who would leave the *refugio* at daybreak and make the five-hour ascent of the Volcano. With binoculars, we could see them reach the crater by 9 or 10 a.m. and by early afternoon they would be back from their strenuous daily ascent, deeply tanned, their eyes reddened by fumes from the crater. In the evening, sitting by the fire, they sang German *lieder* accompanied by an accordion. One night I noticed that the management, annoyed, had turned off the lights at midnight, leaving them to find their way to bed in the dark. The war was not entirely over, evidently.

When Saturday night came I thought we should not ignore each other any longer. This was 1948 and the war had been over for three years. To break the ice I went to them and suggested that we all have dinner together. Some of us made new friends that night, forgetting our links to the war and our European pasts, thinking only of our lives in Chile.

In 1949 I was sent to Montevideo to represent our Commission at two international conferences, one organized by the Food and Agriculture Organization (FAO), on nutrition in Latin America, and the other by the International Labor Organization (ILO), on manpower training and productivity. This latter was a prelude to a number of very successful skill-training centers and institutes for management established in Latin American countries with assistance from the ILO, the UN's oldest specialized agency. By then the amount of advice given to the governments by the UN and its specialized agencies had increased significantly, and the Latin American governments were taking great advantage of it.

More than forty years have passed, but I recall our time in Chile as one of our most interesting traveling experiences. I can picture this spectacular land of nature's violence, its hundreds of volcanoes, the snow-capped Andes, and its picturesque haciendas between Santiago and Valparaiso in the Central Valley and Viña del Mar, that elegant resort where I came to discover the Pacific Ocean.

But more importantly, from this exciting mission I could take pride in having shared in the first international efforts for an economic integration of the Latin American countries, and in Prebisch's pioneering efforts to explain to the world the real problems of developing countries.

Turtle Bay

By the time I returned from Chile in 1950, the new UN Headquarters, located on a beautiful spot prosaically named Turtle Bay (translated from an Indian name) on the shore of the East River, were almost completed.[6] We continued to work at Lake Success until our offices moved to Manhattan in 1950. The first day I arrived at the wide, black iron gate in front of the impressive new Headquarters, I felt more pride than ever at having joined the UN. A stream of thoughts came back to me, including the fighting in Normandy and my dream of joining the UN one day. I thought of

---

6 The New York site was chosen after a long search. The Europeans preferred Geneva; the Russians favored a site in the United States. Robert Moses, then the powerful official planner of New York City, proposed the city to the Rockefeller family. John D. Rockefeller, through the New York City Council, donated $8.5 million to the UN for the purchase of the Turtle Bay site along the East River between 42nd and 48th Streets, an area full of slaughterhouses, warehouses and slums. New York City acquired, then gave the land, an area of 16 acres, and waterfront rights, to the UN; it became one of the most expensive pieces of real estate in New York.

those who did not come back and did not have the chance I had now, working at what was to be the nerve center of world-wide activities promoting peace.

From the gate I contemplated the four buildings which comprise the Headquarters: the low, domed General Assembly with its gently curved roofline; the 39-story glass and marble Secretariat Building; the low, rectangular Conference Building alongside the East River; and, on the southwest corner of the site, the elegant building later to be the UN Library, the Dag Hammarskjöld Library, a gift of the Ford Foundation.

Forty-five years after its completion, the UN Headquarters in my view still represents one of Manhattan's most interesting works of architecture; it has not become dated despite all the daring and powerful skyscrapers built since the 1950s. The basic design, the work of an international architectural team led by Wallace K. Harrison, an American, included contributions by such world figures as Le Corbusier and Neumeier, who later designed Brasilia, Brazil's new capital. In planning the Headquarters they had held to two basic principles; to create the most efficient working conditions for the delegates, providing them with a spacious and handsome hall for the General Assembly, well appointed Council and conference rooms; and, for the Secretariat and UN staff, a well coordinated and arresting set of connected buildings.

The tall Secretariat building, where my office was located, appeared to me like a giant matchbox standing on end, its all-glass front reflecting the sky and the abstract silhouettes of the buildings across First Avenue, its two narrow sides made of beautiful green Vermont marble. I entered the gate and passed beside the circular fountain that dominated the forecourt, later graced with the sculpture "Single Form" given to the UN by Barbara Hepworth, whose work Hammarskjöld admired.

One of the elevators lifted me to the 25th floor, where the Department of Economic Affairs was to be settled. I wanted to find out whether my office would face the river or Manhattan, for each side offers dramatic contrasting views. Each officer has an office with one, two or three window sections depending on his or her grade in the organization. The metal furniture is light grey, and purely functional. The wall partitions are easily removed to change the size of an office at will. Under each windowsill is an up-to-date air conditioning system to balance the climate of the building's east and west sides to compensate for the heat generated by the sun catching the glass structure in the morning or afternoon.

An American friend, Glen Bennett, a former professional musician and a legendary figure at Headquarters, was the director of the office of the Architectural Committee and later headed the attractive corps of UN guides. He took me on a tour.

The interior decoration for the General Assembly hall, the chambers for the Security Council, the Economic and Social Council and the Trusteeship Council, were not yet fully finished. Not until 1952 did the Assembly meet in its hall. This magnificent modern structure, with a 77-foot ceiling, was being fitted with more than one thousand blue and green seats for the delegations and the public. This was where delegates of the member nations from throughout the world were to meet, the closest thing to a "Parliament of Mankind" ever assembled. Artists and artisans from Scandinavia were still working on the Council Chambers' decor. That of the Security Council, often seen on television, was the work of Norwegian Architect Arnstein Arneberg and includes a large mural by Per Krohg of Norway symbolizing the promise of peace and individual freedom. The Trusteeship Council Chamber was designed by Danish artists while the Economic and Social Council Chamber is a product of talented Swedish designers.

In my first year in the Secretariat I spent many days working in the Economic and Social Council Chamber. The Economic and Social Council (ECOSOC) meets there twice a year. I was assigned to some of its sessions as well as to those of the Second Committee of the Assembly (Economic Committee), as Assistant Secretary, the Secretary always being a high ranking officer of the Secretariat who helped the President of the Council or the Committee in the debates, which I had to follow very carefully.

At night I often was in charge of approving the precis, the official summaries of the lengthy proceedings. I was required to wait until the precis-writers from our language divisions had completed their work, which I had to check carefully for accuracy before they were reproduced overnight for distribution to the delegations the next morning. This was precise work that often kept me at the office for long evening hours; often I didn't get home until eleven o'clock or midnight. Professional personnel were not remunerated for this overtime—it was a privilege that went with the job. Fortunately, my assignment changed after a time of this rather tedious work.

* * *

Once the UN was settled on the East River we decided to leave Great Neck. We moved to New Canaan, Connecticut, where Natalie's sister and brother-in-law lived. New Canaan had been an important New England shoemaking center in the early nineteen-hundreds. Later in the century a considerable number of summer residents were drawn to the town. Many of their descendants make it their home, helping to create the residential community that New Canaan remains.

What interested me about New Canaan was the feeling of being in the countryside and breathing fresh air. Many of the houses were on small estates, but ours was in town. Life there offered us many amenities, including the chance to meet families who shared our intellectual and cultural interests. Here also were opportunities to participate in the activities of various local groups interested in world affairs. My wife became active in the local UN Study Group. Unfortunately I did not spend enough time in New Canaan, and hardly saw my children even at night.

During the General Assembly, I worked with the Second Committee in Charge of Economic Affairs. Each day I took an early train to Grand Central Station. In the fall, when I was working with the Second Committee, I would meet co-workers in the Delegates' Lounge in the morning, where the delegates arrived from their hotels around 10 a.m. before taking their places at 11 in the Assembly Hall for a plenary session. The Delegates' Lounge is a high-ceilinged, imposing beige-colored rectangular room. Its massive plate glass windows open onto the UN garden along the East River, and one of its walls houses the grand mural of the Great Wall of China offered to the UN by the Communist government when the People's Republic joined the organization. I always liked to contemplate the colorful assemblage from all corners of the world who constituted this first "Parliament of Mankind."

The delegates would stand in small groups, greeting one another, exchanging pleasantries or milling around, waiting for other colleagues to arrive and exchange notes on the day. Over the hubbub of voices one could hear from time to time the resounding voices of the young women at the reception desk paging the delegates or calling out messages over the public-address system. After decolonization in the '60s that increased the number of UN members to 150 from 57, we would see many delegates wearing their national costumes. The Africans were the most colorful, particularly the Ghanaians and the Guineans with their bright togas and caps contrasting with the dark business suits of their colleagues from the Western delegations.

Just before 11 a.m. they would edge toward the General Assembly Hall for the session about to start, occupying the seats bearing the nameplates of their delegations. The President of the Assembly, likely a foreign minister from a developing country elected each year for this important function, was already at the high podium of green Vermont marble which dominates the entire room. At his right sits the Secretary-General, on his left the Deputy to the Secretary-General.

The Hall resembles an immense bowl of very bright colors with its green and blue chairs, and is decorated with two abstract murals by Leger. One of these, resembling a fried egg, gave the room an air of noisiness, yet in its modernism it appeared appropriate for the time. Across the room, half way up, behind wooden walls and glass partitions, one could see the radio, television and interpreting staffs in their booths, setting up for action. The public and press sections, on elevated blue-seated tiers at the rear, were already filled.

There was drama and excitement in the hall as the President rapped his gavel and announced; "Will the delegates please take their seats! The plenary session of the General Assembly is now in session."

But the world of the delegations was not my world directly nor that of my colleagues. We belonged to the Secretariat, one of the six executive arms of the UN, the one which does the work while the leading organ, the General Assembly, debates, makes resolutions, votes on budgets and gives us its directives.

The World of the Plaza: Life in the Secretariat

Working for the Secretariat never failed to surprise me. It was a unique experience. Where can one find in the entire world a place where one's colleagues are of all different nationalities, from all corners of the world, most of them belonging to the intellectual elite of their countries? Many have studied in Europe or America but retain their own national characteristics, religion and culture. Some keep their own way of dressing, particularly those from Asia. One can see young women from India wearing graceful saris in the office. Clubs were formed for artistic, cultural and athletic pursuits after hours and on weekends. There are concerts, films, lectures and topical discussions. Many staff members from abroad are entertained by American families in the New York area. But most of all, close friendships develop among people of different national backgrounds in the absence of discrimination based on race, color or religion.

Over the last four decades the UN staff grew and grew as the organization's workload progressed. Now more than 15,000 men and women from some 150 countries are employed by the UN Secretariat, about one-third of them at New York Headquarters and the others in UN offices and centers around the globe. Another 10,000 work for various other UN organizations. Among many types of specialist working for the United Nations, the interpreters are a breed apart. They need a first-rank education, must know several languages and their work is exhausting. In the first years' sessions of the General Assembly in New York, "consecutive" interpretation was the rule, instead of the simultaneous interpretation customary today. Such stars as the popular Kaminker brothers could repeat Andrei Vishinski's speeches without a flaw. They had worked with the League of Nations and, with a few others, were born in Russia before the Revolution of 1917. Educated in France, they spoke Russian, French and English perfectly.

The trouble was that consecutive interpretation was time-consuming, slowing down the meetings considerably. But it was precise and required for all debates of the Security Council. Many delegates would leave the Chamber for a cigarette during the translations. Later, simultaneous translation became available for all meetings and, thanks to a small dial linked to each delegate's desk and to the seats in the public gallery, one now can simultaneously hear the speeches in the UN's five official languages: English, French, Russian, Spanish and Chinese.

* * *

In May 1946, on the day I joined the United Nations, I took the oath of allegiance, as do all members of the Secretariat:

> I solemnly swear to exercise in all loyalty, discretion and conscience the functions entrusted to me as an international civil servant of the United Nations, to discharge these functions and regulate my conduct with the interests of the United Nations only in view, and not to seek or accept instructions in regard to the performance of my duties from any government or other authority external to the Organization.

As a result, I had contracted special obligations and responsibilities which made me no longer an ordinary citizen of the United States.

It is important to understand the principle of independence and primary loyalty of the United Nations staff, one of the tenets of recent international law, as spelled out in Article 100 of the Charter. The idea that individuals may actually have to place their duties to the UN above those of their own country may be difficult to understand for an outsider, but in practice there are few situations where such a choice faces the staff. The overwhelming majority of their duties do not raise problems of national loyalty. National interests are represented by the delegates of the governments, not by the staff, and the Secretariat has little opportunity to influence policy statements or discussions.

It does not mean that an international civil servant is a world citizen. Yet, in an informal way, one could say that he or she is the closest to what might be called a "world citizen." I have tended in this book to refer to myself using that term. I certainly felt that way when I worked for the UN, but there is no world citizenship as such and we are unfortunately still far from ready for world government on this planet.

The title "citizen of the world" may remind some of Garry Davis, an American who, in the '50s, renounced his citizenship and proclaimed himself a world citizen. He wrote a best-seller, *The World Is My Country*. Many thought he was a crackpot. His life grew lonely as he wandered across the world. No country wanted to recognize him without a national passport, nor his ideas about world government. Yet famous people praised him. French Nobel laureate Albert Camus, author and philosopher, was among them. Albert Einstein sent him a telegram of congratulations for having had the courage to state his position against what he called "the militarization of people by governments;" Einstein would have liked to have seen the United Nations become a supranational institution with enough independence and power to be able to solve the problems of international security.

The unique character of the international civil service was imparted and the independence of its employees was instituted by Sir Eric Drummond, the first Secretary-General of the earlier League of Nations, based on the concept of integrity and excellence of the British civil service. In a recent letter, Carlos S. Vegega, Vice Chairman of the International Civil Service Commission, summed up the professional and personal circumstances of international civil servants.

> . . . dedicated, effective, exposed, versatile and reserved. Dedication is the willingness to go to different places, many of them very difficult (Haiti, Bénin, Uganda, Cyprus) [entailing] many frustrations. [As to] exposure, as we say in Spanish *estabas siempre en el candelero listo para ser quemado* (you are always dangling over a fire, knowing you could be burned), but knowing your exposure you always did your duty even with risks for yourself and your family. Versatile you were; you were an economist, a political affairs officer, and a manager, all jointly and successively, as needed. All of this with a lot of reserve, discretion and never putting yourself on a par with our political masters . . . .
>
> But what is for me *the most important aspect is that you were not an exception, but rather the rule.* You were and I am surrounded by hundreds of colleagues who reenact your experiences daily, quietly, and effectively with only the reward of a job well done..[7] (the italics are mine).

The rule of independence was well respected by the staff in the first years of the UN, except by the Soviets. Their government did not authorize staff members to stay more than five years in the Secretariat. For Soviet citizens, working for the world organization meant being designated by their government rather than to submit to the normal process of direct competitive recruitment. After serving five years they had to return home and, instead of serving the Organization as true international civil servants, they were held by their government to continue to serve the interests of the Soviet Union. Since the breakup of the Soviet Union, the policies of the various member states have not yet become clearly observable.

Another important rule determines the recruitment of the international staff. It asserts that paramount consideration in the employment of staff and in the deter-

---

7 Personal correspondence to the author dated 25 January, 1992, in the author's possession.

mination of the conditions of service shall be given to securing the highest standards of efficiency, competence and integrity. Further, it expects that due regard will be paid to the importance of recruiting the staff on as wide a geographical basis as possible. The juxtaposition of these two rules has created enormous difficulties for the Administration. Highest standards of efficiency, competence and integrity are clearly the first requirement, but those priorities increasingly were ignored in favor of concern to achieve a balance of nationality at all levels. It is of course normal that, in an international organization, the staff should reflect in its composition the variety of cultures and nationalities represented in its membership.

Giving priority to nationality over competence has unfortunately increased the role of governments in the recruiting process. Soon it became a practice that certain posts belonged to specific countries and should be filled only by their nationals. In other words, where a candidate was from became substantially more important than his or her professional qualifications. My colleagues and I strongly opposed this idea. When the number of member states increased substantially to 150 from 57, the new member states, mostly from the Third World, quite rightly wanted to have some of their citizens appointed as staff members in the Secretariat, where there was indeed a great imbalance in the representation of nationalities. In 1947, according to UN sources, thirteen nations, nine of which were NATO states, occupied 121 of 402 posts in the professional and higher grades not requiring language qualifications. It was then that the policy changed and the factor of competence became not the first requirement but the second, after that of geographic distribution.

The Assembly requested the Secretary-General to determine "desirable ranges" allocating a minimum number of staff for each region of the world in accordance with population. Considerable pressure was put on the Secretary-General by the delegations for the appointment of their candidates, and the Secretary-General and Secretariat unfortunately were not always able to resist the pressures. In addition, because of the shortage of qualified civil servants in the developing countries, some governments limited the appointments of their candidates to five years and would not allow them to become career international civil servants. This, of course, diminished the loyalty of this new staff to the UN.

* * *

The top appointments were always made on a political basis, and did not necessarily lead to selection of the best candidates. By agreement, the five great powers had managed to reserve for themselves the following posts; the Department of Security Council and Political Affairs to a Russian; the Department of Social Affairs to a Frenchman; an American was Chief of Administration; a Chinese headed the

Trusteeship Department; and an Englishman directed the Economic Affairs Department to which I belonged.

The latter was David Owen, already mentioned as the second international civil servant, hired in London at the very beginning of the Secretariat. A scholar, historian and economist, he had been private secretary to Sir Stafford Cripps. He was a kind and friendly Welshman, liked by everyone. His department at Lake Success prepared reports for the Economic and Social Council centering on Europe and its postwar problems. At the start, its economists included, in my Division, four Americans, two Frenchmen, two Englishmen, a Belgian, a Dutchman and a Greek. The staff grew rapidly.

An internationally famous Polish economist joined us. He had lived in England since the war, taught in British universities and had published major papers on growth. Unfortunately, he trumpeted as he spoke English, his thick accent filling the air beyond his office to the point of seriously bothering others. The floor of the vast Sperry Gyroscope plant at Lake Success had been divided into cubbyhole-like offices with removable partitions only eight feet high for walls. Under the best of conditions we lacked the privacy we needed for our type of work. Despite several appeals to the man to quiet down, he was never able to do so, especially when explaining his theories to visitors.

Another economist of international repute brought aboard by David Owen was Hans Singer. This German refugee, who became a British citizen, was a super analyst and a prodigious worker. He published many innovative papers as well as a few books on international development and the fundamental problems of underdeveloped countries, which were then being understood for the first time.

On my return from Chile I found some changes in our Lake Success office. The head of my division, an American, had brought with him a few technically well-qualified Americans. Although personal politics were never discussed, I and some of my European colleagues felt a somewhat constrained atmosphere reigned at the office. Three members of our division were among those later ousted from the Organization at U.S. government request during the McCarthy period. They had refused to answer questions concerning their pre-UN activities when called before the U.S. Senate Internal Security Subcommittee, invoking the Fifth Amendment. I don't believe their alleged Communist affiliations were ever proved.

Although many in the UN thought that the attitude of the Secretary-General had been weak in allowing the FBI to carry its investigations into the UN building, thus violating its extraterritoriality, cleaning out the Secretariat of its so-called American Communists continued. The witch hunt Senator Joseph McCarthy engineered wrongly destroyed the reputations of valuable people, and in particular the life of Abraham Feller, the Secretariat's legal counsel. He was so badly harassed that he committed suicide by jumping from a window, although he had not been proven to be a Communist. Others, like Gustavo Duran, a popular senior staff member also pursued by McCarthy, were later completely exonerated of charges. A Spaniard who had become a naturalized U.S. citizen, Duran had led a colorful life before joining the UN. He had been a General in the Spanish Republican Army, fighting heroically during the Civil War. He also had advised Ernest Hemingway when the author was writing *For Whom The Bell Tolls* and is mentioned in that novel.

I hasten to add that an infinitely small percentage of Americans on the UN staff were held under suspicion and that it was just a coincidence that a few were from our division, which also included a known Communist Argentinian and a Chinese who left the UN to join Mao Tse Tung in attacking his own delegation.

Besides my work as an economist, on various occasions I was asked to represent our Department at periodic coordination meetings in the office of the Secretary General. There I met Andrew Cordier, the Secretary-General's Executive Assistant, a stocky and congenial history professor from the Midwest, who chaired these meetings, and did much to put some order in the house, avoiding the kinds of confusion that often happen in a budding organization like the UN. For many years he was in charge of General Assembly Affairs and a great expert on the interpretation of its rules of procedure. When he retired he became Dean of the Graduate School of International Studies at Columbia University and, for a short period, its President. At those meetings I also met Ralph Bunche, one of the Secretariat's all-time great figures. He earned the Nobel Peace Prize for his role as a mediator in the Arab-Israeli conflict, after the assassination of Count Folke Bernadotte. There was a chance for me to join his group in Palestine, which would have changed the orientation of my UN career. I missed this exciting assignment, having gone instead to Santiago with the ECLA.

I could not name all the friends from the Secretariat who helped make my days there so congenial and unique. Yet I must mention a few. Many colleagues had fought in the Second World War. These included Stéphane Hessel, the program coordinator in the Department of Social Affairs. A graduate of the *École Normale Supérieure*, France's top school, he had headed a French Resistance network during the war. Captured by the Gestapo, he was sent to Buchenwald, from which, it was reported, he escaped by being spirited out of the camp in a sealed coffin, passing for dead.

Another hero was Brian Urquhart, who later became Under Secretary-General for Special Political Affairs, whom I have known since the UN settled in New York.

A paratrooper who served in the British Army in North Africa, Sicily and Europe, he survived the most incredible accident when his parachute did not open. Crashing to the ground from a height of 1,200 feet, he broke every bone in his body. Miraculously, he completely recovered after a long hospital stay.

There also was Robert Muller, from Alsace-Lorraine, a friend and later an Assistant Secretary-General who, during the German occupation of France, had fought with the *maquis*[8] while still a student. He joined the UN as an intern, having won an essay contest on the subject of world government. Now retired, he is the Chancellor of the University of Peace, a highly respected author and lecturer and a real prophet of the UN.

One thing I admired most was the manner in which we at the Secretariat were able to work together despite our vastly different backgrounds and experiences.

For example, Rev. Emmanuel de Breuvery, a Jesuit priest, was one of the most remarkable persons I met at the Secretariat. When Mao Tse Tung came to power, he was expelled from Shanghai in 1951, where he was teaching economics at the French Catholic University. He was a member of the French delegation to the UN Economic Commission for the Far East when Dag Hammarskjöld recruited him to serve in the Secretariat in New York. Tall, handsome, distinguished, with a strong, friendly personality, he always wore his clerical collar under his well-cut black business suit. He invited respect. He was a close friend of Teilhard de Chardin, who spent some time in New York. At the UN, Breuvery was named head of the important Division of Natural Resources in the Department of Economic Affairs. His deputy was Joseph Barnea, a Jew from Israel, one of the sharpest minds in the Secretariat. I knew them both well. They formed a perfect team. I became a friend of the Father, who came to visit us in Connecticut. He traveled extensively. When I was in Uganda as Representative of the UN Development Program in 1964, his itinerary brought him to Kampala to discuss a forthcoming technical assistance project. He came to our house for lunch. When we had finished talking, he asked if he could sit alone in the living room to read his breviary. He installed himself on the couch in front of the coffee table and, with a twinkle in his eye, asked me to bring him a scotch and soda—*bien tassé*, (a strong one) he added. He placed the glass in front of him, at which point I left him to his meditation. This was when I remembered that he had a heart condition and that this might have been good for him. An hour later he was on his way, resuming his busy schedule of visits. He had had three earlier heart attacks, but did not want to stop traveling. He died in New York shortly after.

---

8 Resistance fighters named for the scrub-covered mountainous terrain where they hid and from which they raided the Germans during the Occupation.

At Headquarters my work on programming our technical assistance to developing countries brought me into frequent consultations with Father de Breuvery. He explained to me the scope of the pioneering work his division was engaged in, surveying the world's mineral, water and energy resources. In those early years they already had imagined a new international order for the seas and oceans, and had conducted one of the first studies on exploitation of the seabed. His division had surveyed various international river basins, setting the stage for river development projects such as the Mekong in Southeast Asia and the Senegal in West Africa. Vast coordinated regional basin projects were later undertaken by the UN. Father de Breuvery had foreseen the world energy crisis and convened the first UN conference on new sources of energy—from the sun, the wind, the sea and geothermy—in Rome in 1961.

In my years in the Secretariat I met many other outstanding men and women in a variety of fields, often experts in their own countries before joining the World organization and all enlivened with the desire to put their knowledge and energy at the service of humanity. Of course, they were not all like that, and there were Secretariat members who did not carry their weight, often recruited under political pressure or in accordance with the principle of the geographic distribution of posts. Fortunately, there was almost always a competent deputy to that person who could carry the responsibility of the office behind the scenes. Given the UN's universal character, one could not expect complete homogeneity in the quality of the staff. One must remember that the UN still is a new organization. Its administration cannot be compared to those of national governments which have operated for hundreds of years.

* * *

People have often asked whether I was frustrated during my career as an international civil servant. I tell them yes, many times, but there was always the feeling of serving the noble cause of peace, and the knowledge that international civil service, because of its newness, complexity and the diversity of its staff, could not be perfect.

We all had bad moments, but never for very long. I refused to become a cynic. I realized the complexity of the task of bringing humanity to progress and sometimes the lack of man's willingness to do it, but I had faith in the human spirit. I knew it would take time to improve the lot of the poor, particularly in the developing countries, but among my colleagues in the UN, doing the same pioneering work, I was never discouraged and remained an optimist. All of us working at the UN were, of course, dedicated internationalists.

One feeling I am sure most of my colleagues shared was the tremendous satisfaction of bringing about some human improvements in the poorest countries of the world.

As far as Headquarters staff was concerned, I felt it absolutely essential to protect in the future, more so than in the past, the integrity and independence of international civil service. I believed the powers of the Secretary-General should be better protected so as to put him or her always in a position to reject pressures in staff selection. The excessive concern that has existed over nationality distribution of posts should be curbed; competence and merit should be the overwhelming factors in staff selection. In recent years a system of competitive written and oral examinations has been instituted, which has greatly improved recruitment for the lower grades of the professional staff.

A career in international service is not easy. It requires high degrees of integrity and may involve considerable risk, often in unstable political conditions or unhealthy climates. These posts often include financial hardships and severe disruption to family life. Even higher prices have been paid by the hundreds of UN soldiers killed in peacekeeping operations in various parts of the world and UN staff members who have been kidnapped or imprisoned or who have disappeared in the course of their duties. In recent years danger has increased significantly for staff members posted abroad, particularly on UN-conducted operations in militarily unstable countries like Somalia where the UN must use ground and helicopter attacks to intervene against a warlord, or in Bosnia-Herzegovina where the UN is taking care of refugees in a country torn by a war intent on killing civilian populations to produce "ethnic cleansing."

But, I no longer must tell my friends that the UN is not only a Headquarters on the East River; daily, the news covers field activities all over the world which require quick decisions and innovations at every turn, as well as a devoted staff on the spot. The UN is peacekeeping missions protecting both sides of many disputes; it is negotiations in the Congo, Cyprus, Afghanistan, Asia, the Middle East, Latin America, the Caribbean, and other areas of conflict and war; it is the hard work of technical assistance in the Third World; it is relief operations in Ethiopia, the Sudan, Bangladesh, and Cambodia; it is great and vast humanitarian enterprises in Somalia and Bosnia and other dangerous war situations which require thousands of staff members in the field of operations—never losing sight of the need for technical assistance and economic development. The UN's mission demands of its representatives the ingenuity, courage, and stubbornness of true pioneers.

* * *

Life at the UN Secretariat also has its more relaxing side. UN Day, October 24, the anniversary of the ratification of the Charter, marks a day of celebration for the UN staff in New York and in many communities across the world.

In the early years at Headquarters, Dag Hammarskjöld added the greatest brilliance to these festivities. He arranged the annual concert given in the General Assembly Hall, which could be converted in a few hours into a splendid concert hall. The secret was a monumental movable platform which can hold an entire symphony orchestra and provide enough space for a ballet. I saw many philharmonic orchestras there on UN Day. One year Hammarskjöld selected Beethoven's Ninth Symphony as one piece for the occasion, and it was that symphony that Eugene Ormandy conducted at the UN Day concert following Hammarskjöld's death at Ndola. Famous musicians such as Pablo Casals, Yehudi Menuhin and Victor Borge performed there, as well as actors such as Danny Kaye who did so much for the Children's Fund, joking on stage with Hammarskjöld, calling him "Hammy", just short of disrespect but well taken by him and very amusing. A huge ball followed in the surrounding halls where staff, delegates and guests danced until the early morning hours.

The Secretary-Generals

I worked at UN Headquarters and in the field between 1946 and 1970 under three Secretary-Generals—Trygve Lie, Hammarskjöld, and U Thant—and on occasion dealt with each of them. The Chief Administrative Officer of the United Nations is the Secretary-General. He heads the Secretariat, and, besides his administrative role, has the important duty of drawing to the attention of the Security Council any matter which, in his opinion, threatens the maintenance of international peace and security. These two responsibilities demand selection of a truly outstanding person.

During Kurt Waldheim's mandate, I was no longer at Headquarters. Accordingly, I knew little about him until recently when, on his having become President of Austria, we learned that he had lied about the extent of his service in the German Army during World War II, a deep embarrassment for the whole world and for all of us in the Secretariat.

Why the UN did not seriously demand a full study of Waldheim's activities when he was being considered for the position remains a mystery. The case seems an unfortunately clear demonstration that what the member states want most is to find a politically-acceptable candidate for what is often described as "the most impossible job on earth." Candidates must have the highest intellectual qualifications, background, international experience, tact and ability to negotiate and be acceptable to East and West. Otherwise he or she could not function as Secretary-General. This has traditionally eliminated United States and Soviet citizens and any other candidate too outstandingly on one side or other of the Cold War. The search for a suitable candidate is not only a long one, but factually ends up with selection of a compromise choice. In 1946 Paul Henri Spaak, the well-known Belgian statesman, was the strongest candidate for the post but the Russians did not want him. Trygve Lie, who was then about to be appointed President of the General Assembly was selected instead, while Spaak was elected President of the Assembly.

Trygve Lie, a former Foreign Minister of Norway experienced in labor politics, was essentially a pragmatist, hardly prepared for the job. He was anti-Nazi and anti-Communist, but as a socialist, he was acceptable to the Russians. Lie was at the head of the UN during the difficult McCarthy period, and had to settle all problems of the installation of the Organization in New York and the recruitment of the staff. He was far from being an ideal Secretary-General but he was brave to have taken the job, the first Secretary-General called upon to deal with Middle East problems and the creation of the State of Israel. He ran into trouble in 1950, as the Soviets believed he had influenced the vote of the Security Council in favor of UN intervention in Korea. As a result, the USSR stopped all communications with him and, on Nov. 10, 1952, Lie decided to resign.

Dag Hammarskjöld was elected to replace him. He was the Secretary-General I knew best. I had the greatest respect and admiration for him, as did all my colleagues, and for me he was the model of the international civil servant. Before his election as Secretary-General he was minister in the Foreign Office in Stockholm, a most respected economist and financial expert, brilliantly representing his country in the Councils of the Organization for European Economic Cooperation. U.S. Ambassador Freeman Matthew, to whom I had talked about Hammarskjöld at a friend's home in The Hague, had seen him perform in the OEEC. He told me he had cabled the State Department in Washington, "If Hammarskjöld is willing to take the job, grab him."

The first time I talked to Hammarskjöld, shortly after he had taken up his duties, we were sitting together in the Secretariat building lobby waiting to give blood to the Red Cross. He had simply joined the staff and waited his turn.

A few weeks later Hammarskjöld decided he should know each professional staff member and the projects on which they were working. This was a big commitment on his part. His visits to all the offices in the Secretariat building spread over several weeks.

When he came to my office I was in charge of the office of technical assistance for Latin America. Among more than a hundred projects, he chose to discuss one called Economic Integration of Central American Countries, consisting of agricultural and industrial projects in the various countries, based on selected complementary aspects of their economies, for the purpose of developing a Central American common market. Hammarskjöld, as an economist, was extremely interested in this innovative project, which was carried out successfully for several years. Alas, political conditions between countries later deteriorated to the point where economic cooperation among the Central American republics greatly suffered until recently.

Hammarskjöld was a man of high moral principles and ideals. He felt that no life is more satisfactory than one of selfless service to your country and humanity. His deep religious faith was depicted in *Markings*,[9] a book which illustrated his profession of faith, his understanding of life, and his absence of fear.

He was indeed without fear when he challenged the great powers in the search for solutions to the conflicts in the world and, as I will describe, came to create a new kind of preventive diplomacy and action when the Congo crisis broke out in 1960.

U Thant, a Burmese who succeeded Hammarskjöld, was quite different. I corresponded directly with him and his Chef de Cabinet from Port-au-Prince, during the Haitian crisis in 1963, as he was concerned with the safety of our mission there. An educator and a Buddhist, he was a quiet man, highly religious. My friend Robert Muller, his personal assistant for a few years, said U Thant was a good ethical statesman. He was humble, unobtrusive, never impatient or irritated. He considered simplicity and kindness the highest values a man could seek.[10] His friendships with Pope Paul VI, Pablo Casals and Norman Cousins were well known. Brian Urquhart, who worked closely with him and wrote most of his political speeches and reports, said he became very fond of him. U Thant showed courage and firmness in the various crises which plagued the Organization during his mandate. He was strongly against the Vietnam War and was criticized for this by Washington. When, at the request of Egypt, he took upon himself the responsibility of withdrawing the UN Emergency Force from its position as a buffer between Egyptian and Israeli troops, he was rightly blamed for "caving in" to Nasser, the Egyptian dictator. Yet it was stipulated in the agreement concerning the Force that one of the parties can request its withdrawal at any time. It was thought that Thant should have resisted, since it was obvious that departure of the UN Emergency Force would precipitate the resumption of hostilities between Egypt and Israel.

---

9 Dag Hammarskjöld, *Markings*, translated by Leif Sjöberg and W.H. Auden (New York: Alfred A. Knopf, 1966).
10 Robert Muller, *They Taught Me Happiness* (New York: Doubleday, 1978).

U Thant had little time to occupy himself personally with the problems of the Secretariat and, as a result, his mandate was not always well appreciated by the staff.

Successes and Failures in Maintaining Peace

It is not my intention to write a history of the United Nations. Yet I feel that my readers should know about the UN as a political organization and its limitations where they occurred in solving problems related to the maintenance of peace.

Why hasn't the United Nations succeeded in preventing war? More than one hundred local and regional wars have taken place since the UN was created. The United Nations is not a world government or a suprastate; although the General Assembly is the closest thing to a Parliament of Man that has ever existed, it is not a world legislative body. It produces only "resolutions," which are recommendations addressed to the member states. The UN has no strength to enforce them. Every country, rich or poor, powerful or weak, regardless of size, has an equal vote in the General Assembly. Any problems affecting the world can be discussed here. The decisions made represent world opinion but have only the moral authority of the world community. But when there is agreement, many of these recommendations have led to a multitude of actions on the part of the member states, for the greatest benefit to humanity.

The UN has not succeeded politically because of its lack of sovereignty. Its member states, in almost all cases, do not want to concede portions of their own sovereignty to the Organization.

The Security Council is the organ of the UN expressly created in San Francisco to maintain world peace and security. The Charter expected that the "big four"—the U.S., USSR, UK and China—who had won World War II would carry together the brunt of world responsibility for keeping peace. The Council, which comprises fifteen members, has five permanent members (the big four plus France), each having veto power. Without unanimity among the Permanent Members there was bound to be a stalemate in the work of the Council each time a Permanent Member opted to use the veto. This happened almost immediately after World War II, when an ideological feud which brought on the Cold War developed among the Superpowers. The UN could not then play a full role in the maintenance of peace, and in many instances had its hands tied.

The Council, however, while successful in solving a number of conflicts endangering world peace, has almost always been used only as a last resort, after bilateral negotiations failed, when the Council's Permanent Members deemed to act together. In recent years, however, through consensus, considerable improvement has taken place.

The UN's ability to stop war might have been quite different if Article 42 of the Charter had been implemented. It enables the UN to take urgent military measures against a threat to peace; the Security Council can call upon its members to apply coercive measures, such as economic sanctions, and "take such actions by air, sea or land forces as may be necessary to restore international peace and security." Under that Article, members are obligated to make forces available to the UN on the decision of the Council, in the form of national contingents for combined international enforcement.

A Military Committee was created in 1946. The Chiefs of Staff of the member nations met periodically but were unable to undertake anything constructive. The process was repeated year after year with lower level meetings. A French military officer and Committee member admitted to me that he had rarely had anything to do during his day at the office. It was a hopeless situation. At some point the Chiefs of Staff represented on the Committee reached an agreement by consensus on only two-thirds of the articles proposed for the international force, but the Russian, British and American representatives finally failed to agree on various technical aspects of the proposal. After that the Military Committee made no further progress.

In 1950 I happened to attend an incredible event in the Security Council when the North Koreans invaded South Korea. It was the first time in UN history that a large international military force was authorized and went into action, in conformity with Article 42, under the command of U.S. General Douglas MacArthur, the U.S. constituting the bulk of the force. That day the Russians boycotted the Security Council over the question of the admission of Red China. Had the Russians been present at the Council meeting they would have exercised their veto and killed the authorization.

On the whole, the United Nations record in maintaining peace is by no means a complete failure. The UN gave valuable help in resolving such conflicts as the Berlin Crisis in 1948-49 and the Cuban missile crisis in 1962. As many will remember, much of the political activity of the United Nations in the first years of its existence was concerned with Palestine and the creation of the State of Israel. Before World War II Palestine was administered by the British under a League of Nations mandate. In 1947 the General Assembly endorsed a plan, prepared by the United Nations Special Committee on Palestine, for the partition of the Territory into two separate states—one Arab, one Jewish—with an international status for Jerusalem. I remember how high our expectations were in those days. This Plan, however, was not accepted by the Palestinian Arabs, and war broke out. The UN assembled and sent out its first peace mission to the area in 1948, with the appointment by the General Assembly of Count Folk Bernadotte as UN Mediator for Palestine, to promote peace and settle the Palestinian problems.

Then came the tragic day when we learned by radio that Bernadotte had been assassinated by a Jewish terrorist group—some members of which later became well-known figures in Israel. This assassination outraged the world, but the assassins were never punished. Secretary Trygve Lie replaced Bernadotte with Ralph Bunche, who had served as Bernadotte's deputy. With an incredible perseverance and great talent as a negotiator, Bunche was able to arrange separate cease-fire agreements between each Arab country concerned with the conflict and Israel, an outstanding achievement for which he won the Nobel Prize for Peace. He also organized a group of UN military observers to supervise the truce and to act as mediators.

Other interventions by the UN followed, first with the UN Emergency Force sent to the Middle East after the outbreak of the Suez Canal War between Egypt and Israel, the United Kingdom and France in 1956. Many ships had been destroyed by bombing and the Canal could no longer be used. It was our section in the Technical Assistance Administration which helped provide the needed international help and equipment to restore traffic on the Canal. For this purpose we appointed Lieutenant General R.A. Wheeler of the U.S. Corps of Engineers to head the total operation.

Dag Hammarskjöld went to Egypt to negotiate the establishment of a UN Force on the Egyptian side of the Sinai Desert with Gamel Abdel Nasser, the President of that country. The Israelis had refused to accept the Force on their side of the line of demarcation. The UN Force stayed there 10 years, keeping the peace in the area. It was withdrawn at Egypt's request, in accordance with a clause specified in the agreement, but the Security Council could have decided to maintain the Force as it was obvious that war would resume. In fact, shortly after, in 1967, Israel launched a major surprise attack on Egypt and destroyed the entire Egyptian Air Force while it was still on the ground. Egypt capitulated and was occupied following the lightning "Six-Day War." U Thant, the Secretary-General at that time, was blamed for not having put pressure on the Council.

Other UN peacekeeping operations included the Congo in 1960 and the United Nations Force in Cyprus in 1964 (to which I was an advisor). Then, in 1973, United Nations Emergency Force II was established as a buffer between the Israeli and Egyptian forces following the Yom Kippur War. Finally, the United Nations Interim Force in Lebanon was created. These forces comprise armed contingents drawn from the armed services of various member states. They maintain peaceful conditions along the armistice lines of international frontiers, guarantee internal law and order and administer buffer zones and territories after the cessation of hostilities, while efforts continue to help negotiate a peaceful solution of the conflict, as in Cyprus. They have never been enforcement forces.

My reflections on my experiences in the Cyprus peacekeeping operation appear in Part IV of this work; here I wish to single out the UN Congo Operations, which I carefully followed although I was not an actual part of them.

I had been scheduled to be part of the Operation, and my name placed on the short list of senior officers selected to fly to Leopoldville as part of the initial UN staff. To be designated by the Secretary-General for this type of mission is the UN equivalent to a command performance. But at the last minute it was decided that I could not be spared in Port-au-Prince, where I was head of the UN mission. I only participated in a sad peripheral to it, following the airplane accident which killed Dag Hammarskjöld and his party in Ndola, Northern Rhodesia, in 1961. This was when the body of a member of the group, a Haitian, was sent back to his country to be buried.

I wish to describe some aspects of the Congo Operation nonetheless, because it was perhaps the most vivid demonstration of the difficult tasks the UN can face. It also revealed the talent that Secretary-General Hammarskjöld had already mastered in confronting the large powers in certain types of east-west conflict.

In 1960, ten years after Korea, the Congo, a wealthy African colony, was suddenly granted its independence by Belgium. The Belgians had trained virtually no native public servants. They thought, wrongly, that their own personnel would stay at their posts to assist the new government. Instead, when their nationals left in droves, law and order completely broke down: in a blood bath, thousands of Belgians were killed.

At the request of the Congolese authorities, the Security Council authorized Secretary-General Hammarskjöld to assemble a UN Force to provide the newly-created government with the military assistance it needed. Order first had to be restored among competing tribes which, by that time, were scrambling for power. But the UN mandate was primarily to preserve the integrity of the new state against Belgian troops and mercenaries who had landed in Katanga Province and which refused to join the Congolese government. There was also danger of the intervention by foreign powers.

Without departing from the Charter, Hammarskjöld created a new UN role through a doctrine he called "Preventive Diplomacy," which was endorsed by the Security Council. Hammarskjöld's premise was that it is extremely difficult for the United Nations to exercise any influence on problems which are clearly and definitively within the orbit of ongoing daily conflicts between power blocs.[11] He argued that where conflicts arise in non-committed areas of the east-west political struggle, the UN, through an "executive action" on the part of the UN Secretary-General, can offer solutions which avoid aggravating the big powers' differences, thus filling a power vacuum and forestalling the extension of existing conflicts. The Congo crisis provided the first test for a practical demonstration of the Secretary-General's doctrine. The executive action was to be conducted by the Secretariat and involved establishing and directing a large international police force. Many in the Secretariat became involved in this new operation. From afar I watched the unfolding of the new adventure with enthusiasm and trepidation; I knew the Council had authorized the force without the backing of France or the USSR.

During the first months the UN operation faced an incredible situation. The Belgian troops still there were fighting the Congolese, destroying all hope for the UN to restore normality. The Force, under a UN Chief of Staff, included contingents from Ethiopia, Ghana, Tunisia and Morocco, posing an important problem of coordination, however well handled.

Joseph Kasavubu, the President-elect of the new Republic and Patrice Lumumba, the Prime Minister, were constantly at loggerheads. Both had requested U.S. help from President Eisenhower, who referred them to the UN. As the assistance did not arrive fast enough, the lanky Lumumba, a naive, inexperienced revolutionary leader, pleaded his country's case before the UN. Somewhat awkwardly he threatened in a public statement to go to the Soviets if UN help was not made available immediately. The press thought he was a Communist, but Brian Urquhart, who with Ralph Bunche was in daily contact with him, says Lumumba was neither a Communist nor a Soviet puppet. Yet during the early UN presence in Congo, the western powers feared a Soviet takeover, while the Russians objected to the transporting of UN troops to Congo by the American Air Transport Command. They were also critical of the UN for having failed to advance rapidly into Katanga to fight Moise Tshombe's secessionist forces.

Tshombe, the Katangan Prime Minister, refused to join the new Congolese government. He wanted independence, and obviously was not anxious to share with Leopoldville the revenues of the province's vast copper resources, exploited by *Union minière du Haut Katanga*, a powerful Belgian consortium.

Then another major difficulty arose. Both Nikita Khrushchev and Charles de Gaulle criticised the operation because neither liked the personal initiatives taken

---
11 Dag Hammarskjöld, *Annual Report to the 15th General Assembly* (New York: United Nations, 1960).

by Hammarskjöld. De Gaulle called the UN *ce machin* (that thing); the USSR and France refused to pay their share of the cost of the venture, creating a deep financial crisis for the operation.

These were days of high drama at the UN. Khrushchev, furious, wanted to abolish the office of Secretary-General and replace it with a Troika, with three top officials representing the three power blocs of the world, which would have killed the independence of the Security Council forever. He demanded Hammarskjöld's resignation. In a memorable speech before the General Assembly, the Secretary-General replied to him, saying to the Delegates: "It is very easy to resign; it is not so easy to stay on. It is very easy to bow to the wish of a big power. It is another matter to resist. I've done so on many occasions. If it is the wish of those nations who see in the Organization their best protection in the present world, I shall do so again."[12] Except for the Soviet bloc, the Assembly gave him a standing ovation never before heard in the Hall.

The most critical aspect of the UN mission, carried out by *Opérations des Nations Unies au Congo* (ONUC), became its role in preventing the secession of Katanga. The Secretary-General had appointed as his representative at Elizabethville, the Katangan capital, a French colleague and friend of mine, Georges Dumontet, who was the Secretary of the Economic Council. He was a competent, calm and poised international civil servant who got along well with Tshombe and kept the situation under control for a while, but the Katangan government brought in a number of French military advisors on the side of the Elizabethville government. It was felt that he should be replaced by someone with different nationality. The Secretary-General then appointed Connor-Cruise O'Brien, a member of the Irish Foreign Service, a courageous, perhaps too highly-spirited man to be given such an assignment.

The Belgian government by then had agreed to withdraw its military personnel from Katanga, but the Katangan government had hired a large number of mercenaries from Western Europe to lead their own soldiers against the UN forces which at the time consisted mostly of Ethiopians. The UN troops were to use force only as self-defense, their role being to protect civilians against tribal violence. In accordance with his instructions, O'Brien was trying to solve the problem without engaging the UN contingent against Katanga. They secured such strategic points as the Elizabethville airport and radio station. Hammarskjöld, in New York, fearing that open hostilities between the UN forces and Katangan secessionists would take place, decided to meet Tshombe himself. Under no circumstance did he want the

12 Ibid.

UN to start the fighting, as this would have violated the UN mandate.

Arriving in Leopoldville from New York on a trip that was supposed to be routine, he learned that fighting had broken out in Elizabethville and that the UN command had moved against the European mercenaries, and a solid battle was engaged, something Hammarskjöld had wanted to avoid at all cost. He left immediately for Ndola, a small town located in the Northern part of Northern Rhodesia, now Zambia, close to the border of Katanga, where he was to meet Tshombe.

Leaving Leopoldville the evening of September 17, 1961, his plane signaled its presence to the Ndola airport tower as it was making an approach to land. It was in the middle of the night, the lights of the airport were on, but the pilot, a captain of the Swedish Air Force, and the rest of the crew did not know the area. They flew too low, and some six miles from the airport the aircraft brushed the top of a cluster of trees on a low hill, cut a path in the woods, crashed and then exploded. The crash killed all passengers on the spot, except for one who died two days later of deep burns at the Ndola hospital without regaining consciousness. Hammarskjöld, the only one thrown clear of the wreckage, died of multiple fractures. A UN and Swedish investigation concluded that the accident resulted from human error.[13]

The death of Hammarskjöld was an irreparable loss for all of us at the United Nations. His funeral in Uppsala was attended by dignitaries from throughout the world. Brian Urquhart, his personal assistant for so many years, wrote: "None of us knew Hammarskjöld really well, but he had come to occupy a unique place in our lives, thoughts and affections by the nature of his leadership and his character."

As noted, I was at the time on post in Port-au-Prince, Haiti, as UN Resident Representative, when Hammarskjöld died in Ndola. The news, which reached us by radio, filled me with great sadness. I immediately called a meeting of our field personnel—most of them from the Specialized Agencies, and local staff—and talked to them about Hammarskjöld and what his death meant to us in the UN and to the world. I told them that Hammarskjöld had been an idol in the minds of many international civil servants at Headquarters. I said he was certainly, to me, the Secretary-General who, as no one else, had fought for the principles of the Charter

---

13 In 1992, more than thirty years after the crash, two UN officials who had served as UN representatives in Katanga, George Ivan Smith and Connor O'Brien, convinced the Swedish government to reopen the investigation of the death of Hammarskjöld. According to the *UN Secretariat News* of October 1992, Smith said that a "senior French diplomat" had given him taped interviews with mercenaries who had worked for European mining interests in the Congo. The interviewees indicated that they knew of a plan to use two DeHavilland planes specially equipped with machine guns to force the pilot of Hammarskjöld's plane not to land at Ndola. Smith alleges that the European industrialists who controlled Katanga feared Tshombe would cave in to Hammarskjöld's entreaties, which would not work in their interests.

and had been the champion of multilateral diplomacy all along. It was my belief that, had he lived, his influence would have taken the UN to great heights. A great leader, a man with high principles and personal dignity, had been lost: a man who could perhaps never be replaced as the head of the Organization.

A week later, after the crash victims had been identified, I was advised by cable that the body of Serge Barrau, a Haitian UN security officer in the Secretary-General's ill-fated party, was to arrive at Port-au-Prince two days later. I went to receive the coffin at the airport with a small honor guard from the Presidential Palace. It was a sad moment. After a religious service at the cemetery, a representative of the Foreign Affairs Ministry gave a eulogy of the victim and spoke of his youth in Port-au-Prince. At the grave I said the following words: "We are here to salute the memory of a man of courage who was . . . on an errand of peace . . . to defend the integrity of a new African nation . . . . I know what both independence and Africa mean to the people of Haiti . . . . In the name of the UN I want to offer our deepest sympathy to his family and tell the Haitian people that Serge Barrau shall always be remembered in the UN for the sacrifice he made in the cause of peace."

After the resolution of the military conflict, the UN, having maintained the integrity of Congo as a nation (later to be called Zaire), had another vital long-term function to carry out. Under our technical assistance program we recruited literally hundreds of technicians and experts who went to the Congo as UN personnel to replace the departed Belgians. Their jobs were to help run the various Government services and train the Congolese, a task without which the country would have remained chaotic. Still in Haiti, I assisted the UN Bureau of Personnel in the recruitment of many Haitians authorized by their Government to leave their country to help the new African nation. It just happened that trained Haitians, with their African background, were the most readily available candidates we could find. They were anxious to serve in the Congo as advisors in education, agriculture and social services. A few were even appointed as judges. I knew that many of them were happy to leave the increasingly harsh ambience of Haiti, in those days under the cruel dictatorship of Papa Doc Duvalier.

Many of my colleagues from New York and the UN Specialized Agencies were also sent to Leopoldville (later Kinshasa), to help solve the Congo's many critical problems of nation-building, but, alas, the country is still in deep trouble due to the excesses of its present leader.

* * *

At UN Headquarters, the years following Hammarskjöld's death were disappointing, to say the least, in particular for us in the UN Secretariat. We saw the Security Council unable to develop an effective common approach to dealing with potential conflicts. The Council was not putting sufficient pressure on the conflicting parties to resolve their differences by peaceful means. Its members would have brought results using their resources of persuasion and, if necessary, practical leverage by reaching a consensus. But clearly the member states did not have the necessary political will and this demoralized many of us in international civil service.

There were also new problems in the General Assembly. After decolonization, the Third World held the voting majority, since so many new states had joined the Organization after 1960. It was often reported in the news media that the delegates from developing countries always sided with the East. The U.S. Delegation felt threatened by this, and Daniel Patrick Moynihan, the U.S. Representative, later a Democratic Senator from New York, in 1980 called the UN a dangerous place.[14] Yet the UN Secretariat made a tally of votes during those years and concluded that, despite appearances, the Third World had voted more often with the West than with the East.

It was at that time, however, that the American public lost confidence in the UN. In the first years of UN existence, Americans had warmly welcomed the organization. According to a Gallup Poll, 87 percent of Americans thought the UN was still doing a good job in 1959, but gradually the public faith declined. In March 1981 a Roper Poll indicated that only 10 percent of the American public thought that the UN was highly effective in keeping the peace.

We all remember the end of the '70s and into the '80s when the United Nations became the object of deliberate criticism from U.S. conservative groups. A real campaign was mounted against the Organization, supported by the Heritage Foundation, recommending that the U.S. leave the UN. Daniel Patrick Moynihan had accused the U.S. of "complacency," due to a failure to perceive that a distinctive ideology was at work (among the Third World's members) and that the U.S. had to deal with it. In 1975 the Assembly in one of its resolutions condemned Zionism as a form of racism. The U.S. Senate called for a prompt hearing to reassess the participation of the United States in the UN. In the following years the U.S. Delegation to the UN justifiably tried to counteract the propaganda against the U.S. in the General Assembly from the Soviet Union, and increasingly from the Group of 77, the unaligned contingent of underdeveloped countries. Some of its delegates were vilifying U.S. positions, accusing the U.S. of being the leader of international imperialism. In reply the American delegation contended that the New International

---

14 Daniel Patrick Moynihan, *A Dangerous Place* (New York: Berkeley Books, 1980).

Economic Order proposed by the Group of 77 was simply an attempt by the Third World to grab the wealth of the industrialized countries.

This point of inflammatory rhetoric, as it was called, came to a climax when the U.S. Deputy Chief of Mission to the UN, Ambassador Charles Lichtenstein, declared that he would look forward to the day when he goes to the Hudson River to wave good-bye to UN delegates sailing into the sunset. It was indeed a very bad period for everyone at the UN, including the Secretariat, the morale of which was at its lowest ebb. The U.S. leaving the UN and the UN leaving New York would have had the effect of isolating our country. It would have been a real disaster for international relations and incidentally a great financial loss for the city of New York. Fortunately, at the highest level of the U.S. administration, there was no real intention to leave the UN. However, we did withdraw from UNESCO.

The unfortunate part of this crisis was that the United States began to delay the payment of its dues to the Organization and it is still in arrears in the payment of its contribution to the UN regular budget to several of the Special Agencies, and to the fund for peacekeeping operations. U.S. conservative organizations continued into the '80s to bash the UN, claiming that the Secretariat had too many people and staff salaries were too high. They wanted reforms in the Secretariat as a condition for the United States to pay its contribution to the UN budget. The reforms were carried out and more than 1,200 staff members were dropped. Congress authorized the payment of the arrears but incredibly only by installments over the following five years.

With regard to staff competence, on the whole the Secretariat was an easy target. In my view the majority of the staff is as competent as the levels of UN prevalent salaries enable, and they are not sufficient to attract the very top people. UN salaries are, at present, lower than those the best people can command in government and in industry in Western Europe and in Washington. The best proof of that is that the U.S. government, even twenty years ago, paid a differential to U.S. government senior personnel who took positions in the UN Secretariat and the Specialized Agencies to compensate for their loss in salary. This practice, the subject of askance glances from other countries, however, encouraged some U.S. government employees to work for the UN. When I served in Jamaica as head of a team of experts, one of them, a senior official of the U.S. Department of Education in Washington, D.C., was receiving such a differential to balance his loss in salary while working for ILO.

Fortunately, a number of governments came to the Secretariat's defense against these attacks. Canadian Ambassador Stephen Lewis in 1985 told the Fifth Committee of the General Assembly during the debate on the UN financial crisis that by any objective standard, the UN Secretariat is not poorly administered, especially compared with some other multilateral institutions or, indeed, many national or local governments. He suggested that few national governments subject their accounts committees books and balance sheets to the same searching process as the UN. Further, he suggested that the budget of the United Nations is, relatively speaking, well handled and the people who do the analysis and the administration are first-rate people."[15] But these remarks could apply as well to the majority of staff members in the Secretariat.

On UN Day, 1986, UN Secretary-General Xavier Perez de Cuellar publicly observed that through the 41 years of the existence of the United Nations, there has been no instance of its staff failing to respond to a situation, to implement an agreed decision or to carry out a program simply because of administrative and budgetary weakness or inefficiency. He suggested a reason for the relative weaknesses of the Organization by saying that, important though they are, the administrative and budgetary issues should not eclipse the far more crucial question of whether the Member-States recognize that multilateralism, of which the United Nations is the dynamic embodiment, is the only viable response to the nature of today's problem and the realities of the interdependence of nations.

Challenges and Accomplishments

*We the Peoples of the United Nations have resolved to promote
social progress, and better standards of living in larger freedom.*
Preamble of the UN Charter

The UN Economic, Social and Humanitarian Programs
There is another crucial side of the UN, in which I worked almost my entire career but about which the public knows little. It is the work done by the United Nations and its Specialized Agencies, under Article 55 of the Charter which states that one of the many purposes of the Organization is "to cooperate in solving international problems of an economic, social, cultural and humanitarian character, and to promote respect for human rights and fundamental freedoms for all," and that the UN be "a center for harmonizing the actions of nations in attaining these common ends."

---

15 *Records of the General Assembly* (New York: United Nations, 1985).

This has opened the way for a large variety of UN programs which since the '50s have considerably advanced the cause of world development and peace in assisting developing countries in their efforts to progress.

According to a 1992 study of United Nations Development Programs (UNDP) based on UN statistical data, much progress has been made in the Developing World, but the extent of deprivation is still alarming. Average life expectancy is now 63 years, 17 years more than in 1960, but 14 million children die every year before they reach the age of five. The mortality rate of young children has been halved in the past 30 years, but in the poorest nations the rate is still 115 per 1000 live births. Nearly 1 million children in sub-Sahara Africa are infected with HIV. Nearly 1.5 billion people lack access to health services and 1.3 billion lack access to safe water; 1.2 billion people still barely survive in absolute poverty. Still over 100 million people were affected by famine in 1990, and more than a quarter of the world's people do not get enough food and nearly a billion go hungry.[16]

It may be surprising to learn that farm production, which was at a very low level in 1950, has grown faster in the developing countries than in the developed ones, in fact twenty-five percent faster on a per-capita basis. Industrial production has more than tripled in the Third World from 1960 to 1980, growing some forty percent faster than industry in the developed countries, due in part to the tremendous increase in such countries as Taiwan, Korea, Brazil, Thailand, India and a few others.

Of course, this is not all due to the UN, but to combination of the efforts of the countries themselves, of bilateral and multilateral assistance, international trade and also the expansion of multinational corporations across the world. Although the UN system of multilateral aid assistance is representatively a small part of the total aid (approximately 15 percent), it has played a key role in bringing these results about. But progress has widely varied from country to country, as I was able to discover in the course of my field missions. In the poorest countries comprising the majority of world population, where population growth was high, the standards of living are still desperately low; the averages mentioned above can be misleading.

The need for technical assistance and aid to the developing world continues to be real and urgent. Today forty to fifty percent of the world's population still lives in deprivation, is undernourished and in poor health, with insufficient shelter. On a worldwide basis the resources exist or can be developed for all of us. Our planet can produce all the food needed but, when too much is produced in one area, surpluses often cannot be transported to areas which desperately need them. These imbalances

---

16 *Balance Sheet of Human Development for the Developing Countries; Human Development Report,* UNDP (New York: Oxford University Press, 1992), 14-15.

threaten the lives of millions and are a serious cause of conflicts and wars. I am convinced that there is an indissoluble link among peace, development and social justice. Secretary-General Perez de Cuellar pointed out when he accepted his reappointment in 1986 that the more affluent members of the Organization must understand that their high degree of development cannot be isolated from the welfare of the poor peoples of the globe. Instead, greater cooperation between them and the developing countries is imperative, so that the latter may reach, within the shortest possible time, economic and social standards consistent with human dignity.

Where the UN worked

I feel privileged to have been able to work in the two principal world development efforts of the UN: first, in the early years, on some of the Secretariat's development studies; and second, in the operational programs it created in the '50s—the Expanded Program of Technical Assistance, followed in 1960 by the UN Development Program (UNDP), the largest technical program in the world, in which I served both at UN Headquarters and in the field. I also worked in close liaison with the Specialized Agencies, the Children's Fund (UNICEF), the UN Environment Program, the Fund for Population Activities, the World Food Program and the Office of the High Commissioner for Refugees, the achievements of which have been universally recognized.

C.V. Narasimhan, the brilliant Indian who was *Chef de Cabinet* of two Secretary-Generals, argues that one of its greatest contributions to world development since the Second World War has been in the field of ideas and concepts. The UN has insisted that "economic development" should be superseded by "development" which includes higher literacy rates, participation of the people in the political life of the country, development of their own initiative and self-reliance, and an efficient public administration as well as increased wealth or economic growth—in other words, all aspects leading to the modernization of societies. Development of this sort leads to a top-to-bottom transformation requiring not only the pre-World War II notion of capital investment, but an integrated approach including a change in values, motivations, and institutions—a very long-term proposition involving development of all human resources and gradually leading people to the ability to live in a democratic society.[17]

The United Nations, first through the work of its expert working groups and its World Conferences, conceived new strategies for development. Through its statistics and other studies, it made the world aware of the population explosion and the

---

17 C.V. Narasimhan, *The United Nations: an Inside View* (New York: UNITAR, 1988).

urgent need for population control. At the UN Conference on the Environment in Stockholm in 1972, the world became aware for the first time of the need to maintain a global ecological balance. Later in the '70s the United Nations raised the question of the need for a new international economic order, calling for a new set of relationships between the rich and the poor countries. This question of paramount importance to our future has not yet been solved, as I discuss later. It has raised perhaps the most serious economic and social controversy between North and South as to what is the proper approach to achieve world prosperity. This vital issue was debated for several years on the East River, in Paris and elsewhere without so far having produced any new practical result.

In my first years with the UN, when relatively little was known about the economics of the Third World and how to go about development in those areas, our studies in the Department of Economic and Social Affairs pointed out key structural differences between the fully-developed and the less-developed countries. The governments of the latter too often concluded that industrialization was the only key to development. They had a tendency to finance show-off projects which had little to do with national development priorities. In some of the studies in which I participated, the UN and the Specialized Agencies advised those countries that the development of their rural areas was more often the key, and that rural people had to be taught how to pull themselves up by their bootstraps. Then we outlined policies for human resources development. We made case studies of state enterprises in certain countries, most often badly managed and uneconomical, and we encouraged the development of private enterprise. In the '60s we and the United Nations Food and Agriculture Organization (FAO) started a World Campaign against Hunger aimed at increasing food production for the people, too often neglected in favor of profitable exportable cash crops. UNESCO, the International Labor Organization FAO, the World Health Organization and other agencies advised governments on education, training, health care and proposed helpful policies for governments of developing countries. Thus, the UN system became a unique assortment of "think tanks" giving the developing countries an awareness of their development potential and the types of policies they should follow to achieve results.

There was no doubt, as Robert Muller stated, that "a great effort on the part of humanity was being made through the UN, to understand better the problems of our planet and to begin to envisage and execute needed programs to meet some of those goals."[18] What is rewarding is that these problems are now being tackled every day in the developing countries, thanks to the work of thousands of international civil

---

18 Robert Muller, *New Genesis* (New York: Doubleday), 28.

servants assigned by the UN and its agencies at the far corners of the world, as the world can no longer dispense with their services.

In 1952 the UN created an Expanded Program of Technical Assistance to the developing countries. By then I felt I had done enough economic reporting and wanted a change and a piece of the action. A Technical Assistance Board, headed by David Owen, had just been set up to coordinate the program which was being carried out by the Specialized Agencies and the UN Secretariat and to distribute funds to them. At UN Headquarters we created the Technical Assistance Administration (TAA) to assist in the fields of economic and social development not covered by the Specialized Agencies, such as public administration, industry, transportation, economics, social and community development. I joined TAA. Our Director-General was Dr. Hugh Keenleyside, a Canadian with an impressive diplomatic and administrative background. He had been his country's Ambassador to Mexico and its federal Minister of Mines and Resources in Ottawa. He had successfully conducted the first comprehensive UN mission sent to the Third World, to advise the Government of Bolivia on the revamping of its economy. This had clinched his appointment to the new TAA. Another mission had been sent to Haiti, the poorest country in Latin America, to survey the resources and recommend a variety of important development initiatives.

TAA was indeed a very busy shop, making a start on identifying problems and seeking effective ways to provide help to governments and people in the Third World. I was Acting Chief of the program for Latin America. We were sending experts recruited worldwide to train with local personnel in 20 Latin American republics and the Caribbean. We also gave fellowships and set up conferences and demonstration projects. Some Latin American countries asked us to provide a number of administrators to improve their public administration services, in my view one of the most needed aspects of development. Dispatching executive personnel to work as part of the national administrations on a long-term basis, modernizing their services and training their civil servants, was a successful aspect of our program.

TAA staff in New York was widely diversified. The ten program officers I supervised were all Latin Americans. Our staff meetings were conducted in English and Spanish, and much of the correspondence to the governments was drafted in Spanish. My knowledge of the language, already quite good, improved substantially during my assignment. My Latin American experience gained in Santiago was now especially handy, as my work involved programming the assistance after appropriate discussions of priorities with the governments, as well as supervising projects and the evaluating the results. In those first days I learned a lot and enjoyed these stimulating activities.

In accordance with the UN principle of geographic distribution of posts, a Latin American was slated to take over my position as soon as someone suitable could be found. In 1955 Alejandro Oropeza Castillo was appointed head of the office. He had been Governor-General of the Province of Caracas, Venezuela. What he did not know about international organization he made up for with a keen knowledge of the Latin American scene and great political acumen. I stayed on one more year as his deputy to coach him in his new functions.

I moved then to the European and Middle East Office to become chief of the program for eleven countries of the Middle East and three in North Africa: Morocco, Tunisia and Libya. The head of the Office was Taghi Nasr, an Iranian, a former minister of the National Economy under the Shah. Taghi, short, stout and bald, had the herculean strength of a wrestler and a pleasant round smiling face. He held a doctorate in economics from the University of Brussels and spoke French and English fluently. We got along famously. His sharp mind and great sense of humor made him extremely popular on our floor. His working habits were perhaps not those of a strictly organized American business office. We gathered in his office like in a tent in the desert for a gathering of friendly acolytes. His door was always open for enlightening discussions. Taghi would crack a joke at the opportune moment, yet made quick decisions, his judgment almost always sound. I remember him as a man who knew how to create a happy atmosphere around him, a rare quality in life.

One of the remarkable aspects of UN technical assistance, of which the public is largely unaware, is that it is financed by voluntary governmental contributions pledged at a Special Conference, quite independently of government assessments to the UN's regular budget. Under TAA, these voluntary contributions totaled only about $30 million dollars a year. But after 1965, under the much larger United Nations Development Program constituted by the merging of the Expanded Program and the Special Fund, the total of these contributions rose to $1 billion, making it the largest program of technical assistance and pre-investment in the world. In 1966, from UNESCO, I joined UNDP as Coordinator of the assistance extended to Africa which alone then accounted for more than $200 million in projects. It may be interesting to note that the managing directors of UNDP have all been Americans, since the beginning of the Program. This makes sense in view of the importance of the United States contribution, which has amounted to approximately twenty-five percent of the total over the years. All have been well-known public figures who had made their reputations before joining UNDP. The first was Paul Hoffman, who had had a successful career as President of Studebaker, then as head of the Marshall Plan and of the Ford Foundation. He was over 70 years of age, still remarkably young for his years. He had the approach of a businessman and oriented the program toward pre-investment, consisting of feasibility studies for the development of the countries' natural resources, infrastructure, education, training and health projects. Our preoccupation was to make the assisted country ready to absorb capital investment in the public or private sector. Hoffman used to tell us that production and productivity in the underdeveloped countries depend on investment, and that investment, public or private, will not venture into the unknown. Therefore, the job of the UNDP was to lay the effective groundwork for investment. The UN Development Program is anything but a giveaway of resources. All along we have been building the cornerstones for these countries' futures.

Hoffman had two senior deputies with the title of Assistant Administrators, Myer Cohen and Paul-Marc Henry, with whom I worked closely, each with a notable personality of his own.

Myer, an American who had served as a senior official of the United Nations Relief and Rehabilitation Administration (UNRRA), had been our first Resident Representative in Yugoslavia. A demanding, tough manager, he was in charge of all staff and organizational problems as well as the actual programming of the assistance, seeing that all of us correctly followed the complicated program procedures. I remember him as a great executive.

The other, Paul-Marc Henry, a bon-vivant with a brilliant mind, was the flying ambassador and negotiator of projects all over the world with the recipient governments. It would have been hard to find someone more dynamic. He had cordial relations with all political leaders and high level bureaucrats in the developing world, particularly Africa. His memory was phenomenal. He knew the details of most of our 4,000 projects, touching virtually every type of development endeavor, including agriculture, livestock, forestry, fisheries, housing, disease control, public administration and fiscal policies and many other fields. The programs also included a number of capital development projects financed by the UN Capital Development Fund.

At review meetings we were always amazed when Paul-Marc was able to give us guidance and instructions practically without consulting his notes. He was a French career diplomat and the product of the famous *École Nationale d'-Administration* created by de Gaulle after the War, the top training center for French government leaders. Rather than a continuous career at the Quai d'Orsay, he had preferred the life and ideals of an international civil servant, so he had joined the

UN. When he left UNDP he became head of an important OECD study group in Paris. Then, resuming his foreign service career, in 1984 he had no hesitation in filling the dangerous post of French Ambassador in Lebanon, just after his immediate predecessor had been assassinated at the height of the street fighting in Beirut. French Embassy personnel then were always under constant threat of attack by extremist factions.

The current administrator of UNDP, William Draper III, is a dynamic executive, a successful businessman from California's "Silicon Valley" and a former President of the U.S. Export-Import Bank in Washington. His predecessors were, respectively, a former President of the Bank of America and formerly a U.S. Congressman.

Under Draper's leadership, UNDP has made human development the center of its program. In the foreword of a 1992 study conducted by the UNDP staff, he says, "The message that comes on loud and clear from the *Human Development Report* is that the international community must strengthen its support to global human development, not only through increasing aid, but through improving developing countries' access to global markets to make resources available to developing countries for urgently needed investments in their people." The report, prepared by a team of eminent economists and distinguished professionals establishes that the gap between developing countries and developed countries is worse than anybody could have imagined and reveals an appalling distribution of income: the richest 20 percent of the world's population receive 82.7 percent of the total world's income, while the poorest 20 percent receives only 1.4 percent; the richest 20 percent of the world's people get at least 150 times the income of the poorest 20 percent. If this situation is not improved, it will become a source of constant conflict and wars.[19]

The public should know also that UNDP projects are anything but giveaways; a recipient government's contribution toward such projects is usually three to four times that of the UN and is conditional on the signing of strict agreements. The effectiveness of the Program was increased in the '60s when programming and evaluation were decentralized and especially when coordination of the activities of Specialized Agencies' personnel was placed in the hands of the UNDP resident representative at the country level. In 1970 a major Capacity Study, conducted by Sir Robert Jackson, reviewed the whole system and concluded that the Specialized Agencies programs should be coordinated more strongly from New York. There had been some improvements, but not enough. Even Hammarskjöld could not bring this about as the Agencies have their own governing councils and statutes. A restructuring of the system should address this particular aspect.

19 UNDP, *op. cit.*

On the whole the system, though heavy, has functioned well. But spreading UNDP funds over fourteen agencies, tends to diminish the impact of the Program. It would be better to concentrate the resources on a more limited number of projects of global importance for world development. This is under study.

As I experienced many times in the field, the multilateral assistance provided by the United Nations presents considerable advantages over bilateral assistance. I believe more world aid and international assistance should be channeled through them. The UN programs are apolitical, bilateral assistance is not. National interest most often is the motive of bilateral donors, but this may vary; countries support countries with which they have strong ties. Thus France and Britain give assistance primarily to their former colonies. Now the world leader in terms of money, Japan concentrates its aid in the Asian region and uses it often to encourage trade with Japan. On a bilateral basis the U.S. has come now to assist only countries whose politics are in harmony with its own interests.

In the future, as expressed in the UNDP's *Human Development Plan*, the motivation for aid should no longer be to fight communism but to eradicate poverty. There is now a concerted move to get both sets of countries (donors and recipients) to spend 20 percent of the aid money on human development projects.

Multilateral assistance presents other clear advantages, as I often observed the UN and its Specialized Agencies normally enter into a partnership with a developing country more easily than can a single donor country. The recipient country does not feel dominated by the UN, as it might by a powerful bilateral partner. Advice from a UN expert is usually better received, particularly in such fields as economic planning, fiscal policy, public administration reforms and other advice which touches on national pride or sovereignty. The UN can undertake large-scale regional projects, such as the development of the Lower Mekong River, cleaning up the Mediterranean Sea, or developing the Senegal River Basin, involving several countries more easily than can a single donor country, providing the core of the assistance to such projects, and incorporating a number of bilateral projects from various donors willing to lend their help.

Finally, the UN Development Program has been praised by everyone. Vernon Walters, U.S. Permanent Representative to the UN during the Reagan administration, told the U.S. House Foreign Affairs Committee that, compared to its work in political fields, the work of the UN in the economic and social fields had been better than anyone could have predicted in 1945.

* * *

As part of my UNDP work and in the '60s, I had the privilege of working directly with the humanitarian agencies of the UN as UNDP Senior Liaison Officer with the three most important agencies: UNICEF in New York, the World Food Program in Rome, and the United Nations High Commissioner for Refugees in Geneva. I represented the UNDP at the meetings of their governing boards and helped plan joint field projects for specific countries.

Like UNDP, the programs of these Agencies are financed from voluntary government contributions and are very popular with donors and recipients. They are considered among the best managed UN operations. No one needs to justify the existence of UNICEF, which has saved the lives of millions of children in the developing world, or of the World Food Program, which has done outstanding work not only in distributing surplus food provided by industrialized countries as emergency relief but as a tool for increasing domestic food production in the Third World. I was personally involved in planning several food-production projects which have been very effective in Morocco, Algeria and Tunisia.

UN assistance to refugees and their resettlement has unfortunately become, in today's world, a mammoth operation, and extensive programs have been conducted with considerable success by the office of the High Commissioner for Refugees. It was the prime Specialized Agency I worked with in Uganda in the '60s, where I helped plan resettlement projects during the visit of Prince Saddrudin Aga Khan, then the High Commissioner for Refugees.

I've also worked in close cooperation with the Fund for Population Activities, newer, but still a vital UN agency. At the current rate, the world's population will double in just over thirty years, and we need to control population growth. We badly need such a Fund. UNFPA is now conducting about 1200 projects in 90 countries, at the request of their governments, training personnel, assisting family planning clinics, counseling services and even census-taking, an essential part of population planning.

Other UN activities deal with many problems paramount to the survival of our planet, such as environmental protection, chemical weapons control, international agreements on outer space, human rights and many others which will be emphasized in Part V of this book. Here I will mention only the importance of UN World Conferences, which often are not sufficiently understood by the public. The 1970s and '80s have generated global meetings on the environment, population, food, education, women's rights, trade and development, employment, human settlements, development cooperation among the developing countries themselves, science and technology transfers and the law of the sea. These world conferences draw countries together to study critical problem areas which would otherwise not receive priority government attention. They are necessary to understand the interdependence of our planet and to take a global approach in solving the problems. Before the United Nations Environment Conference in Stockholm in 1972, the issue of the environment was not a global one. It is now, thanks to that Conference. That meeting led to creation of the United Nations Environment Program (UNEP), which is performing a valuable role in carrying out many cooperative projects, one of which is a major cleanup of the Mediterranean Sea. A second World Conference on the Protection of the Environment was held in Rio de Janeiro in 1992.

* * *

To me, educating the people of developing countries is the long-term solution to most of their problems. In 1964, after the completion of my mission with the UN Peacekeeping Force in Cyprus, I was named for a tour of duty to a UN Agency doing just that, but which became highly controversial and from which the United States withdrew. It was the United Nations Education, Science and Cultural Organization (UNESCO) in Paris, in which I worked for a most interesting two years. I was originally scheduled for assignment as an economist in the new field of educational planning. But because of organizational delays I was offered instead the post of chief of the UNESCO Field Personnel Division, in charge of administering some 1200 professors and other experts in over one hundred Third World countries. This tour of duty, for which I felt qualified after so many years of experience in national and international public administration, had been made possible through an exchange of posts with Gertrude McKettrick, an American well known in UNESCO, who wanted field service experience and was assigned for two years to Tanzania as UNDP Deputy Resident Representative. Such personnel exchanges among Agencies were useful in developing a diversified staff able to serve in various positions in the UN system.

I enjoyed this stint in administration, even if some UNESCO experts around the globe occasionally gave me the impression at times of behaving like primadonnas, in contrast with the experts of other UN organizations, in the attempts of some to find exceptions to the rather rigid UN staff rules. Many were, however, highly competent advisors to governments, their expertise varying from the restructuring of complete national educational systems to the setting up of a new university or the improvement of primary and secondary education, the teaching of science, literacy, cultural activities and communications including the use of radio and television programs for education. Dealing with these experts during their visits to headquarters and trying to solve their administrative problems was never dull. The Director of Personnel at UNESCO was Gerard Bolla, a Swiss lawyer trained in the

U.S., with a great deal of experience in various parts of UNESCO. We worked very closely under an American, John Fobes, in charge of the administration of the Agency and on crises, with the Director-General, Rene Maheu, a brilliant French educator, but prone to burst into anger. To a large extent, Fobes was the man who kept UNESCO's administrative machine running smoothly for a number of years, as far as this could be done. The situation became chaotic, after he left, under Amadou M'Bow, the new Senegalese Director-General who served two terms and was defeated seeking a third. M'Bow ruined the reputation of the Agency by his mismanagement and the politicization of the organization, so much so that the United States, the United Kingdom and Singapore withdrew from it in 1964.

Another reason why the U.S. left UNESCO was the threat to the free flow of information involved in UNESCO's well publicized Declaration for a New World Information Order. The Third World governments wanted to use the news media to further their national ideologies and regulate information in their countries. They complained that they had to depend too much on foreign news media for their information needs. Indeed, as much as 85 percent of the news crosses international borders through only four major Western-based news agencies: United Press International, the Associated Press, Reuters and *Agence France-Presse*.

A resolution following the Declaration on the so-called McBride study of media was finally negotiated to unanimous adoption and referred to a process leading toward "a New World Information and Communication Order" (NWICO) Western media nevertheless continued to feel that the door was open to national measures which would restrict the free flow of information. Today, as a result of the efforts of Spanish scientist Frederico Mayor, the new UNESCO Director General, even the strongest Western critics admit that NWICO is no longer a threat and that the UNESCO program is restricted to promotion of greater freedom for the media.

Thanks to Professor Mayor, appropriate reforms of the Agency have been almost completed and Western countries are pressing the U.S. to rejoin UNESCO, although this has not yet happened.

Jack Fobes retired to North Carolina, where he is waging another battle, this time for the support of the universality of UNESCO. He has created an association, Americans for the Universality and the Renewal of UNESCO and U.S. Participation in the Work of the Organization at the Earliest Possible Time. Most American educational and scientific associations support it and seek the U.S.'s rejoining. Thanks to Fobes' efforts, Americans are gradually recognizing that we have a major stake in assisting the development of education through the multilateral structure of UNESCO. The agency's activities support scientific cooperation, especially concerning the environment, facilitate the exchange of all kinds of information, and promote cultural development and mutual understanding. I am convinced that being part of UNESCO is, for all Americans, an important way to maintain peace and understanding among peoples. Whether it is in education, environmental protection or arms control, we must realize that all people must now come together because only through the sharing of our resources, in mutual respect, can we hope to solve the problems assailing this planet.

Two Unfinished UN Agenda Items

If it is true, as Gardner says on page 335 of this book, that the present division of the world is between those who see only the self-interests of their limited groups and those who see the broader interests of the human as a whole, the discussion following is a patent illustration of this idea. It concerns the so-called "New International Economic Order" and the resources of the sea bed.

In the 1970s the Third World countries declared in a widely publicized Manifesto that the existing world development system was unfair to them, and that they had been short-changed by the colonial powers and did not share enough of the world's wealth and resources. Through the UN they proposed a "New International Economic Order" (NIEO). It took the form of a single package of redresses they sought from the industrialized countries; the package deeply disturbed the industrialized countries. Some of them, including the United States, rejected the proposal outright.

My main reason for raising this issue, and a second one on seabed resources, is that they best illustrate the serious controversy still dividing the developing and the developed countries vis-a-vis the sharing of world resources, an issue which was at the heart of our activities in UN development programs. Their respective positions indeed remain far apart and, until they come to a better understanding, I doubt that rapid progress, particularly regarding the first issue, can take place to reduce the gap between the poor and the wealthy on our planet.

The package of redresses was a program of action submitted to the UN in 1974 by the so-called Group of 77, the nonaligned countries (later numbering about 125), in the hope of creating a better balanced world economy, and of correcting the inequities that beset it. The group represented all the newly independent nations, constituting the vast majority of the United Nations membership since decolonization. The founding fathers of this non-aligned movement were Joseph Tito of Yugoslavia, Jawaharlal Nehru of India, Gamal Abdel Nasser of Egypt, and Sukarno of Indonesia, all in the '50s, while President Boumedienne of Algeria became one of its most active promoters at the beginning of the '70s.

The goal of the proposed New International Economic Order was no less than to change the conditions in which blatant inequality exists between the industrialized and the poor countries, with power and affluence overwhelmingly concentrated in the former. The developing countries are not developing rapidly enough and depend too much on the industrialized world for goods and resources. In fact, the poverty gap is widening between the two worlds instead of narrowing, thus perpetuating the underdog status of the poorer people.

The package put forward to correct these injustices included an expansion and diversification of trade to enable developing countries to obtain fairer and stabler prices for their commodities and increase their share of the world's manufactured goods. It also proposed measures to increase industrial and food production and assistance for social and institutional improvement.

According to its proponents, NIEO was meant to benefit the rest of the world and give stability and strength to the global system. One argument advanced in its favor was that the U.S. had a great deal to gain from larger export markets to the developing countries. In recent years these countries had bought more than forty billion dollars annually of U.S. goods and services, nearly one-third of U.S. total exports. NIEO also claimed that the U.S. would benefit from an assured supply of raw materials from the Third World on which it depends for its industries—half of its copper, 94 percent of its cobalt, 83 percent of its tin, 57 percent of its aluminum, 41 percent of its tungsten.

While the NIEO was undoubtedly one of the hottest items debated in the halls of the United Nations, consuming a lot of time and energy in the '70s and into the '80s, in the end it did not produce any tangible result. The industrialized countries, principally the U.S., dissociated themselves from the proposal, which was put indefinitely on the back burner and never reached the stage of actual negotiations.

The obstacles to a New International Economic Order were indeed many. First, economic growth slowed down in the '80s, creating balance of payments difficulties in the market economies. In these circumstances the industrialized countries were not ready to increase their level of aid and, in fact, tightened their purse strings. The partisans of free market ideology, particularly the multinational corporations, were solidly against NIEO because they feared the threat of new regulations as well as the possibility of further nationalizations of foreign investments, although adequate compensation had been pledged.

Another fear was that the package of proposals included the possibility of setting up cartels among the producers of raw materials, much like the Organization of

Petroleum Exporting Countries (OPEC). Michael Manley, at the time Prime Minister of Jamaica, a persuasive and charismatic leader of the Third World (whom I knew when I was assigned to that country for four years), wanted to create a cartel for marketing bauxite, his country being a leading producer of that ore, the raw material from which aluminum is made. His proposal, on the heels of the formation of OPEC, scared the industrialized countries, the object of most cartels being primarily to raise prices for the consumer.

A more restricted meeting of 27 developed and underdeveloped countries, invited by Valery Giscard d'Estaing, President of France, to a North-South conference, fared no better. After two years of discussions they also got nowhere, the political will of the developed countries for agreement being definitely lacking. Another decisive obstacle to NIEO was a request for restructuring the two principal international financial institutions, the World Bank and the International Monetary Fund, an initiative strongly resisted by the U.S. and other Western countries.

Finally, at the beginning of the '80s, a gigantic debt problem started to confront the developing countries, pushing NIEO preoccupations into the background. The debt crisis has to be resolved in a satisfactory way, first of all, and NIEO seems definitely shelved for the time being, the Group of 77 realizing that their proposal will not be entertained soon.

But there still is much good will in the industrialized world for helping Third World countries, and their problems will have to be taken one at a time, not under the type of revolutionary package proposed by NIEO.

The sharing of the resources of the seabed for the benefit of all countries was another matter which reached the UN agenda and created an ongoing interest among us at the UN and in the rest of the world. In 1967, at a dramatic meeting on the Law of the Sea, the biggest piece of international legislation ever discussed in the halls of the United Nations, Ambassador Pardo, the Maltese representative to the UN, told the General Assembly that the seabed is the legacy of all human beings and that its resources should be exploited for the benefit of mankind as a whole. This declaration made a tremendous impact on the delegates, who saw in this new resource a way to accelerate world development. Seabed resources consist mainly of manganese nodules and other minerals, but oil and gas reserves exist that are of great future value. At this stage, only eight pioneering companies, either state or private consortia, exist in the world and are ready to exploit these resources. Ambassador Pardo's statement also caused a sensation because he recommended the creation of an international agency as a part of the UN, which would administer the oceans and ocean floor resources beyond national jurisdictional limits. At that time the U.S. did not seem opposed to the idea, and President Lyndon Johnson the year before had said at the dedication of a research ship that "we must ensure that the deep seabed and the ocean bottom are and remain the legacy of all human beings."[20]

In 1970, after three years of hard work, a Declaration of Principles on the Law of the Sea was approved by most countries as a package covering navigation rights, the limits of continental shelf, sea pollution, fishing rights and the resources of the seabed. The Declaration reiterated that the sea was the common heritage of mankind. UN people rejoiced as everything seemed to go along positively. The Declaration of Principles was signed by 108 countries, including the United States, with one against and 14 abstentions, the latter mainly the socialist countries which later declared themselves supporters of the Declaration. A convention, to be called "the Law of the Sea," remained, however, to be ironed out.

The drafting of such a comprehensive Convention took a few more years. It involved perhaps the greatest assembly of world jurists and government officials ever convened under the UN for discussion of a single issue since the framing of the UN Charter in San Francisco. I for one was pleased to see that the Convention included the statutes of an International authority to administer the resources of the seabed suggested by Prado. The authority would give concessions to exploiting companies and realize profits to be used for the benefit of world development. For several years the U.S. had been represented at the conference by Ambassador Elliot Richardson, a distinguished lawyer, a Republican and former U.S. Senator from Massachusetts, and several times a Cabinet member in Washington under both Republican and Democratic administrations, who was very favorable toward the Convention.

In 1981, however, when the Convention was ready and presented for signature to member states as a package of new legislation, it was a matter of deep disappointment that the American government—although having previously accepted the Declaration of Principles—under the new Reagan Administration, almost alone among the nations of the Earth, rejected the part of the Convention dealing with the exploitation of the seabed. Since it was a package to be approved as a whole, the U.S. had to disapprove the Convention altogether, although it had no objection to the rest of the document. The Convention was approved by a vast majority of countries as the first comprehensive treaty governing practically every aspect of the uses and resources of the oceans. It is recognized as a remarkable ecological charter

20 Narasimhan, *Op. cit.*, 236.

of world importance. Its implementation is now being prepared without U.S. participation at Headquarters of the Authority in Kingston, Jamaica.

The U.S.'s rejection of the Convention was a shock to me and many others. Apparently, the decision was deeply influenced by the maritime lobby in Washington. Under a free market outlook there is always the desire of some to possess more, and to operate without restraint, in this instance turning down the generous principle that some world resources of the seabed could be shared with the poorer people of the world. This rejection was one of the few exceptions to our sincere desire as a nation to construct a better world. I hope that the U.S. will later change its position and sign the Convention.

In the same vein, I was disappointed that we did not always abide by decisions of the World Court, even though the U.S. is not the only power to do so. This is undoubtedly weakening the prospect for a world of law, which we have already supported as the main basis for constructing a world at peace.

Another aspect of the whole issue of international assistance to the Third World which considerably slows development is that international cooperation too often is a one-way street. Industrialized countries are entitled to see a much greater effort on the part of developing countries to put their houses in order, reduce corruption, improve their public administration and reform their fiscal systems. In the field I saw the desperate need for this daily. This is not only a question of morality but a necessity if the aid extended is to be absorbed without waste. Too many scandalous examples of neglect on the part of governments exist in these areas.

The developing countries also should take strict measures to prevent the sheltering of their assets in Switzerland and other western countries by their wealthy compatriots. Some heads of countries with staggering national debts have large personal fortunes invested abroad despite the desperate need for capital investment at home.

Looking back to fifteen years of work at UN Headquarters, I wish to leave my reader with four central ideas:

- In the political field, the UN has shown many shortcomings, but it has not been a failure. It has not been able to fulfill all the dreams of the Charter, but during the Cold War the world was not ready for it. In the view of many, the UN has accomplished a great deal, and there are signs that it can do much more in the future. Its peacekeeping operations, not even envisaged under the Charter, have prevented some dangerous local conflicts from degenerating into wars;
- The UN programs of international cooperation in the economic, social and humanitarian fields have been successful and have enormously helped world

development. Most of the world problems which are of a global nature should be tackled through the UN;
- No one can deny the good will and the hard work done by the Secretariat and all UN workers around the world. Under extremely difficult conditions they certainly have done their best, sometimes at the cost of their lives. They deserve to be respected. They undoubtedly could accomplish more if they were given the financial means.
- The UN's role is no longer an issue. The world is far better off and safer with the existence of the United Nations than without it. This has been said by almost everyone except those few who have a political axe to grind, and this has been confirmed by all U.S. Secretaries of State since the creation of the Organization, and by all the world leaders. Dean Rusk, Secretary of State under President Kennedy, summed up my wish in his memoir when he wrote of the UN as the symbol of the kind of world the U.S. tries to build.

I turn now to my field experiences in the Third World which cover another fifteen years in some of the least developed nations of our globe, the most exciting and fulfilling time of my life.

PART IV

SIX MISSIONS TO THE THIRD WORLD

Tales of Morocco, Haiti, Uganda, Cyprus, Jamaica and Bénin

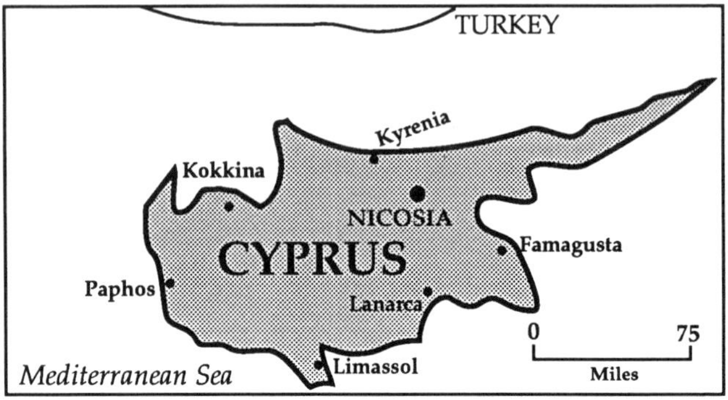
TURKEY
Kyrenia
Kokkina
NICOSIA
CYPRUS
Famagusta
Paphos
Lanarca
0
75
Miles
Mediterranean Sea
Limassol

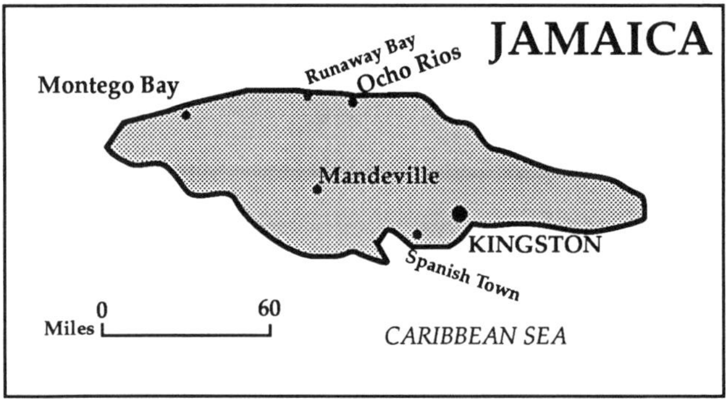
JAMAICA
Runaway Bay
Ocho Rios
Montego Bay
Mandeville
KINGSTON
Spanish Town
0
60
Miles
CARIBBEAN SEA

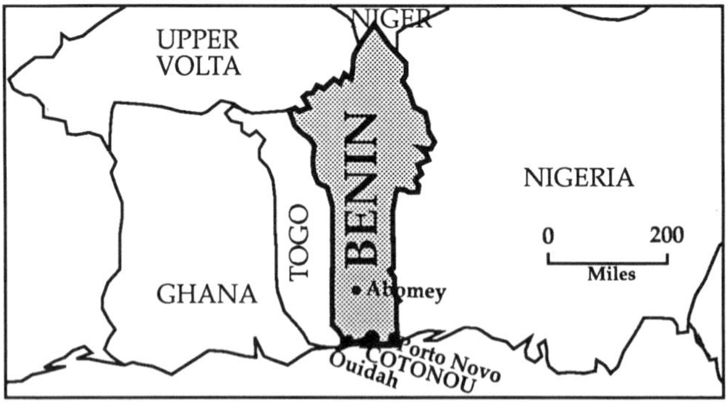
NIGER
UPPER
VOLTA
BENIN
NIGERIA
TOGO
0
200
Miles
GHANA
Porto Novo
COTONOU
Ouidah

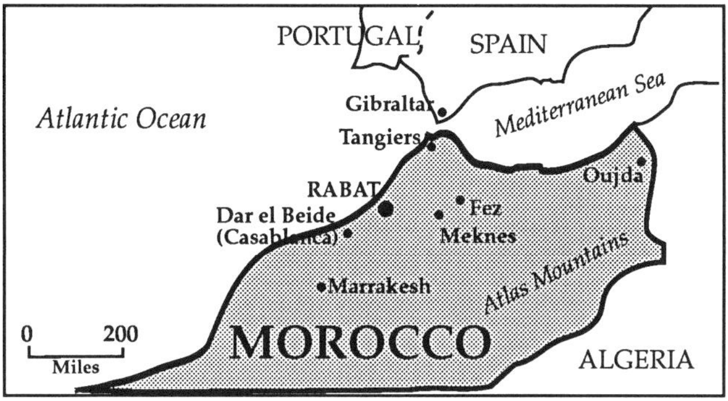
PORTUGAL
SPAIN
Atlantic Ocean
Gibraltar
Mediterranean Sea
Tangiers
RABAT
Oujda
Dar el Beide
(Casablanca)
Fez
Meknes
Marrakesh
Atlas Mountains
0 200
Miles
MOROCCO
ALGERIA

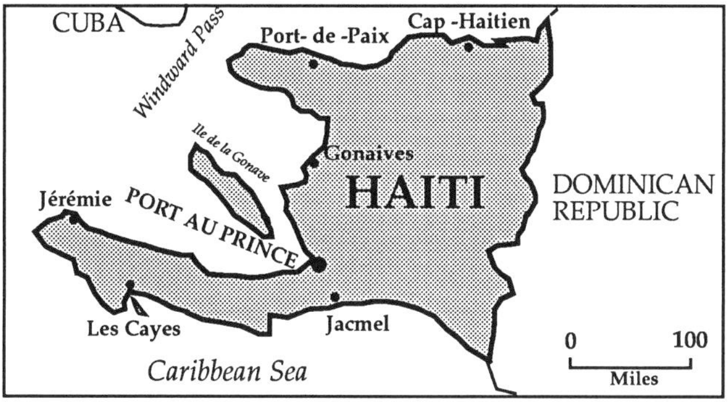
CUBA
Windward Pass
Port- de -Paix
Cap -Haitien
Ile de la Gonave
Gonaives
HAITI
DOMINICAN
REPUBLIC
Jérémie
PORT AU PRINCE
Les Cayes
Jacmel
Caribbean Sea
0 100
Miles

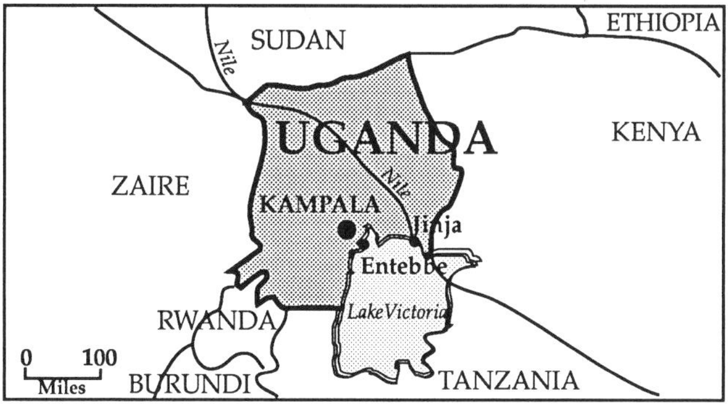
SUDAN
ETHIOPIA
Nile
UGANDA
KENYA
ZAIRE
Nile
KAMPALA
Jinja
Entebbe
Lake Victoria
RWANDA
0 100
Miles
BURUNDI
TANZANIA

PART IV

SIX MISSIONS TO THE THIRD WORLD

Tales of Morocco, Haiti, Uganda, Cyprus, Jamaica and Bénin

Introduction
The following stories describe my work for the UN in six countries—Morocco, Haiti, Uganda, Cyprus, Jamaica and Bénin—some among the most underdeveloped in the world. In Cyprus (1964) I was part of one of the first UN peacekeeping operations. In Morocco (1957-1958), Jamaica (1970-1974) and Bènin (1974-1975) I was what we call a Project Manager advising the government on planning and implementing specific development projects in community development, youth employment, and the preparation of a four-year national plan, respectively. Those particular jobs required more the qualifications of a generalist, which I was, than those of a narrow specialist, and I used to good advantage my knowledge and training in economics and social development and in planning management and law.

In the two other countries, Haiti (1959-1963) and Uganda (1963-1964) I was head of the UN Mission with the title of Resident Representative of the United Nations Development Programme. I dealt with all the assistance extended by the UN system. This involved negotiations with the government regarding the country's program and its various projects, the management of the mission, the coordination of our efforts with those of the bilateral programs and other aspects. It required a thorough knowledge of the problems of the country and its people at all levels. To gain this knowledge, I traveled extensively in the rural areas. The job of UNDP Resident Representative is by all standards one of the most fascinating that can be entrusted to a member of the Secretariat, and I felt privileged to have been selected.

I enjoyed thoroughly my days in the field; I worked hard and tried to give my best. There were inevitable frustrations, but those years gave me a new perspective on the problems of the world which I could not have gained elsewhere. I made many friends, and I can honestly say that on the whole I personally received much more than I gave.

During those years my belief in the vital importance of people's self-reliance grew stronger. Additionally, I became firmly convinced that governments must improve public administration, stimulate free enterprise and develop democratic institutions if we are to obtain lasting peace and equity among peoples.

While one or two of the countries in which I served have made steady progress toward democracy, others still struggle on its threshold. Regardless, there are still immense tasks ahead in education, population control, health, food and industrial production and, most importantly, government reforms. Without those reforms, the recipient countries cannot benefit fully from the help extended to them and cannot make rapid or steady progress toward a better life.

In trying to summarize my experiences in those countries, I find I firmly agreed with Joan Anstee, a brilliant UNDP Resident Representative colleague in Latin America in the '60s who later became a UN Under Secretary-General and served as Special Representative of the Secretary-General in Angola, an African country nearly destroyed by civil war. At an early stage of our UNDP work, she perfectly captured the role and attitude of international civil servants in the field when she wrote:

> As I try to sum up my impressions of this period in my own mind, the most significant of all is that, whereas I have tried to make my own modest contribution, I have in fact learned very much more than I have taught, not only about development problems as such, but about the whole intricate pattern of human life and problems all over the globe, and the basic similarity of human needs, sentiments and aspirations, irrespective of race, color, creed or social standing. . . . First, we must not become so mesmerized by the tempting magic of facts and figures—GNP, national income per capita and the rest—as to forget the human individual whose welfare is the ultimate goal of our endeavor. Second, to be successful in a program of this kind one must be constantly in touch with everyday reality and the life of the people of the country one is called upon to serve. Not only are some of my richest and happiest memories of occasions spent in remote areas, often in acute discomfort, but these experiences have been of inestimable value to me in helping to understand the problems we are called upon to help solve.[1]

---

1 United Nations Development Programme, *Generation; Portrait of the United Nations Development Programme* (New York: UNDP Division of Information, 1985), 21.

MOROCCO: FIRST STEPS IN SELF-RELIANCE

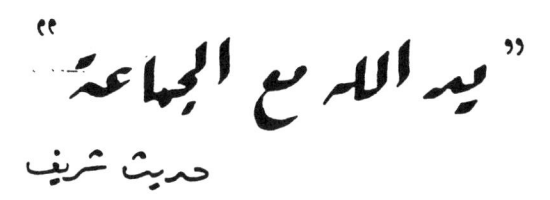

"يد الله مع الجماعة"
حديث شريف

God's hand guides those which join together to reach a
common goal

El Hadis
Traditions

MOROCCO: FIRST STEPS IN SELF-RELIANCE

A National Community Development Program
This is the story of my exciting one-year mission in 1957-58 to Morocco, to plan a national community development program in an emerging newly-independent Islamic country. I seek to explain the importance of this work for the people of that country and its national development. I tell of my team's travels and experiences among the tribes in the rural areas, and my life and that of my family in Rabat and our visits to the fascinating old cities of Marrakesh, Fez and Meknes, during which we were able to learn much about the Moroccan people.

What is self-reliance? It is having confidence in oneself to do something without depending on others, to show initiative and the willingness to work for one's own improvement and that of the community in a committed, cooperative spirit. Alexis de Tocqueville, the French philosopher, wrote at the beginning of the nineteenth century that the spirit of self-reliance displayed among the people in American cities and towns amazed him. He found that as soon as there was a problem to solve, a citizen committee was formed and action taken without the intervention of authorities.[1] But self-reliance is markedly absent in the rural areas of the Third World. After World War II, development experts began to wonder if local, national or regional communities in underdeveloped areas could become more self-reliant, could learn to use more resources for themselves, to assert their own value systems, to have confidence in their ingenuity—in other words to be less dependent on their governments, international organizations, foreign governments or giant corporations—when trying to attain a better life?

In the 1950s and '60s this was what the UN was trying to do in promoting programs of community development in the Third World through new methods and special techniques: creating conditions leading to economic and social progress for entire communities with their active participation and, to the greatest possible extent,

---

[1] de Tocqueville, Alexis, *Democracy in America* (New York: Knopf, 1980).

on their own initiative. In the French-speaking countries these techniques were known as *animation rurale* and *participation populaire*. As far as I was concerned, community development was a new element for national development in the Third World and perhaps an ingredient for a beginning of real democracy in those countries.

In the poorer countries of the Third World, up to 80 or 85 percent of the population live in rural areas. Most are illiterate, ill-fed and in poor health, and have been like that for centuries. Change must take place if the country as a whole is to progress, and the best change that can occur is to change the mentality of the people. The governments and the international community can extend to them as much technical and financial help as they want in agriculture, health and other fields, but in the end it will leave little durable effect if, in the process, they are not taught how to become self-reliant and to participate actively in the improvement programs extended to them.

In the '50s, when I was in charge of technical assistance programming at UN Headquarters—first to the twenty republics of Latin America, then to eleven countries of the Middle East including North Africa—I became convinced developing nations should request more assistance in community development. Because of my deep personal interest, I kept abreast of the progress made by community development in Latin America. I also followed some of the U.S. and UK assistance schemes in India and Pakistan and later became aware of the first efforts in that field in Africa. Wanting to know the techniques used, I attended a series of training films depicting the activities of community development workers in the villages of India, who advised the *Penchayats* (the assemblies of notables of those villages). International assistance to this kind of project, it seemed to me, was the heart of human development, helping men, women and children to become masters of their own fates. I became most enthusiastic about community development and wanted to participate in this work, go overseas and help governments and communities plan such projects. As a UN programming officer I wanted to see for myself whether this new strategy could make a real difference in people's lives.

Soon an opportunity arose which led to my personal involvement in this exciting new endeavor. One day in the fall of 1956 I was in the Delegates' Lounge at UN Headquarters when I saw the President of the newly independent Republic of Tunisia, Habib Bourguiba, standing alone, evidently waiting for someone. He had arrived in New York the day before, to head the Tunisian delegation at the session of the General Assembly. I did not know him, but had seen his photograph in the *New York Times*. With some hesitation, I went to him, and introducing myself in

French, I said I was sure he knew that, as a member of the UN, his country was entitled (as was Morocco, which also had just joined the UN) to receive UN technical assistance. I explained I was in charge of our programs for the Middle East and North Africa. If he wished, I could arrange a meeting to discuss Tunisia's needs with his staff and the procedures to request assistance. He was very interested.

A few days later, Dr. Hugh Keenleyside, a former Canadian Minister of State and Ambassador who headed the UN Technical Assistance Administration, chaired a meeting with members of the Tunisian and Moroccan delegations. Soon after, a small UN mission was dispatched to Tunis and Rabat to discuss a priority program of technical assistance with the two governments. Several weeks later we received a list of requests for help in education, vocational training, agriculture, industry and social development, all top national priorities which, according to their nature, we forwarded for execution to the UN Specialized Agencies concerned.

Among the requests was one from Morocco's Ministry of Labor and Social Affairs, endorsed by His Majesty the Sultan, for one UN expert in community development to explain to the government what community development was all about and, if relevant to the needs of the country, to assist them in planning a national program. The request explained that the government was hoping that community development could assist the efforts already undertaken to help its rural people organize themselves, improve their villages and later participate in regional and national development projects they were planning.

The UN Bureau of Personnel looked for some time for a suitable candidate for the post, particularly for an Indian, since at that time India was considered the most advanced in that field. Although there were a few excellent experts none was available who could speak French, an essential requirement in the case of Morocco.

I was finally selected because I had a thorough knowledge of the principles of community development, and had experience in planning projects requiring large amounts of coordination among the various ministries and at the regional and local levels. The public administration of Morocco, having been set up by the French, was familiar to me. I spoke French fluently and the UN thought I would get along well with the Moroccans and the many French advisors still working in the country. I was American, an acceptable nationality to the Moroccans, and this, too, was considered a plus. My name, submitted to Rabat for clearance, was approved immediately. It was decided that the planning would take one year and that subsequently I would be replaced by someone who had experience in village work to run the pilot projects I would help develop.

I arrived in Morocco in July 1957, shortly after the country had gained its independence from France. The young Moroccan leaders were burning with the desire to tackle the economic and social problems of the rural areas and *medinas*, the native market cities. Just a few weeks before I landed in Rabat the *Route de l'Unité* in the north, a road more than 100 kilometers long crossing the Rif Mountains and linking the former French and Spanish protectorates, had been completed entirely by volunteers from all walks of life, including many civil servants from the ministries in Rabat. This symbolic achievement had received great publicity, even outside the country, and clearly demonstrated the will of this new country to do something for and by itself after so many years of domination by two foreign powers.

France's Protectorate over Morocco lasted from 1912 to 1956, a total of 44 years during which the Sultan's government, the *Maghden*, existed parallel to that of the Protectorate. The *Maghden* had practically no power, the main policies being dictated by the French and Spanish administrations. It was at the historic International Conference of Algeciras, in Spain, that the western powers settled the question of French and Spanish rule over Morocco, confirming the "open door" policy established by the Berlin Conference in 1880 on the future of Africa. Through the Nineteenth Century, North Africa was the target of several European efforts at colonization. Eventually Great Britain recognized French preeminence in Morocco in exchange for its own exclusive influence over Egypt. Spain had agreed with the French on the exact division of their respective zones, of which Spain's was smaller.

Before the Protectorate, the country had been anything but independent. From the first century BC until the fifth century AD, Morocco had been a Roman province, which then was occupied by the Visigoths and the Byzantines. By the 8th century the Arabs had taken over, and the Berbers, the indigenous people of North Africa, had been conquered and had rallied to Islam. Yet for several centuries the country had been the scene of incessant infighting among its tribes. There were major rebellions by the Berbers against the dynasties which ruled Morocco. Finally, in the middle of the seventeenth century, the House of Alawi took over. It still rules Morocco.

The French pacification of the tribes continued until 1934, marked from 1921 to 1926 by the formidable rebellion of Abed al Krim, the leader of the Rif tribesmen, who was finally crushed with the help of the French Foreign Legion. I had heard stories about this war from my aunt Lucie, my father's sister, who had served with the French Red Cross on the front in Morocco as a director of the *Foyers du Soldat* (a French equivalent of the American USO) in a critical period in which the French nearly lost the war. During my adolescence in France I had also learned much about the great pacifier of Morocco, the venerated Marshal Louis Lyautey, a brilliant soldier and statesman, the real father of modern Morocco. The modernization of the country was mainly the result of his leadership and was indeed an amazing accomplishment. Yet, in the process, traditions and tribal customs had suffered considerably as a result of the introduction of western technology, urbanization and new patterns of living. Understanding the full impact of the French and Spanish occupations on tribal life was necessary for the work my team was undertaking in the rural areas. For this we traveled widely in the various parts of the country.

I, as were all who traveled in Morocco before and after World War II, was struck by what the French had done to develop the country in such a relatively short time. They had built an excellent network of roads; modern European-type cities shot up right beside the traditional *medinas*. They had developed mining to a high degree, built important irrigation systems leading to the development of large private agricultural estates run by French managers. They had set up schools, hospitals and clinics. In brief they had created a remarkable infrastructure. French government financing and private investment had made Morocco the showcase of France overseas.

Most important for our future UN projects, the French had also put in place a rural development scheme, called *Modernization du paysannat* (Modernization of the Peasantry), a program including many agricultural consulting and education centers, as well as more than one hundred small government cooperatives which, however, were not genuine because they were not run by the farmers themselves. This program, remarkable as it was and involving a large number of French technicians, was conducted by the Protectorate in a much too paternalistic manner to change the people's ways. The *fellahs*, the small farmers, had little to say. They were not learning how to take personal initiatives. It was now time to educate them differently and teach them new methods of participation in development. Despite the French efforts, 93 percent of the rural and 77 percent of the urban population were still illiterate on the day of Independence, according to French sources.

Our work in Morocco was not all easy, since it consisted of showing the people that they could, by their own efforts, do much to improve living conditions in their communities. For this new methods and technologies were needed which would reveal to the people what they could do for themselves and how to acquire the desire and the know-how which would enable them to progress.

Meeting Moroccan Leaders

As part of my briefing before arriving at my new post, I spent two useful weeks at

Khavala in Greece, on the Turkish border, to observe in progress one of the successful UN programs in community development.

On September 15, 1957, I arrived in Rabat, the Moroccan capital, for a one-year mission. Before my family joined me I lived at the *Hôtel de la Tour Hassan*, located near the famed tower of the same name, the city landmark, where visiting foreign officials usually stayed. The hotel had been converted into a government hotel school—the guests were served by students smartly dressed in red and white uniforms comprising a red fez, a shirt with wide sleeves and narrow cuffs under a short red jacket adorned with black embroidery, and white trousers with a sash. The food was European and excellent.

I was happy to see Rabat again. Not a very large city at the time of my 1930 visit, it had changed little since. The elegant white public buildings of the Protectorate now housed the Moroccan administration, with no apparent difference. The first Sunday after my arrival I took a walk to the district that had been known as the *Résidence Générale*, now the seat of the Moroccan government ministries. Some looked like sumptuous villas, hidden behind gleaming white walls, surrounded by beautiful gardens. The avenues were wide, bordered with palm trees, the whole area looking much more like a chic seaside spa than the center of an administrative city. I walked to the commercial part of the city which, while much like it had been in 1930, now boasted a number of new and modern stores. It was Sunday, an ordinary day in Islamic countries, and the shops were open. I also paid a visit that day to the *medina* and the garden of the Casbah of the Oudayas, along the Oued Bou Regregg and its estuary, a site which had impressed me so much on my 1930 visit.

The next day I began a series of calls on the government officials who had generated the proposed project. My first visit was to the Minister of Labor and Social Affairs, His Excellency Abdallah Moulay Ibrahim, who had requested my coming to Morocco. A member of the Cabinet, he was also one of the most prominent figures of *Istiqlal*, the powerful nationalist party which had fought for independence and included both liberal and conservative politicians. In his early forties, a kind man of rather small stature, with a handsome face and deep brown eyes, he had enormous charm. I liked him immediately. He welcomed me with great cordiality and, even before we started to talk about the project, invited me to a *diffa* (a Moroccan dinner) he was to give a few days later at his home. Sorbonne-educated, speaking French with distinction, Ibrahim had a most aristocratic background and was said to be a descendant of the Prophet, therefore worthy of the title of *Moulay* (*mullah*), the religious equivalent of "My Lord." I learned later that he was sometimes called the "Red Sheriff" by political opponents because of his frank leanings towards the left of the Moroccan political spectrum. He was deeply interested in social development. Being extremely compassionate to the poor, he wanted to find ways to improve their deplorable conditions.

I also had a meeting with Abderrahim Bouabid, also a liberal, the Minister of the National Economy and Vice-President of the Council of Ministers, perhaps the most brilliant man in the Cabinet. He considered our project a promising effort to start democracy at the grass roots level. He thought it would help later in establishing modern municipalities in the rural areas, a goal for which he was striving.

I also called on the Minister of Education, His Excellency Sidi El Fassi, in contrast a conservative with traditional views close to the Sultan, and President of the *Istiqlal*. He was extremely important to me, since his ministry was working on a basic education program assisted by UNESCO which closely related to what we were going to do and required close contact with us.

Shortly after my arrival I was invited by a highly controversial figure in Moroccan politics, Madhi Ben Barka, to discuss the project with him in his office. Barely five feet tall and very young, he was certainly the most lively politician in Rabat. Now Chairman of the Legislative Assembly, his long-term secret ambition for Morocco, I was told, was to see the Kingdom one day replaced by a republic. As a result, he was carefully watched by the Sultan.

I accepted his invitation, but made sure I was accompanied by someone from the Ministry. Ben Barka greatly impressed me with his keen intelligence. He kept me in his office for at least two hours. Several years later I read in the international press that he had had to flee Morocco. He had been kidnapped on a Paris street and was subsequently murdered in a villa in the suburbs of the French capital.

These early meetings and what I later learned gave me a valuable insight into Moroccan politics. On the surface the situation appeared calm and the monarchy seemed stable, but there was no doubt that much infighting was taking place behind the scenes on the part of political opponents, conservative and liberal, a type of struggle for change that often exists in developing countries. Yet I did not think that it would have a detrimental impact on the development of our project. Of course I was careful not to proffer any judgments or take sides in these matters. The attitude of an international civil servant on mission is to maintain at all times the greatest tact and discretion, the only objective being to attend to his or her duties, the interests of the United Nations and those of the country he is serving.

Two weeks later I was introduced to His Majesty the Sultan at a Royal Palace garden party. His son, the Prince Consort, later King Hassan II, was at his side and had just been appointed Chief of Staff of the Army by his father. Both expressed deep interest in the assistance the UN and its specialized agencies were extending to their country and wished me well with our project. The Sultan, Mohammed Ben Youssef, later changed his title from Sultan to King Mohammed V. Two years earlier he had come back from exile, first in Corsica, then in Madagascar. His exile had been an unfortunate French decision, taken against a popular leader when there was much political trouble in the country. It brought about independence earlier than had been expected.

It was a wonderful occasion for me to pay my respects to the King of a traditional Islamic kingdom, whose power is at the same time temporal and spiritual. Separation of church and state is a concept alien to Islam and this should never be forgotten when dealing with a Moslem country like Morocco. Few young Moroccan leaders would have preferred to see their country become a republic instead of remaining a kingdom, and as history proved in the years after I had left the country, the few attempts which took place to destroy the monarchy or assassinate King Hassan failed. Mohammed V was adored by his subjects, but unfortunately died prematurely in 1961. His devoted son, who succeeded him as Hassan II, is an astute monarch and a friend of both the U.S. and France, and assumes an important voice in the concert of Arab nations.

During my first weeks in Rabat I considered it important to establish cordial relations with people from the French Embassy, as France had remained the most influential advisor in Moroccan affairs. It was important that the French support our project since they were still assisting the country in rural development. I met the Ambassador, Alexandre Parodi, a former High Commissioner of the French Republic under de Gaulle, a hero of the French Resistance during World War II, recently appointed to Rabat. His Minister-Counselor was Charles Roux, whom luckily I had known in New York when he was acting French Consul-General. Through their introductions I was able to discuss tribal problems with two top French experts, one the creator of the *Paysannats* and the other an ethnologist known for his work on the populations of the *Maghreb*. I also met the Director of the National School of Public Administration in Rabat, who was training the kingdom's new young administrators. All responded to my questions with interest and cordiality, but probably wondered why the Moroccan government had requested UN assistance in the field of rural development in which France had already done so much.

The government gave me offices in one of its buildings in the center of town. The following week Fouad Faraj of Lebanon, my immediate assistant and a man who had been responsible for community development in his own country, arrived in Rabat. He spoke Arabic and French. Then we were joined by two "associate experts" from The Netherlands, sociologist Frank Schmidgall and anthropologist Adrianus Kater. Both were fluent in French and, under a special agreement between the Dutch government and the UN, had been selected to reinforce the team and carry out needed research and act as assistants to me. After a difficult search, we hired two Moroccan secretaries who knew English, and we were in business. In the following days our team had fruitful meetings with the experts of the UN specialized agencies in agriculture, health and education, for the purpose of coordinating our efforts.

With The Tribes Across Morocco

The first phase of the mission was to familiarize ourselves with the problems of the rural areas. We drove across the country, visiting the tribes and meeting government officials such as provincial governors, *super-caïds* and *caïds* appointed by the Sultan and in control of the interior. In Morocco the rural population is composed of tribes. A tribe may number thousands, covering several villages and sharing a common ancestry, language, culture and name. Most are sedentary tribes as nomadism has practically disappeared in Morocco.

On those visits we often were accompanied by someone on the staff of the Ministry, but even when we were not we had no communications problems as the *caïds*, administrators for the rural areas, spoke French. There was always someone in the village as well who could speak that language. Fouad Faraj spoke excellent Middle Eastern Arabic.[2] However, he had no trouble conversing with the people and he was a very good interpreter.

Exploring the country proved a source of great enjoyment. The views were sometimes breathtaking, the scenery always full of contrasts. Rugged mountains with altitudes ranging from 2000 to 4000 meters divided Morocco into three principal regions: the mountain interior in the east called High, Middle and Anti-Atlas; the Atlantic plains in the west; and the arid and semi-arid Eastern and Southern regions. The countryside was sparsely settled. Everywhere, the people we met were cordial and attractive. The total population of the country at the time was about 10 million, 80 percent of them in the rural areas. Yet the birth rate in North Africa is among the highest in the world, and as a result the population doubles every 20 or 25 years. When we were there, half the people were under twenty years of age and 40 percent under 14; this gives one an idea of the burden all these young people represent for the economy, since they are not yet contributing to the national product.

With the exception of a small group of Jews in the cities, the people are all

---

2 Moroccan Arabic is only a vernacular of the language.

Moslem, and there is a striking contrast between the rural and urban populations. The civilization of the latter, mostly Arab, is considerably influenced by European society. In contrast, the rural people, mostly Berbers, live in tribes in the mountains. They have stayed isolated for many years, and consequently have remained attached to their traditions much more than the city dwellers.

On fieldtrip from Rabat we crossed the coastal plains that produce important harvests of wheat and corn and where cattle are raised. We passed modern agricultural estates where tractors were used, and where productivity was, according to extension agents, six times higher than in the traditional sectors. In the same region the small farmers, the *fellahs*, still used primitive cultivation methods. The *fellah*'s plough, made of wood, sometimes without a metal blade and pulled by a camel or horse, only scratched an arid ground. The government intended to change the tribal system from its decline, into modern community structures to be called *communes rurales*, which were to be installed gradually. The *fellah*, obviously, whether settled or nomad, had not yet been prepared for such a transformation. Community development would definitely help in that respect. Our visits to the tribes confirmed that much had to be done to awaken the *fellah* and develop his initiative, a process which undoubtedly could take several years.

Our trips also exposed us to the irregularities of the Moroccan weather and its bad effects on crops. We confirmed what we had been told—if the winter is too dry or if the spring is too rainy, the harvest collapses. When the weather is fine in the *Rharb* (a northwest region), the *Haouz* (south) suffers, and when the *Haouz* prospers it is the *Rharb* which is drowned in humidity. Only in rare years were the *fellahs* self-sufficient.

Our trips to the semi-arid regions of eastern and southern Morocco, made of plateaus of grazing valleys extending to the foothills of the Atlas Mountains, acquainted us with the land of the Berber tribes. Fifty miles east of Marrakesh we went to see the administrative organization and the technical services of the *Cercle d'El Kelaa des Srarghnas*, a district including an impressive irrigation system developed by the Protectorate, in an immense plain at the foot of the Atlas Mountains. With an area of a million acres and a population reaching 168,000 inhabitants, its four tribes were administered by four *caïds* and one *supercaïd*, all under the authority of the Governor of the Marrakesh province. This was an excellent area to start one of our pilot projects, which could double as one of the future *communes rurales* where between 8,000 and 10,000 people would be settled.

In the north and center of the country we visited typical Moroccan villages with populations seldom over 1,000 inhabitants, called *douar*, literally "circle of tents."

In the south these villages are called *ksar* (plural *ksour*). Each *douar* owns its collective lands, protected by customs law and inalienable. The heads of clan families form the *jemaa*, the assembly of notables of the *douar*. It manages the collective lands and repairs the *seguias* or irrigation canals where they exist. It also maintains the mosque and has other duties. We recommended that until the *jemaas*, duly strengthened, could be replaced by the *communes rurales*, they should have a central place in our program of community action. Moroccan tribes represent about one-third of the population and, at that time, owned half the land in the country. We found the *caïds* in charge of the villages quite cooperative. They were appointed by the Sultan. Properly trained in the community development approach, we thought they would be suitable agents for the program. A special corps of assistants to the *caïds* for community action would also be created, since the *caïds* already had many administrative responsibilities.

Since the *fellahs* were mostly idle during the off-season, there were developmental works in which they could engage. At the time, they were not protecting the soil against erosion, which was considerable because of the turbulence of rivers (*oueds*) during the rainy season. Droughts in the summer, caused both by climate and by man, who indiscriminately cut trees, contributed to devastating floods. Clearing stones from the fields to enable more extensive ploughing was not done either, except in certain areas. We thought that a number of projects in those areas could be easily started or strengthened, applying community development principles. Other more important programs such as terracing and the planting of fruit trees on slopes had already been started with great success under the French in various parts of the country, and could also be expanded.

We concluded that there were abundant human resources which could be put to work, if properly motivated. There was much to do in the *douars* to improve living conditions, starting with housing. The typical hut of the *fellah*, called *nouala* in the coastal area, was made of reeds and straw with a thatched roof. Inland they were called *rhaina*, a tent made of a woven fabric of goat and camel hair brought by nomads from the high plateaus of the south. Other houses were made of beaten earth with a cement terrace supported by poles, usually poorly maintained. Much improvement could be started in that area.

Our visits to the rural areas also acquainted us with the ways people lived. On one of our trips, near the Atlas foothills, a less developed area, we traveled along a green valley and passed many oak forests. We met a Berber family at their *casbah*. Adults and children all came out on the terrace to greet us with great excitement. They showed us their crude household and the primitive stove on which they cooked their meals. As we talked with them two young women who belonged to the family came along, bearing on their backs enormous loads of faggots from a distant wood. Nearby we saw women wearing black shawls and rolled turbans harvesting hay, and men loading a cart pulled by one horse. Evidently the women took a large part in farming activities. All these people were very poor, but seemed happy.

On another expedition that took us south of Marrakesh on the other side of the Atlas Mountains on the edge of the desert, we spent the night at the simple but comfortable *Gite d'Étape* at Ouarzazate, one of the stopping posts the French set up about every hundred kilometers in isolated regions to accommodate tourists and French officials visiting the Protectorate. The next morning we walked into a nearby oasis, which, compared to the aridity of the scrubby and desert landscape surrounding it, was green and restful. Small boys displaying the agility of monkeys climbed up a palm tree to fetch fresh dates for us. Farther east we passed the famous Gorges of Todra, driving along the almost-dry river and fording it at various intervals. The *casbah* (houses) in the *ksour* of South Morocco are chocolate brown in color. They look like forts and are often surrounded by an outer battlement-like wall with holes for the weapons once used to protect the tribe against attack from other unfriendly tribes. Although these *casbahs* are made just of dried mud rammed into shape like concrete, they include no cement but give an impression of great solidity.

We stopped at one of the villages near the Gorges of the Oued Dra and were greeted by members of the *jemaa* on the little village square. They invited us for a small gathering inside a tall *casbah* where a French Army officer was still stationed, assisting the *caïd* with police work. We passed through a dark corridor and I noticed on the floor a heap of dates covered with dust, which I was told was a food reserve for the winter. What a strange way to store their most precious crop, I thought. We climbed for a formal gathering to a large unfurnished room in the building's tower, which boasted a large bay giving us a superb view of the arid countryside.

Before we made further acquaintance with the notables and talked about the problems of the community, we were served the traditional mint tea, passed around in glasses which were far from crystal clear. Servants brought two tall earthen teapots, one of boiling water and green tea, the other with mint leaves and boiling water. They started to pour the hot beverage into our glasses. Before taking a drink I noticed several flies on the edge of my glass, and on those of my companions. The French Army officer, who was used to flies, paid no attention to them and continued to talk to our hosts. There was little we could do but put our glasses to our lips and drink the beverage; it would have been an insult to refuse it.

The next day, farther east, we investigated conditions for the project in the oasis of the *Tafilalet* at Erfoud, on the edge of the Sahara Desert. However, arriving late, unannounced, and dead tired, we found there was no room available in the hotel, not even in the *fundunk*, the traditional Arab lodging for travelers. I remember we slept in a shed, with no sanitary facilities, all wooden shutters closed. I returned to Rabat thoroughly ill and had to stay in bed with fever and pneumonia for a whole week. This was the only time I suffered from our incursions into the deep interior of the country.

Over the course of these months our team had discussions with many officials at the central government level in Rabat as well as at the provincial and local levels. Midway through our mission, having convinced almost everybody of the significance of community development and of the importance of the techniques of popular participation for national development, we were able to recommend a detailed national program, which included: understanding at all levels of government of the need for developing initiative and participation among the *fellahs*; identification and training of the natural leaders in the communities in the methods and techniques of community development; orientation of various local administrators (*supercaïds*, *caïds*, *sheiks*, etc.) and later of the elected representatives after the rural communes were set up; training of special technical personnel in the various ministries in the provinces and at the local level in the community development methods and techniques they should use to assist the people of the *douars*. Finally we recommended the preparation of two pilot projects, one in Lalla Mimouna in the *Rharb* and one in the south at El Kelaa des Srarghnas.

Our recommendations for such a program were widely distributed and finally approved by the government in most of its aspects, and the launching of community development in Morocco was authorized in the summer of 1958 by an interministerial commission created in Rabat, which undertook to obtain from the Treasury the funds necessary for the pilot projects. As planned, I returned to UN Headquarters at the end of my mission to resume my functions there. In 1959, John Bowers, an Englishman and former Director of Fundamental Education in UNESCO, continued my work. After taking up his duties in Rabat he reported to the UN that the project was well in hand thanks to the enormous work of preparation, planning and coordination by Jean Richardot and his team. Katherine Shippen, in a book in which she describes a number of successful UN projects in developing countries, included our pilot project at Lalla Mimouna. She wrote, "Lalla Mimouna was one of those shabby villages, its people restless, hungry, and discouraged and many left the town and tried to take up their lives elsewhere. But Lalla Mimouna is a changed place now. The United Nations experts studied conditions in rural areas of Morocco. They selected one village to work on—one small place where the government, the UN, and the villagers could cooperate in bringing people to a better life. They knew that if they were successful here, other villages would imitate them."[3]

When our final report to the Government of Morocco was published by the UN, the Technical Assistance Administration found it so useful that they sent copies to all French-language African governments to serve as a guide for the preparation and execution of their own national community development programs.

As a follow-up on the introduction of community development in Morocco, I must mention two very important large-scale projects undertaken by the government. One started during our mission there, the other two years later. Both projects were based on the principles of self-reliance that our assistance had helped develop in Morocco. Both projects had significant influence on the self-esteem, initiative and personal development of the tribes, as well as on increased agricultural production and in reducing the high rate of unemployment in the parts of the country where these programs were implemented as we were introducing community development in Morocco.

The first one was called *Operation Labour* (Operation Ploughing). The *fellahs* settled in the *Chaouias*, the great cereal producing coastal plain, had rarely been able with their antiquated equipment to complete ploughing a soil hard as rock before the rainy season. This changed in 1958 when the government made the bold decision to purchase sixteen hundred U.S.-made tractors to plough the fields and to organize the *fellahs* into cooperatives for distributing fertilizer and seed. Our team participated in the official dedication of the operation, with King Mohammed V driving the first tractor. *Operation Labour* continued over five years, ploughing a total of one million hectares (2.5 million acres), during which the farmers reimbursed the cost of ploughing and the *jemaas* learned how to manage the cooperatives and obtain credit, something new to most of them. Production and yields increased substantially, although the critical time targets fixed by the Government could not be fully reached, and the operation was a considerable success.

The second government scheme, called *Promotion nationale*, a larger project covering many parts of the country, consisted of using the abundant rural manpower, particularly during the agricultural off-season, to help build up the infrastructure of the country including roads, irrigation works, earth dams, erosion control devices, stone removal from tillable areas, terracing and the planting of fruit trees. Without

---

3   Katherine Shippen, *The Pool of Knowledge; How the United Nations Share Their Skills* (New York: Harper Row, 1954), 22-28.

the use of this low-cost manpower, much of the needed infrastructure work would not have been undertaken due to lack of government funds. In no way did the work resemble forced labor. The workers were volunteers, wages being paid partly to them in money—a low daily wage—and partly in food bought from U.S. surpluses with Moroccan currency. This vast operation resulted in the opening of many jobs all over the country, revolutionizing the countryside, and was a great way to fight unemployment and underemployment. The project first provided a labor supply for large projects of national interest carried out by agencies of the Government. Second, it encouraged and supervised projects for community improvements, initiated by the village people along the lines our team had recommended, i.e., the communities' proposing the projects they wanted to carry out.

The *Promotion nationale* program, directly attached to the office of the King, continued successfully for a few years, its one difficulty being that of finding enough trained agents to supervise the operation. Thus it was in Morocco that one of the first programs of "food for work" was started. These projects, carried out later on a large scale in the Third World, used U.S. and other food surpluses, in cooperation with USAID, the UN World Food Program and numerous non-governmental agencies such as CARE, Roman Catholic and Protestant organizations. It was sometimes said that "food for work" projects did not encourage local agricultural production, because the people, if they were fed, lost their incentive to farm. This was not my experience in Morocco. Of course these projects must be well planned and controlled to avoid waste and the dishonest use of the supplies, and they should not become permanent.

Our project had contributed something important to the people of Morocco by showing them how to increase their self-reliance. But we, in turn, as a team, had greatly benefited by knowing the people, by learning something of their culture and by having had the privilege of participating with them in vital aspects of the country's development in its first years of Moroccan independence.

A UN Family In Rabat

For my family, our year in Morocco was exciting and enlightening. Generally speaking, UN staff and their families in the field mix more freely with the local people and have closer personal contacts with the country's officials than do technical assistance personnel of bilateral programs conducted through the embassies. Embassy personnel often keep to diplomatic circles and the foreign colony socially, while UN experts have their offices in the Ministries of the host countries, and, as a result, we came to know quite a number of Moroccans. Day by day we were in contact with a civilization new to us, and on a personal basis we surely received more than we gave.

School had just started. Carole, who was 15, enrolled in the French *Lycée de jeunes filles* of Rabat while Nancy, 9, was registered at *Institut St-Gabriel*, a Roman Catholic private school run by French nuns. Soon both became fluent in French. They enjoyed their new schoolmates and teachers and coped with the strict, hardworking regimen of French schools. For transportation we bought a Dauphine, a small Renault new on the market. For reasons of safety, the schools insisted that a family member transport the children, not a family friend or chauffeur. Natalie drove our daughters to school, took them home for lunch, and back to school, then home again after each school day. Both schools were far from our home in Agdal and this absorbed much of her time.

The house was furnished with local furniture. We had brought our own refrigerator from the States, the only appliance we were authorized to transport at UN expense. In the winter heating was by kerosene stoves. Although Morocco was classified as semi-tropical, heat was needed during the winter as the Atlantic coast was subject to rains and windstorms and household interiors stayed cold and clammy for three to four months. Kerosene was the normal way to heat houses in Rabat, central heating being an exception. We got used to the smell of kerosene when we lighted our stove.

We hired a Berber cook, Saadia, and Fathma, an Arab maid, who served as our laundress and worked during the day downstairs in the house basement. The two women did not get along well. This should have been expected, as the relationship of these two ethnic groups was never very smooth, to say the least, and they often insulted each other. The Berbers are the indigenous tribesmen of Morocco from the Atlas Mountains of Eastern Morocco and the Kabylie plateaus of Algeria. When the Arabs in the eighth century conquered the country, they settled in the plains, built the cities and took the Berbers under Islamic tutelage, many of them rallying to Islam. Saadia wore a *djllabah* and the veil of Arab women. She and Fathma at times exchanged insults in their vernacular Arabic, since Saadia was very proud of being a Berber. One day, when the Fathma called her *sale Berber* ("dirty Berber," in French) during one of these arguments, Natalie asked, "Are you a Berber, Saadia?" She then proudly pulled back her uniform to show Natalie the white skin of her thigh to prove her Caucasian background. Saadia's face was always tanned, the only part of her body that was.

After a time Saadia wanted to show us how she lived in the *medina*, so one day she invited us to come to a couscous dinner in the cooperative apartment building in which she lived. Following a number of tortuous narrow lanes crowded with people, with shops and small courtyards on each side, we reached our destination after asking several times where she lived. Her apartment, consisting of a kitchen and one room, was on the third floor of a very old building. An outside Roman staircase, still strong with some of its tiles, led to it. Her room, impeccably kept, was a little cubbyhole, hardly big enough for her bed, so one of her friends had loaned her a larger room which opened on the third floor courtyard, to receive us. We arrived to the distinctive aroma of couscous in the room. First she offered us mint tea, served as always in small glasses, made with two silver teapots because two infusions had to be used, one boiling water over mint leaves and the other over the green tea. Saadia dived under the bed which served as a couch and pulled out two cones of sugar, wrapped in blue paper, to sweeten the potent beverage. She broke the sugar cones into large pieces, using a little copper hammer, and plopped them into the pots before pouring.

When we left Morocco we were sad to leave her. We liked her and she had been a great help. Although she was poor, she had purchased a beautiful all wool white *djellabah* and a white veil with blue embroidery as a parting gift for Natalie. Her generosity had been boundless.

During the day my work placed me in contact with many Moroccan government officials with whom I maintained cordial but formal relations. Each office call had to start with a glass of mint tea, brought in by the *huissier* (usher), called a *chaouch*. By the end of my stay my system was reacting negatively to mint tea, but protocol demanded one drink three glasses of it before serious conversation could begin.

Moroccans rarely invited foreigners to their houses. We met quite a few American and European couples at Embassy receptions and I met men at government functions where women were not invited. These contacts were extremely useful to explain the purpose of my mission.

Visiting The Old Cities Of Morocco

On weekends, when I was free, we took fascinating trips across Morocco in our little Dauphine, visiting its cities and some of the mountain sites in the Middle Atlas.

Among our favorite destinations was Marrakesh, some four to five hours from Rabat on the fine roads built by the French during the Protectorate. Driving south we first had to cross the fertile plain, *Chaouia*, then later a zone of arid plateaus. Finally, after crossing a mountain gap, leaving behind us the solitude of the *bled*, we suddenly faced one of the most striking panoramas in the world. On the horizon stood the majestic high barrier of the Atlas range covered with snow and, at its foot, loomed the celebrated oasis city of Marrakesh, still far away, like an apparition enveloped in the golden mist of the late afternoon. Behind its formidable ramparts lay thousands of triangular roofs and flat terraces, all of various earth colors. Hundreds of palm trees jutted against the sky in clusters, the whole scene dominated by the tall sturdy silhouette of the *Koutoubia*, the 250-foot high mosque of Marrakesh, one of the spiritual beacons of Islam.

We reached the foot of the city's ramparts, passed under the monumental *Bab-er-Robb* (literally the "Gate of Grape Juice"), and entered the city, driving along its wide avenues. Our first stop was the internationally-known Mamounia Hotel, an ancient Saadian palace, where Winston Churchill used to paint and find peace and solitude in the hotel gardens, a riot of flowers, mosaic fountains and high pink walls. Soon after we arrived at the vast square called *Djema el Fna*, meaning the "meeting of the dead," an allusion to the terrible tortures and executions publicly held in the square years ago. Now it was a never-closing market and, above all, a place of entertainment where people enjoyed the ancient tales of *raconteurs*, the snake charmers, dancers and musicians from the Atlas Mountains or from across the desert.

We also saw the Bahia, a marvelous palace built by the great Vizir Bah Ahmed with its Moorish gardens, evoking dreams of the thousand and one nights. On a different trip, at 10 p.m. one evening I went to the *souks* accompanied by a guide to purchase rugs in a shop located at the end of a narrow street with tricky little stairs leading to a basement where the rugs were displayed. The *souks* were completely deserted except for a few groups of men whose appearance was not too reassuring. Anything unpleasant could have happened to us, but we reached the shop without trouble and I was glad, the transaction being completed, to rush back to the hotel. Why I did this I don't know. It took a certain amount of daring, even of foolishness on my part, to go to the *souk* at night just to buy Berber rugs before leaving town, even though it was to be my last visit to Marrakesh. We bought two lovely rugs with black and brown designs on a white background that we are still using after so many years, long before Moroccan rugs could be found in the United States.

The next day we ventured south of Marrakesh in the direction of the High Atlas. Just before the road crossed a gap in the mountains leading to the other side of the range toward the desert, some Berber boys stopped us, offering amethyst crystals embedded in rock, which we bought. Farther on we stopped at an inn called *Le Sanglier qui fume* (the Smoking Boar) with its picturesque sign showing a boar with a pipe in its mouth. We spent the night there, ate good food, and decided to climb the rocky hills facing us. The climb was hot and dry. On the way back to the inn, at the bottom of the road, was a rushing stream. There was a question of where we would cross the stream. I chose one spot which meant fording the stream using stepping stones. My female companions were not too sure about this, so they watched me from the bank. You can guess what happened. I slipped and fell into the stream up to my waist. It was cold but refreshing. I suddenly realized that I had brought only one pair of shoes and socks, and one pair of trousers despite my wife's warning to take a spare of each. The incident ended amid roars of laughter from my family as they crossed the stream at a much safer place. I stood shivering, wondering what to wear to go to dinner. I explained my predicament to the innkeeper, a Frenchman, who loaned me attire for the evening. As night fell the children amused themselves with small animals in cages which were there for their benefit. We heard a yelp and a burst of tears as Nancy came running to us. The monkey had taken a little nip out of her, but her feelings were hurt more than her arm.

Sunday afternoon on our way back to Rabat we again passed through Marrakesh and headed north. While passing through the small town of Ben Guerrir an accident occurred which could have had unpleasant repercussions for all of us. I was driving. As we neared the center I saw a big *fellah*, perhaps thirty years of age, coming from the opposite direction, teetering on his bicycle toward our side of the road. There was no other traffic. I slowed down and kept going, my car far to the right of the road. But the *fellah* did not seem to know how to ride a bicycle. Unexpectedly, he suddenly crossed the middle of the road, landing on our car's fender. He rolled off his bicycle, falling heavily on the pavement right in front of us. He lost his turban, injuring his scalp, and lay on the ground. We could hardly believe this was happening.

Natalie and I got out of the car and soon saw that he was not too badly wounded. With great presence of mind my wife took her red satchel from the car, knelt and started cleaning his wound with zephiran chloride, a foolproof antiseptic which she carried with her at all times. By then, having seen the accident, people began to gather in some numbers around us, perhaps as many as fifty, enough to make us wonder how this was going to turn out for us. I remembered then reading about what had happened just one year before Independence when Arabs had cut the throats of many Frenchmen, women and children in their homes at night during a famous uprising in Meknès. There was much chattering in Arabic around us that we did not understand. They finally calmed down as they looked at Natalie, a perfect stranger, caring for their friend, lying on the ground. It was obvious she had gained their respect, while we had been instead expecting a flow of insults and threats.

At that point we looked up and a French gendarme had arrived on the scene, still stationed there to help the newly organized Moroccan police in the rural areas.

"You have done enough, you have done enough, Madame!" he said. Natalie reluctantly gave up ministering to the Arab. I said, "Get a doctor." Ten minutes later, a two-wheeled mule-drawn cart, not very clean, arrived, and they hoisted the wounded man into it unceremoniously—he was quite a heavy man—to be taken to a clinic or the closest hospital. After that we were accompanied to the local gendarmerie where we had to declare our identity and occupation. The French officer in charge congratulated Natalie on taking care of the man. He told us we were lucky that the accident had not occurred during one of the recent troubled periods of the Protectorate as we probably would have been in danger of being maltreated, if not lynched.

From Rabat by car one could go to Meknès and Fez and back to Rabat in one day and even see the Roman ruins of Volubilis and the little holy Arab town of Moulay Adriss in another marvelous excursion. The *medina* of Fez, one of the greater centers of the Moslem world, left us with the feeling of having visited the oldest city on earth. It seemed older than Jerusalem. From the surrounding hills on which we stood, Fez appeared like a sea of flat roofs in a symphony of greys, beiges and ochres, its mosques and minarets dominating the sky. It was noon. A sort of dampened clamor was coming from the *souks*. The warm air over the city seemed to vibrate from the intense heat, rising from the buildings all day in the heat of the sun.

We entered Fez through the European quarters built by the French under Lyautey. It had wide avenues and tall apartment buildings, and we passed the *mellah*, the Jewish quarter. We reached the *medina* and the narrow crowded streets lined with hundreds of little shops displaying their goods and artifacts. As we walked, following an incredible flow of humans, literally taken along by the incessant stream of men, women and children in all kinds of garb, of donkeys loaded with merchandise, it was hard to slow our pace.

The atmosphere hung heavy with pungent aromas. Many of the shops bordering these tortuous alleys sold art objects made by local artisans still capable of reproducing the same graceful artifacts made in Andalusia in the sixteenth century when it was part of Islam. We watched the dexterity of these Fasi workers, seemingly responding only to their subconscious, copying the gestures of their ancestors. They were transforming copper, silk, rare woods, silver and gold into an infinity of graceful crafts, trinkets and other art forms which could make wonderful gifts. We still own one of their hanging lanterns with its colored glass cut in lozenges.

Then we arrived at the *Quaraouijne*, the grand mosque of Fez, and the *medersas* or Islamic schools occupying the center of the city. Someone compared their role in the spreading of religion and culture to that of Notre Dame de Paris and the Sorbonne in the Middle Ages. We visited one of the *medersas*. The students lived there in a sort of seedy old palace, its walls and patios covered with delicate mosaic designs.

On the way back to Rabat we stopped in Meknès, the city created by Sultan Moulay Ismail with its monumental gates called *Bab Berdaoui* and *Bab Mansur*. Not far from there we went to Volubilis on the promontory of a vast plan, the only important Roman ruins preserved in Morocco, including an arch of triumph and a forum.

Then we visited Moulay Idriss, the holy city of Morocco. Seen from Volubilis the village looked like a triangle of tight little white cubes anchored to the flank of the mountain. Idriss, a prophet chased out of Arabia, had arrived there long ago as a refugee. Accepted by the Berbers, he became the saint of Morocco. Periodically, on the occasion of the *Moussen*, a national festival, hundreds of tents are pitched on the hills as pilgrims flock from all over the country to sing, pray and offer sacrifices. The village, framed by beautiful olive groves, lay close to a most incredible narrow gorge and standing at the center was like a magnificent painting.

But it was in Rabat itself that we became most familiar with Arab life. On Throne Day we saw the Sultan going to pray with his retinue and a spectacular fantasia of tribal men on full-blooded Arabian horses.

One of the most attractive pastimes in Rabat was to sip Turkish coffee in the late afternoon on the terrace of a little bar which faced the entrance of the Casbah of the Oudayas, with its monumental chocolate brown battlemented walls. We would then walk back home through the *souks*, stopping in front of some of the shops, fascinated by the lengthy and animated bargaining taking place. Sometimes we would pass near the mosque at prayer time. In those years the electric clock had not yet replaced the *muezzin* announcing the hours of prayer from atop the minaret. *Muezzins* often were chosen from among blind men, who would not be tempted to look below at unveiled women resting in the patios of their houses. Down near the mosque entrance we observed men washing their feet in a decorated fountain before entering, while artisans halted their work to kneel to the East.

One day in the month of *Ramadan* our family was invited to a dinner at the home of the deputy minister of my Department, who was married to a French woman. All the guests including children arrived just before sunset. At the precise stroke of seven o'clock, the famished guests set upon the buffet with gusto, after an entire day of fasting. It was a matter of who could get there first. There was certainly no protocol then, but who could blame them.

Later we were invited to an elegant Arab wedding in Casablanca by a young friend in the government who had studied in the United States and was one of the rare Moroccans who spoke English in those years. His brother was getting married to his cousin, the daughter of his uncle. This type of marriage between close relatives is not unusual in the Moslem world. Nobody sees anything wrong in it. It is in the tradition that a marriage with a very close relation belonging to your parental lineage is much preferred. As a matter of fact, it is highly recommended to keep the boys in the family for the girls in the family.

By the end of our stay in Rabat I had been invited to quite a few Arab houses, often without my wife, according to custom. They all had an inside patio on which the rooms of the house opened, but their doors were usually closed. In wealthy families the patio was tiled and there were small mosaic fountains and flower basins. The host's welcome is formal but always very cordial. If a meal was served, female servants, veiled and silent, usually dressed in robes with bouffant trousers, would bring trays, crystal glasses or plain glasses, depending on the luxury of the home.

The food, in earthenware under straw conical covers, was served on low round tables around which the guests and hosts sat. With three fingers we were required, as elegantly as possible, to take the food with the right hand, directly from the plate. This is a must—be it small bits of *seksou*, lamb or breast of chicken. One dips them in a peppery and pimentoed sauce, terribly hot but delicious. If *pastilla* is served, you again must break the layers of pasta *(pâte feuilletée)* used for this famous sweet and delicate dish taken at the beginning of the meal, stuffed with bits of sugared pigeon. For me it was one of the daintiest and most succulent dishes I ever tasted in Morocco. It was usually followed by the traditional couscous, a mainstay. Servants constantly passed napkins and warm water to clean the hands.

As the end of our stay approached we had to sell the household furnishings we had acquired locally, bearing in mind the UN's tight policy on transporting household goods. This rule differed dramatically from that of the U.S. Foreign Service, whose personnel could take practically their entire household to their new posting and have it shipped home at the end of their mission. For UN people, selling one's own articles before leaving was a must. We had placed an ad in the morning paper. That afternoon, on returning from the office, I was taking my usual walk in our neighborhood of Agdal. Natalie had told me, before I left, that an Arab woman had called on the phone to say she wanted to see our refrigerator, which was for sale. In those years there were few refrigerators in the stores and those of departing foreigners were much sought after. I had just returned home when the bell rang and a young woman in a white *djellabah* presented herself, wanting to see our appliance.

I took her to the kitchen. She was fairly tall, though wearing leather *babouches* (sandals). All I could see were her eyes as she wore a white and blue veil over the lower part of her face. She asked a number of questions in excellent French. It seemed to me she must have been a teacher or the wife of a middle class Moroccan, likely a civil servant. The exchange went on for a few minutes.

As the electricity was not on and it was getting dark, I could not exactly distinguish the color of my interlocutor's eyes. Suddenly Natalie and Nancy began to laugh. They could not believe I did not recognize Carole's disguise. As she pulled down the veil, we all burst out in a roar of laughter. I must admit that they had had me. I was completely befuddled by Carole, who had put on the *djellabah* and veil Saadia had given to my wife.

In that economy, still starved for important household articles, we had no trouble disposing of the things we had to leave behind. To top it off, on the eve of our departure Nancy, to our great relief, was able to find a home for her two little kittens, Josie and Nappy.

* * *

Since we served there, Morocco has continued to progress with little upheaval or setback, staying as it was then a conservative and traditional kingdom. The people still solidly support their King. Although there were several attempts on the life of Hassan II, they failed. At present the predominant foreign policy issue is the conflict over the southern territory of Western Sahara, now in the process of being settled with UN help.

The *fellahs* undeniably have progressed since we were there, and their standard of living, though still low, has substantially improved in the last two decades. As in many countries there are serious economic difficulties, but Morocco is one developing nation which has held together well and can be proud of her accomplishments since Independence. It was indeed a privilege for me to have participated in these efforts.

HAITI: MISSION IMPOSSIBLE?

The Tragic Tale of a Fractured Country

HAITI: MISSION IMPOSSIBLE?

The Tragic Tale of a Fractured Country

A Challenging Job Offer

Haiti is one of the most fascinating countries I know. Its political, economic and social problems seem hopeless, but despite the extraordinary difficulties I met there in the early '60s, Haiti still retains for me all its exotic flavor and charm. So I keep hoping. I hope that the efforts have not been entirely wasted and that one day the Haitians will learn to govern themselves and prosper.

When David Owen, the Chairman of the United Nations Technical Assistance Board (TAB) offered me the post of UN Resident Representative in Haiti in the fall of 1959, Natalie and I had no hesitation in accepting. I was excited about the challenge directing the UN's programs in one of the most underdeveloped countries in the Third World. A UN "Res. Rep.," as he or she is called, is an international diplomat heading the UN missions of experts and technicians, advising the country on its economic and social development, coordinating all UN technical assistance activities, including those of the specialized agencies, and dealing with the government at the highest level. Besides, Natalie and I loved Haiti. We had been married in Port-au-Prince in 1941. We loved its beaches, its dramatic mountains and valleys, its people and their folklore and arts.

What Is Haiti?

Haiti is different things to different people. For those who only hear about it in the news, it is just a very poor country, a violent Caribbean island recently ruled by two ruthless dictators, Papa Doc and Baby Doc Duvalier. For many others, it is a "magic island," the land of the mysterious Voodoo religion practiced by the peasants.

Robert and Nancy Heinl [4] described it as a fragment of black Africa which had dislodged from the mother continent, drifted across the Atlantic and grounded in the

---

4 Robert and Nancy Heinl, *Written in Blood* (Boston: Houghton Mifflin, 1978).

Antilles. Before it became independent, it was the famous St-Domingue, "the pearl of the Antilles" which, thanks to slavery, became the richest French colony on earth in the 17th and 18th Centuries.

In 1791 the slaves revolted, murdering thousands of French planters, their wives and children. After a terrible 13-year guerrilla war, a powerful French force of 20,000 men sent by Napoleon Bonaparte ravaged by yellow fever and convinced that the slaves would never give up, surrendered to the slaves, and in 1804 independence was proclaimed.[5] This was an incredible feat which surprised and amazed the whole of Europe. Haiti was the first and only slave colony to win its own freedom by military victory and the second country in the Western Hemisphere, after the United States, to gain its independence. Haiti had followed gloriously in the steps of the French Revolution, at the cry of liberty.

But all this is in the distant past. The glory did not last. Today the country has six million people—poor, ill-fed and still malaria-ridden. Of all countries in the Western Hemisphere, it has the lowest life expectancy, the highest infant mortality, the lowest ratio of hospital beds, the lowest ratio of medical doctors (1 for 15,000 people), the lowest literacy rate (10-15 percent), the lowest agricultural yields and the lowest per capita consumption of electricity. In the rural areas the people still live in primitive conditions, isolated, never participating in the political life of the country.

The Tragic Fate of a Fractured Nation
How does one account for the fact that, after 175 years of independence, Haiti is still so violent, so wretchedly poor, wallowing in ignorance and misery? One could answer simply by saying that independence came too early, but I suggest there are four principal reasons for its abysmal backwardness: the paucity of its natural resources; the economic split of its society; the ignorance and the superstition of the rural masses; and the history of corrupt governments that Haiti has known since independence. The latter, in my view, has been the greatest obstacle to progress.

The population of the French colony of St-Domingue was divided into three groups: the white masters or planters, the *affranchis* or freed slaves (mostly mulattoes), and the slaves. The 1791 census indicates there were approximately 40,000 whites, 28,000 mulattoes, and half a million slaves. Only two classes remained after independence: the mulattoes, who took the place of the whites at the

---

5 Knowing he would soon lose Haiti and needing money for his European adventures, in 1803 Napoleon decided to rid himself of all New World encumbrances and sold New Orleans and Louisiana to the United States.

head of society, and the mass of illiterate slaves, who became free. Since then, the elite have contributed little to the advancement of the peasant class. The mulattoes have continued as a closed caste-oriented society possessing education, wealth and prestige, in which light skin—although less now than before—is still the object of pride and privilege. [6] Some blacks have prospered and there is now a small middle class. Certain of them have reached the upper class. There have been several black presidents and many black members of government. Economic considerations became more and more an important criterion, if we believe a Creole proverb which says, "The rich black is a mulatto, the poor mulatto is a black."

Among the poor, ignorant, Creole-speaking and voodoo-practicing people of the rural masses, the legacy is purely African. When I was there they seemed to express no apparent desire to be close to the upper class, as they continued to pass on their African heritage to their children. This lack of communication and cooperation over the years is still no doubt one of the greatest deterrents to the economic and social progress of Haiti.

The lack of natural resources is another major obstacle to development. There is no oil, only some copper ore—now almost exhausted—and some bauxite which is no longer exploited by an American company. The main resource is agriculture, but the shortage of arable land (only 15 percent of the total area) and a number of other major factors—primitive techniques, illiteracy, poor health, malnutrition, erosion, lack of access roads, rugged mountains hampering communications—limits agricultural production. Further, the peasants have cut most of the trees to make charcoal. As a result, Haiti is among the most eroded countries on earth. Its future depends on arresting the erosion that sadly continues with each torrential rain that carries its soil to the sea. The country suffers from periodic hurricanes, violent floods and drought. So generalized is poverty that peasant farmers seldom produce more than they need for day-to-day survival. Manufacturing is little developed. Artisanship has progressed and produces beautiful handicrafts, while assembly industry for export has become the most important source of employment in Port-au-Prince.

Health, illiteracy and religion are other major causes of underdevelopment. There are dramatic deficiencies in the diet. People suffer from malaria, tuberculosis, parasitic infections and other diseases. Infant mortality was as high as 20 percent of live births when I was there, and mortality among those between the ages of one and four is thought to be as high as 25 percent. As many as 15 percent of all infants

---

6 In the 18th century, the courts of St-Domingue recognized as many as 10 major and 200 minor blood combinations

die during the first eight weeks of life, many from umbilical tetanus. These conditions are slowly being corrected by a devoted number of small medical services which are hampered by limited financial resources, and by a large number of foreign charitable organizations.

Close to 85 percent of the people are illiterate. The Haitian peasant has always lived in fear; first of his parents in childhood, then of his political and religious leaders. Thus, until recently, he preferred to live in isolation in his mountains and valleys and not to participate in the affairs of the country. But what he still fears most is the wrath of the *loas*, the voodoo gods, even more than the *chefs de sections*, the traditionally harsh representatives of the government in rural areas.

While the mulatto elite adopted French culture, including Catholicism, the peasants kept voodoo as a religion, although after 1860 African rituals were fused with Catholic liturgy, a factor which made Haitian voodoo different from African cults. Although not officially recognized, and looked down upon by the mulatto elite, Dr. François Duvalier supported voodoo and was one of its followers.

Voodoo deals with the spiritual forces of the universe. It came from Dahomey[7] and includes the invocation and placation of numerous *loas* or spirits, including magic, cults of the dead, music and dance. At the summit, above all the *loas*, is the Christian God, the *Bon Dieu*, good and omnipotent. There are hundreds of *loas*, and some are linked to Catholic saints and look like them in their representations. In Haiti, many people still believe in *zombies* and *bakalous*.[8]

The deficiency in education is still frightful in Haiti. Only 12 percent of school-age children were going to school in 1970. The instruction imparted in the rural schools is poor, causing an extremely high dropout rate. The children are taught in French, which few pupils comprehend. Haiti has two languages: Creole is spoken at home by the peasants and by the elite with their servants; French, the official language, is spoken and understood only by the upper and middle classes, representing about 10 percent of the population. Creole is a complete language, an African version of old French from Normandy and Brittany, used by the slaves to communicate among themselves and with their white masters. It was the *lingua franca* of the slaves who came from different parts of Africa, each with their own tribal language.

---

7 Now called Bénin.
8 A *zombie* is someone presumed to have died, been buried and then resurrected to become the permanent slave of the evil person who engineered his death; a *bakalou* is an evil spirit said to make devilish bargains with people, bestowing upon them some greatly desired power in exchange for the death of a member of their family—then another and another. Source: James G. Leyburn, *The Haitian People*, (New Haven: Yale University Press, 1966) and O. Ernest Moore, *Haiti, Its Stagnant and Shackled Economy* (New York: Exposition Press, 1972).

Until recently, French was compulsory in the schools; but recently Creole has become the learning language during the first school years in the rural areas, it being realized much too late that the children could not master French sufficiently to properly learn the basic elements of education in hygiene, farming, etc.

In Haiti the power has always been centered in the hands of a president. With the exception of the 19 years of American occupation (1915-1934), the presidents have ruled with absolute authority, often as cruel dictators. President Duvalier declared himself President-for-life and bestowed the same title on his son, Jean-Claude. The administration has always been corrupt, the civil service and the finances of the state always in a precarious situation.

Such were the conditions that prevailed when I arrived in Haiti in 1959, one year after Dr. François Duvalier (called Papa Doc) had been elected President of the Republic.

Papa Doc

When I landed in Port-au-Prince to take up my new duties as UNDP Resident Representative, the Haitian Government had failed to meet in full its counterpart obligations under our technical assistance agreement, and my first task was to put strong pressure on the authorities to reverse the situation. However, I had no idea of the conditions under which the program would have to operate, nor the regime of terror later imposed on the Haitian people by the *Tontons Macoute*,[9] as my mission unfolded. During my three-and-a-half years in Haiti, I came to know Papa Doc, his greed for power, the cruel and constant war he waged against the opponents of his regime, and the inner workings of his government.

I had cordial relations with the Ministers with whom I had to deal. Their authority was, however, limited, all important matters being referred to the President for final decision. My work in Port-au-Prince was certainly the most difficult of my career as an international civil servant. Yet I loved the Haitian people.

A few days after my arrival, I was invited to meet the President and present my credentials. This was to take place in the glittering white National Palace on the Champ-de-Mars, a wide park-like thoroughfare lined with high stone pedestals topped by statues of Haitian Independence heroes—Dessalines, Toussaint-L'-Ouverture, Christophe, and Pétion. My official car, flying UN colors, left me at the entrance to the Palace. Accompanied by two guards in bright uniforms, I climbed the monumental marble stairs to the *Salon d'Attente* adjoining the President's office. After a wait, I was finally asked to come in to meet the President. As I was about to

---

9 Meaning: bogeymen, in Creole; the private militia of the President.

cross the threshold into his office, I was brusquely stopped by two officers of the guard who proceeded to search me for weapons. Given the nature of my visit, this was a shock. (Later I found that this was standard procedure at the Palace.) I was even more surprised when, on entering the office, I noticed two officers of his private guard standing at attention on each side of the President, who was seated at an enormous mahogany desk. One had a submachine gun pointed at me, the other a cocked carbine. I could also distinguish part of a revolver on the desk, half hidden by papers, which he later resituated on a small table at his side.

President Duvalier, a small dark man, then 52, was wearing enormous glasses with thick lenses. He extended a limp, clammy hand to me. In his soft, hardly audible voice, he greeted me without a smile or apparent feeling. After the usual first exchange of words we started a conversation during which I did most of the talking. I described briefly the projects we were supporting, all essential to the progress of the country, such as improvement of the infrastructure, agriculture, health, education, the training of civil servants and vocational training. I expressed the hope that the Government would meet its obligations regarding each of the projects.

I explained the need for the Haitian Government to make available, in accordance with already signed agreements, the required monetary contributions—then in arrears—as well as the local counterpart personnel without which the projects could not operate smoothly. He agreed, and the money was later obtained to the satisfaction of UN Headquarters.

The President expressed an interest in my earlier experience in Haiti in 1941-42 with the Standard Fruit & Steamship Company. It had installed collection counters everywhere in the rural areas where peasants could bring their bananas and sell them to the company. I stressed the fact that it was the first time that the small farmers had been able to get instant money for their efforts at growing a cash crop for export. I said I was sorry that the company had had to leave Haiti.

As Papa Doc knew very well, it was former President Dumarsais Estimé, his friend and mentor, who had destroyed this new industry in 1947 by refusing to renew the company's contract. Estimé gave the concession to eight senators who were his friends. They knew little about the export of such a perishable fruit and as a result, two years after banana exports fell from seven million stems to just about 200,000; the industry never recovered and Haiti no longer exports bananas. But the President expressed no regrets about this, even though the banana export industry could have been a savior for the economy.

As we talked, I wanted to discuss the crucial problem of rural development, and tactfully remarked that the six percent of the regular national budget earmarked that year for rural services, including agriculture and education, was only a tiny fraction of what was needed to bring about a significant improvement in this most important sector of the economy. I told him that the UN hoped that Haiti would increase expenditures for this sector so that an expanded program of assistance could be undertaken. He agreed that it was needed but the high cost of the army had to be met first. This was essential, he said, for the security of Haiti and could not be reduced. He meant, of course, the security of his regime. On this discouraging note, after nearly two hours, the interview ended, leaving me more discouraged.

I met with the President a few times after. He did not like to receive foreign officials and left most discussions to his ministers. I saw him at official functions at the Palace or at parties, where he always arrived late, walking like a zombie and giving handshakes as cold as ice. His cold hands could have been from fear, but it was well known that he suffered from a heart condition and diabetes.

Who was this man who practically destroyed his country and acquired the reputation as one of the world's worst dictators? François Duvalier was born in 1907, the son of a Justice of the Peace, a black from the poor middle class of Port-au-Prince. He attended the *Lycée Pétion* in Bel-Air, a popular district of the capital. After graduation from the Medical School of the University of Port-au-Prince, he began a practice and married a mulatto, Simone Olive Faine, who bore him four children, including Jean-Claude, his only son. Because he was a medical doctor, Duvalier was able to join the American-Haitian Health Cooperative Service in the 1940s and was given a scholarship to the University of Michigan to study public health and epidemiology, but did not graduate. Back in Haiti, Duvalier was appointed Under-Secretary of Labor. Later he was made Minister of Labor and Public Health.

Somewhat an intellectual and deeply interested in African culture and voodoo, Duvalier determined that his country should turn away from the Euro-American culture. He wanted the people to find their inspiration in *negritude*, a new philosophy and African mystique developed by Senghor, the French-educated President of the Republic of Sénégal, and other black intellectuals of French expression in West Africa. François Duvalier became a member of the *Griots*, a group of *noirist* intellectuals with leftist tendencies who demanded social justice for the masses. He was an admirer of Dessalines, Lenin and Franck Fanon. Because of his political ambitions and somewhat extreme views, Duvalier was a strong adversary of the regime of President Magloire in the '50s and had to go into hiding to escape arrest.

In 1957, after Magloire's fall, Duvalier declared himself a candidate for the Presidency. With his announced desire to work for the betterment of the masses, and the support of the army, as well as the favorable view of his candidacy by the United

States, he won the election handily. As always in Haiti, there was, of course, the usual amount of fraud during the election, but he took over the Presidency with considerable support and encouragement. However, almost immediately after the election, his enemies declared open war against him, and from 1959 to 1963, during my days in Port-au-Prince, planted bombs exploded at random, people disappeared mysteriously, Army officers found themselves purged, while hundreds of Haitians were jailed and tortured—many died in front of firing squads.

A half a dozen or so invasions were attempted by small groups of exiles who came from Florida and across the border from the Dominican Republic. All were repulsed. One, however, came so incredibly close to success that Duvalier actually had packed his suitcases and was ready to leave his palace for the safety of the Colombian Embassy.

Two other tragic events, striking examples of the way Duvalier pursued his enemies, deeply shocked the population. The first was his relentless search for Clément Jumelle, in hiding for 21 months. He had been Finance Minister under President Magloire. I had met him then and was impressed by his sincere desire to help his country. He had a Ph.D. from the University of Chicago and was the most highly-trained Haitian official. In 1955 he had been a friend of Duvalier and had helped him when he was in hiding. He had been a candidate for the presidency in 1957. But Papa Doc considered Jumelle responsible for recent bombings in Port-au-Prince and wanted to eliminate him. With Jumelle in hiding, Duvalier sent one of his top *Tontons Macoute*, Capt. Jean Beauvoir, with his goons to kill Jumelle's brothers. They were shot in cold blood while asleep, and the man who had sheltered them was tortured to death. Seriously ill with uremic poisoning, Clément Jumelle was forced to come out of hiding to find medical help in Port-au-Prince.

One night, disguised as an old woman and accompanied by his wife, he rang the bell of the Cuban Embassy. A doctor was called by the Ambassador, but it was too late to save him and he died that night. His body was taken to his mother's house on Avenue Charles Sumner. The funeral was arranged for the next day. As the funeral cortege slowly approached the Church of the Sacré-Coeur, followed by hundreds of sympathizers, a police car screeched to a halt beside the hearse. Two men jumped out, threw the wreaths and flowers on the ground, grabbed the coffin and drove away. The body was taken to the Palace, to Duvalier, who viewed it and ordered that it be taken to a cemetery near St-Marc to be buried with voodoo rites. Jumelle, a devout Catholic, was buried without a priest. The stopping of the funeral and the stealing of the coffin appeared as a scene in Graham Greene's novel *The Comedians*.

The second outrageous event began at the door of *Collège Bird*, which I passed every morning on the way to the office, and concerned Clément Barbot and two of the President's children. Barbot had been Duvalier's most loyal and oldest friend, his principal aide and counselor and hatchetman. He had been the head of the *Tontons Macoute*, protecting the President at all times, and acted for him during the latter's heart attack. But Duvalier became suspicious of Barbot's loyalty when the latter had close contacts with the U.S. Marine Mission and Embassy. He believed Barbot had discussed his mental state (which was the subject of many rumors) and also his misuse of American aid. As a result, Barbot had been arrested and imprisoned by Duvalier in Fort Dimanche. After 16 months he was released and placed under house arrest, but he escaped and went into hiding and with a small group of men decided to wage a merciless war against Duvalier.

On April 26, 1963, as I was driving to my office I saw one of the Presidential limousines taking Duvalier's children, Simone, 14, and Jean-Claude, 12, to *Collège Bird*. It was suddenly attacked by the occupants of a car which had been following. The driver of the limousine and the two *Tontons Macoute* bodyguards were shot, but the children were spared and managed to get into their school. This attack was the first coup by Clément Barbot's men, as Barbot had sworn that he would succeed in destroying the President.

The *Macoute's* search for the assailants of the children's limousine was savage. Oddly enough, the President did not think of Barbot as the perpetrator of the attack because he felt that there was only one man in Haiti who could pick off the bodyguards from a moving car. He had to be a super marksman. This made him immediately suspect Lt. François Benoit, the star of the Haitian Army rifle team. Duvalier sent his goons to look for him at his modest home in Bois Verna, a house I passed four times a day by car. Arriving in front of the house in this bourgeois neighborhood, the *Macoute* in cold blood murdered Benoit's father—a retired judge—his wife and a neighbor who were calmly sitting on the front porch. They mowed down the servants and even Benoit's pets, leaving the bodies in the street to be eaten by dogs and rot in the heat. Then they set fire to the house, which I saw burning. Fortunately, the Lieutenant's pregnant wife was not at home.

Lt. Benoit, however, did not perpetrate the killing at the College. He had been purged from the Army a few days before and had taken asylum in the Dominican Embassy. When the President became aware of this, in a rage he sent his henchmen to the Embassy to capture Benoit. This was the first time since 1915 that the sanctity of asylum in a Latin American embassy had been violated. The Chargé d'Affaires and the guards of the Embassy succeeded in chasing out the *Tontons*, who then occupied only the grounds.

Upon hearing of this, the President of the Dominican Republic, Juan Bosch, was irate. He immediately put his army on war footing and threatened Duvalier with an invasion of Haiti and a bombing of the Palace. This created an international diplomatic incident. Duvalier broke relations with Bosch and placed the conflict on the agenda of the UN Security Council. René Chalmers, the Foreign Minister, went to New York to defend his country's actions. As we watched all of this, a commission from the Organization of American States came to Port-au-Prince to investigate the situation, holding off the threatened invasion. Then, a few days later the *Tontons* found Barbot, the real author of the Collège Bird incident, hiding in a cornfield on the edge of the city. They set fire to it and Barbot, forced out, was shot.

As the years passed Duvalier became more violent and machiavellian. He decided to eliminate 19 officers of his guard who were imprisoned in Fort Dimanche, all of them friends of his son-in-law, Lt. Col. Max Dominique, the husband of Marie-Denise. The night of the execution, he selected 19 other officers of the guard, including his son-in-law, who were given rifles with one bullet each and were lined up facing the 19 officers to be executed. Behind each officer was a soldier with a submachine gun aimed at his back, with orders to kill anyone who did not pull his trigger at the order of "Fire!" Duvalier participated in the execution, shooting some of the victims with his own gun. The following day, Mrs. Duvalier interceded for her daughter and son-in-law and they immediately left Haiti for Europe.

During all those years, the United States Government was very concerned about Haiti, not only because it represented—in the words of Secretary of State Dean Rusk—"a kind of political cesspool right on our back step," but because we could not think of Haiti without being appalled by the miserable condition of her people. Washington thought Haiti was an open invitation for the establishment of a Castro-type dictatorship. Actually, Duvalier was an opportunist, not a Communist, but he had quite a few communists in his government, and a deal with Castro was not an impossibility.

Duvalier practiced voodoo and had made Zacharie Delva, a well-known *houngan* (voodoo priest) a top official in his government. It was rumored he held secret ceremonies in the Palace with him and other spiritual advisors. It was known at the Presidential Palace that President Kennedy hated the Duvalier regime. Ironically, voodoo was the only weapon the Haitian President could use against him. It was known that a chief *bocor* (a special voodoo priest) helped Duvalier cast an *ouanga à mort*[10] on the U.S. President.

---

10 A voodoo spell or curse meant to harm or kill someone. A French journal of astrology had predicted that Kennedy would be assassinated on November 22, 1963. It happened that 22 was

Ultimately Duvalier wanted to be President-for-Life like his political hero, Jean-Jacques Dessalines, who had made himself Emperor-for-Life. First he thought of calling an election to give him a new six-year term. But other presidents had tried this and had been ousted each time. So in 1961 he dissolved the two Chambers and decreed new legislative elections for a unicameral 57-man National Assembly. On the ballots, printed in the Palace, were the names of the Duvalierist candidates, and above the list, in place of the usual heading, the words: "République d'Haiti, Docteur François Duvalier, Président de la République."

With no opponents, the returns came in at 1,320,748 votes for the list, while it was estimated that there were only about 1 million persons eligible to vote in the country. Since the President's name was printed on each ballot, it could only be construed that François Duvalier had been re-elected. How could he then refuse to serve his people another term after such a mandate? The world was shocked at the news. The *New York Times* of May 13, 1961, wrote it was "the most outrageously rigged election ever seen in Latin America." Later, Duvalier declared himself President-for-Life.

I don't think Papa Doc was greatly interested in personal enrichment. He did not live ostentatiously, in contrast with his son Jean-Claude and his son's wife, Michèle. However, a great deal of money was accumulated in Swiss banks for his family, and real estate was acquired in France. The funds President Duvalier sorely needed were for his pet projects at home, such as the construction of a new town he called Duvalierville. He raised this money from a compulsory contribution of 10 percent deducted from the salaries of Haitian civil servants and from cash to be supplied by shopkeepers who were threatened with arrest or were mugged if they did not immediately deliver.

The Treasury was being plundered on a grand scale, as some of the President's friends diverted non-fiscal funds into their own pockets. These funds included proceeds from monopolies such as tobacco, rice, and sugar which should have been shown in the regular budget because, according to international standards of public accounting, non-fiscal accounts wre blatantly irregular since they invite all kinds of corruption. Having them was strongly criticized by the U.S. Embassy, the International Monetary Fund (IMF), myself and our UN fiscal expert. We made several formal presentations and wrote our Headquarters, but nothing was done to change

a sacred number for Duvalier, as he always scheduled important state events on that day of the month. When the prediction came true, Duvalier credited his *ouanga* with it and, a short time after, he sent an emissary to Arlington National Cemetery to collect some soil from Kennedy's grave in order to protect himself and Haiti from any harm that could come from the dead President's spirit.

the system until later when, as a result of continuous pressure from the IMF, some improvements appeared, although the fiscal system needed a complete overhaul.

Helping the Haitian People

Haiti was one of the first countries in the world to be assisted by the United Nations. Starting in the 1950s, the UN mission supplied experts for periods varying from a few weeks to several years in many priority fields such as basic education, agricultural extension, community development, cooperatives and credit, poultry and livestock raising, veterinary science, public administration, monetary and fiscal problems, vocational education, rural industries, hotel management, civil aviation, eradication of diseases and social welfare. Jointly financed by the newly established UN Special Fund and the Government of Haiti, in 1959 our program also included two major pre-investment projects: an irrigation and agricultural development scheme in the north, in the area of Port-de-Paix, demonstrating the proper growing of food crops by small farmers to be grouped in cooperatives, and an important first-time cattle raising project in the Plains des Cayes in the south for meat and dairy products and for the training of veterinarians.

We also assisted the Government in the creation of an Economic Planning Office (CONADEP) and the preparation of an economic development plan, something entirely new in Haiti. The country had been thoroughly surveyed by a team of UN experts in 1948-49 and a large number of recommendations for government reforms and for development projects and programs had been formulated, to be undertaken when funds would become available—which meant, in the largest part, with foreign financial assistance in view of the lack of domestic savings.[11]

Bilateral assistance was important. The largest program was that of the U.S. Government (USAID), particularly in the fields of agriculture, rural education and health. The French helped in several education programs and set up a teacher training institute. The Germans were busy in underground water projects in various parts of the country, while the World Bank and the Inter-American Bank were providing loans for a variety of agricultural and industrial projects and regional development schemes. There was no duplication in any of these projects, which were well coordinated.

The UN program was proceeding fairly satisfactorily. Progress continued until 1962 when the political situation markedly deteriorated. The terrible acts perpetrated by the *Tontons Macoute*, people's fears, the violations of human rights and the instability of the country as a whole began to adversely affect technical assistance

---

11 *Mission to Haiti* (New York: United Nations, 1950).

and the efficiency of our work. Although there were other harsh dictatorships in the world where foreign assistance continued to be granted on a much larger scale than in Haiti, I was personally concerned and wondered whether we should continue our assistance to a government such as that of Dr. Duvalier. I was able, through my own channels, to keep my headquarters informed of the full situation. I also took all possible precautions to see that our funds would not be jeopardized. I was always ready to go to the government and demand that its counterpart contributions to assisted projects be made available in time. I often obtained satisfaction, thanks to my personal visits to Antonio André, President of the Banque Nationale, the central bank of Haiti, who was authorized to release Government funds. He was a trusted friend, fighting for us at the Ministry of Finance and at the Palace. I made sure that we would never transfer the property of UN equipment to the Government until a project was completed and on several occasions threatened to send the equipment to another country if we were not satisfied.

Despite my firm attitude, I remained popular with the ministers, who respected my demands and sometimes did their best to change the situation. The UN did not stop its assistance, nor did the other donors. We did not, however, approve new projects, but only completed existing works provided the Government met its obligations.

Another reason for continuing our assistance was that most of the projects were rural development initiatives concerned with the building of the infrastructure of the country (irrigation, conservation, health care and education) which would be useful at a future time when political conditions would improve. Another fear was that some Haitians trained abroad under our fellowship program would not return to Haiti or that some of the counterpart staff in our projects would leave the country for political reasons. But even in these exceptional cases, not numerous, it could be expected that one day they would return to their country to serve a new government.

More serious would have been the cancellation of projects of a humanitarian character, affecting the life of poor people already in a dangerous state of malnutrition and health. For this reason, UNICEF and the UN World Food Programs as well as other non government-agencies continued their programs in health care, relief work and food-for-work activities.

One incident, however, brought about the end of the World Bank financial assistance to the important national program of road maintenance, carried out by the Italian contractor Techint. Its many trucks at the depot had been requisitioned by Papa Doc to transport hundreds of peasants to Port-au-Prince to demonstrate in his favor on a Sunday at a mass rally in front of the National Palace. A Haitian employee of Techint had tried to prevent the use of the trucks for such a blatant political purpose. During the night he was savagely killed. His dead body was nailed to the entrance door of Techint, as if he had been crucified. This gruesome spectacle deeply shocked us all. A photograph was sent to the World Bank in Washington but, to my knowledge, was never made public by the Bank. Techint, however, left Haiti immediately and its important project was canceled.

Towards the end of my mission, in April 1963, at the time of a threatened invasion by the Army of the Dominican Republic, Duvalier became scared and, at one point, was ready to leave the country. I was convinced that if all the diplomatic representatives in Port-au-Prince, duly mandated by their governments for this purpose, had gone to the Palace and together made a strong representation to the President to the effect that the international community could no longer tolerate the behavior of his Government, he would have left Haiti.

This could have been combined with an embargo on oil imports[12] and the temporary cancellation of all aid to Haiti. Several ambassadors shared my personal views, but some either did not dare or did not want to take such a position. The French Ambassador in particular was against any curtailment of assistance or *démarche* of all ambassadors together, as, he said, de Gaulle was in personal correspondence with Duvalier. I wrote a confidential memorandum to my headquarters recommending that in the eventuality of Duvalier's departure a Council for External Assistance to Haiti be created, including the principal donors, to assist a provisional government in implementing needed reforms and control the spending of funds, pending new elections.

None of the above were ever undertaken, leaving me angry and frustrated. But soon after, the U.S. withdrew its aid mission. I still maintain that the international community lost various opportunities to rid Haiti of Duvalier without recourse to forced intervention in those years by not presenting a common diplomatic front. As a result, Duvalier continued to rule until his death peacefully in bed eight years later. His dictatorship had lasted 14 years, followed by 15 years under Jean-Claude's rule—a total of 29 years during which the country fell into complete ruin, the two regimes causing untold death and destruction.

A Colorful Social Life
During my first months in Port-au-Prince, social life among the Haitian elite, the diplomatic corps and the business community continued at the same fast rhythm as in my earlier years there. I received numerous invitations, declining some because

---

[12] A move finally taken in 1993 to force a solution to a political crisis.

of my work, but I could not ignore them even if I had wanted; they provided the contacts I needed and scads of information about what was going on in the island—through the *Télédiol*, the famous Haitian grapevine—that I never would otherwise have gleaned. I must also admit that at these receptions at private homes and hotels, often in beautiful flower-filled gardens of tropical ambience, one could meet the most attractive cosmopolitan people. Life had a glamor you would not have expected in a place like Haiti. Yet one could feel a little guilty in attending some of these parties with displays of luxury and high living which contrasted with the poverty and misery in surrounding Port-au-Prince, even though we know these contrasts exist in most capitals of the developing world and elsewhere. In Haiti, somehow, it seemed worse. But, they were part of the life of Port-au-Prince associated with tourism, and without them, this picture would be incomplete.

When I left Connecticut for Haiti in the fall of 1959, our daughters' school year had started. Natalie stayed in New Canaan with them until the end of the school year, so my family did not join me in Port-au-Prince until July of 1960. During my first weeks there, I lived at the *Hôtel Sans Souci*, an attractive former plantation house located in town near the Champs-de-Mars, where foreign service personnel usually stayed on arrival pending the finding of a suitable house. A long driveway planted with very tall royal palm trees led to the hotel. Behind it, a swimming pool and a deep beautiful tropical garden formed the right kind of decor for the formal dinners and *soirées dansantes* the *Sans Souci* gave on Thursday nights under a sky studded with stars.

Each of Port-au-Prince's fine hotels had its own night in the week for this kind of chic entertainment for the beautiful people of Port-au-Prince and tourists discovering the culture and music of the country. The show, always a brilliant one at the *Sans Souci*, featured folk dancers executing St-Domingue minuets in colorful costumes of the colonial period, Congo dances, and sometimes a voodoo-type spectacle accompanied by drums. A lively local band played popular meringue tunes, and Viennese waltzes and Hungarian polkas for the enjoyment of the dancing guests. I attended a few of those evenings, but I missed my family, wishing June would soon come so Natalie could join me.

Monday was the evening for the *Hotel Oloffson*, where I had stayed in 1941 when I came to Port-au-Prince to join the Standard Fruit Company. The Hotel, a white, exotic gingerbread mansion with several turrets, pointed roofs and a wide verandah, resembled a Charles Addams house. It rose up on a small hill at the end of a lane lined with gigantic palm trees. The hotel's style had changed greatly. Its *soirées* were well attended by tourists who flocked to see their brilliant pseudo-voodoo shows with dancers and drummers—*Baron Samedi*, the best known *loa*, leading the ballet with his cane, his top hat and black dress coat, associated in the minds of people with President François Duvalier. The Baron's emblems are a skull and crossbones, and he lives in cemeteries.

In those years the *Oloffson* was managed by an American from Long Island, Al Seitz, who succeeded in attracting a repeat clientele of well-known American and English jet-setters, including writers, artists, journalists, and some just plain lovers of its picturesque ambiance and famous rum punches. The hotel boasted a Sir John Gielgud suite and even one called "John Barrymore," although I don't know if he actually slept there. Truman Capote visited several times.

The hotel became famous world-wide from a scene in Graham Greene's novel *The Comedians*, and in 1967 in the film of the same name starring Richard Burton and Elizabeth Taylor. It showed the luxurious swimming pool where the Minister of Health, Dr. Philipot (a fictional character) was drowned, his throat cut by the *Tontons Macoute* in the worst days of Papa Doc's regime. Curiously enough, I dealt with the Minister of Health, an engaging young Duvalierist, not a doctor, who had nothing to do with Dr. Philipot in the novel except his name, Philippeau. The hotel had 30 rooms, was always booked solid all winter, and it is told that Burton, who portrayed the owner in the film, had to stay elsewhere on a visit to Haiti two years later because a clerk, not recognizing him, was unable to find him a room.

By December I had had enough of hotel life. I wanted a quiet place where I could work in the late afternoon and evening. Horace and Gordana Ashton, an American couple and friends since our first stay in Port-au-Prince in 1941, invited me to join them as a paying guest in their extraordinary mountaintop home, Villa Rosa. From it one had a beautiful view of the bay where, in the distance, often in a haze, one could see the mysterious, primitive and rarely visited island of La Gonave. Another American friend once said, "It was worth going to Haiti just to stand on the porch of the Ashtons and look at the view."

The French doors of my room opened onto a terrace with an elegant stone balustrade. After office hours I could work there in peace and admire the constantly changing sky, the surrounding mountains and the bay. Each evening brought a glorious sunset, the sky aflame with rose and gold. As the sun was setting, the lights of the city below would suddenly shine through the mantle of darkness enveloping it, giving the illusion of dancing and twinkling candles in the warm atmosphere of the night. From time to time the hum of an approaching plane sounded in the dark distant sky, growing in intensity as the lone craft flew over the bay, its projector beam pointing its sharp descent toward the airport.

A Voodoo Ceremony

Horace and another American, Stanley Reser, who had stayed over after the American occupation, were probably the only white men in Port-au-Prince expert on the rituals of the Voodoo religion, fascinated by its supernatural character. Horace knew several *houngans*. One evening he invited me to join him for a ceremony far out in the country—far afield from the usual tourist affairs.

We left by Jeep at twilight, crossed a mountain range into a dark valley, crossed a river on the only bridge in that area, forded a couple of streams and passed a few deserted hamlets where the people were already shut up for the night in their *cailles*. On the other side of the valley we could see the Morne silhouetted against the dark blue sky, becoming lighter as the moon rose over the horizon. Then we heard the gentle beating of drums, and the faint singing of the women as we approached the *houmfort*, the small unpretentious rustic ceremonial temple.

Horace explained that the circle of family, friends and neighbors who had asked the *houngan* to hold the ceremony for them had to pay him a handsome sum, and they also needed authorization from the *gendarmerie* to hold the ceremony. The service we were about to see was held for the benefit of a newborn infant. The family had come with many others to worship the spirits, thus assuring that this would bring luck and happiness to the infant for the rest of his life.

On the way to the ceremony, Horace and I talked at length about voodoo. He insisted that it is a true religion, recognized by serious anthropologists. As such, Voodoo helps its followers over the difficulties of birth and death and all life's hurdles in between. God, the *Bon Dieu*, the supreme being, and all his pantheon of spirits, called *loas*, can be approached directly. For each follower's prayer there is a corresponding spirit that is invoked, and when a *loa* comes down on earth he may "mount" a worshiper in a phenomenon called "possession." This reveals to the audience the divine will.

I did not know for sure whether Horace strongly believed in Voodoo but he was fascinated by the relationship in it between the living and the dead, and he seemed to take it quite seriously. He said that there was great flexibility in Voodoo ceremonies and that the service might well continue with what is called in Creole *rétirer d'en bas de l'eau*, (recalling the spirits of the dead below the waters), where they are supposed to have gone at the time of death. This was to protect a deceased person. If the deceased is not recalled one year and a day after death, Horace said, he or she would become a wandering evil spirit who would avenge itself against its relations by inflicting upon them all kinds of vexations and illnesses.

When we arrived the ceremony had just started. There were perhaps 100 people, most sitting under the *tonnelle*, a large shed roofed with corrugated metal, also called *peristyle*, in front of the *houmfort*, the temple itself, which looked like a large *caille*. It had a wooden altar littered with sacred objects, on which offerings to the gods were displayed, including bottles of wine and liqueurs and various dishes of food brought by the family financing the ceremony. Together with the fee paid to the *houngan*, the purchase of these offerings usually left the family in debt for many months, but they believed the gods required sustenance and the faithful must make sacrifices to please them. Above the altar, against the walls, were a cross and images of saints identified with certain *loas*, as Haitian voodoo is a mixture of Catholic ritual and animist cult. Most visible in the badly-lit *tonnelle*, around the central post or *poteau-mitan* supporting the roof from which the spirits are supposed to descend to earth, seven *hounsis*, young girls at the service of the *houngan*, were standing in long white robes and turbans, about to start a dance procession. They were directed by a *mambo*, the voodoo priestess who assisted the *houngan*. Before the ceremony the *houngan* had designed voodoo tracings with flour on the ground to honor the *loas*, beautiful intricate signs representing various deities such as Damballah (the serpent), Legba (god of crossroads), the Marassas (twins), etc.

As there is no assigned place for the public, we soon moved to the other side of the peristyle to get away from the increasingly unbearable and frantic beating of the drums. The *houngan* then called on Legba, a *loa* who is the guardian of crossroads, saying in Creole, "*Papa Legba, ouvre barrière pou moin!*" ("Papa Legba, open the gate for me!") This started the rituals of the service which included a series of benedictions, genuflections and responses, as well as chants orchestrated by the *houngan*. Certain rites were similar to those of the Roman Catholic mass.

During the service, which lasted several hours and tired me considerably, we saw three possessions. One occurred of a middle-aged woman who suddenly felt she was "mounted" by a *loa*, the woman becoming the god's horse, and taking the characteristics of the deity. The sudden lodging of the *loa*[13] in the head of the woman generated a violent shaking of her whole body and the shouting of some incoherent words from the god possessing her. She danced in a disorderly way around the *poteau-mitan* and embraced various persons, growing completely hysterical and finally losing her balance and falling in a swoon to the ground. The trance continued for some time, her face contorted in pain, as she was probably threatened by the *loa*. As she was regaining her senses, Horace said she would remember nothing of what had happened to her that night.

There were many interruptions and much *clairin* (raw rum) was being con-

13 I never learned which *loa* it was.

sumed, but nobody seemed drunk. All voodoo ceremonies are excuses for having a good time, and someone said that 90 percent are an occasion for a *bamboche*, a joyous party; that was the impression I got. We saw the sacrifice of a chicken and a goat.

We drove back to Port-au-Prince in the middle of the night. It was 3 a.m. Horace was still excited by the service. The *houngan* certainly exercised a great deal of power over these poor, ignorant and gullible people. My mind was seldom off my work, and an idea struck me. I thought that if one could mobilize and train *houngans* as community development agents they might exercise the needed leadership at the community level and teach people to modernize their ways; a thought, of course, on reflection, I rejected, since most *houngans* are illiterate and would not wish to renounce their privileges and sources of personal influence and revenues by destroying voodoo in the process. Only basic education of the masses (a very long-term task) by specially-trained teachers would make people gradually abandon this terrible deterrent to progress.

A Romantic Gingerbread House

In the spring of 1960 I began to look seriously for a house to rent, one that suited my function as a UN representative and met the need for entertaining that my job entailed. I found the loveliest gingerbread house still in good condition in Port-au-Prince. Its gingerbread embellishments mimicked lace and, with the peaked eaves, added atmosphere. It had a garden of five acres with beautiful trees and a long cobblestone walk which led to the gate. In front was a rotunda-shaped terrace bordered by a white stone balustrade, tropical plants and potted palmettos. The branches of a giant African tulip tree with its red flowers hovered over the terrace and the steps leading to the verandah entrance.

I cannot resist describing it and telling its story. It was a two-story house, each story with its own verandah extending along the front of the building, each with gingerbread balustrade, the gingerbread repeated symmetrically under the roof, giving the house much elegance. The first floor featured a long living room and a dining room with fine mahogany furniture and two magnificent crystal chandeliers from Czechoslovakia. On the second floor there were a number of bedrooms, each with tall French doors opening on the verandah. Lying on the bed of the master bedroom one could see the entire bay and the mountains toward Montrouis and St-Marc, a breathtaking view. The house was topped by turrets on each side from which one had a panoramic view of the Cul-de-Sac Plain, its sugar plantations, and the airport beyond the top of the royal palm trees, the bougainvilleas, the oleanders and the hibiscus in profusion in the garden below. The whole property was enchanting.

It was indeed a masterpiece of its genre, and an outstanding example of Haitian architecture, but the rent I paid ($400 U.S.) was so low that no one could criticize me. It was simply luck that I got it, but it lent a touch of prestige to our UN mission, for in many posts, the UN looks like a poor cousin compared to the embassies. Of course we were not in Haiti to put up a front, but in the developing world, perhaps more than elsewhere, appearance counts if you want to be taken seriously.

Tonton Lyle's house, as it was called, had a most interesting history. It had been designed at the turn of the century by a Haitian architect, Léon Mathon, a graduate of the *École des Beaux-Arts* in Paris, for a German trader, Gustav Keitel. A beautiful drawing of it is included in an album of all the remaining gingerbread houses in Port-au-Prince, considered an endangered species, by American artist Angela Harrington Phillips. The Lyle house in my view is the most elegant one. Herr Keitel cemented on the wall near the entrance a marble plate inscribed *Licht, Luft und Liebe*. He knew the fine art of living. Married to a Haitian, he enjoyed his little palace until the declaration of war in 1914 when he was drafted by the Germans. His closest friend and relative, Pierre Nadal, a member of a well-known mulatto family of Port-au-Prince, had kept both his French and Haitian nationalities, something quite common in those days among those who considered themselves of French culture and ancestry. Nadal was also drafted, but into the French Army. They parted, embracing each other, hoping that if they were on the same front they would not have to fire on each other.

Later, the house belonged to a British merchant. In 1933 when the Duke and Duchess of Kent spent their honeymoon in Jamaica, they wanted to visit nearby Haiti. The British Minister chose the house for the visit of Their Royal Highnesses. They apparently enjoyed it, as they slept in it several days during the period of receptions given in their honor.

Terror in Port-au-Prince

The job of a UN Resident Representative is almost a 24-hour proposition. I had to travel often to the rural areas to visit our projects, enjoying the serenity of the Haitian countryside. During the first two years of our stay and despite a political situation that is always difficult in normal times under a dictator, we lived a happy life in our dream house. We entertained quite often as a part of my job.

As we went along, more opposition to Duvalier arose, always to be brutally repressed. The atmosphere of malaise in Port-au-Prince grew to one of real fear. The *télédiol* spread stories like wildfire of the crimes perpetrated by the *Tontons Macoute*, including the arrest and disappearance of various senior officers of the Haitian Army. At the beginning of that period I did not think that I should restrict my contacts to the Ministers and friends of the Duvalier regime—who seldom invited foreigners to their homes—just to please the Government. We had friendly relations with Haitian intellectuals, cultured persons who had studied in the United States and Europe, whose approach to life was cosmopolitan and who could by no means go along with the regime. Some were natural targets for the Government, likely being watched in their daily activities, such as Dr. Dantes Bellegarde, an intellectual of great distinction, one of the most remarkable men I have known.

He had occupied posts such as Minister of Education in preceding political regimes, and had been Haiti's Ambassador to Paris, Washington and the United Nations. A tall man close to 75 years of age, he was living a quiet life as a retired Haitian patrician. He had published several books on the history of his country, on the problems of education and on the U.S. occupation. I took great pleasure in conversing with him and in learning more about Haiti and the Haitians. Although a peaceful man, he was targeted by Duvalier as one of his enemies.

He had light skin, and was not in favor of the *negritude* movement embraced by Duvalier, which sought to return the black people to their African roots. He also was a strong critic of voodoo, but because of his reputation, indeed his celebrity, in his own country and abroad, they hesitated to get rid of him, either by expulsion or murder.

However, the *Tontons Macoute* had tried. One day he was closely missed by a bullet shot through an open window which ended up in the wall of his bedroom. I suspected the house was being watched, but I did not think I should stop my occasional friendly visits. Still I always parked my car, easily recognizable with its diplomatic plates, away from his house. It is likely that the government knew of my visits, but I heard nothing about this. Fortunately, Bellegarde, despite two attempts on his life, was never arrested and died peacefully several years later in his bed in Port-au-Prince.

The situation became even worse in the third year of my mission. Intimidation, arrests, tortures and disappearances continued, and even foreign residents became suspicious to Duvalier. Several European businessmen were expelled, including Bernard Dietrich, Australian publisher of the *Haitian-Sun*, who later wrote the bestseller *Papa Doc*. Monseigneur Poirier, the Archbishop of Haiti, a Frenchman, and several priests from Brittany and Belgium were also ousted. Papa Doc was excommunicated. Fort Dimanche, the Port-au-Prince prison for political prisoners, where tortures took place, was full, its walls spattered with blood.

Soon an 8 p.m. curfew was ordered and checkpoints installed at the entrances of the cities and their various sections, manned by armed *Tontons Macoute*. One had to get out of one's car and present identity papers before one could proceed.

Three very competent senior civil servants working at the National Bank, two with Ph.Ds from the University of Paris, were secret opponents of the regime. Their views became known and they were in danger of being arrested. They had made plans to flee. We had worked together and were friends; I respected them and considered that if they should succeed in leaving Haiti they should be helped in finding new connections abroad. I was later able to introduce them to various international organizations. One obtained a job with the International Monetary Fund, where he had a very successful career, one with the UN and one with the UN Economic Commission for Latin America in Chile. This, no doubt, was in the interest of the country. Pursued, they escaped the police and were able to reach the Brazilian Embassy. I drove to the Ambassador's residence, a place well-guarded by the police, to see them under the pretext of visiting the Ambassador. Taking refuge in an embassy is common in Latin America since, by mutual pact, embassies are considered sanctuaries for political escapees. At an appropriate time the Ambassador arranges for a safe-conduct with the Government, allowing the fugitive to be taken to the airport and flown to exile.

I also secretly helped other civil servants from the Ministries of Agriculture and Education who felt they wanted to leave. They succeeded in being recruited by FAO and UNESCO in Africa, where their services were needed. Although doing this was far from my terms of reference, I had no hesitation in taking the risk. I simply could not remain indifferent to such cases in light of what was going on in the country.

Later the situation changed. With the President's approval I was able to set up a substantial recruitment program in Port-au-Prince, involving the interviewing qualified Haitian educators and judges needed to fill positions in the administrations of the newly established State of the Congo (later Zaire) left vacant by the departure of the Belgians.

Then the situation worsened. The *Tontons Macoute* became more visible and threatening. One day, while driving downtown near Boulevard Harry Truman, I inadvertently started to take a wrong turn. A *Tonton Macoute* saw it, ran towards me and from a distance of five or six feet pointed his gun, ready to shoot, yelling words in Creole I could not grasp. Probably drunk with *clairin*, he looked like an absolute madman. People had been killed for less than my mistake in those days in Haiti. What to do to calm him down? I decided to smile, opening my arms in a gesture of complete astonishment, feinting surprise that he had not recognized me. I laughed and said to him in a mixture of French and Creole, "Don't you recognize me? I work for the United Nations." This stopped him for a moment. He lowered his gun and asked for my papers. I extended my identity card, which he carefully examined. He was unable to read it but he saw on it the stamp of the Ministry of External Relations. This calmed him completely. He apologized, saluted, and let me go.

The confidentiality of our official communications was constantly in jeopardy. Whenever I had to dispatch an urgent telegram to New York in the evening during the curfew, I preferred to drive downtown in my official car to the Western Union office and give it myself to the night employee there. I feared that, if I used the service of a messenger, the message would be copied immediately to the Government. Our cables, in those days, unfortunately were always sent in clear, as UNDP had no codes in its field offices until later, because we dealt mostly with technical assistance matters not considered confidential. We only had one weekly diplomatic pouch. Since mail was censored, when I had confidential letters I resorted to giving them to reliable persons, usually one of our people taking a plane that day who would be willing to mail them in Miami. Carrying these letters involved a little risk at the airport but the practice was widespread in Port-au-Prince.

Going out at night during curfews was always hazardous, and involved being stopped at checkpoints. We lived on a steep hill. Two houses down the road, at the corner of the street, was a large villa with a front terrace commanding a view of both streets; it was the residence of one of the most feared *Tontons Macoute*. As I approached his house, a guard would beam a light on the car to identify the vehicle. I could see a machine gun pointing to the road. Recognizing my car with its diplomatic plate, they never did stop me, and I could proceed down the hill without further trouble.

Persona Non Grata

Then came the beginning of 1963. My relationship with the Government became more difficult, until the day in May when Papa Doc declared me *persona non grata* in somewhat dramatic circumstances. Duvalier, more hysterical than ever, had the *Tontons Macoute* stop all vehicles on the road and search their occupants for weapons and money, sometimes undressing women, a complication to which our experts and their families coming to the city were exposed in several instances. As international personnel, our people should not have been searched after declaring their identity, and I made several strong representations to the Minister of Foreign Affairs so that this practice would be stopped immediately.

I finally concluded that it was no longer safe for the families of the experts to travel in the country or even stay in Haiti, when a highly influential and raging *Tonton Macoute* at the Palace issued an insane statement to the effect that rivers of the blood from white people would soon flow down the streets of Port-au-Prince. Reproduced in all the local newspapers, it scared the foreign colony to the extreme. The UN experts agreed to stay to carry on with their jobs, provided their wives and children be evacuated.

I notified New York, and Secretary-General U Thant accepted my proposal. I had to communicate his decision to our experts and their families living away from the capital so we could make plans for their departure. The livestock project at Les Cayes in the south peninsula included several families whom I asked to come to Port-au-Prince for an urgent staff meeting. The only way to advise them promptly was to use an old private telephone line linking Port-au-Prince to a Government sugar plant located in that town. The plant was managed by a man we knew well but who we later learned was a *Tonton Macoute*. The message was telephoned by one of my assistants when I was busy outside the office. I did not want our conversation to be divulged too early to the Government but someone heard the message and reported its contents to the Presidential Palace. I was accused of wanting to get the UN out of Haiti.

Tension in Port-au-Prince skyrocketed. Two days later I received a call from the Deputy Minister of Foreign Affairs to a meeting at the Ministry attended by all the Secretaries of State, the entire Cabinet except for the Foreign Affairs Minister himself who was in New York to discuss the Haitian Government's request for a Security Council meeting on the threat of the Dominican Republic to invade Haiti. The Ministers were in fact meeting as a kangaroo court to judge me. I was asked why I wanted the UN Mission to leave Haiti, a gesture they considered unfriendly on the part of someone like me who, in the words of the Deputy Minister, had always been considered a great friend of Haiti. They wanted to know if I had decided this move with the U.S. Ambassador, Raymond Thurston, since the USAID Mission was also leaving Haiti. I replied that the UN Secretary-General had instructed me to evacuate only the families, not the experts, and that this had nothing to do with the decision taken by the American Government.

I was also asked whether I considered the present situation explosive. I told them that it was indeed explosive, particularly with regard to tourism. The Haitian Government was most anxious not to discourage tourists from coming to Haiti. The Ministers expected that I would say the situation was not explosive so they would be able to quote me to the press and reassure tourist agencies and public opinion.

Haiti was then the object of lengthy articles in the *New York Times* and the *Miami Herald* and in the European press, discouraging visits to the island.

I was then asked to issue an immediate order to stop the departure of UN dependents. Of course I was not prepared to do that since at that moment the UN families, including my wife and daughter, were on their way to the airport to board a Pan American plane my office had contracted to take them to Miami where they would stay a few weeks to see how the situation would develop. The Deputy Minister who had made the request was furious at me for my negative attitude. The meeting was over. I rose and took leave of the Ministers.

The same evening, at my house in Dupré, I received a visit from a protocol attaché with a note from the Palace inviting me in the name of the President to leave the country within 48 hours. It was the first time in history that a UN Resident Representative, an international civil servant and therefore a neutral official, had been expelled from a member country.

My staff and all the UN experts in Port-au-Prince came to the airport. Most of the chiefs of the Diplomatic Missions in Port-au-Prince, many of them personal friends, came to say good-bye. It was a sad occasion for me, after working so hard, to leave so many friends and acquaintances behind. The entire mission signed a letter to U Thant justifying my position and thanking me for helping them get their families out of the country. A few days later U.S. Ambassador Thurston also left Haiti, officially for consultations in Washington. But he did not return, as the Haitian Government did not even allow him back for his personal belongings. The Commander of the U.S. Marine Mission was also expelled.

The international press had reported my expulsion and the British Ambassador, Gerald Corley-Smith, expelled a year before from Port-au-Prince and now in Quito, Ecuador, sent me a telegram at UN headquarters saying, "Congratulations, Jean. Welcome to the Club." Although it was a new situation for the United Nations Development Program to have a representative expelled from one of the member countries, no one blamed me and soon after I was appointed as the first UNDP Resident Representative to Uganda. Various books published later about the Haiti crisis and Papa Doc mentioned my departure. Among them was this quote:

> The United Nations continued to maintain a full-fledged staff of technicians in Haiti to assist the country's economic progress, despite the fact that the UN Resident Representative, Jean Richardot, had been expelled during the U.S.-Haitian showdown of May 1963, on the curious charge that he had shown unfriendliness by insisting—at the request of UN headquarters in New York—that the Government give exit visas to 31 members of the families of UN technicians. The expulsion of Richardot was particularly ironic because he

was generally known to be one of the warmest friends the Haitian people had among foreigners.[14]

Haiti Revisited

After I left Haiti under such adverse circumstances, my name was put on a blacklist, but I continued to be interested in the fate of the Haitians, with the hope that one day there would be some change in the island and I would be able to go back to see my friends.

I learned about the death of Papa Doc in 1971 when I was in Jamaica. He was replaced by his son Jean-Claude, named President-for-Life by his father at 19 years of age. He knew little of affairs of state, and apparently was only interested in fast cars and women. The same small group of Duvalierists I knew continued to rule the country, Jean-Claude's mother in the first years playing an influential role. The regime was perhaps less harsh than before, but violations of human rights reported by Amnesty International continued. There were still tortures and killing by the *Tontons Macoute*. Economic conditions had somewhat improved. Jean-Claude noted his father's political revolution and decided his would be an economic revolution.

In 1971, Bob Folsom, the U.S. Chargé d'Affaires, and his wife Florence, had returned to Port-au-Prince for a tour of duty. They were close friends from our early days in Haiti, in 1941, when Bob, then Consul, had signed the marriage certificate the U.S. Embassy had delivered to us. They had not seen us for years and, since we lived in nearby Jamaica, they invited us to spend a few days with them in Tonton Lyle's house which they had rented. However, after inquiring discreetly at the UN office, they had phoned us in Kingston that the visit was not advisable, as it was still too close to the events of 1963 and my eviction. One year later, during my assignment in Jamaica, I was visiting the Regional Director of the International Labour Organization for the Caribbean in Port of Spain, Trinidad, when an occasion for me to go back to Haiti presented itself. This was to have unexpected repercussions with quite a comical twist. As we were having lunch, my colleague told me he had to go to Port-au-Prince ten days later to represent the ILO at a meeting of the Caribbean Tourist Association for which the Government of Haiti was acting as host. The conference was, in part, to deal with the question of youth tourism in which my project in Jamaica was interested. ILO headquarters insisted that someone be there to represent the Organization as Observer, but the Regional Director did not have time to go. He suggested that I attend the conference in his place. I immediately

---

14 O. Ernest Moore, *Haiti, Its Stagnant Society and Shackled Economy* (New York: Exposition Univ. Press, 1972).

accepted the proposal, and a substitution of name was arranged with the Secretary of the Conference.

As an official delegate to an international meeting of which it was the host, I was sure that the Government of Haiti would not, if I attended, create any trouble for me. I thought that it would be quite an interesting experience and an opportunity to see our old friends, so I invited Natalie to join me. Both my friend in Trinidad and I assumed that the Haitian Government had been advised of the switch so we no longer thought of it.

One week later Natalie and I arrived by plane at the Dr. François Duvalier International Airport and walked across the tarmac to the main building where the registration of arriving delegates to the meeting was in progress. We were greeted by the Conference Chairman, the Haitian High Commissioner of Tourism, Monsieur André Théart who, when I was in Port-au-Prince eight years before, was Minister of Agriculture. We had had frequent meetings and enjoyed cordial relations.

When I greeted him in the airport he did not seem to want to recognize me and said, "I think I must have met you somewhere!" After being welcomed by the Secretary-General of the Conference and having registered, we met Gordana Ashton who had come to pick us up. When we arrived at her house, where we were to stay, we learned from her son, Marc, who had been in the airport that afternoon, that our arrival had caused some commotion and that the Government had put me under surveillance. Théart asked Marc to tell me to be sure not to attend an official reception to be given by the President at the National Palace for the delegates two days later. Nevertheless, I attended the Conference as observer without incident. A Haitian lawyer friend to whom I had explained the situation advised me to attend the reception with the other delegates because, he said, "You would seem to snub the President otherwise." I decided to attend the reception and see what would happen. Natalie declined and stayed with our friends.

On the appropriate day, as I stood at the end of the reception line in the main salon of the Palace with my colleagues, waiting to be introduced to the President, I saw Théart at the head of the line announcing the name of each guest. The President was sitting in an imposing gilded armchair with, on one side of him, his mother, Madame Simone Duvalier, acting as First Lady, and on the other the Foreign Minister. Théart gave a startled look when he saw me, probably thinking I had not received his message. I smiled at him, confident that, whatever he felt, he could not do anything but announce my name and that of the agency I represented. I greeted the President, Madame Duvalier and the Foreign Minister, who was no other than the Deputy Minister who had requested my expulsion in 1963! What could he do about my being here? This was becoming more and more interesting!

A few minutes later, all the delegates having been introduced, the party moved to a sumptuous buffet in an adjacent room. I was immediately surrounded by the Deputy Minister, Théart, and others who had recognized me. They were quite excited, greeting me profusely, giving me the Latin American embrace, saying how glad they were that I had come back to Haiti! They invited Natalie and me to a barbecue at Ibo Beach the Government was hosting the next day.

My lawyer friend had been right. My going to the reception had indeed turned things around. All I wanted from this incredible, almost comical, adventure was to be able to go to Haiti freely from Jamaica if I wanted to see my friends. As a result, we have been able to visit the island on several occasions in the years since.

* * *

In 1975 I retired from the UN and was asked by the Agency for International Development of the U.S. State Department (USAID) to advise the Government on the administrative reform of the malaria control program in Haiti, a vast project which had been going on for 20 years with a view to eradicating malaria in the island.

Haiti was still the only Caribbean country where the disease had not been eliminated. I accepted the offer. The project was a tripartite effort involving the government of Haiti, the World Health Organization and the United States. From the end of 1975 to the summer of 1977, I lived again in Haiti with Natalie, in a period of relative political calm. Much progress in the fight against malaria was expected from a new campaign distributing malaria tablets to the peasants, and through the spraying of houses and swamps with DDT to kill the anopheles mosquitoes, particularly in the south, where the incidence of malaria was the greatest. The disease, still among the worst health enemies of the Haitian people, caused untold numbers of deaths every year in the countryside.

Service Nationale des Endémies Majeures (SNEM) was part of the Ministry of Health. My work was rewarding. My duties consisted of monitoring the use of U.S. funds (which over the years had already cost the U.S. taxpayers about $20,000,000), and of reorganizing management in its relationship with the Ministry and other health care programs to implement concrete improvements in the administrative aspects of the work. Over the 20 months I was there much progress was accomplished, which was noted with appreciation in the report of the Inspector-General of USAID after his visit to Haiti in the summer of 1976.

To fully control the disease, aerial spraying should have been undertaken. But this was very costly and out of the question in Haiti. Drainage of swamps was part of the program and accomplished some good results. At times the results seemed elusive, the number of positive malaria cases showing considerable variations in conjunction with hurricanes and excessive floodings. Yet the campaign was not totally ineffective; when I left malaria no longer existed in many areas below 500 meters altitude. There was little danger above that altitude, a fact that enabled the organization to focus its efforts in only 52 of the country's 560 rural districts, almost all of them located in the South Peninsula.

* * *

After I left Haiti in July 1977, the Haitian political situation did not improve. Jean Claude Duvalier, *Président-à-vie*, married a mulatto divorcee, Michèle Bennett, who wanted to run the Government as much as her husband. Corruption continued. The luxurious life of the President and his wife resembled that of the Marcos in the Philippines. It was reported that Michèle bought dozens of furs in Paris for herself and her friends so they could wear them in the tropics at receptions in the air-conditioned rooms of the National Palace. They spent huge amounts of Government funds on themselves and their friends. The head of the Human Rights Society in Port-au-Prince was arrested, and the press muzzled on several occasions. Very little had changed in Haiti.

The visit of the Pope in 1986 marked the start of popular revolt against the Duvaliers; at the end of his visit Pope John Paul II gravely announced that things must change. Haitian Catholic priests moved the people to act. Disturbances in provincial towns were followed by widespread riots and a general strike in the Capital. Jean-Claude began to panic. Michèle, who thought she would prefer to live abroad now that millions of dollars had been spirited to Swiss banks and real estate purchased in France, actually pushed her husband to resign.

After they fled early in the morning of February 7, 1986 on a plane provided by the United States, a provisional three-man council started to govern the country, headed by General Namphy, a Duvalierist, albeit not a bloody *Tonton Macoute*, but not a real leader either. Eighteen months elapsed before the scheduled presidential elections. Several candidates, including two who had been living abroad,[15] conducted regular electoral campaigns. But on election day, November 25, 1987, some Army officers and *Tontons Macoute* prevented people from voting, massacring more than 30 of them at the polls without opposition from the Provisional Government. This strategy appeared to many to have been initiated by Army officers and Duvalierists wanting to regain power and nip democracy in the bud.

The United States and other nations halted their aid immediately, but no other

---

15 One was Marc Bazin, a former official of the World Bank.

action was taken to topple the ineffective and guilty Provisional Government, clearly allied to the perpetrators of the monstrous election day crimes. A new election was scheduled for January 1988 by the Provisional Council, on its own terms. The principal presidential candidates withdrew their names, save one, Leslie Manigat, who with the Army's support was elected. A well-trained economist, Manigat had lived in exile during Papa Doc's years. As President he was just a lackey of the Army, and several weeks after he took office he was evicted and sent into exile by General Namphy, who proclaimed himself President. A few months later, General Prosper Avril took over the Presidency and with the Army under his control gave Haiti a new dictatorship.

It was a grave mistake to think that the departure of Jean-Claude Duvalier in 1986 would solve Haiti's problems. His unlamented abdication did nothing to reduce political instability and it created serious new economic problems. One of the keenest observers of the Haitian scene, Robert Rothberg, observed that the major obstacle to development in Haiti is the failure of the elite to see its true interest.[16]

Late in 1986, there were small signs that some members of the elite had started working for the common good. These included some health professionals and business people I met in Port-au-Prince in 1986 where I went to assist the Americares Foundation in organizing the distribution of pharmaceuticals to the poor. At that time the masses, the poor, were awakening under the spell of a young priest, Jean-Bertrand Aristide. It was my hope that Haitians would now group together, put an irresistible pressure on the Government to hold elections as soon as possible, and to take the road toward democracy. Then the international community would be able to help a new Government tackle the enormous problems of economic and social development. In the words of my friend Scott Behoteguy, former director of USAID in Haiti, money alone won't do the job, though plenty will be required to overcome the factors which have helped to make Haiti synonymous with ecological disaster, political squalor, and economic backwardness. Haiti cannot solve these many problems alone.

Is Haiti Beyond Hope?

I was naive to think that Haiti was ready in the 1960s for the challenging transformation required to place the country on a firm footing toward democracy. I had shared my views with my Headquarters, but at the time it was not thought that the UN should pressure the government. Fortunately, today the thinking is different. Several years passed and, at the end of 1990, general elections were held, including

---

16 Robert Rothberg, *Haiti, The Politics of Squalor* (Boston: Houghton Mifflin Co., 1972).

the first presidential election held democratically and supervised by the UN and the OAS.

The winner was Rev. Jean-Bertrand Aristide, the young priest who for a decade had carried a courageous fight from his parish in Port-au-Prince against the Duvalier dictatorships to defend the rights of the Haitian poor of whom he is the self-proclaimed champion. He was elected with a majority of 67 percent, the mass of the people voting for him. Shortly after, a coup attempt was led by Roger Lafontant, the former head of Jean-Claude Duvalier's brutal secret police, who tried to take over the National Palace. The coup failed; among the victims were seven conspirators who were hung up by Aristide supporters and burned to death by placing lighted tires around their necks.[18] Soldiers loyal to Aristide later stormed the Palace and regained control of the beleaguered nation, freeing interim President Ertha Pascal Trouillot, who had been seized by the assailants as a hostage.

The new President had been inaugurated February 7th, 1991. Although he was confronted with the perennial and overwhelming economic and social problems of the country, he initially appeared to have been able to control the Haitian Army and to draw it to his side. Although his knowledge of government was limited, there was hope that Haiti had started on the road to democracy, with the promise of substantial economic and financial aid from a number of countries including the U.S., France, Germany and others. But one year later the new president was ousted and sent to exile by the military government. At the time of this writing a democratic government had not been restored in spite of ineffective sanctions against Haiti and extended diplomatic negotiations and strong pressure by the Organization of American States, the UN, the U.S. and others. These negotiations include an arrangement by which the sanctions would be lifted if the President would return to Haiti and grant amnesty to the military leaders who had ousted him, and appoint a new Prime Minister. The return of President Aristide was scheduled for October 30, 1993.

We all hope there will soon be a durable solution to this everlasting conflict between the elite and the military on the one hand and the mass of people and their representatives on the other. The first group must recognize at last that their interests are totally and indissolubly linked to a clear improvement of the situation of the masses, that their way of running the country has been wrong ever since independence, that they need to be more generous vis-a-vis the poor and clearly help them, and that the role of the military should be confined to the maintenance of law

---

18 A torture called *Père Lebrun* which Aristide unfortunately condoned. He tolerated such conduct through a declaration he made on the steps of the National Palace before his ousting.

and order.

The masses and those who represent them must also realize that, even if they have been terribly victimized over years of neglect, "an eye for an eye" will only prolong the present situation and lead them nowhere.

In any case, we know that an intervention by force in Haiti would not be the solution, nor would a UN or U.S. trusteeship. We can only hope that both sides will see the light and that the efforts of the international community in mediating this endless crisis will succeed in soon bringing back stability to this unfortunate nation and finally help install democracy for which there was, very unfortunately, only a faint spark of hope when the new president was democratically elected in 1990.

UGANDA, THE PEARL OF AFRICA:

BEFORE AND AFTER IDI AMIN

UGANDA, THE PEARL OF AFRICA:

BEFORE AND AFTER IDI AMIN

A New Mission
When I was appointed UN Resident Representative in Uganda, to coordinate the work of the United Nations missions and develop a comprehensive program of technical assistance just after the country became independent in 1962, I was intrigued by what I would find on arriving at my new station in the heart of Africa. British colleagues in New York had told me that Kampala, the capital, was a pleasant post, much looked after by British civil servants, and that the country was lovely as well.

Besides what I had learned in my technical briefings about the country, I had been very much impressed by the picture Winston Churchill had painted in 1908:

> *The Kingdom of Uganda is a fairy tale. You climb up a railway instead of a beanstalk, and at the end there is a wonderful new world. The scenery is different, the vegetation is different, the climate is different and most of all people are different from anything elsewhere to be seen in the whole range of Africa. In the place of naked, painted savages, clashing their spears, and gibbering in chorus to their tribal chiefs, a complete and elaborate polity is presented. Under a dynamic king, an amiable, clothed, polite and intelligent race dwell together in an organized monarchy. An elegance in manners springing from a naive simplicity of character pervades all classes.*[18]

Churchill had called the country the "pearl of Africa." He was describing the Kingdom of Buganda, only a part of Uganda, then a British Protectorate, and the *Kabaka*, its King. When I got there Uganda's independence had just been declared. Soon after, a whole set of new problems would beset the Government of Prime Minister Milton Obote and change the country altogether.

Who could have believed, then, that in the '70s, under monstrous dictator Idi Amin, the fabric of this beautiful country would be completely destroyed, hundreds of thousands of people would be killed or murdered, and Uganda would become

---

18 Churchill, Winston S., *My African Journey* (New York: WW Norton, 1989), 56.

victim to civil war, foreign invasion and economic disaster.

The country is now being rehabilitated—a gigantic task. Fortunately, Uganda has valuable basic resources which will help, but it will take years before it will recover to the state in which I had known it. It will probably lose forever some of its idyllic character, and the charm under which my family and I, as well as many others, fell.

* * *

It was with great expectations that I left New York to take my new post. In 1963, the usual route to Uganda from New York was to fly to London, and from there to board a British East Africa airliner (still propeller-driven in those days) bound for Nairobi. After a few hours we landed in Bengazi, on the edge of the Libyan desert, at about 2 a.m. for refueling. Our plane stopped far out on the tarmac. All passengers in transit, mostly British, walked a long way to a wooden barracks-type shed close to the small airport building, to quench their thirst with a soft drink and admire the dark blue sky, scintillating with stars in the middle of a beautiful desert night.

We resumed our flight toward the Nile Valley. In the early morning I woke up to see below the russet tones of an immense plateau. From place to place little puffs of dust indicated where small herds of animals were on the move. I could not identify them because we were too high. Frightened by the noise of our engines the wild beasts were veering from right to left, not knowing from where the danger came. We were above Kenya. To the east one could see majestic Mount Kenya, 18,000 feet above sea level. Yet this huge mountain did not seem as high as it should have because the West Kenyan plain beneath it is already at 8,000 feet. I did not get the awesome impression that I had when flying along the highest peaks of the Alps in Europe, the altitude of which is considerably lower.

Soon we prepared to land in Nairobi, and smoothly touched down at its brand-new looking airport. I had three hours before resuming my flight to Uganda. I took a taxi to get an impression of the city, admiring its large avenues, modern buildings and flowers everywhere. The air was light, the temperature perfect. What impressed me most was the carpet of blue jacaranda petals on the ground under the tall blue jacaranda trees I had never seen before.

Our flight to Entebbe (the Uganda airport) was in a slow, low-winged Vokker, and lasted two hours. Flying east over Kenya and Uganda was a pleasant discovery. While the east coast of Africa can be hot and extremely humid, about one hundred miles inland, east of Nairobi, one comes to a high tableland—seven to eight thousand feet above sea level in Kenya, three to five thousand feet in Uganda—which extends across all of East Africa to the Mountains of the Moon on the western Zaire border.

We soon crossed the Rift Valley, practically on the Equator, and were over Uganda. I saw not a land of steaming jungle but of rolling hills in the south and in the west, and of plains in the northern triangle where the White Nile emerges from Lake Victoria to wend its meandering way North.

Our plane slowly descended over the blue waters of Lake Victoria, one of the largest lakes in the world, and after a graceful banking of its wings landed on the short airstrip of Entebbe. Entebbe was then a lovely small administrative center created by the British on the shore of the Lake with giant trees in a park-like setting. Its name was to become world-famous when, fifteen years later, the airport became the theater of a spectacular raid by the Israeli Air Force to free the hostages of a hijacked aircraft which had been given permission to land there by Idi Amin.

After landing I found the countryside just as Winston Churchill had described it: green, luscious, peaceful, a nice climate not at all equatorial. As a matter of fact, I never found Uganda's climate unpleasant, although it could become slightly oppressive as one traveled in the northern areas. The people on the road between Entebbe and Kampala seemed happy. Entebbe was less then an hour by car from Kampala, the capital, also a charming modern small city.

I would ply between Entebbe and Kampala on this picturesque country road many times, since the Ugandan Government still occupied buildings of the former British administration in Entebbe and was only beginning to settle in Kampala, the country's new capital. The UN and its agencies already had a number of experts on the spot, advising the Government, gradually replacing the departing British and beginning to make their contributions to Uganda's development.

I was put up at the Grand Hotel, the best in Kampala, where British civil servants and their families usually stayed before settling into a house. It was indeed a very comfortable establishment looking over a pretty public garden. During my first week there I paid a courtesy visit on Prime Minister Obote and was introduced to various Ministers.

I liked my job. As head of the UN in Uganda, I represented the Executive Chairman of the UN Technical Assistance Board, David Owen, the 10 organizations of the United Nations which participated in the Expanded Program of Technical Assistance and Paul Hoffman, the Managing Director of the UN Special Fund. We had already had two Special Fund pre-investment projects operating in Uganda—the Aerial Geographical Survey and the Kampala Technical Institute—and a third project, in the field of irrigation surveys, was under consideration. Over the two years of my assignment the Technical Assistance program developed rapidly and covered economic planning, housing and physical planning, manpower planning, agricultural statistics and credit, tse-tse fly control, fisheries, irrigation development, mass communication, adult women's education, health education and meteorology—all these fields reflecting the highest national priorities. In all, the projects involved the services of 37 experts in 1963-64, as well as fellowship and equipment. In addition, a number of UN agencies including the UN proper, UNICEF, WHO, UNESCO and ILO were helping Uganda from their regular budgets. We were gradually replacing the British who were leaving the country.

UN assistance also provided for the development of East Africa as a whole in the form of regional projects. At that time Kenya, Tanganyika (later Tanzania) and Uganda formed a common market of about 25 million people representing considerable economic development potential. Unfortunately, the common market was dissolved in 1977 because of political conditions in the area. The British had also created for the three countries an efficient organization called the East Africa Common Services which included the railroads, the airlines and a number of agricultural and medical research and development services, all very important for the economic progress of the entire region.

The UNDP representatives in the three countries—Amishadai Adu, in Dar-es-Salaam, Bernard Chidzero in Nairobi and myself in Kampala—would meet periodically to discuss helpful projects concerning the three countries. My colleagues were extremely competent. I enjoyed working with them immensely.

Adu, a tall distinguished looking Ghanaian about fifty-five, who often wore his tribal toga at receptions, was well known in administrative circles in Africa and England. He had been trained by the British Civil Service, and had earned the reputation that comes with being the first African District Commissioner in Ghana. After independence he was in charge of high level administrative affairs under Kwame Nkrumah, becoming his right hand man. When he offered his services to the UN, we grabbed him. Later, after he served UNDP, he was elected Deputy Secretary General of the British Commonwealth, and later, a few years before he died, Chairman of the UN International Civil Service Commission in New York.

Bernard Chidzero, a Rhodesian[20] and much younger than Adu or I, had been a brilliant student at Oxford and at McGill University in Montreal and had served as an economist with the UN Economic Commission for Africa. Later he became a high official at United Nations Conference on Trade and Development and in 1992 was almost elected Secretary General of the UN.

We met a few times at the New Stanley Hotel in Nairobi, the well known

---

20 Rhodesia later became Zimbabwe.

rendez-vous for tourists going on safari and a favorite place of Ernest Hemingway and actor William Holden.

On one occasion the meeting was in Tanganyika and I drove by Jeep all the way from Kampala to Dar-es-Salaam with two colleagues, to meet with Adu and Chidzero. This long trek of more than 1,000 miles enabled us to see wildlife on the way and to visit the Amboselli Game Park in Kenya, on the Tanganyikan border. We put up for the night in a warden's house in the middle of the Park. It might have been 9 o'clock. My companions were either getting ready for bed or exchanging stories, but as it was hot inside I decided to take a stroll and to observe the rising moon and the star-studded sky. I walked towards a small river nearby, bordered by a vegetable garden. Coming close to the riverbank I did not distinguish, a distance away, the dark form of a hippopotamus, his nose close to the ground, who had left the riverbed to maraud in the garden. All of a sudden I saw his head looking up. For a second he hesitated. Then, suddenly, his big brown mass and short legs turned and scrambled in my direction. Hippopotami can run very fast. I ran toward the cottage; I don't think that I had ever sprinted faster. When I arrived, breathless, the hippo had stopped some distance behind me. I told my friends what had happened. The game warden gave me a severe, well-deserved reprimand because I should never have taken a walk alone at night in those surroundings.

After stopping at Arusha, a small city at the foot of Mount Kilimanjaro we arrived in Dar-es-Salaam. We were then planning two large regional projects. One was an East African regional University with new campuses in Nairobi and Dar-es-Salaam to complement Makerere College in Kampala and triple existing facilities. This project was implemented but the universities in each capital turned out to be national rather than regional. The second project was a vast East African cattle development scheme, provided one could lick the tse-tse fly which was decimating the cattle. Through renewed efforts and by establishing feedlots and other livestock services the East African region could ultimately become a very large producer of meat for local consumption and for export.

These two special projects were being studied and promoted by UNDP in New York. Sir Hugh Foote, later Lord Caradon, a well-known British diplomat and former Governor of Jamaica and Nigeria, was sent to the three East African countries as UNDP Senior Consultant. His mission was to discuss at the highest level of Government the implications of these projects. I assisted him in this task and together we made rounds of the Ministries concerned in Uganda. I much enjoyed working with him.

Shortly before he came to East Africa he had been the UK's representative in in the 4th Committee and the Trusteeship Council when they dealt with the Rhodesian question. In 1964 he wrote a couple articles for British periodicals about the work UN people were accomplishing in the newly independent countries of what had been British East Africa, naming my colleagues and me. Between two trips to Kampala he wrote me a flattering letter in which he noted:

> ... you have obviously made a magnificent start in Uganda. Your reports are distributed in the New York office as models of what such reports should be and you are always spoken of as the perfect Resident Representative. Your name and reputation are very highly regarded. It is sufficient for me to say that this does not surprise me at all.

Kampala

We enjoyed life in Kampala at that time. Natalie and Nancy, our younger daughter, arrived before school started. Nancy, who was fourteen, could not gain admission to the Aga Khan school, the only one suitable in Uganda, which was full. We had to send her to a British private school in Eldoret in the Kenya Highlands, more than four hundred miles away. Nancy did not like it because of its stern discipline and loneliness. When I tried to telephone her from Kampala, I was told that it simply was not possible to talk to the students by telephone. We went to see her once. She did not return to the school after the Christmas holiday, but for a different reason.

We were able to rent a house on Kololo Hill, where most embassies had their residences. Our landlord was the Government, which owned a large number of houses built during the Protectorate for British colonial civil servants. One of these had been reserved for us. It was a small ranch house in the middle of a large property with English gardens and servants' quarters. There was no glass in the windows, but steel bars instead as a safety measure against the many robberies that plagued the city. While life was pleasant in Kampala, one did have to contend with the theft problem, which put one's property in constant jeopardy. It was also an admission that Prime Minister Obote could not provide adequate police protection. Armed robbery was organized by regional gangs, operating from Nairobi, which disposed of stolen goods including cars and auto parts.

We had to hire a night watchman, called an *Askari* (soldier), to patrol the garden. He was a forbidding-looking big fellow from the north, but with a marvelous smile when we talked to him. He spoke only Swahili to us. On rainy nights he wore a heavy khaki military overcoat to protect himself from the tropical downpours, standing guard at the house entrance which hardly sheltered him. One night after a party we were awakened at 2 a.m., the *askari* yelling at the top of his lungs. I asked him what was the matter. He pointed out two men escaping through the hedge near the garage at the end of the garden. Still yelling he chased them but did not catch them. I ran into the house and called the police. The thieves had torn out the three padlocks of the garage door and were in the process of removing the wheels of our new Peugeot when the *askari* realized what was happening and gave the alarm. They fled. My complaint to the police was only one among many. They came but their investigation brought no results.

To leave a car on Kampala streets at night was to issue an invitation to thieves. Even traveling from city to city at night was dangerous and rarely attempted. If a breakdown occurred out in the country one ran the risk of being attacked. I read in the papers that a white missionary had thus been murdered and his body left on the roadside near his car. The killers had taken the gold from his teeth. In Kampala, however, one was safe and, except for robberies, I heard of no other disagreeable incidents happening to the foreign colony.

Kampala was a very clean town. The center of the city featured nothing remarkable except for the new Parliament Building and an entrance arch leading to it. The first 15-story high-rise, Embassy House, was built during our stay. I was able to transfer the UN office to this building, on the floor between those occupied by the U.S. and West German embassies, the tiny office the Government had first given us being completely inadequate.

While the stores and other buildings along the street lacked all but an occasional distraction, passers-by were most interesting to observe. Some wore traditional dresses. Buganda women wore vividly-colored long skirts to the ground, their garments elegantly draped around their large bodies. In the old days, the ideal for a husband in Uganda was to have an enormously fat wife, and girls were fattened up with milk until they could hardly walk.

Kampala was built on seven hills, like Rome, and because of its high trees, green open spaces and tropical vegetation it was relaxing to drive from our home in Kololo to each of the other hills. A golf course close to the center of town gave Kampala a resort appearance.

By far the most interesting parts were the hills to which we paid several visits in the early days after our arrival and during which we learned about Uganda's fascinating history.

One was the Hill of the Royal Tombs, Kasubi Hill, where the *Kabakas*, the Kings of Buganda, were buried. This hill, also called Mengo Hill, had a traditional palisade of elephant grass protecting a vast conical shelter with thatched roof, under which burns the sacred *Gombalola fire* that is extinguished only on the death of a *Kabaka*.

Behind this most venerable building stood the palace of the *Kabaka*, occupied when we were there by his Highness Edward William Frederick David Walugemba Mutebi Luwangola Mutesa II, 35th *Kabaka* of Buganda, "possessor of almighty power and knowledge."

The *Kabaka* had been crowned at age 14, dressed in barkcloth, the traditional cloth of the Kingdom of Buganda. As part of the Coronation ceremony he had received the allegiance of the chiefs of his Kingdom, the congratulations of the British Protectorate and the blessing of the Anglican Church, as he was a Protestant. He was peaceful and debonair, while Mutesa I, of whom he was a direct descendant, had been an extremely cruel king, killing people on the slightest whim.

In 1945 Mutesa II, known in international circles as "Freddie" from his schooldays in London, had been exiled to London by Governor Sir Andrew Cohen, following strong differences of views between the British Government and the Buganda, who did not want Uganda to join the Federation of East Africa. Freddie spent almost 10 years in exile in England and returned to Uganda in 1955, amid scenes of indescribable joy on the part of his people.

It was hard for me to realize that Uganda had been subject to Western influence for barely one hundred years while West Africa had for several centuries been in contact with Europe and had developed more. Mutesa I had been the first Buganda king to admit foreigners to the country, in 1860.

At independence Mutesa II had become the National President of Uganda. We met the *Kabaka* several times later, at official receptions in Entebbe. He was informal, and said he had followed the work of the UN ever since it started in Church House, when he was in exile in London. He had attended Magdalen College in Cambridge in 1945.

The first foreigners to reach Uganda had been *Kiwahili*-speaking Arabs from Zanzibar, whose language, popularly known as Swahili, later became the *lingua franca* of East Africa. They tried to convert Mutesa I to Islam but were able to stay in Buganda only eight years, when Mutesa sent them back to Zanzibar. In their stead he accepted the French Catholic missionaries who came from the north and started converting the Africans. Mwanga, who succeeded Mutesa, made a contract with Protestant missionaries from England and for a while there were great rivalries between the two missions. The next *Kabaka*, Daudi Chiva, Mutesa's son, chose to become a Christian in 1897, and embraced the Anglican denomination.

The other hills of Kampala are no less important than the Kasubi Hill. We first went to Rabaga Hill, on which was erected an imposing Roman Catholic Cathedral. It was Sunday. The immense nave was full of the faithful, testimony to the success of the Roman Catholic church among the population. The Catholic missions in Uganda were introduced a century before by a Frenchman, Charles Martial La Vigerie, Archbishop of Algiers. His French priests, the *Pères Blancs* (White Fathers), who had converted the Muslims of the Sahara to Catholicism, wore Arab clothes, a red cap and a rosary around the neck. Pushing their way south across the African desert, they created the Central African Mission in 1878 and ended up at the court of Mutesa I.

Another hill, Namirembe Hill, the Hill of Peace in the language, is the site of the Anglican Cathedral. Both the Catholic and Protestant churches brought Christianity to Uganda, converted the tribes and created schools. This explains why the Ugandan tribes, particularly the Buganda with their *Kabaka* and their Parliament, were more advanced than those in Kenya and surrounding areas.

On a smaller hill, Kibuli Hill, a mosque is erected. Although Islam was introduced by the Arabs of Zanzibar, this Mosque looks more Indian than Arabic because it was built rather recently by the followers of the Aga Khan, the Ismaelis, originally from Persia, a vital community in Uganda when I was there. They had done much to develop the country in trade, industry and education. The Aga Khan hoped to see Islam assume a front rank in the cultural development of East Africa, financing social services and building mosques in various parts of Uganda. He had advised his followers to become Ugandan citizens, to mingle with Africans and to marry them. They had slowly started doing this and their leader, whom I knew, had married a cousin of the Kabaka.

While there is no doubt that both Christian and Muslim religions have made great strides in Uganda, there is still in the rural areas the religion of Uganda, which centers on the spirits of the dead as in other animist religions of Africa. Ugandan peasants still believe that the *Muzimu*, the spirits who live near the graves of their ancestors, remain in contact with their descendants, and can take possession of one's soul and torture it.

The last hill of Kampala is the Hill of Learning, the site of Makarere College, an impressive institution, unique at the time with its modern university campus in the heart of Africa. The British had started it in 1922 as a technical college, opened a medical school in 1924, and by 1937 it had become the center of higher learning for the whole of East Africa, giving courses in Medicine, Veterinary Science, Education and Art. In 1953 it included an interracial university college of art and science linked to the University of London, with 450 undergraduates from the various East African Countries and a staff of 110 mainly from England, the U.S. and Canada. Visiting the Makarere campus was always a pleasant experience for me, where I met a few visiting American professors.

Obote's Politics

Within a few months after my arrival, the United Nations Development Program was rapidly becoming one of the most important agencies helping Uganda. As in other parts of Africa the country was also receiving assistance from a number of Western nations, including the United States and Israel. Britain still contributed the greatest amount of aid in grants and loans, although this was declining. There was optimism in Kampala about the future of this newly independent country that all friendly nations wanted to help. A brilliant celebration took place on the First Anniversary of Independence, October 9, 1963, which had closed 70 years of British rule in Uganda. Two weeks later, with great pomp, the Government celebrated UN Day on October 24th, on the front terrace of Parliament Building, under a striking new Coat of Arms above the main entrance. Facing the beautiful gardens which surrounded this handsome example of modern architecture the Minister of Foreign Affairs, Hon. S. N. Odaka, MP, delivered a speech to perhaps one thousand people, followed by my message to the Government in the name of the United Nations. There were other manifestations including the participation of UN experts, films and receptions.

The Minister hosted a huge diplomatic reception at his home. One of my wife's favorite stories was that a dish of fried locusts was passed around to the guests by the Minister himself during the cocktail hour. Natalie at that moment was talking to the Israeli Ambassador's wife, who ate the locusts, apparently without trouble but not realizing what she was eating. Natalie asked, "Do you know what you ate?" "No," she replied, and when Natalie explained, "They were grasshoppers, a Ugandan delicacy," the lady jumped a foot off her chair and looked completely aghast. In the evening in Kampala one could see groups of children trying to catch grasshoppers under the street lamps as they flitted about drawn by the light, either to sell them or to eat them for supper.

The Israeli Ambassador and his wife were popular in Kampala in those days. Unfortunately this did not last under the regime of Idi Amin. In addition to Western donors, Israel's assistance was significant. It consisted of important projects in the North helped by specialists from the kibbutzes. Israel was also invited by Obote to train the Army. This of course displeased the British, who had created the Uganda Military Forces. The Israelis had responded enthusiastically, as they were anxious to increase their presence in Africa. Uganda was not unknown to them. Years before the creation of Israel the Jews, looking for a home, had considered Uganda as a possible place to settle. In fact in 1902 Neville Chamberlain offered the Karamoja in the North of Uganda as a home for the Jews. Theodore Herzl, the founder of the Zionist Movement, had sent emissaries to survey the area but it was found unsuitable for settlement. The Zionists would have preferred the nearby Highlands of Kenya which, however, were not offered.

* * *

While everything was going well after Independence with regard to our technical assistance, and excellent cooperation had been developed among the various foreign missions, there was no doubt that the Ugandans were suffering serious growing pains in governing themselves. And Obote was having increasing difficulty in governing. This was characterized by in-fighting behind the scenes among the tribes and the political leaders to satisfy purely personal ambitions. This was of course to be expected because of the existence of three separate kingdoms, and their resistance, particularly that of Buganda, to integration into the new Government of Uganda. Obote as Prime Minister understandably wanted integration for the sake of national unity but, from what I could observe, he was not the kind of statesman who could deal capably with complex and delicate situations. Some found him arrogant. He was incredibly ambitious, unwilling to compromise or to wait for a better day.

Obote came from the Lango tribe in the North, the same area as Amin, and was not well accepted by the Buganda people. He went to a Protestant mission school, and later attended Makerere College to become a teacher. There he met Julius Nyerere, the future Prime Minister of Tanzania. They became friends, and it was in Tanzania that Obote took refuge when he was ousted from power in 1971 by Idi Amin.

Obote shared Nyerere's political views and was an African socialist and partisan of the one-party state. His *Common Man's Charter*, published in 1968, was very similar to the Arusha Declaration of Tanzania. He wanted to become the only head of the Government and, in a daring and disastrous move, he got rid of the *Kabaka*, who since Independence was the National President. He arrested five of his own ministers whom, he said, were plotting against him. Idi Amin, then a colonel in the Army, was put in charge of the coup against the *Kabaka*. Using artillery he assaulted the State House in Kampala; the *Kabaka* escaped and fled to Britain. Amin, for his exploit, was promoted to Brigadier-General.

Obote then suspended the 1962 Constitution and appointed himself President, to the displeasure of the peoples of Buganda and of the other Kingdoms. Four years later he abolished the Kingdoms and created a republic.

Uganda remained part of the British Commonwealth, but Britain was much displeased when Obote nationalized a number of major enterprises, mostly British, particularly banking and coffee institutions in which the Ugandan Government took a 60 percent interest. This also made him the immediate enemy of business circles in Kampala. And, finally, he used the brutal power of Amin and the Army to control the various tribes.

In the few meetings I had with him and Peter McLean, my counterpart, I never found that he was deeply interested in development, leaving this to his Ministers and their Permanent Secretaries. His entire time seemed to be spent in asserting his political position.

On Safari

Our work in the field was progressing satisfactorily. Quite often I had to go on safari to visit our experts on the job or to talk to district authorities about the planning of new development projects. We were still at the stage of building up our program and these trips, often accompanied by civil servants from the Ministries, were an essential part of my job. They also taught me a lot about the country. I found them fascinating, not only because I discovered the country, but because I got to experience the wild beasts in their natural environment, almost as if I had been a tourist visiting the game parks. I traveled days on end across the plains and the hills under the immense blue and violet vault of the East African sky. I felt free, transported into another world. As Isak Dinesen had so beautifully said about Kenya in *Out of Africa*:

> The views were immensely wide, made for greatness and freedom. The chief feature of the landscape and of your life in it was the air . . . in the middle of the day the air was alive, like a flame burning, it scintillated, waved and shone like running water. . . .

I was under the spell of the bush, but I felt something rewarding: I was working with the Africans participating in the building of a modern Uganda, and the training of its human resources.

The term *safari* in East Africa is not restricted to the hunting or photographing of wild beasts, with or without an organized tour. Any trip of a certain length, for business or otherwise, is called a safari. When I went on safari I took a brand new office station wagon, a Peugeot 404 which I had been authorized by UN Headquarters to purchase from a local dealer. We had the first new model 404 in Kampala. Although a French car, it was extremely popular in British East Africa. That year it had won the grueling East African Safari rally, the toughest circuit in the world. The

Peugeots were excellent cars for rugged East Africa: the only fault we discovered was that when driving fast on the unpaved sandy rose-colored roads across the bush, they had a tendency to slide on slippery gravel surfaces. This happened a few times during our trips, fortunately without creating a real accident. One therefore had to be cautious at the least curve in the road, a difficult thing to teach an African driver. Mercedes-Benz were also popular in East Africa, favored over the Peugeots, and held the road better.

I had an excellent chauffeur, George, a *Muganda*[20] to the core, who loved his kingdom and was very faithful to us. He spoke English well and knew about the country's politics. His father had been Chief of Police in Kampala. We liked George. He was quite proud to wear his pale blue uniform with the UN insignia. He lived with his wife and children in a cottage on our property.

One day we drove to Toro to visit an irrigation project at its inception, stopping first to pay my respects to the King of Toro, George Rukidi III, at his residence, a comfortable country house much like a Latin American hacienda. The three little kingdoms of Buganda, Ankole and Bunyoro, with the Kigezi district, constitute the Western Province of Uganda. King George was a tall man, perhaps six feet four, with dark complexion and lively expressive eyes, who welcomed us in a most friendly and informal manner. The District Officer, still a Briton, was with him with two local Ugandan technicians. Following a short meeting, we worked together for the rest of the morning at the site of the future project in Mubuku. The purpose was for the expert from the Food and Agriculture Organization to demonstrate, on a one-thousand-acre tract, modern irrigation and agricultural techniques for crops suitable for export and the domestic market. In the afternoon we drove to Kilembe mine in the west of the Province, at the foot of the Rivenzori, the famous Mountains of the Moon, where copper and cobalt are mined. It is the most important and well-known mining enterprise in the country and the reason why the British built the Uganda Railroad from Mombasa to Kasase near Kilembe. The ore is first transported to Jinja in the east of Uganda. Thanks to the water power of the Owen Falls at Lake Victoria, a smelter treats the ore before it is exported.

It was at Jinja that John Speke, the famous British explorer who discovered Uganda, had first seen the River Nile leap over the falls with all its thunder. The power generated by the falls is tremendous—not from the height, which is only 12 feet—but cascading from its width of over 500 feet, carrying an enormous volume of water at an average rate of 620 tons a second. The historic spot is what is

---

20 A member of the Buganda tribe. The area is called Buganda and the Buganda are the inhabitants of Buganda; Muganda is the singular for Buganda.

commonly called the source of the White Nile, although it actually starts southwest of Lake Victoria in the mountains east of Lake Tanganyika and flows into Lake Victoria as the Kagera River.

No wonder the principal industrial complex in Uganda started at Jinja. Electricity had indeed transformed life in this part of Africa. Close by were breweries, weaving industries, the Nyanza Textiles (run by Europeans with African labor using Ugandan cotton) and a cement plant, Tororo, sixty miles further east. The Nile can provide a surplus of electric power for export to Kenya nearby, Nairobi being only 325 miles away. In the future this industrial center will develop further. It will be possible to transform a much larger part of the 400,000 bales of cotton produced each year in Uganda and meet the needs for millions of yards of textiles required to clothe the population of East Africa. The mill I visited operated only at one-fourth capacity.

Driving around in Toro that day we passed a few tea estates. I admired the neatly trimmed rows of tea, a fairly low bush kept at a height convenient for picking. An Englishman named Meredith had about 130 acres planted in tea on an estate of about 640 acres. Fortunately for him, the land had been acquired before 1916. After that date the British Protectorate decided that large estates could no longer be purchased by European and Asian settlers. British policy was that the land should be preserved for the Africans. Uganda was not a colony like Kenya, where thousands of former British Army Officers became gentlemen farmers after the First World War. In Toro several tea estates were in the hands of the Uganda Company, a government enterprise managed by Europeans.

As an independent planter, Meredith lived with his wife in a well-built home surrounded by a large English garden with a profusion of flowers, in an ideal climate at an elevation of 5,000 feet. He managed hundreds of workers whom he described as courteous. In those days he had little difficulty with them. They were illiterate and shy. Surrounded by a beautiful natural landscape of rolling hills and tall trees, with cattle in the meadows, it seemed that he and his wife led an idyllic and at the same time lucrative existence. Jim Ilett, a British UN economist we came to know in Entebbe with his family, contemplated running a tea estate in Toro at the end of his assignment and living this kind of life. I met him again several years later at our New York Headquarters. He told me that, having studied the situation carefully, they decided not to settle in Uganda since the country was becoming unstable and living on an isolated farm would constitute too high a risk. When he left the UN, they instead went to live in Ontario, Canada. They were fortunate not to have settled in Uganda as they would have been there during Amin's reign of terror. I also was lucky to have been able to serve in Uganda before the change of regime, although in the last months of my stay in Kampala clouds were appearing on the horizon caused by the political infighting between Obote, a man from the north, and the Buganda, who were gradually losing their power in the country.

Murchison Falls

My daughter Carole came from Mount Holyoke College to see us for the Christmas holidays the first year we were in Uganda. I drove to Entebbe to meet her plane in the early morning and drove her through the Entebbe Botanical Garden—perhaps one of the most beautiful in Africa—so she could admire its giant trees and myriad tropical flowers. I drove to a part that was a true jungle, with lianas hanging from tree to tree, so she could see the exact spot where the first Tarzan movie, with Johnny Weismueller, had been filmed in the '30s.

During the holidays we decided to safari to Murchison Falls where, into a misty gorge, the Nile makes a spectacular plunge of 130 feet from a high plateau to the marshy plain unfolding towards the Sudanese border. We took the Peugeot and asked George to be our driver for the trip, and paid all expenses out of pocket.

Driving through the kingdom of Bunyoro we reached Paraa and Baker's View, the spot where, in 1864, Samuel Baker, the famous British explorer, traveling with his wife Florence, became the first white man to see Lake Albert and its waters flowing north into the Nile across a most desolate unpopulated area. Contemplating the scene I could not but be in awe of the tremendous courage and endurance of the first white men and one woman who walked across Central Africa. In his journal, Baker tells that his wife, who had walked with him all the way, almost died in a swampy river near Lake Albert. Baker said later he was horrified to see her sinking in the weeds, her face distorted and perfectly purple. Porters carried her, unconscious, for seven days while her husband marched by the side of her litter. When she awoke, she was delirious, having a violent succession of convulsions. Thinking it over, the men put a new handle on the pickax that evening and sought a dry spot to dig her grave. But that night Florence awoke. When her husband himself woke up a few hours later he found her calm and well again. Two days later she was ready to resume the journey.

We continued our drive towards Murchison Falls. Speke had discovered the Victoria Nile and the part of the river flowing northwest from the Victoria, but it was Baker who first saw the falls of the Nile and named them after Sir Robert Murchison, President of the British Royal Geographic Society. Baker's discoveries ended the controversy between Burton and Speke about the source of the White

Nile. He called the lake 'Albert,' making Lakes Victoria and Albert the two sources of the Nile.[21]

We arrived at Murchison Lodge at twilight. The lodge sits on an escarpment of the Nile from which one can see many animals on the banks. It had a central unit including a restaurant, and a large number of cottages for tourists spread over a garden with walkways leading to the restaurant. These paths were bordered by bushes and small trees. The night was pitch dark. Away from the center there were no lights. Each night roving elephants would invade the garden, munching on leaves. We could hear them, but as they were dark themselves we could not see them. We did know, however, that they were close. It was eerie. Fatal accidents could have happened easily had someone bumped into the wild beasts, and more than one tourist was afraid to go to the restaurant at night. Yet we had to if we wanted to eat. Back in our little cottage after dinner we could hear the elephants just a few paces away.

The next morning we boarded a boat to go up the Nile to the Falls. This was a memorable journey. The riverbanks teemed with animals. We saw many monkeys in the trees, jumping from branch to branch. With my binoculars I could see the lovemaking of two baboons under a tree. On the same bank, mouths agape, were a number of enormous crocodiles, some easily 20 feet long. The launch came close to the banks. Two enormous crocodiles waddled into the water just a few feet away. We saw many pelicans, marabout storks and snake-birds.

As we neared the falls, the scenery on each side of the river became even more spectacular. The grass was a sparkling green. Trees of all kinds and shapes with overhanging branches crossing over the branches of other trees formed a striking background for all kinds of beasts wandering between the forest and the river. It was like an exotic wonderland. Very close to us, literally hundreds of hippopotami were in the water, the tops of their heads and short ears above the surface, peering at us with their brilliant small eyes. We saw five or six buffaloes under the trees. Two waterbucks were playing on the other bank, chasing each other, followed by a herd of elephants on a stroll.

As for birds, I cannot adequately describe them. There were ibis, herons, skinners, their large red heads under their wings. And then the river widened into a great basin and, far in front of us, we saw the Falls glistening in the sun. As we drew nearer the rumbling of the water filled the air, becoming more and more pronounced, gradually deafening us completely. At a respectable distance our launch stopped, as the turbulence of the waters at the base of the falls did not permit a closer approach.

---

21 *Exploration of Africa* (New York: American Heritage, 1963).

Before leaving the next day we drove through Murchison Falls National Park. We saw a lioness and her cubs finishing the carcass of an antelope under a tree; we met a large herd of elephants crossing the road. Respecting the rules of the park, we stopped the car and patiently waited at a distance. In National Parks the beasts come first. The parks preserve wildlife in its natural surroundings, enabling it to live in liberty and at peace. They protect the animals against poaching. Yet Africans living near the parks consider them as potential meat and a threat to farming as they roam at night killing cattle and being a threat to their own lives and occupations. The UN had helped the Game Parks which have a vital importance, on scientific grounds, for the survival of animal life. Their great value as an attraction to tourists from all over the world is a source of considerable revenues to the country.

Two little incidents happened just before leaving Murchison Falls National Park. An isolated bull elephant was about to cross the road. We stopped the car to let him go, but suddenly his ears flapped and, turning half way, he violently roared and began to charge towards us. George, with admirable presence of mind, slammed the car into reverse and gunned away at a great clip. Seeing us retreat, the elephant stopped and turned away in contempt. A moment later we saw a rhinoceros cross the field some 60 feet in front of us. I wanted to take a picture of this rarely seen animal and asked George to stop. I quickly alighted, but this made George very nervous. In fact the rhino, having seen us, was changing his course. He was wounded in the leg, blood dripping from it. For a second there was danger. I snapped my picture and regained my seat as the animal pursued its course away from us.

We returned home impressed by the way the game parks were kept in Uganda. Later, under Amin, poaching became the rule and the herds were decimated. The restoration of the game parks is now a prime Government objective.

* * *

On our way back, in the middle of Bunyoro, without knowing, we had passed through a tse-tse fly-infested area. We were stopped at a control station. One tse-tse fly was found in our station wagon, which could have stung any of us and given us sleeping sickness.

A few days later we hosted a luncheon at our house for a team of experts from the Food and Agricultural Organization who had come from Rome to advise the Government on cattle development and related health problems. The head of the team was Chief Veterinary Officer of the Food and Agriculture Organization, a Scottish doctor with long experience who had previously worked for many years in East Africa under the British. He was sitting on Natalie's right at luncheon. In the course of conversation she told him that Nancy, our younger daughter, had had her spleen removed following an accident the year before at camp in New Hampshire. She said Nancy was with us in Uganda. He became alarmed and said, "Do you know that in the course of twenty years of service in this area, I have not seen one single cow with a removed spleen that did not die? Without her spleen your daughter cannot fight infection. If she contracted malaria, for instance, she would not be capable of fighting the disease. You should take her out of this area. You should write to the Institute of Tropical Diseases in London or the Pasteur Institute in Paris and ask their advice as to what to do with your daughter. I urge you to do so."

The next day I wrote the two letters. Shortly after, the reply from Paris arrived, recommending that Nancy be sent to Europe or the United States. At the end of Christmas break she returned with her sister to the U.S., where she stayed with the family of friends for three months pending Natalie's return. Our family life in East Africa had ended. The irony of it all was that the Institute of Tropical Diseases two weeks later took a completely different view, saying that it would not be wise to send Nancy back to the U.S. in the middle of winter where she would be at greater risk than in East Africa of catching an infectious disease. By then Nancy had left, and we believed we had taken the right decision, although it singularly upset the rest of our mission in Uganda.

* * *

A few days before Natalie left Uganda I paid a visit to Karamoja with her, a region in the north of the country, near the Ugandan border with Sudan and Kenya. This was a closed district. It was a day's drive from Kampala, with temperatures well over 110°F, in a dry, oven-like atmosphere hard to bear.

This primitive area, populated by about 150,000 people and their cattle, had been a problem for many years. Their health left much to be desired and medical and social services were being strengthened. The only human diet was a mixture of milk and blood, like the Masai in Kenya. This does not harm the animals, but it is not a sufficiently diversified diet for the humans.

The men still go around naked. For years the British tried to make the Karemojong wear clothes like others and become more self-reliant, with little success. When we were there in 1964 the women were still half naked and the men, except for a dark little blanket over one shoulder, wore nothing at all. They went naked not only in the countryside but also in the town of Moroto where I saw them shopping at one of the stores. Their hair was arrayed in elaborate coiffures, matted with colored clay.

These are semi-nomadic pastoral people. They graze their animals until the grass is gone, then move to another area. I discussed with the district commissioner and his assistant the need for digging deep wells at various locations and controlling overgrazing under a project which would receive FAO assistance. In Karamoja, life revolves entirely around cattle. A young man about to be married must give a bride prize, as many as 60 to 100 head of cattle, depending on the quality of the girl. Cattle rustling and fighting among the tribes were current and for this reason the Ugandan Army maintained a detachment of soldiers in the Karamoja to police the area.

A Visit to Zanzibar

My last trip within East Africa before returning to the United States in May 1964 was to Dar-es-Salaam, the capital of Tanganyika, to take leave of my friend Adu, our Senior Representative for that region. Dar was the port of embarkation for Zanzibar, the nearby island, with its rich historic past. I had always wanted to visit this exotic island, the name of which seemed to come from a tale of *The Thousand and One Arabian Nights*. My wish was to be able to spend two days there and try to recapture some of its past.

The city was created more than 1,000 years earlier by the Shirazis who had sailed down from Persia. Later it had been the base from which to explore East Africa. It was from there that Burton and Speke had started their journeys to discover the sources of the Nile. It was also the port of departure of Dr. Livingston's explorations. One could still visit the house where he lived and from which he had assembled caravans for his African safaris. Stanley had also started from Zanzibar to find Dr. Livingston in 1871, and again on an exploration of the shores of Lake Victoria in 1874.

In the days of the African explorations the town of Zanzibar had a population of 100,000, including Africans, Arabs and Persians. Its port was visited by ships from all over the world, including Yankee Clippers. It was a place of transit for slaves and ivory. Its humid tropical climate was ideal for growing spices and the island had become the world's greatest producer of cloves. In 1890 it became a British Protectorate. More recently, its fascinating past and its handicrafts had attracted tourists and the island was flourishing.

But a few months before my visit to Dar-es-Salaam, Zanzibar was the theater of an abominable tragedy: a savage coup by the blacks against the Arab minority. All of a sudden this torpid little island had become an island of terror. Several thousands, mostly Arabs, had been killed, and the Sultan dismissed, in a revolution led by a redoubtable black leader trained abroad, a Maoist Communist named "Bloody Babu." Anyone who could be called a colonialist was arrested, expelled or killed.

Just a few weeks before I arrived in Dar, the British civil servants still there had been ordered to clear the island by April 30th, their servants having been strictly forbidden to help them pack. More than 2,000 persons were crammed in detention camps. The island had become an armed camp.

Tourists were forbidden. This seemed to be the end of my project. But the day I had planned to go the ban was lifted. Thanks to Adu, who seemed to know everybody in Dar, I became the first American authorized to land on Zanzibar after the coup. The hop by small plane was only twenty minutes from Dar.

Needless to say, under the circumstances I could hardly recapture the spirit of the old Zanzibar. As soon as I landed I felt like I was in a concentration camp. Policemen with Russian burp guns patrolled the streets. I saw few people. The narrow lanes and their shops selling chests, ivory, amber beads, silver trays and jewelry were deserted. The palace of the Sultan was abandoned, some buildings demolished. Only one or two *dhows* could be seen sailing in the harbor.

I tried to find information on the new regime for my own satisfaction. Since I was a UN official I was received by the Director of the Ministry of Information, sitting in his office with an East German assistant beside him. There were a number of Communist advisors helping the Revolutionary Council. The police and the militia were being trained by East Germans. But Zanzibar was still a member of the British Commonwealth. The U.S. still had a consulate. The young foreign service officer in charge was named Frank Carlucci who, twenty-years later, was to become Secretary of Defense in the Reagan Administration, replacing Caspar Weinberger.

U.S. interests in the island had been mainly the building and maintenance of a $3 million space-tracking station, one of sixteen around the world to communicate with orbiting astronauts. The Zanzibar Government summarily forced the U.S. to dismantle the station. It was at that time that William Attwood, U.S. Ambassador to Kenya, a friend from New Canaan whom I had just visited in Nairobi, warned the East African governments that what was happening in Zanzibar should concern them, as Zanzibar was becoming another Cuba at the doorstep of Africa.

That night I slept in the best hotel in the city. It was shabby, the fan did not work and my room was infested with mosquitoes. My visit was a shocking experience of the takeover of a small country by a Communist gang.

I completed my trip with a tour of the clove plantations and a friendly conversation with a young Persian managing one of them, who told me about his happy life in the island before all these events had come to pass. Zanzibar was another African country which had gone by the wayside. On the plane to Egypt a few days later, on leaving Uganda, I recognized Babu as one of my flight companions. He was heading for Moscow for consultations. A few days after I left Dar-es-Salaam the governments of Tanganyika and Zanzibar signed an agreement by which the two countries became one under the name of Tanzania with a socialist Government under Muralimu Julius Nyerere as President. This immediately stabilized the situation of Zanzibar but created new problems.

* * *

My mission ended at the end of May. Peter McLean, the Permanent Secretary in charge of Central Planning in the Office of President Obote, wrote to me in the name of the government:

> You arrived in Uganda at a time when we were about to lose a good deal of our experience on technical assistance due to the departure of the British staff. Nevertheless, we have over the last year, with your help and guidance, regained a fair measure of 'expertise' in dealing with the United Nations and its Agencies in the field. I am personally most grateful to you for all you have done. You can, with justification, feel you have made a real contribution to Uganda's development.

During my last week in Uganda I took leave of my colleagues, local officers and friends. I was to be replaced by Kenneth Robinson, transferred from Somalia, a competent agricultural economist from Trinidad, West Indies, with long UNDP service in Africa. One of my last jobs, two days before I left, was to ship our cat, Pixie, and our dog, a poodle named Valentine, back to the States. In the middle of the night I took them to Entebbe so they could meet the giant cargo plane which came in at 2 a.m. When I took the animals in their crates to the belly of the plane I saw they would travel in the company of perhaps twenty wild beasts including lions, bound for various European zoos, and the Peugeot which had just won the East Africa Rally, on its way for exhibition in London's Trafalgar Square.

Idi Amin's Legacy

To my good fortune I was no longer in Uganda when Idi Amin seized power. Yet I feel that this story would be incomplete if I did not comment on the tragic fate of the country after I left my assignment.

Amin, among the most cruel dictators ever known, was born and raised in northwestern Uganda, in an area called the Nubia along the Nile River, at the boundaries of Sudan and Zaire, the former Belgian Congo. He was a member of the largely Kakwa animist tribe, but at age sixteen became a Muslim. Like many young men from the Northern territories he enlisted in the Ugandan Armed Forces. These recruits were regarded as foreigners by the Buganda.

Amin was big, his six-foot-four height quite imposing. First an army cook, he grew in popularity when he became heavyweight boxing champion of the Ugandan Army. Fifteen years later, when I arrived in Uganda, he had worked his way up to officer status. At the great annual Tattoo, a festival held at the National Stadium of Kampala to which we had been invited by the Prime Minister, he paraded with the troops, clearly visible in his uniform at the head of his company. A Muganda I knew, seated by me, pointed him out saying, "There is big Idi Amin, leading his company. He is an ignorant, an illiterate, and a brute. But wait a while. One day you will see him at the head of the Ugandan Army. He is ferociously ambitious and licks the boots of his superiors starting with the British officers, and will use any means to advance."

Amin had served in the Colonial Kenyan Army, the King's African Rifles, where for the first time he revealed his penchant for savagery. During the pacification of Karamoja he was in charge of stopping the stealing of cattle between the Pokos, a Kenyan tribe and the Karamajong people. In order to get the confession of the rustlers arrested by his soldiers, the sanction was to cut off their genitals if they would not confess their crimes and reveal where they where hiding their arms. It seems incredible that the British officers still in charge would not undertake criminal proceedings against Amin. According to George Ivan Smith, a former UN senior advisor in East Africa who later wrote a book on Amin, [22]Sir Walter Courts, the Governor of Uganda, had warned Obote that Amin should be watched on his return to the Ugandan Army. Obote decided against prosecuting him. Amin was then a major. When British officers went home, creating vacancies, he was made a colonel.

In January 1971 Obote had gone to a Commonwealth Conference in Singapore, taking a risk in absenting himself from the country. What he did not know was that Amin had planned his assassination. While Obote was away the plot was discovered by soldiers faithful to Obote, and Amin decided to take over the Government before the President's return. The takeover was bloody, with much of the resistance being staged by soldiers from Lango and Acholi—Obote's ethnic group.

There was little British reaction to Amin's takeover. Apparently London knew about the plot but was not opposed to it because Obote was regarded as a socialist and the British wanted rid of him. Britain recognized the Amin regime almost immediately.

According to Smith, who was able to talk to psychologists and medical men, Amin suffered from a form of epilepsy. His decisions were erratic. Virtually incapable of writing, he could not read complicated documents; they were read to him. He gave all orders and instructions to his ministers orally.

22 George Ivan Smith, *Ghosts of Kampala* (New York: St. Martin Press, 1980).

Amin dissolved Parliament, organized his own administration with the backing of the Buganda, the Church and business. Although it was he who had several years before carried out Obote's orders to expel the *Kabaka*, he arranged for the return of the body of the former King, who had died in England, and gave him an impressive funeral in Kampala, thus increasing his own popularity among the Buganda.

Under pressure from Mohamar Ghaddaffi, the Libyan dictator to whom he had turned for financial support, Amin undertook to convert the Ugandan people to Islam and make the country a Moslem state, although barely 6 percent of Ugandans practiced Islam. Summarily he expelled the Israelis and the Asians, a disastrous decision since the latter had been responsible for industrial and trade development in the country.

Prisoners were treated cruelly. Enemies of the regime disappeared or were killed by Amin's gangsters in faked car accidents or in cold-blooded slaughters. It was reported that Amin would kill his victims with a sledge hammer over the chest or by running over their bodies with tanks, cutting off the genitals and displaying them to the Press. It was estimated that several hundred thousand people were murdered or disappeared during Amin's reign. Amin started a war against the Catholic church and arranged for the murder of Archbishop Luwum in February 1977. This outrage was reported by the world press and generated general indignation against the regime. Foreign embassies were closed in Kampala, including that of the United States.

The magnificent Mulago Hospital, built by the British in Kampala as a gift at Independence, was stripped of everything including equipment and pharmaceuticals. Only a few nurses remained. The economic situation deteriorated precipitously. The price of a single egg on the black market, the only place where one could buy food products, reached one dollar. Corruption was at every Government level and, unfortunately, various Israeli, British and American firms were involved in shady transactions.

Not the least monstrous in Amin's reign of terror was, in my view, the passive reaction of the international community. Amin, a Hitler admirer, was practicing pure and simple genocide against the Buganda. No power raised even a finger because it was an internal problem. Further, he behaved abominably when his turn came as head of state to become President of the Organization for African Unity (OAU). He addressed the General Assembly of the United Nations. The French, Israeli and UK delegations left the Hall in protest during his degrading performance. The irony was that Amin could not even read his speech. He stood at the rostrum, sweating, dressed in the military uniform of a Marshal, exaggeratedly bemedalled like a black Herman

Goering. His speech was delivered by his Ambassador, and all he could do was stutter a few additional sentences in English and Swahili at the end. This was an extremely degrading spectacle for the world body.

Claiming it should be part of Uganda, in November 1978 Amin invaded the Kagera Salient, a part of Tanzania located southwest of Lake Victoria. Nyerere's army repulsed him and pursued his troops into Ugandan territory, taking the towns of Mbabara and Masaka on the road to Entebbe and Kampala. But it was not until March 1979 that Amin's forces were defeated by Tanzanian soldiers after bloody fighting, despite the assistance of a 3,000-soldier contingent from Libya and considerable Soviet equipment including heavy armored troop carriers and tanks. The Libyans, trained for desert warfare, were befuddled by the battle conditions imposed by the Ugandan terrain. At the end of the war, Uganda had lost more than 1,000 soldiers, Ghaddaffi around 600 and Tanzania close to 400. The war had cost hundreds of millions of dollars on each side, and the number of civilians killed in both Uganda and Tanzania totaled several thousands.

To think that Amin can now quietly wind down his days in Saudi Arabia simply because he is a Moslem defies understanding. His legacy will be felt for a long time in Uganda and hopefully will eventually lead to a reconciliation of the tribes and the development of a deservedly united and peaceful nation.

Since Amin, several men have served as interim presidents, still amidst severe political and social chaos. One was Godfrey Binaisa, a former Attorney General, the father of a Middlebury College student I welcomed at my home in Vermont in 1984.

Through a fraudulent election, Obote, despite his limited popularity, returned to power for a second five-year period. It was a second reign of terror during which many people were killed or arrested. The country was overrun by groups of Amin's former soldiers and, reportedly, of Tanzanian soldiers turned thieves.

Limited international assistance to Uganda resumed after Amin's departure and consisted of many relief activities and the restoration of social services. I was invited by the International Labor Organization to go to Uganda for one year to carry out a manpower survey. The request for this assistance was, however, premature and the assignment was called off.

The situation in the country was still chaotic. Describing conditions in 1981, Maury Miloff, a young Canadian assistant UNDP program in officer in Kampala, reported that the economic and security situation in Kampala was a terrible mess. There was hardly anything in the market, and lots of shooting every night. Shooting would start when night was falling and would continue until just before dawn. The principal concern of the UNDP resident representative, Melissa Wells, was the famine in Karamoja. She can be credited with saving many lives among these pastoral people.

The lives of UN experts were in danger. A UNESCO couple was murdered by bandits in their beds in Kampala. Miloff told of his own very difficult existence with his pregnant wife, Helen, who was trying to make a safe little nest when there was shooting outside their door every night. Their friends and neighbors also lived in fear, emotionally drained. Nevertheless, Miloff concluded that an organization like UNDP is needed in such a tragic situation as Uganda. It was, more than ever, an expression of commitment of people to the people and of cooperation among nations.

To make matters worse, Uganda is now one of the African countries hit hardest by AIDS. The fact that health services, doctors and nurses were reduced to almost nothing during Amin's years makes it nearly impossible to fight the disease. The Government has launched a vigorous education campaign, preaching the need for fidelity; trucks carry the inscription in large white letters: "AIDS—Zero Grazing," meaning "don't fraternize in the meadows, be faithful". The people have nicknamed the disease "Slim" because AIDS victims lose weight rapidly. Since 1982 the number of declared AIDS cases has grown from 19 to more than 2,000. AIDS most affects those who travel between cities, particularly truckers and barmaids, who test, respectively, 33 and 76 percent positive, for the HIV virus. The World Health Organization is trying to help save the country in various ways.

Yoseri Museveni

Since 1986 Uganda has had a new leader, Yoseri Museveni, a young patriot educated in Tanzania before Amin took power. He returned to his country by going back to Tanzania to form an anti-Amin guerrilla organization called the National Resistance Movement (NRM). The NRM raised an army of patriots from various political factions and the Front for National Salvation (FRONASA) which Museveni camped north of Kampala in an area known as the Luwereo Triangle. From this strategic position he was able to take over the capital and the Government, forcing the last dictator, General Tito Okello—who had taken power from Obote in 1985—to flee to the north.

The new President has adopted a peaceful approach to the rehabilitation of his country. Anyone who would lay down arms could join the Government, no questions asked. This approach seems to have worked. With the country finally at peace, the NRM is trying to reconstruct from the immense waste left after 15 years under three brutal dictatorships.

Will Museveni succeed? His ten-point manifesto stresses participatory democracy, security, national unity, national independence, social services, the defense of human rights and a mixed economy. Museveni's Government is a nationwide coalition of political and social forces which have pledged to usher in a new and better future for the long-suffering Ugandan people. The economic program calls for a mixed economy allowing activities to be carried out by private enterprise jointly with the state in elected sections, the state gearing the economy towards the desired goals. Museveni rejects both the laissez-faire of pure capitalism and over-nationalization of the socialist economies that burden the state at the micro-economic level. It remains to be seen how such a balanced program can be carried out successfully. There is hope, however, that solid progress can be achieved. The President has the confidence of the international community. A consortium of donors, including the World Bank, the UN and its specialized agencies, are now helping Uganda in its difficult recovery.

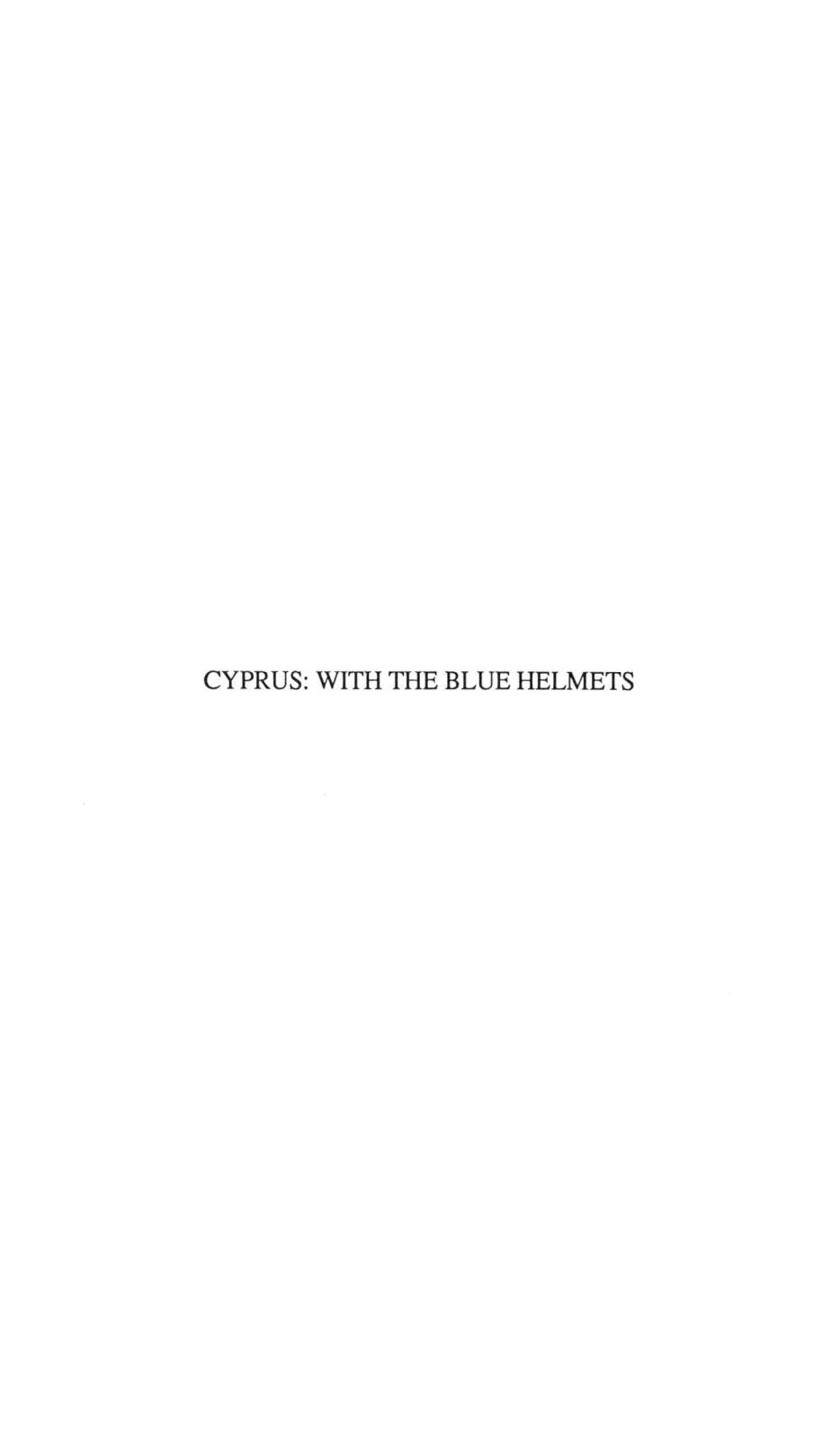

CYPRUS: WITH THE BLUE HELMETS

CYPRUS: WITH THE BLUE HELMETS

An Unexpected Assignment

My expectations were high when I left Uganda in June 1964. I was scheduled to take up a two-year tour of duty in Paris with UNESCO. I had first to return to my home in New Canaan, Connecticut to prepare for this new assignment.

From Entebbe I flew to Cairo, where I stopped for two days. I wish I had been able to stay longer to get to know the city and perhaps visit Alexandria, to find out whether the fascinating ambience of Lawrence Durrell's *Quartet* could still be felt there.

Cairo was preparing for the official visit of Nikita Khruschev, the Soviet leader. In his honor Gamal Abdel Nasser had decorated the city and the long route to the airport with literally thousands of Soviet flags. The street names in English had been erased and replaced by Arabic names, creating great confusion for foreign tourists. I found Cairo crowded, noisy and dusty. I made a quick visit to the Pyramids and paid a call on my colleague, UNDP Resident Representative Jan Van den Heerden, a Dutch civil engineer recently transferred to Cairo from his post as head of our vast Mekong River development project. With so little time on my hands, instead of visiting the city he advised me to spend a few hours relaxing around the pool at the Hilton Hotel, in a pretty garden.

The next day I flew to Paris to discuss with UNESCO their projects in Uganda. Then, after a "bumpy" flight to New York, I reached New Canaan, happy to be back with my family. I had hardly returned when the phone rang and the Western Union girl read a telegram to me from UN Headquarters advising me that the Secretary General had selected me to urgently join a small group of senior staff members assigned to the newly created peacekeeping operation on the Island of Cyprus. I had been appointed Advisor to the General Commanding the UN Force in Nicosia. The Cyprus operation was considered an Emergency and, as in the case of the Congo crisis, such missions are command performances for the staff. There was no way that personal preference could be expressed in the matter. UNESCO was not particularly pleased with the news that I would not be available but agreed to wait three months for me, which was the period for which the UN Peacekeeping Force had been initially authorized by the Security Council. Our family plans to live in Paris were in limbo, since nobody had any idea as to whether I would be released that soon. Disappointed, the family stayed quietly in New Canaan for the summer.

The next day I went to the UN for a briefing. Field Service and the Bureau of Personnel had been very busy since March 1964 when the Security Council had authorized the Secretary General to raise a peacekeeping force for Cyprus. The Force would preserve international peace and security, use its best efforts to prevent a recurrence of the fighting between the Greek and Cypriot communities on the island, and restore law and order.

Behind the Cyprus Crisis

The background of the Cyprus crisis was enormously complicated. How the problem reached international significance in the '60s and why its solution had fallen into the lap of the UN should interest my readers, if they want to understand its full importance internationally and the role of the United Nations Peacekeeping Force in it. A brief recounting of the island's history leading to the crisis seemed helpful, and I made it a point in my briefing to spend some time in the Dag Hammarskjöld Library to review the history of this beautiful little island, where Aphrodite had been born and which had been the theater of so many invasions in the past.

When Cyprus became independent in 1960 it had a total population of 560,000, about 80 percent of Greek and 20 percent of Turkish origins. The two communities occupied distinct zones on the island, with the Turks in the northeast only 40 miles from the Turkish mainland. The rest of the island was inhabited by the Greek Cypriots, but there also were hundreds of villages of mixed Greek and Turkish population. It struck me that, when independence was declared, it was the first time in more than twenty-five centuries that the island had not been ruled by foreign powers.

The Mycenean Greeks were the first to invade, in the second millennium BC, and then the Phoenicians, the Assyrians and the Egyptians in successive invasions. The Persians were there in 540 BC. Despite these invasions, Greek culture was able to flourish there. Then came the Roman occupation, which made Cyprus a province of the Roman Empire for two centuries. By the first century AD Christianity had been introduced on Cyprus. Then for 900 years it was part of the Byzantine Empire until the decline of Byzantium brought the Crusaders and Richard the Lion Hearted on their way to the Holy Land. The country was governed by the Knights Templar, and then under the secular dynasty of the French Lusignans who for three centuries until 1489 were the kings of Cyprus. After that, for almost 400 years, until 1878, the island was under Turkish occupation.

By then Cyprus was of great interest to England, as a major strategic location in the eastern Mediterranean. The British were able to lease the island from the Turks. In 1925 Britain declared Cyprus a crown colony. From that point the situation on the island grew tense, soon degenerating into a political crisis involving the Greek and Turkish Cypriot communities and Greece, Turkey and the United Kingdom.

The Greek people of Cyprus had one great desire. Instead of being colonized, they wanted union with Greece, *Enosis*, as they felt they were blood brothers of the Greeks. They revolted in 1931 but did not succeed in rejecting British rule. Again after World War II the Cypriot people asked Britain to apply the principle of self-determination and grant them independence. The refusal of the British Government, coupled with its rejection of *Enosis*, led to another violent and bloody armed revolt, the "Cypriot Liberation War," by the Greek Cypriots in 1955. The struggle involved numerous acts of terrorism and executions led by EKOA, a nationalist movement directed by retired Greek general George Grivas. This struggle in the mind of the Greek Cypriots would lead them to Union with Greece. It was during these violent days that one morning we learned at my office in New York that the son of one of our British colleagues, Wilfred Benson, the young manager of a bank in Nicosia, had been killed by terrorists as he was leaving his office. His father never recovered.

All along, the Turkish Cypriot community and the Turks in Ankara had wanted their own brand of self-determination: partition. But partition was an extremely difficult proposition in a country whose population was so intermixed geographically; many Greek villages were located in the proposed Turkish area, and, as mentioned, many mixed villages contained both populations. Instead of partition, and as a result of a tripartite agreement drawn up at Zurich and London in 1959 by NATO powers (Britain, Greece and Turkey) and representatives of the Greek and Turkish Cypriots, the island was declared an independent republic.

Before leaving New York I studied the Zurich-London Agreements as part of my briefing, and found them so complicated I doubted they could work for Cyprus. They included the creation of a Greek Cypriot President and a Turkish Cypriot Vice-President, each elected for five years from communal polls, each having a veto power over decisions of the House of Representatives concerning foreign affairs, defense or security. Under the Agreements, *Enosis* and partition would be forever prohibited. Britain would retain sovereignty over two areas containing British military bases and the Cypriot civil service and security forces would comprise 70 percent Greek Cypriots and 30 percent Turkish Cypriots.

To further complicate the matter the treaty had created two communal chambers, one for each community, with rights to impose taxes for the areas of each community and authority in the matter of religion, cultural affairs, education and personal status. Each of the five largest towns would be divided into Greek and Turkish municipalities, each with its own council.

Greece was also allowed to station 950 men on the island, and Turkey 550, while the President and Vice-President could together request either mainland government—Greece or Turkey—to increase or reduce these contingents. Further, under the Tripartite Agreement the basic structure of the republic could not be altered or amended. This was a total dictum, completely negating all real sovereignty for Cyprus. It was so rigid that it could not function properly.

Great bitterness was expressed by both the Greek and the Turkish Cypriots. In the interests of peace, the island's Greeks had to make considerable concessions: they accepted limited independence instead of *Enosis*; the Turkish Cypriots gave up partition but received in exchange disproportionate powers in the constitution regarding the number of civil servants and security forces representing their ethnic group and this was bitterly resented by the Greek Cypriots.

Independence and Civil War

Finally elections were held in 1960. Archbishop Makarios was confirmed as President of Cyprus and head of the Greek Cypriot community, Dr. Fajil Kuchuk presiding over the Turkish Cypriot community. The two communities, which had been at peace for long periods in the past, were now irremediably split, bringing about a complete deadlock in the Government and leading to civil war.

Communal fighting started in November 1963, accompanied by acts of terrorism in various parts of the island, conducted on both sides by irregular forces which had been storing weapons and ammunition for a number of months. There were many casualties.

The British forces in Cyprus, 7,000 men strong, conducted peacekeeping operations. They wanted to protect their bases and did their best to stop hostilities, but did not want to become a "permanent fire brigade" for Cyprus. They then proposed an international force made up of NATO units. This was accepted by the Governments of Turkey and Greece. Makarios vehemently objected, predicting an unpopular settlement under NATO. A shrewd diplomat with a reputation for being devious, he sought the support of the Soviet Union. The Soviets sided with him, describing the proposed NATO peacekeeping force as an armed invasion and a crude encroachment on the sovereignty, independence and freedom of the Republic of Cyprus, and an attempt to place Cyprus under the military control of NATO. For these reasons the Soviet Union announced to the U.S., Britain, France, Greece and Turkey that it could not remain indifferent to developments so close to its southern borders.[23]

With civil war and chaotic conditions on the island, and Turkish troops ready to embark for Cyprus early in 1964, the situation day by day assumed greater international significance. A war between Greece and Turkey was far from impossible. The British suggested the sending of a UN Peacekeeping force.

At the same time Makarios requested an emergency meeting of the UN Security Council, to ask the UN to become responsible for the solution of the Cyprus problem, to rule out the partition proposed by the Turks and, perhaps, to ultimately obtain the return of the British bases to Cyprus. He was ready to accept a UN peacekeeping force. The force was unanimously approved by the Security Council, and the Secretary-General was authorized to appoint a mediator for the purpose of promoting a peaceful solution and an agreed settlement of the problem confronting Cyprus.

The United Nations Force in Cyprus (UNFICYP)

It took the Secretary-General three months to declare the Force operational. He had to find countries willing to supply troop contingents and equipment acceptable to Cyprus, the Greeks, the Turks and Great Britain. The search was directed to relatively small neutral countries: Sweden, Austria, Ireland, Canada and Finland provided the necessary troops, in addition to the 3,500 Britain had agreed to contribute, bringing the total to about 6,500. The countries which contributed units to UNFICYP paid the expenses of sending these contingents, as the UN did not have financial provisions for this kind of intervention.

As in other UN peacekeeping operations, the troops were not expected to engage in combat. They were to arrive there after a cease-fire. They were only to act as a buffer, interposing themselves between the contending factions, which had agreed not to shoot at each other. But there were serious clashes in various parts of Cyprus even before the UN peacekeeping forces arrived, particularly north of the capital in the Kyrenia region. It was obvious that each party was trying to consolidate its position and overpower its enemy before the UN forces landed. Such was the situation on the island when I arrived in Cyprus in mid-June.

23 UN Document S/5534 (February 8, 1964).

In July 1964, I flew into Athens, changing plane for Nicosia. The flight above the blue Mediterranean was short and beautiful. As we approached the island, only about sixty miles wide at its widest, we could clearly see two green mountain ranges extending from East to West with the highest peak, Mount Olympus (6,400 feet) in the Southern range, called Troodo, which covers nearly half of the island. Heavily forested with cedar trees it is widely known for its famous Kikko monastery. We flew over the Northern range, which forms a narrow belt along a rocky coast with lovely sandy coves and the fortified historic Turkish town of Kyrenia. A few minutes later we landed in Nicosia.

The UN staff was lodged at the Hotel Palace Ledra, where everything happening was the subject of bar and lounge discussion, and where visiting diplomats and journalists stayed. Later those, like me, who were attached to the Force moved into smaller hotels.

Each morning we would attend the meetings held by General Kodendera Subayya Thymayya, the Indian officer commanding the Force. A Sandhurst graduate, he had had a sterling career, had served in World War II and been promoted to Chief of Staff of the Indian Army. In 1950 he had been in Korea with the UN Forces. He was tall, distinguished, easily approachable, and I liked him. He was well aware of the vital importance of the non-military aspects of the conflict, the areas in which I had been sent to assist him. I found him sincere and kind. His valuable services ended at his sudden death in Cyprus in December 1965.

At each morning meeting the unit commanders reported on the situation in their sectors and what the unit had done to prevent the recurrence of fighting. The "blue berets" or "blue helmets" as they were equally referred to, were highly visible, patrolling the streets of Nicosia and the country roads. But one thing soon became quite apparent. The troops, understandably, were not keen on being confused by the Cypriots with the occupying forces. The Greek Cypriots did not want to recognize the British contingent as part of UNFICYP, although they were an integral part of the Force and conducted themselves as such. The Finns, on their arrival, were rumored to have ridden 50 miles on their bicycles from the disembarkation to Nicosia rather than being transported in British lorries. The maple leaf was prominent on all Canadian contingent vehicles.

The largest UNFICYP military contingents came from NATO countries, with Great Britain, Canada and Denmark representing more than 50 percent. The rest, as mentioned, were mostly from neutral European countries: Austria, Finland, Ireland and Sweden. Those from Ireland and the Scandinavian states had already participated in previous UN peacekeeping operations in Suez and in the Congo.

In addition to the military units including brigades, regiments, companies, squadrons and other groups, about 170 civilian policemen and security officers, forming United Nations Civilian Police (UNCIV POL), had come from Australia, Austria, Denmark and Sweden and later from New Zealand. They wore their national uniforms with blue headband and blue berets, and were an integral part of UNFICYP. The contingents were deployed across the island, each having its own sector closely covering the six Cyprus administrative districts.

UNFICYP also included a civilian staff of advisors to the Force commander, of which I was a member. Most of us, totaling about 50, came from the UN Secretariat in New York, including administrative personnel, political and legal advisors, public information officers and other specialists. The Secretary-General's Special Representative in Cyprus, Galo Plaza, a former President of Ecuador who had served the UN in the Congo, was conducting discussions and negotiations with the feuding parties towards achieving the objectives of UNFICYP's mandate and settling the Cyprus crisis. UNFICYP kept close contact with him, while, daily, in accordance with its mandate, it did its best to prevent a recurrence of fighting, to restore law and order, and to contribute to a return to normal conditions.

One did not have to be in Cyprus long to realize that the Greek and the Turkish Cypriots interpreted quite differently the mandate given to the Force: the Turks thought UNFICYP was there to save them from the Greeks, the Greeks thought it was there to help the Government suppress the Turkish rebels.[24] A further major difficulty was that when we acted as negotiators trying to solve some of the two factions' most critical problems, they refused to talk to each other. As a result, I was required to go from one party to the other across the "green line" dividing the two Nicosian communities. This line marked the farthest Turkish advance in street fighting. It went through the slums of the city and along the old Venetian wall which enclosed Nicosia, a tangle of barbed wire, cement-filled drums and abandoned barricades. At various points, I could see on one side of the line a Turk red crescent flag and, opposite, the yellow and white flag of Cyprus, with soldiers milling around each side of the line waiting for something to happen. There were dozens of daily incidents and problems for us to solve. I shall relate only three of them, each distinct but dramatic enough to make my life anything but boring and to teach me some lessons on human behavior.

Saving the Citrus Crop

The Canadian troops were responsible for policing the roads and escorting Greek

---

24 Charles Foley, *Legacy of Strife* (New York: Penguin Books, 1964).

and Turkish Cypriots making specific trips important to the survival of the economy. One of those tasks was to facilitate arrangements between landowners and farmers so that watering and harvest operations could continue without heavy crop losses. This came up particularly with regard to citrus, an important part of the agricultural production of Cyprus. Without watering during the summer, the crop would have been lost.

Often the owners lived far away from their fields and had to be escorted to their properties to avoid incidents. On a July morning in 1964, I was asked by the Government to take under military escort an older Turkish Cypriot, a wealthy landowner who owned important orange and grapefruit orchards in the center of the island. Like thousands of other Turkish Cypriots he had left his village in 1963 at the order of the Turkish Cypriot Community leaders and was resettled as a refugee in the Turkish Community in Nicosia. Moving freely from one part of the island to another was restricted and, being Turkish, he could have been attacked while crossing Greek territory had he been alone on the road.

He had made no arrangement with the people who worked for him before he left, so his orchards had not been watered. His workers were Greeks, as the village in question was one of the hundred mixed villages of Cyprus.

The trip's purpose was to draft a watering contract between those workers and the old man, in the hope that they would be willing to work for him. I had taken with me an interpreter and the Ministry of Agriculture had sent along one of their lawyers to help. An officer of the Canadian contingent also accompanied us with a couple of men in an armed command car. We were following in our UNFICYP car with a driver from our office.

I did not know what to expect when we reached the village. Would the Greek people who knew the old Turk be friendly to him or consider him an enemy? Since my arrival, I had heard so much about the hatred between the two communities and the acts of terrorism perpetrated in various parts of the island that I was curious to see the reception they would give him.

We arrived at the center of the village at noon. There, a large café with a front terrace, perhaps twenty people were quietly having a drink before lunch under the canopy. When we stopped in the middle of the small plaza, and the people at the terrace saw the old man alight from our car, they immediately recognized their former neighbor. There was much excitement. Two came toward us and, to my stupefaction, embraced him. They kissed each other on both cheeks. Soon everyone on the plaza knew who had returned to the village. Evidently our friend was extremely popular.

They asked me to join them for a drink. I accepted, hoping to create the climate for concluding the arrangements we came to complete. And indeed, after lunch, we visited the orchard and were able to discuss the work to be done with the parties involved. With no difficulty we came to an agreement as to how, when and where the work was to be carried out and what would be paid for it. By 4:30 p.m. everything we came for had been settled and our Turkish landowner would have liked to stay longer to talk to his old friends.

We drove back with him to Nicosia, everyone completely satisfied by what had been accomplished. I could not believe it. On one hand were the two official communities, the Turkish Cypriots and the Greek Cypriots, hating each other, at each other's throats, waging war against one another to the point that a large UN Peacekeeping Force had to be brought onto the island to act as a buffer between the fighting parties to restore law and order. On the other was this manifestation of brotherly love and friendship toward a former inhabitant of the village.

This remarkable experience taught me that often, when men start hating each other and groups become enemies, it is their leaders who push them to do so. Terrorists start scaring people and create conflicts and war between ethnic groups. For centuries Greek and Turkish Cypriots had lived together in the mixed Greek Villages and it was only at certain periods that conflicts arose. It was the desire of a few for power which created such situations. Tragically, it is nothing new.

The Raid on Kokkina

In August 1964 the Government of Cyprus refused to allow a Turkish relief ship to land supplies for the Turkish Cypriot community. Furious, the Turkish Government retaliated by sending its Air Force to bomb many villages in the northwest of the island, which was reputed to shelter some Greek EKOA terrorists. The raid took Cyprus by surprise. Many Greek villages were badly damaged, one, in particular, Kokkina, totally destroyed.

The Swedish contingent of the UN Force assigned to the area took care of hundreds of Greek refugees, providing them with tents and food, resettling them near a beach. I went to visit the Colonel at his new command post to ask him what we could do in Nicosia to support their efforts.

I was accompanied by a representative of the International Red Cross in Cyprus, a young Swiss, who had arrived on the island a few days before. As we were driving back to Nicosia and were passing along the fine beaches on that part of the coast, a Turkish fighter plane came zooming over us, turned ahead of us and came back towards us strafing. A burst of machine gun fire spread over the vehicle. In understandable panic my friend abruptly stopped the car. We both jumped from it and threw ourselves into the little ditch along the road, trying to hide behind some rocks. The plane returned, this time aiming at a group of beach buildings, part of a small restaurant a few hundred yards from us. Our car, a beige Ford Esquire station wagon, had not been damaged beyond a few bullet holes in the back. Its roof, painted with a large Red Cross, could not have been mistaken from the air. The plane disappeared on the horizon. Somewhat shaken by the experience, we resumed our trip without further trouble and reported the incident to the UN and the Government.

The destruction of the villages in the northwest and the extensive use of napalm by the Turkish Air Force led the Government of Cyprus to launch a sharp protest to the UN Security Council. The Council immediately requested a detailed UNFICYP report on the Kokkina damage. Alvaro Ortega, a Colombian town planner attached to the staff, and I were asked to survey sixty bombed villages to completely evaluate the destruction. Archbishop Makarios loaned us his personal helicopter and pilot for this purpose. It was a small craft, seating only four including the pilot, completely enclosed by glass, from which we could gain the best possible view of the Cyprus landscape.

We took off from the Palace on a hot, dry summer day, with temperatures over 100°F. The grass looked brown. We could see in minute detail the olive and citrus orchards scorched by the sun and the villages scattered along our route. Here and there we could distinguish military units placed at some strategic points in hidden gullies or around abandoned farms.

We soon arrived over the bombed area above Kokkina. Lifting clouds of dust, we landed in the middle of a devastated little square, its surroundings almost destroyed. Only a few buildings were still standing. The job had been thorough.

As we were busy identifying the damage and taking copious notes, we heard a little meow from behind a broken door that lay on the ground. A white kitten emerged, so small, so thin, but so happy to see human beings. The poor little soul was the only living thing we saw in Kokkina. We had no milk for it but gave it some biscuits we found in the helicopter and took it back to Nicosia hoping to find someone to adopt it.

We landed in other villages, completed our survey, and flew to Paphos, a port on the western coast, to visit a hospital where nearly one hundred bombing victims had been transported. Accompanied by town officials we were trying to make our way to the hospital entrance when a group of Greek Cypriots—men, women and children also coming to visit the victims—stopped us, shouted obscenities and threatened to attack us. We were almost lynched.

The rumor had been that we were a NATO party coming to see the wounded. The Greek Cypriots hated NATO, of which Turkey was a member. The napalm bombs, from NATO, had been made in the United States. We had picked up some exploded parts in Kokkina with the indication that they had been manufactured in Rochester, N.Y. So their anger was well justified. After lengthy explanations by the Paphos officials, we were able to enter the hospital and visit the wards. We saw the wounded, with the terrible burns the napalm caused and wondered how the Turks could have allowed their Air Force to use such atrocious weapons on innocent people in an isolated village? We sympathized with the wounded and their families, counted the victims for our report, and flew back to Nicosia. This was my first personal experience with the barbaric consequences of hatred between two ethnic groups like that manifested 30 years later, on a much larger scale, in the "ethnic cleansing" of Bosnia-Herzegovina.

A Disputed Corpse

Another gruesome incident took place just after our return to the capital. A Turkish plane had been downed in the fighting over the northwest and the pilot, who had bailed out, had been shot by the Greek National Guard. His body had been taken to Nicosia and was in the hands of the Greek Cypriot municipality and kept in their morgue. Turkish Cypriot community leaders in Nicosia asked the Government to allow them to take the body to their community on the other side of the Green Line, so they could honor the flyer before sending his body back to Turkey. A huge procession had been planned after a service in the Mosque. The Greeks categorically refused to deliver the body or to grant others permission to cross the Line to get it. The situation was growing out of hand: the Turkish population had become very excited and fighting could have resumed between the two communities on that ground alone at any moment. One or two days passed without an agreement being reached, despite UN pressure.

My friend, the assistant representative of the International Red Cross who had been with me in his station wagon, eventually saved the day. He offered to pick up the body himself and deliver it to the Turks. Short and stocky, he went to the morgue and, unaided, put the naked body of the flyer on his back, carried it wrapped in a sheet to his station wagon and drove across the Green Line to where the Turkish Cypriots could take it over. This was a peaceful ending to a potentially-dangerous incident, born of the pettiness of ethnic hatred.

I was invited the next day to the Turkish district to attend the ceremonies which had been planned for the occasion. UNFICYP subsequently arranged for a van to take the body to the airport and fly it back to Ankara.

A Critical Food Situation

There were, of course, many other serious situations to handle dealing with refugees, the provision of minimum public services, and food supply, which were solved with the help of UNFICYP before they could erupt into violence and possible resumption of the fighting.

The food situation in the Turkish sector was among the most critical problems we faced. They claimed they were being starved by the Government. They wanted more food to reach the Turkish sector and no more bans placed on the unloading of relief ships from the Red Crescent of Turkey. Their supplies were dwindling so rapidly, they said, that it was seriously endangering the health of their people.

The Greek Cypriot government authorities laughed it off and told me the Turks were lying and had no reason to complain. "They have enough food," they said, "their reserves are still ample and they just want to create trouble." UNFICYP decided with no advance notice to take a quick and thorough inventory of all food reserves in all magazines, warehouses and stores in the Turkish sector and to investigate the supplies at hand in the shops. This was not an easy operation. It had to be done as a surprise and carried out so rapidly that there would be no possibility of the Turks hiding any significant quantity of food.

I was asked to carry out such a food survey and, subsequently, to set up a rationing system for the entire island. Food distribution would be based upon the overall supplies available and to be expected in the near future, and on minimum requirements for the maintenance of health.

To undertake such work and get rapid results, I obviously needed to assign many people to the task. With the help of the Chief of Staff of the Canadian contingent who had some knowledge in this field, I devised a secret plan of action for the proposed food survey, enlisting the help of UN force unit Commanders across the island as well as the UN military policemen in the cities. On a designated day we ordered the opening of all Turkish stores and warehouses. The checking went on simultaneously in all parts of Cyprus. In small villages the survey was carried out by specially appointed road patrols covering several villages in one day.

In three days the work in Nicosia had been completed. All data concerning the rest of the Turkish sector had been tabulated and forwarded by all units to UNFICYP Headquarters. UNFICYP was in a position to show the exact situation to the Government of Cyprus. The findings proved that the Turkish Cypriot food situation was indeed precarious. The Government was forced to pay attention to the situation and immediately authorize the release of food supplies to the Turkish sector. We established a plan for the fair rationing of all the island food supplies.

The Turkish Invasion

The Greek Government in Athens utterly disliked Archbishop Makarios, who was not in favor of *Enosis*. In 1974, ten years after I left the island, the Greek national guard stationed in Cyprus tried to assassinate him and take over the Government after he had demanded the removal of 650 Greek officers of the Guard. A small party attacked and destroyed the Presidential Palace where they hoped to find him. Makarios, tipped off, was able to escape to one of the British bases and was flown to London.

Turkey, fearing for the future of the Turkish Cypriot community, decided to invade the island. A large force was landed in the northeast, against which UNFICYP could do little. The UN Force, however, promptly secured the Nicosia airport.

The Security Council asked for a cease-fire and requested Turkey, Greece and Britain, the three guarantor powers, to start immediate negotiations to restore peace. Despite four days of negotiations in Geneva, the Turks continued to advance, denouncing the cease-fire and finally occupying more than a third of the island. Much fighting resulted in many casualties, atrocities and missing persons on both sides. UNFICYP established a wider buffer zone across the island between the two opposing forces when the Turks reached the limits they had set for themselves. Unfortunately, UNFICYP also experienced casualties of its own. UN soldiers did their best to take care of the refugees, evacuate people located in enclaves, and protect the civilian population.

Since then Cyprus has remained divided. Peace has been kept by the UN Force but political negotiations to settle the Cyprus crisis have been dragging.

An Assessment of Peacekeeping on Cyprus

I left Cyprus in the fall of 1964 to take up my new job with UNESCO in Paris, as the Agency pressured General Thymayya for my release. He had finally agreed, asking UN headquarters for a replacement. I was pleased to have participated in a well conducted and successful UN peacekeeping operation on this beautiful island. But thirty years later, the Cyprus problem is still not settled. One can wonder why.

No one can deny that UNFICYP played a valuable role in protecting international peace, mitigating strife on the island, saving lives, carrying on humanitarian actions and restoring law and order. The Force has been called a model of efficiency and economy. It would be wrong to place blame on UNFICYP for not having settled the Cyprus problem. It was not its mandate. It was not that the UN mediator failed; settlement, in the final analysis, can be made only by the Cypriots themselves.

It has been generally believed that the cost of maintaining the Force has been justified by its contribution to the pacification and normalization of Cyprus over the years. Authorized for short periods at a time, the need for its extensions has been recognized in each instance by the members of the UN Security Council as the best existing solution for maintaining the internal stability of the island.

The efforts at mediation attempted by the United Nations, first through two mediators, General Gyani, then Galo Plaza, and later directly by the Office of the Secretary-General in New York and negotiators in Geneva, have not been successful so far, despite of all they did. The present leaders of the two Cypriot communities, Clerides and Dentash, have pledged a political settlement since 1989. One can hope that they will show the necessary will to bring about a distinct and final end to this long-drawn-out problem. Perhaps after so long the presence of the UN Force has become counterproductive and may be considered a prop for the status quo. If the negotiations are not conclusive, showing that the political will to reach a settlement does not exist, I believe that this should be considered the last opportunity for the UN to offer its good offices to the two communities.

Until the day when the UN has a system to control global and regional conflicts, as foreseen by the Charter, United Nations Peacekeeping Operations must continue. They have demonstrated over the years that they are useful to control violence, maintain cease-fires and provide the level of stabilization required until the other instruments needed for conflict resolution can play their role, such as mediation and peace making. Each UN peacekeeping operation is, of course, different, but the fact that the UN Forces won the 1988 Nobel Prize for Peace is sufficient proof of their outstanding service, and all member states now favor strengthening them.

One thing seems certain: a Peacekeeping Operation under the UN is better than a non-UN multilateral force such as the one used in Beirut in 1984. That force included U.S., French and Italian contingents. In that instance the presence of UN soldiers from neutral countries would have been more acceptable than those from large military powers, with the obvious danger of bringing about direct attacks against the force from the local political factions involved, as happened in Beirut in the tragic killing of 241 U.S. Marines and more than 50 French soldiers.

JAMAICA: OUT OF MANY, ONE PEOPLE

JAMAICA: OUT OF MANY, ONE PEOPLE

Introduction

From 1971 to 1974 I served in a developing country I liked and respected that had been a slave colony for many years. When it became independent in 1962 it inherited parliamentary government from its former masters; thus its people have lived in a democratic society ever since. The majority are of African origin. Although deeply influenced by British ways, they are still seeking their own identity. They are also striving for a correct balance between capitalism and socialism in the shadow of a giant democracy—the United States—which, whether they like it or not, deeply influences their way of life and affects their future.

Here follow the stories of my experiences in that country—the beautiful island of Jamaica—where I was sent by the International Labor Organization (ILO), a Specialized Agency of the United Nations to help solve a long-term national problem: how to integrate turbulent unemployed youth into the national economy. It was an urgent task which, if not properly addressed, risked endangering the stability of the country and its orderly development. I shall describe the island itself and especially certain aspects of Jamaican society I found fascinating and critical to the success of our mission.

A Sprawling Metropolis

On the morning of January 9, 1971, Natalie and I flew from New York to Kingston, the Jamaican capital, to take up my new duties. We had left winter behind us, exhilarated to be going back to the Caribbean, an area we knew and considered a sort of paradise. We had just flown over Cuba and were approaching the north coast of Jamaica, the third largest island in the Caribbean, which stretches 50 miles north to south and 150 miles east to west. Below we could see its rugged mountainous terrain covered by dense blue and green foliage. To the east rose the lofty Blue Mountains (altitude 7,500 ft.), an impressive sight.

Someone once said that to get a good idea of the island you take a piece of glossy paper, crumple it hard in your hand and release it. The result is something resembling a relief map of Jamaica. This was particularly true of the center of the island, over which we were then flying, the famous cockpit country, its mountains and gullies an impenetrable jungle. I was later to discover that part of Jamaica and its fascinating background.

Suddenly, a voice on the loudspeaker asked us to fasten our seatbelts for our slow descent into Kingston, on the south shore at the extremity of a vast plain covered with sugar estates. We were approaching the Jamaican capital and its 600,000 people—one-third of the island's total population. Kingston, a sprawling city, is the largest English-speaking Western Hemisphere metropolis south of Miami.

We were greeted by a few people, after easily clearing Immigration and Customs because of my UN "Laissez-Passer." First was Warren Cornwell, an American, the United Nations Resident Representative and a former colleague at UN Headquarters. He had been in Kingston for two years and was a strong supporter of the youth program. Unfortunately, he had suffered a heart attack a few months before my arrival, and his health remained fragile. With him was a protocol attaché from the Ministry of External Relations, and Owen Batchelor and Vin Lawrence, the two senior officials of the Youth Development Agency with whom I would be working closely. The initial contact between us was warm and I immediately felt we would become good friends and work together harmoniously.

Owen Batchelor, the Acting Director, was about 45 and of fair complexion. He had the fine stature of an athlete. Lawrence, a few years older, was the former Director of the Agency, and had just returned from a long-term assignment in Dominica. Owen was soon to replace Vin permanently and thus become my counterpart at the operational level of the project. But what struck me about Vin was his marvelous smile. He had the head of an African king, his face and eyes radiating kindness. Both became, in fact, lasting friends.[25]

Owen and Vin had been responsible for all the pioneering work which had gone into establishing of the boys' camps, a great institution, as I was about to discover. From the airport we drove into Kingston, about 10 miles, going around the magnificent basin of Kingston harbor, rated the seventh best-protected harbor in the world, which had recently become the largest freight redistribution center in the

---

25 I used to see them during my yearly visits to Club Caribbean on the north shore of the island after I returned from international work. Unfortunately, Vin died in 1987, leaving a void in the hearts of many Jamaicans because of his unfailing dedication to the youth of his country.

entire Caribbean. We soon passed the uptown Square of the National Heroes leading to St. Andrew, a large residential district of villas with gardens and beautiful tropical foliage.

Reservations had been made for us at the Mona Hotel, in the imposing foothills of the Blue Mountains. The Mona was situated among several levels of gardens, in the middle of which was the hotel itself—a former Colonial mansion of the type Jamaicans call a "great house"—quite a few of which still exist in various parts of the island. The view toward the mountains was stupendous. It was a restful, comfortable place often used by British families settling in Kingston.

The next morning I spent some time at the nearby UN office with Warren Cornwell and met some UN experts advising the government in a variety of fields. On returning to the hotel I had a delicious lunch with Natalie, served under the trees around the swimming pool, with the panorama of the city below us. Suddenly there appeared a tiny swallow-tailed hummingbird, called the Doctor Bird, the national bird of Jamaica. He started sucking nectar from a pink hibiscus flower not two yards from us. For minutes we observed this graceful creature, its wings beating at a fantastic speed; you could hear the vibrations.

The garden was lovely with its myriad tropical flowers and rows of royal palm trees, their long branches swaying gracefully in the breeze. It was a moment to linger over before starting on our exciting new adventure.

The UN and the Youth Problem

After lunch Owen Batchelor picked me up to introduce me to the Minister of Community Development, Hon. Allan Douglas, at his office downtown. Douglas, a member of the Cabinet and a Senator, was from Falmouth, the most English-looking little town on the north shore of the island. With him was Senator Hector Wynter, Minister of State for Community Development, the official with whom I would discuss all major aspects of UN participation in the Youth Program at the top level of government, and with whom I would iron out any difficulty which might arise. Of short stature yet dynamic and suave, and sometimes sporting a flower in his lapel, he was brilliant and considered the intellectual wizard of the governing Jamaica Labor Party. A Rhodes Scholar and a man of great culture, he represented his country in international conferences on education and social affairs, and later became the Chairman of the Executive Council of UNESCO.

Hector Wynter explained the basic problems facing youth in Jamaica: "To the Government and to the Jamaica Labor Party, the problem we are now facing with youth is of vital importance," he said.

"We must lick it with all the means at our disposal, as this situation is worsening and may affect the stability of our country in view of the growing restlessness and frustration among young people in the ghettos of our cities. We must train our unemployed boys and girls and try to find jobs for them, a most difficult task in an economy in which unemployment is high.

"One reason for this situation is that many of our youngsters do not have a good home life, with a normal family pattern, as so many are raised by single mothers. Because of the absence of a father, our young men lack the attitudes and the discipline so important in the development of good citizenship and sound character. The mother becomes the breadwinner, relegating the bringing up of her children to a grandmother or other relatives. The consequent breakdown in discipline and the absence of civic pride bring family disasters.

"This is responsible for the large number of youths in the ghettos of Kingston joining criminal gangs. The police and the courts are trying to deal with violence, crime and drug trafficking. Fortunately, most youths are not criminals. But there are unemployable school drop-outs by the thousands in Jamaica. This is where the Ministry comes in, with its Youth Development Program."

Then Wynter and Batchelor described a situation which exists in so many developing countries and with which I was quite familiar: "Many young people leave the countryside, spurning agriculture for the bright lights of the city, only to be disillusioned because they do not have the qualifications for urban employment."

Wynter kept us in his office for nearly two hours—the three of us talking about ways the UN and its specialized agencies could help Jamaica strengthen its program with new methods and techniques for remedial education, vocational training and finding new opportunities for youth employment. The youth situation presented itself as follows:

The number of unemployed in the 14-to-24 years age group amounted to 86,000, an unemployment rate in this age group of 40 percent, or 47 percent of all unemployed in the country. The unemployment rate among young females was considerably higher and growing. It had reached 54 percent in 1972. Our project was involved only with youths aged 15 to 19, estimated to be about 30,000 to 40,000, all lacking the skills needed to find employment.

There was, therefore, an urgent need for expanded training facilities capable of providing out-of-school youth with the skills required for productive employment. To produce the maximum impact, the facilities had to be developed within a well-coordinated, comprehensive national youth program and be properly integrated into the country's overall educational and vocational training programs and the existing pattern of employment.

It was at this stage of the critical situation that the Government of Jamaica had requested United Nations assistance for a project that would constitute a further expansion of some of the measures the Government had already undertaken. It was to include, in part, the upgrading and expansion of the existing youth camps—Chestervale, Cobbla, Kenilworth, Lluidas Vale—and the construction and operation of a girls' training camp at Cape Clear, the upgrading of existing camp instructors and teachers and the training of new ones, and the planning and construction of a permanent training center for staff and voluntary leaders.

At the time of the request, the youth camps offered training to approximately 1,200 young men in agriculture, construction trades, furniture-making, motor vehicle repair, welding, plumbing, and various service trades such as barbering, cobbling, clerking and stenography. Training lasted 18 months and included general education and civics in addition to the vocational training.

The UN allocated close to $1 million U.S. to a two-year project covering provisions for experts and consultant services, 20 UN volunteers, fellowships and equipment for training, and miscellaneous expenditures. The contribution of the Government to the project was budgeted at $3,315,000 Jamaican (approximately $4 million U.S.), for Jamaican professional staff and administrative support, training, non-expendable equipment, adequate premises, and some funds for operation and maintenance of equipment.

The project aspired to a minimum target of doubling the capacity of the camp training system from its level of approximately 1,200 campers. After a number of years the Jamaicans were hoping that the program could involve 16,000 boys and girls, including those who would be members of the numerous youth clubs which existed in the island's towns and villages.

In view of the financial obligation of the Government for this program, I met with officials of the Ministry of Finance and was introduced to Finance Minister Edward Seaga, who in 1980 was to become the Prime Minister of Jamaica when the JLP party to which he belonged again won the general elections. Seaga, of Syrian origin, had graduated from Harvard University, worked initially with the Social Commission and at one time had been Minister of Welfare and Community Development. He was a strong supporter of the youth program, and as Minister of Finance never failed to allocate the counterpart funds needed for the UN project even when available funds were limited.

My first days in Kingston were spent downtown in briefings and planning sessions at the Youth Development Agency, our headquarters. The office was a modest commercial building of Colonial vintage located in a narrow street not far from the harbor and close to the main thoroughfare where shipping companies, banks and a few modern high-rise buildings lined the streets: the heart of the business district. This old part of downtown Kingston was redeveloped a few years later into a modern district including many high-rise buildings, a conference center, hotels and apartments, with even a special building constructed by the Government to house the United Nations Seabed International Authority to which Jamaica is the host. New Kingston, the modern center of the city, uptown, is rapidly expanding, with hotels such as the Sheraton and the Pegasus rising near the old colonial Liguanea Club with its nine-hole golf course where I played a few times.

Once recruited by their respective agencies, the members of our UN advisory team started to join me. The team was quite a multi-national little group. First to arrive was an American, Web Tenney, a former Director of Vocational Training in the Department of Education in Washington. He had also been the Executive Director of the Future Farmers of America, with its membership of 450,000 one of the largest youth organizations in the United States. He was to advise the Government on vocational training in the camps.

Jean Bazinet, a Frenchman, was sent by UNESCO in Paris to advise on remedial education, while Leo Mannaert, a staff member of the International Labor Organization, was seconded to advise on youth employment. Finding jobs for the youth camp graduates in the Jamaican market would be a difficult job, but it was the crux of the matter.

T. C. Liao, a Taiwanese specialist in agricultural extension in youth training and employment, also joined us, sent by the UN Food and Agriculture Organization in Rome, as did a sociologist from Ghana. We needed a competent expert in the training of young women for employment and obtained the excellent services of a woman from Teheran, who had for many years directed the entire handicraft training program of the government of Iran. To these we later added a few short-term consultants. A young Portuguese architect, trained in the U.S. and specializing in the development of resort facilities for the young, came to advise on the possibilities of building tourist camps for young Jamaicans and foreign students—the idea being that low-cost facilities were needed besides the existing tourist hotels. We also had a British construction expert who advised on improved methods for building the camps which, incidentally, were built by the campers themselves, in collaboration with the Jamaican architect consulting with the YDA.

After the first few months we had an efficient team later reinforced by 20 UN volunteers from Europe, Israel and the United States as assistant instructors, who were able to make valuable contributions to many aspects of the Youth Development Program. The UNDP Resident Representative, Sturge Shields, had the administrative responsibility for the new volunteers and devoted much interest to this project. With so many nationalities involved, it was for the team an exhilarating experience as we cooperated with our Jamaican colleagues in a close and friendly atmosphere.

Under a special arrangement between the UN and the Government of the Netherlands I received, as direct assistants, the services of three so-called associate experts, financed by the Dutch, who helped me in a great way. They were young university graduates, carefully selected, who came to help in administration or research. One of them, Pieter Duiker, became my direct assistant in the management of the project. We developed a close friendship. His work in Jamaica led him to a career with the International Labor Organization with long-term missions in Africa and Asia, and finally to a permanent position in Geneva.

The Youth Camps

It was easy to drive to the camps in two to three hours. Chestervale Camp was in the mountains near Kingston; Cobbla was in the center of the island near Mandeville. These were the oldest camps. Kenilworth, a new one, was in the west, near Neg, while Lluidas Vale, also in the center, was still under construction. During the first two years we developed a girls' camp on the north shore, at Cape Clear near Port Antonia. Finally, we created a training camp for instructors and staff at Braco in the Parish (County) of Trelawney on the north coast.

An idea of the boys' camps and of the principles on which they were established can be formulated from a description of Chestervale. Built on the side of a mountain, it housed 250 to 300 campers from 15 to 19 years of age who lived in barracks-like Quonset huts surrounded by classrooms, a refectory and other facilities. The camp director was a small man of about 40 with a warm smile and personality who lived with his wife, a charming woman, in one of the staff cottages. He had lived in London for 10 years as a minister and social worker, helping West Indian communities in a purely urban setting, but he had longed for the island and its mountains. Because of his previous experience, his dedication to youth and his firm but kind manner in dealing with the boys, he was one of the most popular directors of the Jamaican youth camps.

At Chestervale, as in all the other camps, all buildings had been built by the campers themselves under the direction of various Jamaican trade specialists: master masons, carpenters, electricians, plumbers, etc. Thus, there were always some construction or maintenance and repair activities going on, providing training for the boys specializing in the building trades. The camp also offered agricultural training, with vegetable gardens on the slopes following the principles of contour planting, with a view to developing farmers interested in truck gardening. The camp was almost self-sufficient in food, and since the market in Kingston was nearby the camp could sell its surplus, if any, there. Cultivation of flowers had been started, as well as beekeeping and pig and poultry raising. We also started to train boys in lumbering in the forests nearby, and introduced the use of chain saws—a U.S. company donating the saws. Finally, there were various courses in secretarial services, elementary accounting, tailoring, barbering and cosmetology—a large word for hairdressing and beauty care.

Chestervale Camp, surrounded by the higher peaks of the Blue Mountains, stood in a beautiful isolated wilderness. It had been started in 1956, on the advice of George Cadbury of the famous chocolate family, a Quaker. A UN senior staff member and former Assistant Director of the Technical Assistance Administration with whom I had worked, he had come to Jamaica on a long-term assignment to help the Government of Norman Manley, the Prime Minister, in creating its first economic planning services. On weekends he devoted his time to the building of Chestervale Camp, his contribution to the solving of the Jamaican youth problems already discernible in those days.

The main aspect of teaching the youngsters was leadership. The Youth Development Agency (YDA) sought out and trained as leaders the young men who appeared to have the potential for leadership. Character was built through a healthy program of remedial general education, skill training, recreation and leisure. The camp provided a platform whereby the disadvantaged youth could work together with those of more fortunate circumstances. All the camps subsequently were organized around the leadership of the youngsters in all aspects of the training programs.

During the first two years, YDA and the UN team succeeded in upgrading the various aspects of the camp's programs aimed at developing the individual in three main skill areas: technical, academic and social, with personality development and character training basic to the programs. Every recruit who entered a camp had to learn a skill. But because many were admitted at a fairly low level of literacy, they were unable to take the fullest advantage of the training being offered in the various skills. Special classes were therefore arranged to help this group. The skill taught corresponded to the need of the national economy and the employment pattern.

A unique feature of the program was the authority in the camp. Unlike many other institutions, it was based on leadership from the campers themselves as much as on authority from above. Each boy belonged to a *lead* of ten boys and a leader;

each *lead* lived in a dormitory of five *leads* headed by a dormitory leader; each dormitory partnered with another creating a unit called a *round* which was headed by a *round* leader. Leadership training at all levels contributed to the popularity and effectiveness of the program.

In 1968 the Government invited John Bradley, a recognized expert in leadership, to make an independent evaluation of the youth camps in Jamaica. He declared them among the best leadership systems for young people he had seen anywhere in the world. While they gave the youngsters the opportunity to learn a skill, they also developed their personalities, built their character and made them persevere in those disciplines which determine true liberty and produce the good citizen.

In vocational education, Web Tenney, our ILO expert, reorganized and modernized the instruction given in the classroom shops and in practical work, with carefully drawn class calendars, control charts and appropriate standards of attainment. The ILO and UNICEF had provided substantial funds for the purchase of modern tools and equipment for these shops and farms which the campers learned to use when they were employees. We contributed audio-visual aids, motion pictures, slides and screens for instructional purposes to the camps and the youth centers all over the island.

Discovering A Beautiful Island

As I was driving around the country in the first week with Batchelor and sometimes Lawrence, contemplating the scenery of this lovely island, my companions told me much of its history, economy and the way its people lived. Briefings and work sessions with the staffs of the boys camps were, of course, the main purpose of these trips, but I soon became familiar with the landscapes of the 13 parishes, the administrative districts of Jamaica, each of them picturesque and so different despite the island's relatively small area.

Our trips were usually spread over two or three working days out of Kingston, with nights and meals at the camps. They convinced me of the potential of the island for tourism. For instance, the Parish of Portland in the northeast, the most mountainous part of the country, had such a dense and lush vegetation that it was almost a rain forest, yet its peaks reach more than 7,000 feet.

We used to drive from Kingston to the north shore of the island, passing through the most arresting rocky gorges, emerging on the coast, then driving west in the direction of Port Antonio, a well-known port with a colonial romantic past, now visited by cruise ships. In the heyday of the banana trade, it was one of the wealthiest communities in the island. Hollywood actor Errol Flynn made his home there in the

'30s, escaping from Hollywood but continuing to live a glamorous and scandalous existence.

The road along the sea, with its coconut and palm trees and its flamboyants in the yards of village churches, had the charm of a Gauguin painting. We came to a village called Boston Bay in a lovely setting. Between two spits of lush land protruding into the sea, forming a square bay, parallel rows of waves constantly rolled toward the shore, making it a perfect beach for gentle surfing. If we had enough time, we could not resist the pleasure of a quick dip. The place, deserted in the week, was a public beach with rustic cabins under pine trees where local people came on Sunday to picnic and eat jerk pork prepared as in the time of the buccaneers. To swim there was a refreshing pause. What a contrast with the sophisticated resorts of Frenchman's Cove, Trident, and Blue Lagoon, a short distance west.

The famous north shore, with its gentle breezes even in the height of summer, had quite a pleasant climate. At Runaway Bay, west of Ocho Rios, on an open stretch of the coastal plain where sugar cane fields abound, Natalie and I, early in our stay, bought a *rondavel*, one of sixty octagonal huts, very comfortable, right on the beach in a resort called Club Caribbean. It was being built then by six young Oxford men who wanted to share in the exciting, booming business of Jamaican tourism. We spent many happy days there later, on visits to Jamaica in the early spring to relax and swim in the tepid waters of the Caribbean.

Further west, after passing Ocho Rios and Runaway Bay, we came to Orocabessa (Golden Head) where one could visit the homes of Noel Coward and Ian Fleming, hidden in the trees above a gorgeous turquoise sea. Other business and work trips led us to drive through to Montego Bay, Jamaica's leading resort, with its numerous luxury hotels on a hill dominating a famous bay. Reaching the western tip of the island after a work day at Kenilworth Camp in the Parish of Westmoreland, we would drive around the island and pass the famous Negril resort area on the Gulf of Mexico, its wide, flat beach of perfect sand, seven miles long, facing colorful sunsets. In those days, Negril was hardly developed. Large land crabs walked the road at night and equally large mosquitoes hummed a marching tune above them.

All along the north coast a succession of charming little coves dotted our way. The resort of Ocho Rios had beautiful colonial inns hidden behind walls and dense tropical foliage and a few high-rise hotels and a marina where cruise boats anchored. A little farther was St. Ann Bay, a historical, quaint town where Columbus landed in 1494, and Runaway Bay, where the Spanish, pursued by the British, fled the island for good after hiding in its remarkable grottoes.

From the coast, we could go back to Kingston by three different routes, crossing the island from north to south. Two were the most rapid ones, taking us either through a spectacular fern gully or through open country with bucolic scenes of tranquil cattle grazing on the slopes of farm estates, separated by low stone walls as in England.

Bauxite was being mined in those rolling hills by bulldozers which literally peeled the ground, leaving big open scars of red earth. The bauxite companies, all large foreign concerns, were forced by law to cover these giant wounds with new soil so as to restore the land to its original productivity. As a result, the bauxite companies went into farming in a big way, a new source of income for them. Then, coming down the mountain on a road built on the flank of spectacular cliffs, we would quickly reach the plain, cross Spanish Town, the first capital of the island, and finally reach the confines of Kingston, its skyline often misty with smog.

One day we returned from the north shore through the cockpit country, the almost impenetrable area of small mountains and gullies covered by unending tight scrub, which I had seen from the air on the day I arrived on the island. Only one narrow unpaved road served a few sparse villages and hamlets. Crossing the cockpit country even in the 1970s was an adventure in itself. While we drove through it, Owen Batchelor told me the story of this incredible area. During slavery, runaway slaves, called *Maroons* escaping from the cruel treatments to which they were subjected by their masters on the sugar plantations, came to hide in the cockpit country. In this inextricable jungle, literally a maze of pits and sinks, completely safe from recapture, they started a new life. To survive, the *Maroons* raided isolated plantation houses, stealing, and often killing the landlords. They became a serious threat to the people of the colony and had to be dislodged. In 1790 two regiments of British troops landed in Jamaica to search the cockpit country and destroy the *Maroons* in their hideouts. But given the cockpit topography they hadn't a chance to win. Indians were then imported from the Miskito tribe in Nicaragua. They tried to fight the *Maroons* but they, too, failed.

Edward Trelawney, a Governor who gave his name to the Parish in which the cockpit country is located, realized that it was not possible to exterminate the Maroons. He talked with them. A peace treaty was signed by which they were granted freedom and given the land on which they lived as their own. This amounted to letting them have their own government within the colony. This seemed an inadmissible situation to a subsequent Governor, the Earl of Balcarres, who brought dogs from Cuba to attack them. Kept on the run, hunted down, the *Maroons* finally surrendered. Their leaders were shipped to Nova Scotia and later to Sierra Leone in Africa.

I was fascinated by the story. Owen said their descendants still live there, now fully a part of the Jamaican community. We went through the little village of Accompong, the gateway to the cockpit country, talked to a few people on their doorsteps with the inhospitable green hills a backdrop behind their modest homes. They were quite apathetic. I could not believe they were the descendants of the fearless *Maroons*.

Next we drove through another village called Quick Step. People here were aloof, a little suspicious of us, afraid we might be linked to the police—as most of them are engaged in the traffic of *ganja* (marijuana) cultivated on the heights in secret fields that can only be detected by the police from the air.

Some years later, on vacation in Jamaica, we were flying from Kingston to Montego Bay at low altitude in a small commuter plane with only six passengers. The view of the cockpit country, even more forbidding from the air than from the ground, looked then like a succession of small moon craters solidly covered with small trees and bush except for a few clearings in the most inaccessible spots. Obviously, in those clearings *ganja* was being grown. Little columns of smoke could be seen here and there where patches of vegetation were being burned. The terrain below was forbidding. In an emergency, our little plane could not have landed anywhere except by gliding toward Montego Bay way to the north, if we could reach its airport safely.

Natalie and I took advantage of the weekends to visit the island on our own. One weekend, we went to Port Royal on the other side of Kingston Harbor, so large and well-protected that it could contain the entire U.S. fleet. The harbor is bordered on the south side by a narrow slip of sand, with a good road along the seas leading to the airport and to Port Royal, the former headquarters of the famous English pirate Henry Morgan. In the 1660s he preyed on the ships of the Spanish Main. Later, at the climax of his career, ordered by Queen Elizabeth I, Morgan attacked Panama City, the richest prize of Spain in the Western Hemisphere, with three dozen ships and 2,000 men, taking hundreds of prisoners. Loading his ships with gold, silver and other precious goods, he returned to Port Royal a wealthy man, but also a pirate because a peace pact had been signed by England and Spain before he had reached Panama. Therefore, on his return he was considered a brigand.

Port Royal had the reputation of being the sin city of the Caribbean, "the wickedest town in the world." The pirate Morgan's loot was shipped to England from there and auctioned at tremendous profits. Morgan was appointed Lieutenant Governor and knighted, as he promised he was ready to wipe out piracy and turn the West Indies into a peaceful region. Later, in 1682, he was relieved of his function when Sir Thomas Lynch was appointed Governor. Morgan retired to his plantation and drank himself to death.

This was, of course, a fascinating story, but we were even more struck by the famous earthquake which destroyed Port Royal 280 years before. We went to the beach and swam in the deep water, right at the edge of the beach where the cataclysm happened. On June 7, 1692, the earth suddenly opened and in a few minutes part of the city sank into the sea. A tidal wave came rolling furiously over the scene, and drowned more than 1,500 people. There was only one survivor. The ships at anchor were destroyed and only Fort Charles, built a few years earlier with about 200 houses and a church, withstood the earthquake, being away from the center of the impact.

When we visited the yard of St. Peter's Church, we saw among others one old tombstone which attracted our attention with this most extraordinary epitaph:

> Here lies the body of Lewis Galby, Esq., who departed this life at Port Royal the 22d December 1739. Aged 80. He was born at Montpellier, France, but left that country for his religion and came to settle in this Island, where he was swallowed up in The Great Earthquake in the year 1692 and by the Providence of God was, by another Shock, thrown into the Sea, and miraculously saved by swimming until a rescue boat took him up. He lived many years after in great Reputation. Beloved by all who knew him and much lamented at his death.

Both the church and the cemetery were full of graves and other reminders that the British had lost many young army and navy officers from yellow fever in the 18th and 19th centuries when the island was being colonized.

The town of Port Royal is not much these days: small, decrepit, just a big village really. It was rebuilt with linear streets bordered by poor housing. Fort Charles had been strengthened. We visited the fort: its batteries, still intact, had foiled an attack by a 100-ship French Naval flotilla with a British Naval defense of only 16. This was in 1775. Waiting for the French was a young Englishman, sure he would be able to repulse the attack, who was to become the greatest naval hero in British history when he destroyed the French and Spanish fleet at Trafalgar. This hero-in-the-bud at Fort Charles was Lord Horatio Nelson.

After Nelson's departure, another famous naval officer, Admiral Rodney, took over the fort and the command of the British forces in the West Indies, continuing the never-ending fight between the French and the English navies in the Caribbean.

The Jamaican government made great efforts to preserve the town's past. We went to a new museum with its fascinating collection of salvaged treasures lost at Port Royal and in the Caribbean Sea.

On other weekends we discovered various fascinating places in the island and also the artistic resources of Kingston: the National Dance Company of Rex Nettleford, little theaters where witty plays were being given in Jamaican patois.

My wife often accompanied me to the youth camps, sometimes on weekends, as she wanted to meet the campers, talk to the UN volunteers and help in any way she could. We attended parties in the Youth Clubs in various towns. Natalie, along with the wives of the Jamaican directors, was asked to distribute the prizes at graduation exercises in the camps.

Reggae music, which was new and had become a symbol of national identity, was no stranger to us. We were invited by the Agency to two official balls given during Youth Week at the National Stadium in Kingston. To show we shared the campers' spirit, Natalie and I joined the flow of hundreds of young reggae dancers on the floor of an immense hall, getting into the proper rhythm. This went over very well; we were not young any more, but we had a great time.

Violence in Jamaica

While I was in Jamaica the government was trying vigorously to address the serious problem of violence, crime and drug trafficking. The numbers of idle youth, school dropouts, and unemployed in the ghettos of Kingston had considerably increased at the beginning of the '70s. Many young people had left their villages, the cane fields and the banana plantations, hoping to find something exciting to do in the big city. Illiterate and untrained, they could not find work and joined gangs of 15-to 20-year-olds, surviving by stealing and often killing. As the *Daily Gleaner* described: "Those boys knew how to snap out their knives, getting their fingers on the ring at the end of the handle." They also knew how to handle guns, which had come to the ghettos from the proceeds of the *ganja* sold to drug dealers from foreign countries. Every morning the *Gleaner* reported the crimes committed by the gangs the night before. Often these young criminals were shot dead by the police before they could shoot at them. But the police lost men, too. In my view, it required much courage to be a policeman in Jamaica in those days. The gangs attacked banks, even post offices. A postmistress who tried to resist was murdered. Innocent people on the streets, storekeepers, landlords, had also been killed.

In the '70s, Jamaicans who owned villas on the range dominating Kingston sold their properties as it was too dangerous to live isolated. They came down to live in town, starting a boom in the construction of deluxe condominiums. West Kingston was the country's crime cradle.

The Youth Development Agency had opened a training center there. I went to see it twice, during a relatively calm period in the middle of the day. Even the

Jamaican staff at YDA headquarters would not go there during election campaigns, when violence could be at its highest. But even at other times it was still dangerous for a white man to venture unaccompanied into these poorest Kingston neighborhoods, so no member of our UN team went alone. There were always youths loitering on the street corners, reggae music blasting from their portable radios.

The poorest parts of West Kingston were deplorable. People lived in shacks often made of recovered building materials, corrugated zinc, cardboard, and flattened oil drums. The asphalt roads were broken in many places, full of potholes and covered with debris. A Jamaican writer called it a bombsite landscape of live garbage, boxwood, and unlikely greenery.

The situation worsened in 1972. Crime was rampant, law and order challenged every day. The police could no longer cope. Something drastic had to be done. The Government established the famous gun courts, the first systematic and large-scale effort to control crime, initiated by Eli Matalon, the Minister of National Security. Each day, when going to the office, I passed in front of a gun court set up near the entrance of the military headquarters named Up Park Camp. It looked like a concentration camp. There was a large sign, "Gun Court," above the gate. The place was fenced with barbed wire ten yards high enclosing a number of newly-constructed buildings, including the court building itself and prefabricated structures for the prisoners. There was also a tall wooden tower with armed guards at its top, and sentinels at the entrance.

Under the Gun Court Act indefinite detention was the sentence for anyone guilty of an offense such as illegal possession of firearms, or even only of ammunition. One did not have to be caught using a gun, possession was enough. An appeal to all citizens of good will was made by the Minister to help destroy the guns. Everyone having an illegal gun in his possession was invited to leave it at any church or to turn it over to any clergyman. He asked people to search all empty lots, ravines and abandoned buildings to locate discarded firearms, then report to the nearest police station if they found one. Soon the city was covered with large posters with the inscription, "The word is love—come, bring in the guns—NO questions asked—Deadline is March 24th". Matalon ordered the old World War II airstrips in various parts of the island blown up. It was here that the drug dealers landed with their light planes, bringing guns into the country in exchange for *ganja*.

There was one such airstrip close to Braco, our training camp on the north shore. One day I woke up early and went for a walk. I saw a plane landing on the airstrip and packages of marijuana being handed to the pilot. But that day the Jamaican police were hiding in the tall grass and opened fire on the plane, which started burning. The two men on the plane and the two Jamaicans who met it were taken prisoner. Aboard, a supply of sawed-off shotguns and Colt .45s was found—a part of the deal which, this time, was not consummated. A second burnt plane, left on the same airstrip as witness of the fight between the police and the gangsters, could still be seen when I passed on the road near Braco in 1986.

The campaign for destruction of the guns and for drug control was not completely successful, but this tremendous effort went a long way toward breaking the back of the crime situation. The fight continues, but Jamaica is still a violent society. However, the great majority of Jamaicans are as honest as good people anywhere who aspire to a society rid of crime. The police courageously continue their role of keepers of the peace. It can be hoped that gradually the situation will be fully under control. In this respect, Jamaica is no different from big cities in the U.S. and elsewhere, where one cannot walk safely in the streets at night.

"Out of Many, One People"

In all our assignments we had never been in a country where a variety of races lived so harmoniously. The Arawaks were the indigenous population of the islands. A peaceful Indian tribe, they were destroyed by the Spaniards who colonized Jamaica in 1494. The peaceful Arawaks were worked to death, so African slaves were imported by the Spaniards from West Africa to work on the plantations until 1655 when the English invaded and made it a prosperous colony thanks to slavery. At the time of emancipation in 1838, the population comprised mainly Africans and English, with some Spaniards and Portuguese Jews. But later, new importation of labor brought Scots, Irish and Germans as indentured workers to replace the slaves. Further enriching the composition of the population, East Indians were brought in as agricultural workers in 1845. In 1860, Chinese were imported from Panama where they had helped to build the canal. Finally, some Syrians came to Jamaica as itinerant traders, later settling in the towns as they did in so many parts of the world.

The population of Jamaica, now 2.3 million, was 1.8 million in 1970 when I was there—the majority (98 percent) of African descent, with minorities of whites, Chinese, East Indians, Jews and Syrians steadily increasing. The island is a literal melting pot. It is remarkable that its varied ethnic people live in harmony, without tension or racial difficulty, and with considerable intermingling of races and nationalities. There are no descendants of the Arawaks left, so it is rare to find a Jamaican with true West Indian features except for a few, chiefly in the sugar belt. But there are descendants of the Maroons, the fierce bands of escaped slaves who formerly preyed on the sugar plantations.

Gradually, as we were settling in Kingston, my wife and I meshed into Jamaican society, getting acquainted with the rich combination of races and finding much beauty in the diversity. At parties and receptions, among the elite, the racial mosaic was clearly revealed. There were so many types of beauties among the women, a source of fascinating interest. It was not strange to see bronze skinned young women with straight black hair and green eyes, while others, ravishing black skinned beauties, had slightly flat noses and Oriental slanted eyes. Many Jamaicans come from families with mixed African, European, Chinese and East Indian ancestries in different degrees. This in itself created a nation free of racial prejudice. There is unity in the country. Its motto is *Out of many, one people*. There is violence on the island, but not based on race or discrimination. In principle, the differences between people are now mostly economic and cultural rather than racial, and it is work and intelligence, rather than the color of one's skin, which permit one to climb the social scale or the economic ladder.

Still, some remnants of the Colonial past linger. During the colonial period the British frowned on concubinage and mixed marriages, which had been tolerated under the Spanish. The authorities could do little against race mixing and the number of mulattoes increased rapidly. A codification of colored people was established in the colony in Quadroons, Quintroons, and Octaroons, etc., which, according to Sharon Morgan[26] created a terrible sense of inferiority complex in Jamaican subjects that continues to plague them today as it established a new discrimination based not on race but on complexion. It was, of course, to be expected that the offspring of the British civil servants, military and traders with native Jamaicans would become a special group occupying the clerical positions in the government and the private sector headed by the British in the Colonial period. Many of these received a good education in the schools created in the colony, or in England. When independence came, many mixed-blood Jamaicans were the only ones ready to hold executive positions in the island's administration, with banks and in the management of local enterprises. They now share these positions with blacks coming from the lower classes who gradually, through education, can qualify for them.

This is not to say that Jamaica is without certain divisions and prejudices. Which country is not? In my view, Jamaicans present a picture of enviable integration of various racial elements, sharing an African common stock. Even Morgan recognized that integration would follow when one's own family contained a mosaic of cultural heritages. No one stands alone, and this is undeniably a strength for the future of the country.

26 *The Gleaner*, March 27, 1988.

The Election of 1972 and the Youth Program

Well organized under British rule, Jamaica had acquired a large degree of internal autonomy before its independence. Since the Jamaicans who led a free country when independence was declared in 1962 were trained under the British system, the transition to functioning as a parliamentary democracy was easy. The country had the advantage of a well-educated Jamaican elite and a relatively high rate of literacy. The new nation, of course, had serious problems of economic and social development and high unemployment, and suffered from a substantial "brain drain" of professional people, who left for the United States and Britain in search of a better life. Many students at that time were educated abroad and elected to remain either in England or the U.S.

Her Majesty the Queen, represented by the Governor-General, holds the supreme authority in Jamaica, as in all British Commonwealth countries. There is a 60-member House of Representatives elected every five years under universal suffrage, and a Senate of 21 members appointed by the Governor-General on the recommendation of the Prime Minister and the Leader of the Opposition and in proportion to the seats gained in the House. The Cabinet, the principal instrument of government, comprises the Prime Minister and at least a dozen Ministers, who must be members of the House or Senate.

From all my UN experience with countries having recently acquired their independence, I had to conclude that Jamaica was one of the most democratic developing countries I had known. Other developing countries were under a dictator while still others, which had started at independence with a two-party system, shortly after had reverted to one-party rule and abandoned all opposition parties. I admired the fact that Jamaica was a free country in which the press could criticize the government, and where elections—although accompanied by considerable violence—were relatively fair. I found that the men in charge had a sense of fairness and a respect for individual rights that were missing in many Third World countries. In a field as sensitive as Youth Development, it was comforting to find such characteristics in the staff of the Jamaican Youth Development Agency, making cooperation with them pleasant and fruitful.

The 1972 general elections were approaching and a change of government would bring some changes to the national youth program and the future of our UN project. For this reason, we carefully followed the electoral campaign. As pointed out, a period of general elections in Jamaica is never calm. The 1972 campaign turned out to be quite violent; the tactics used by the two political parties (the PNP and the JLP) caused the killing of approximately 400 people. In certain districts of

Kingston in the days preceding the elections, it was unsafe to venture into the streets, and the Jamaicans working with us rejected as too dangerous my suggestions to visit one of our projects in West Kingston, a particularly restless neighborhood. On election day, all foreigners were advised by their embassies to stay off the streets, where gangs were always ready to pick a fight. Their staffs stayed at home. Many Jamaicans did likewise except to go out to vote. [27]

The names of the two Jamaican political parties are somewhat misleading to a foreigner newly arrived in the island. The Jamaican Labor Party (JLP), which had been traditionally considered the party of the poor, had become, by 1970, more and more a party representing the interests of the conservatives, although it claimed it was concerned with the interests of all classes. Edward Seaga, the JLP Minister of Finance, who was running for Prime Minister, was promising to develop the economy and raise the standard of living of all the people.

The People's National Party (PNP), the opposition party led by Michael Manley, since the 1970s has been the party of the people. But for many years before, it had been characterized as the party of the middle class, despite its name. In 1972 its platform clearly favored the masses and opposed the interests of the wealthy. It advocated a welfare state and greater social justice, and promised a redistribution of the wealth. Michael Manley condemned the "rich men," meaning the corrupted politicians who had become wealthy, but not the industrialists and the trade people whose support he needed. Indeed, before the elections, certain elements of the upper and middle classes and civil servants gave their support to the PNP. While Manley appealed to the masses, he also sought the support of the middle class, including professors of the University of the West Indies and other educators, an important group forging the ideas of the younger generation who strongly supported him.

Manley was running under a *Power for the People* banner, seeking to institute a policy of consultation and participation. This, he said, was necessary to bring change and benefits to the people. He was addressing all groups and sects, including the Rastafarians—a sect many thousands strong which reveres former Ethiopian Emperor Haile Selassie as their God—who enthusiastically supported him.

One would encounter Rastafarians in the ghettos and in the countryside. A few times we stopped to say hello to a few rastas sitting on the roadside in some villages as we traveled across the island. They were friendly. Although practically none of them had been to Ethiopia, they considered Africa their natural home. Their souls

---

27 In 1988, in provisions for the forthcoming elections, the heads of the parties, hoping to change the trend, made a pact of non-violence and appealed to the people in the streets to stay calm and to the campaigners not to incite the crowds.

belonged there and they claimed they were strangers in their own land. They braided their hair and colored it reddish with dread-locks hanging to their shoulders. Many dressed in rags and lived as mendicants. The Emperor of Ethiopia had no consideration for them and the Jamaican middle class held them in contempt. When I was there their ranks were growing, and I was told that some middle-class Jamaican youths had joined the sect.

In 1966, when the Emperor of Ethiopia officially visited Jamaica, they all came on their own to the airport to welcome him. The press estimated the crowd at a hundred thousand, a good many of them Rastafarians dressed in white to welcome their idol. Apparently the Emperor was a little frightened by this demonstration of love.

The Rastas were connected with the development of Reggae music, of which the PNP made full use during the campaign. They invited the Rastas to participate in many meetings. The PNP campaign soon took a turn toward Black nationalism with the slogan *Black is Beautiful* advertised everywhere, even on the blouses of young Jamaican secretaries at the UN office in Kingston. The movement espoused *negritude* which had swept Africa, particularly the former French colonies of West Africa.

Manley never failed in his speeches to remind the people of their African roots, saying that they had been brainwashed by a white-oriented society which, however unconsciously, had not allowed the black people to accept their own norms of beauty and excellence. Manley proposed the teaching of African history in the schools and a realistic interpretation of history to help undo the damage by setting present attitudes in a framework of historical truth.[28]

One evening my wife and I decided to go to a lecture in a church hall to hear a professor from an African University. It turned out to be a political meeting. After being seated, we realized that we were the only white persons there among hundreds of blacks. Everybody was staring at us as if we did not belong. Someone rose nearby and loudly said to us: "What are you doing here, Whities? Integrating?" to which Natalie replied, "Why not?" Nothing further happened, but you can see how Jamaican we had become!

The campaign was fully reported in the *Gleaner*, including the charismatic showmanship displayed by Manley. A handsome and elegant speaker with wavy grey hair and white skin, he was adored by the crowds, who called him Joshua. His mother, Edna Manley, a British-born sculptress, was white, while his father, Norman

---

28 Anita Waters, *Race, Class and Political Symbols* (New Brunswick, U.S.: Transaction, Inc, 1985).

Manley, an English-trained barrister and former Prime Minister raised to the highest dignity of National Hero, was a brown Jamaican. He had attended the London School of Economics, and believed in the philosophy of the Fabian societies of England. He was the head of the Jamaican National Workers Union, affiliated to the PNP, and a Senator.

One of the symbols used in the PNP campaign was the "Rod of Correction." From a trip to Ethiopia, Manley had brought back a cane, beautifully carved, a gift from Haile Selassie. This symbol paid dividends at public meetings. The cane was supposed to be charged with spiritual powers, something that Manley and his campaign managers would not, of course, deny. A friend who had attended a meeting told me how it was used:

The rod was placed on the stage in a box in front of the crowd before Manley would arrive to speak. He would ascend the platform, take the rod, hold it up, and slowly face the audience, saying nothing for one or two minutes. He would then extend the rod toward the crowd and smile at them. He did not have to say a word. The people would cheer him, shouting 'Joshua,' and go wild.

Then, according to another witness, at some point in his speech he again took the rod, intimating that because it had supernatural powers it would help them solve their problems. In Kingston, the rod was being talked about everywhere. The Rastas wrote Reggae songs about both it and Manley. One went like this: "Haile Selassie is our God; Claudius Henry is our King; Michael Manley is our Joshua; What a peace of mind, our Joshua has come!"

The rod, the Reggae songs and the Rastas all contributed to the PNP victory. Michael Manley won by a landslide over Edward Seaga in a contest in which personal popularity played a major role.

The UN project for youth development made considerable strides during the first two years, under the Jamaican Labor Party. Its tempo became slower when the People's National Party (PNP) took over after the national election in 1972. There were several reasons for this.

First, the Government had new ideas on social development, and particularly for youth programs. A sort of braintrust in the Prime Minister's office wanted to embark on vast projects which, in our view, were for a different purpose and too ambitious for the resources at hand—both financial and human. The International Labor Organization tried to show them that the programs we had strengthened had shown results, and were best planned to prepare youth for productive employment. The new Government, however, was more interested in devoting its resources to a national literacy program extended to many more adults as well as youth. It created a large number of social centers all over the island, as an extension of the existing youth clubs under the JLP. The Government also thought that a youth program was something so national that it did not believe strangers—even if they were international experts on the subject—could provide much guidance to them. It became a sensitive subject. The Government grew less interested in our advice than in receiving additional equipment from the UN. Our technical assistance project had been extended each year since 1971, and after the fourth year the UN decided that we could no longer continue it. We closed the project, which on the whole had had an important impact on at least one key problem of the country.

Under the PNP the literacy program was successful and the youth camps continued their proven activities. In 1980, when the Jamaican Labor Party came back to power with Edward Seaga as Prime Minister, a new youth training program, derived from our initial project, called HEART (Human Employment and Resource Training Program) was created which covered considerably more ground than the former YDA program. It addressed itself to all youth, not just the school drop-outs as had been the case earlier. It has produced many thousands of trained youth but apparently has yet to reduce unemployment among the youth in any dramatic proportions, mostly due to economic conditions in the island. The crime rate has diminished quite noticeably, however.

A Socialist Experiment and its Consequences
After its election, the PNP government brought about marked changes in the economic and social policies of Jamaica. Michael Manley's aim was to install "a system of democratic socialism, a mixed economy in which each one would have equal opportunities, a society in which private business could exist but would be submitted to certain controls so it would work within the bounds of the national interest and the people's rights and welfare." [29]

An idealist, Manley wanted to get away from the capitalist system which, he said, subordinates people to economic and political exploitation by the wealthy. He stated that the exploitation of majorities by minorities generates poverty and class conflicts and that, under a capitalist system, private business is encouraged to think only in terms of profit. The masses were enthusiastic about his promises. We met him on several occasions at youth meetings over which he presided, and he indeed had enormous charm as a popular leader.

Once in power, his new government established a series of social programs in favor of the people, such as a National Literacy Program, free education to the

[29] PNP statement of December 1974

university level, the abolition of the old master-servant law including minimum wages for house employees. He also started a huge Special Employment Program, giving work such as road maintenance to the unemployed. The Government took over foreign sugar plantations, under lease. About 45,000 acres of land were taken over and leased to 23,000 small farmers under "Project Land-Lease." On the bauxite industry, owned by foreign concerns, Manley imposed a tax on production which increased government revenues six times, helping the country to pay for its oil imports, the value of which had quadrupled when OPEC raised the price of oil in 1973. But this was insufficient for Jamaica's new social programs, and the Government was forced to borrow huge sums of money. Inflation rose sharply.

Efforts were made to curb inflation, and top salaries and rents were frozen. Strict measures were taken to keep capital in Jamaica, but much money slipped out of the country and quite a few wealthy people emigrated.

There were somewhat exaggerated fears that Manley was trying to impose Communism on Jamaica. His trips to Cuba and the later visit that Castro made to Kingston greatly increased these fears. The *Gleaner* became more hostile than ever, particularly after Hector Wynter (with whom I had worked on the youth program) became the Executive Editor of the paper and attacked the PNP leader in his editorials, showing him as a threat to Jamaican democracy. One of the *Gleaner*'s articles called him "the most Messianic figure in Jamaican political history, imbuing himself with magical powers which could lead to a destruction of freedom."

Excessive spending, borrowing and mismanagement led the Manley Government to failure. The resistance shown by the Government to the IMF and its hostility to any domination by the U.S., as well as the ideology displayed by the Jamaican leader, displeased various Western countries. The poor people were, of course, the first to suffer. Fewer and fewer items were to be found on supermarket shelves. The masses became disillusioned with their leader. We noticed that when we were going to Club Caribbean on the north shore in the '70s, the staff of the hotel who had been pro-Manley were favoring a JLP victory, hoping this would restore prosperity to the island and help the food situation. The people could take the restrictions no longer, such as the rationing of food supplies.

In the 1980 election, Edward Seaga carried the JLP to a landslide victory. Michael Manley had tried to change Jamaican society but had not succeeded. He had tried to redistribute the wealth before enough wealth had been created to sustain his policies. To effect a policy of redistribution of income to the poor (i.e., to share the wealth) requires a booming economy. There was a severe deterioration in the balance of payments caused by the decline in the value of bauxite exports. Due to bad publicity in the U.S., reports of tourist muggings in the streets of Montego Bay and the poor attitude and service on the part of hotel personnel, the number of tourists declined. Later, the tourism situation was gradually corrected thanks to the efforts of the Minister of Tourism, P. J. Patterson. The measures he took to teach Jamaicans the importance of tourism and the necessity of treating tourists well helped, but tourism was far from the only source of trouble. Government efforts to reduce its economic dependence on the U.S. and other industrial countries had not worked well. The nationalization of exports, urban transport, some banks, sugar plantations, many hotels, 51 percent of the bauxite companies and all the lands they were mining, reduced Jamaica's dependency on foreign interests. But these takeovers created serious management problems for a country which even before lacked well-trained managers. The economy became mismanaged except for the banks and the bauxite operations. The financial situation of most of the nationalized enterprises was poor before the takeover, and their loans were often already in default. This put a tremendous financial burden on the Government.

The agricultural program started by Manley's government was laudable in its effort to help the small farmers and to increase food production, but there again the acquisition of land for these programs was costly. There was a shortage of foreign exchange to provide the projects with adequate supplies and equipment. Productivity was still low and raising it was something which would take time, so that some projects had to be abandoned and, on the whole, the agricultural program did not have the impact on the economy which had been expected. The sugar and banana industries which are important in Jamaica suffered from the problems affecting these industries all over the world, including lower prices on the international markets.

In conclusion, because of the economic decline which affected Jamaica in the '70s, regardless of one's politics for or against the PNP, one had to conclude that Manley's experiment in democratic socialism had failed and that much would have to be done to restore the economy, which had tumbled into a shambles. Edward Seaga, the new Prime Minister, had inherited a terrible situation. How could he redeem it?

A Reversal to Capitalism
Seaga chose to return to capitalism. In contrast to Manley's views, he skillfully played the "American card" and tried to draw foreign investment to Jamaica and to increase exports. While the Manley economic policies and his friendship with Castro had generated hostility on the part of the U.S., Seaga, on the contrary, cultivated the U.S. He became a friend of President Reagan and was the first Head of State to be

invited to the White House during Reagan's administration. The visit resulted in warm relations between the two countries. A program to promote U.S. investment in the island was recommended by a U.S. Economic Committee on Jamaica chaired by David Rockefeller. Seaga was the first to suggest a Marshall Plan-type program for the Caribbean which became, shortly after, the Reagan Caribbean Basin Initiative (CBI). Jamaica became the prototype of recipient countries under the new program, and of all the Caribbean countries benefited most from it, in 1982 obtaining $139 million, including $110 million in U.S. aid, ranking Jamaica, on an aid-per-capita basis, third in the world (after Israel and El Salvador) in terms of assistance from the United States.

A Promising Future

Despite his efforts in the '80s, Seaga was not able to completely reverse the economic situation in Jamaica, nor to dramatically improve the situation of the people. Some progress was achieved, but foreign investment did not reach the level expected and exports did not rise sufficiently to restore the balance of payments, due to production difficulties and the world economic situation. The Jamaican Governor-General Glasspole, in his 1988 Speech From The Throne said, however, that tourism had reached its highest peak in 1987, exports in the garment sector had increased substantially and the bauxite-aluminum industry's situation was much improved. "The economy of the country rests securely in the four legs of tourism, agriculture, manufacturing and mining, and with the export capability of these sectors, growth is now under way with a steady buildup of momentum."

Michael Manley, in the 1970s, did not want subservience to the U.S. In contrast, in the '80s Seaga considered Jamaica a part of the West. Manley wanted to reorganize the Jamaican economy based on a system of social control and popular participation; he failed, and Seaga rallied to the free-enterprise system.

What may happen in the future? Because of the failure of the PNP experiment and the hostility of the U.S. to it, it seemed likely then that even if the PNP won, its policies would change and become considerably more conservative. This seemed necessary because of Jamaica's economic dependency on the United States and other western countries such as the United Kingdom and Canada. However, the people of Jamaica are still looking for a new identity closer to their African heritage, and they are, in fact, getting this new identity through politics, culture and music. This is all to the good, as they have the right to aspire to be, in all respects, a truly independent nation, a political status that they, in reality, have already attained in recent years.

However, the island's economic future, after 400 years of dependency on the West, will continue to depend on trade and investment from western industrial nations, particularly the United States. This cannot be changed significantly, since Jamaica is only a small island in the shadow of an economic giant. Tourism, mostly from North America, and bauxite will continue to provide Jamaica its greatest annual earnings. The problems of youth and poverty probably can be solved more easily with close cooperation with the United States, Canada and Britain. On the whole, despite the difficult economic and social conditions still existing for many Jamaicans, the country's future is relatively promising.

After more than three years in Jamaica, we left in April 1974, as I had been invited to take up another mission in Africa. My experience in Jamaica had been a most enlightening one, and I am grateful to have had a chance to work on the development of its youth and to live in that beautiful island at a vital and interesting period in its history.

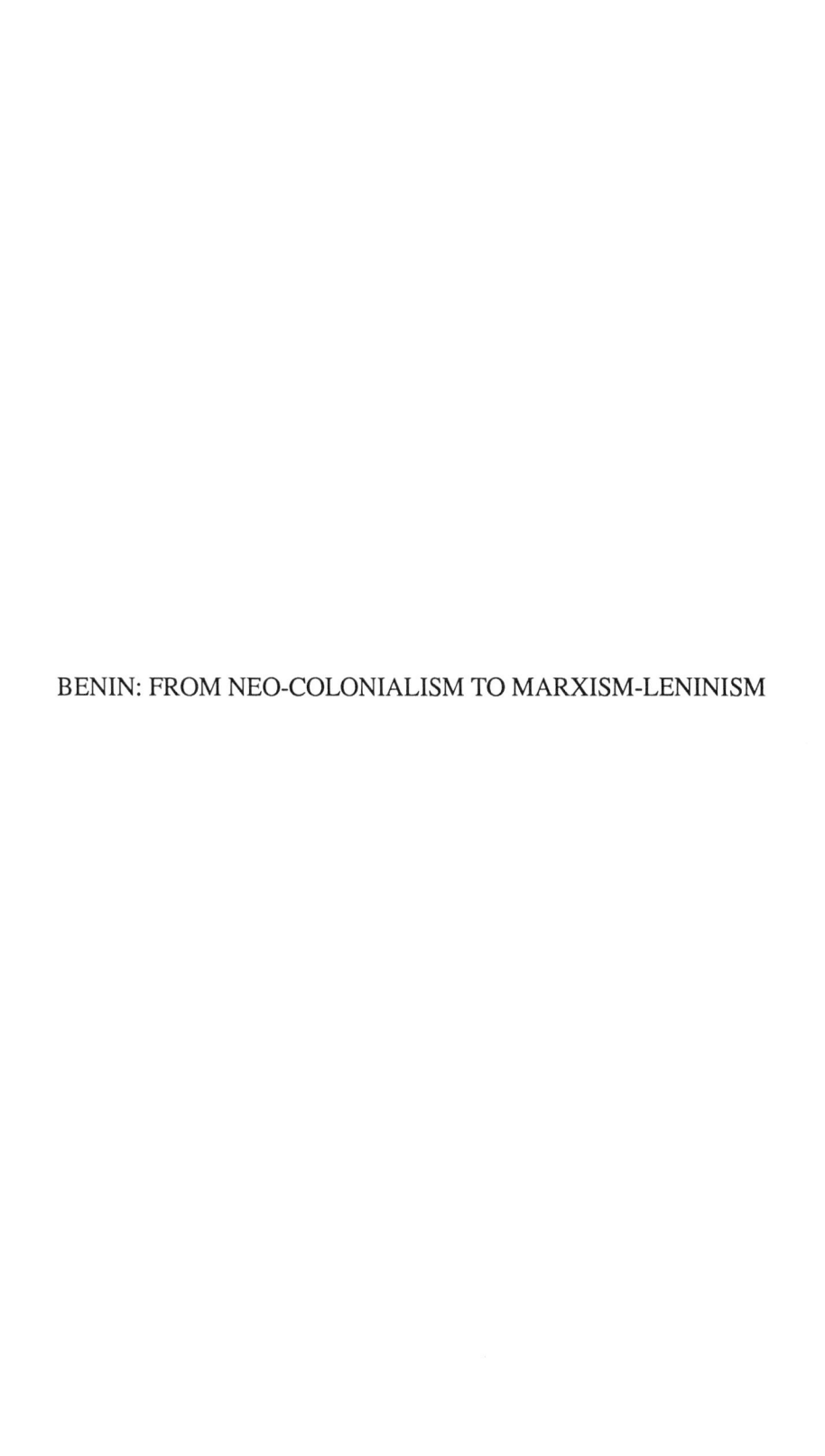

BENIN: FROM NEO-COLONIALISM TO MARXISM-LENINISM

BENIN: FROM NEO-COLONIALISM TO MARXISM-LENINISM

Landing in Cotonou

In April 1974 Natalie and I took an Air France Caravelle from Paris to Cotonou, the capital of Dahomey in West Africa, a country which changed its name to Bénin just before we were sent there. This was to be my last mission before retiring. I was to head a team of UN economists invited by the Government of Bénin to help draft its third four-year Economic Development Plan. Based on an analysis of the country's economic and social conditions, a plan determines the priorities for national development and recommends a program of public investment and projects as a guide to the Government in reaching its goals. I anticipated an exciting professional experience. Bénin was a French-speaking country that also featured several vernacular tongues, and I expected to get along easily with its officials and people. This was to be my third experience in Africa, but my first in the western part of the continent.

We flew over the Mediterranean Sea, Algeria and the Sahara Desert and landed in Niamey, the capital of Niger, for a one-hour stopover. While Natalie and our cat, Pixie, stayed in the poorly air conditioned cabin, I crossed the tarmac to the airport building just to stretch my legs and to test the local temperature. I felt as if I had been thrown into an oven. It was 130°F, but the air was dry. I thought of my UN colleagues stationed in Niamey and considered us lucky to be going to Cotonou where, although almost on the Equator, we would be able to feel the Atlantic Ocean breeze. I observed the local people for a while, admired the attractive handicrafts they had for sale and returned to the plane.

We renewed our flight and soon crossed the majestic Niger River, the most important waterway of the region, with its sluggish yellowish waters. A few sailboats carrying goods slowly drifted with the current. We flew at low altitude over a crowd of people in colorful garb, milling around at a landing near a marketplace in front of flat-roofed buildings the color of clay, like the rest of the landscape. We shortly were over Bénin, contemplating the Atacora range, the most picturesque area of the northwestern part of the country, inhabited by the Sombas, a well-known primitive tribe. From the air we could distinguish their red mud houses, like minuscule castles with turrets. Further south we flew over the country of the Baribas, a land of plateaus good for cattle raising. We reached the south, the country's greatest agricultural resource, where large plantations produced palm oil. Finally we neared the lagoons, approaching the Gulf of Bénin with its endless coconut groves along the coast.

The plane, preparing to land at the small Cotonou airport, described a large arc over the city. As we rapidly descended towards the Atlantic Ocean, we could see the long parallel rows of high waves, their white foam crashing on the shore. Their terrific noise we could not hear from the air, but it soon became part of our daily life on the ground where we lived near the sea in a Cotonou suburb. Framed by the airplane window I could see the city, its European section looking quite new with its linear avenues and streets bordered by small villas in the middle of lush tropical gardens. Beyond lay the native city with its compounds of modest little houses and shacks.

Cotonou seemed welcoming. Our life was to be that of a small diplomatic post, with its advantages and disadvantages and, likely, many surprises awaiting us. We were met on arrival by Kurt Wolf, the West German who was the UNDP Resident Representative, an easygoing and competent man. His vivacious wife had come with him to greet us as well as someone from the Ministry of Foreign Affairs and an official of the Ministry of Planning with whom I was to work.

All Customs formalities simplified, we took the road to the *Hôtel de la Plage*, one of the two comfortable hotels in town at the time, where we put up for a few days before renting a furnished villa. There were few available, but we found one behind the coconut grove bordering the sea. When in the evenings we would go up to the terrace over the garage to feel the cool breeze coming from the gulf and admire the star-studded sky, we could hear the tremendous pounding of the waves on the beach, a roar I will always remember. Our house was brand new, simply furnished, with no air conditioning, but we bought fans. It belonged to a director of the Ministry of Agriculture. In Bénin most houses rented to foreigners belonged either to high level civil servants or to senior army officers who are both professional soldiers and a modern political elite group.

We hired a cook, Julien, who lived with his family in the native district in a neatly kept compound. He was a Class 6 cook, the highest category of cooks trained in the vocational trade schools created by the French. Julien cooked well but spoke little and remained an enigma to us. Possibly he was an informant for the Government on what he heard in our house when the politics of the country started to change.

Our gardener, Bonaventure, quite young, was a Fon from the countryside. Unlike Julien, he was open and friendly. He wanted to improve his status by becoming a chauffeur. In my spare time I gave him a few driving lessons to better his chances of passing the stiff government examination for a permit to drive.

My first days were occupied with making the usual first contacts with Dahomean officials. The Ministry of Planning, a new organ of the Government, was required to furnish us with offices. But not having enough space for its own personnel, they gave us a large bare meeting room at the top of a monumental staircase in a nearby building, which had been a Court. The Ministry did not have money to equip it as a modern office. We got typewriters and a telephone, and hired two secretaries. One was Dutch, married to an African, and competent in English. The other was Dahomean. We were then supposed to be in business.

With the help of a French friend working for the French Bilateral Assistance Program, who was a gifted decorator and wanted to help us, I managed to complete our installation and make the office attractive at practically no cost, using local materials such as bamboo for partitions and handicrafts and potted plants for decoration. This appealed to us but left our Dahomean co-workers unimpressed, since for them furniture, to be respectable, had to be imported from Paris.

Our UN team comprised myself as coordinator and general economic planner and Pierre Cauvin, a distinguished, handsome 50-year-old Haitian, as financial planner. A former official of the National Bank of Haiti, he had considerable experience in African affairs. He had already been a UN financial advisor to the Government of Bénin for three years and was to become my most valued colleague in Cotonou. He knew everybody, and everything about the country. A competent economist, he had taken his Ph.D. at the University of Paris, and was married to a charming Dutch woman named Leni. They had two children studying in Paris. They had barely saved their skins in escaping from Port-au-Prince after Papa Doc had killed Pierre's father and other relatives, who were among the most courageous opponents of the Duvalier regime. When they reached New York, the UN recruited him for service in Africa, a decidedly valuable acquisition for our program. Understandably, Pierre seldom wanted to talk to me about Haiti, although I would have liked him to because I knew his country and its people so well.

Our second expert was a Dutch-American agricultural economist who had taught at Berkeley and had been sent from Rome by the Food and Agriculture Organization. Other experts came later, at different periods, but we were never more than four or five at a time. But we could consult with some of the other UN experts in Cotonou on a variety of local problems.

We worked directly with the Director-General of the Ministry of Planning, my counterpart, a devoted and competent Dahomean who had studied in France, and with three young local economists who had recently returned from a training program in planning in Paris sponsored by the French government.

A Tour of Bénin

After all these initial activities in the two weeks following our arrival, Natalie and I took our first look at the country and through various short trips learned much about its people and their traditions. Bénin is a small country which had 2.7 million inhabitants at the time (now 4.2 million) and can be easily visited in a few days if one wants to give it only a cursory look. It covers an area of about 110,000 square miles, minuscule compared to Nigeria, its giant neighbor to the east.

We first visited Porto Novo, on a lagoon east of Cotonou, a town which had been the capital of Bénin and the first place where the French established their protectorate in 1863. The town was reminiscent of the French Colonial period. We toured the Government compound, settled in a park with giant trees and a few old buildings that had been used as the Ministries, and large villas which had been occupied by senior civil servants during the colonial administration. There I contacted the officers of the Ministry of Agriculture with whom I was to have many visits later.

Contemplating the handsome old villas with their white Venetian shutters, one could easily imagine what life was like at the end of the colonial period and picture the French administrators moving around in this pretty decor. A close friend, Enzo de Chetelat, a naturalized American ten years older than I, whom I had met in Washington at the Board of Economic Warfare, had told me much about Bénin before I had any idea I would work there one day. As a geologist commissioned by the French Colonial Administration in 1925, he had been the first to map the geological resources of the country. This he did on foot or as he was carried in the bush on a litter, in regions infested by the tse-tse fly. His descriptions of life in such spots were fascinating.

He had lived two years in Porto Novo and had given me an unpublished diary of his life in West Africa which read like a novel. Enzo, then a dashing young man of twenty-five, had arrived in Porto Novo at the very spot where we were standing that day, to present his credentials to the French Governor. There he was met by a young man, the Secretary to the Governor, dressed in white uniform and white pith helmet. Ten black colonial guards presented arms. The Secretary escorted my friend in a rickshaw to a bungalow near the Government House. They were followed by five porters carrying his belongings on their heads. How times had changed and how prosaic my arrival in Bénin had been in comparison. The French colonial days had gone, but Porto Novo retained its pleasant ambience. No longer the center of action, it had become quiet, almost asleep, yet I always returned there with pleasure.

Our second exploratory trip was to Abomey, sixty miles inland. It had been the capital of the country in pre-colonial days. Created by the Fon people, a tribe close to the Yorubas of Western Nigeria, it was ruled in the 17th and 18th centuries by the Dahomean kings. They were known all over West Africa for their valor and military skills, their lack of morals and their savagery.

Abomey was then a large town, surrounded by a deep moat. It featured an elaborate court, like a small state. We visited the former palace of the Kings, a vast compound of buildings around a square with tall mud walls and few doors. Nothing much remained to attest to what life had been at the court. As witness of bloody victories in their numerous wars, the palace walls were surmounted by spikes spaced at twenty-foot intervals that held human skulls, and hundreds of skulls also were piled up at the gates. What remained was the gate at which the Kings sat at ceremonies, surrounded by eunuchs, the three thousand wives and the armed women warriors in uniform. Hundreds of banners and umbrellas were carried by servants, sheltering visitors from the fierce sun. There was a constant firing from great guns and small arms to increase the excitement. Parades of the Kings' three regiments of Amazons were held to impress foreign visitors. The women warriors were strong and muscular, not feminine in appearance, armed with muskets and swords and dressed like male soldiers. They were expected to remain virgins and could be put to death for unchaste behavior. A commander of the British Navy who visited Abomey at the time of the blockade of Ouidah wrote of them in 1851:

> *These sable ladies performed prodigies of valor, and not infrequently, by a fortunate charge, save the honor of the male soldiers, by bearing down all before them, discovering themselves, to the astonished and abashed prisoners, to be women, exceeding their male coadjutors in cruelty and all the stronger passions.*[30]

The King's family consisted of a huge community. His descendants, legitimate or otherwise, included a vast number of persons called the royal sib, so numerous that it would have been difficult to find people in all Abomey who were not

---

30 Frederich Forbes, *Dahomey and the Dahomeans* (London: Longman, Brown & Green, and Longman, 1851).

descended from the male or female royalty. This was because members of the royal family were freed of many prohibitions that governed the life of ordinary folk. According to American anthropologist Melville Herkovits, incestuous relations were permitted among them and uninhibited sexual relations were particularly enjoyed by women descended from royalty. If married they could divorce their husbands at will. Married or unmarried they took what lovers they wished.[31]

Little value was placed on the life of individuals at the court of the Dahomean Kings. According to my friend Enzo, the King of Djougou summoned slaves to carry a message to a departed relative. He would say to the slave, "Tell my father that this year has been a good (or a bad) year" or "We have had trouble with a hurricane" or "The crops were destroyed by locusts." The King made him repeat the message several times to be sure the slave would be able to make a complete delivery, then the slave would be beheaded.

The Kings of Abomey had artists working for them in workshops set up around the Court. Dahomean artisans are still famous for their original art forms. We visited the brass workers, members of a closely restricted guild, in a special compound not far from the palace. They make figurines of animals and men beautifully stylized and exquisite. They use the *cire-perdue* (lost wax) method of direct casting for their bronzes, the subject being first modeled in beeswax. Brass castings in Bénin in the last century constituted a most valuable art form. Bénin bronzes carry a high value for collectors; the best from Nigeria are exhibited in the British museums in London. We also saw carvers using various colored woods with beautiful patina, their primitive sculptures representing the earth gods. Dahomean graphic art was also remarkable, with elegant designs incised on *calabashes* and particularly *appliqué* cloth, a precursor of Matisse's work. We bought a few *appliqués* representing exotic birds in striking colors on contrasting backgrounds, as well as other designs of wild beasts, one showing a man caught by a crocodile. The subject was cut according to patterns and sewed on a black background.

As part of our initiation to Bénin, another trip of a few days took us to the northwest of the country. Natalie and I accompanied a small team of World Bank experts planning a rural development project to be assisted by the Bank. We held discussions with Government officials at Natitingou, the only little town in the Atacora mountains, the country of the animist Somba tribe.

Fifty years ago the Somba men still went naked. They had not been influenced by Christian or Moslem civilizations. Self-sufficient, they knew how to make their

---

31 Melville Herkovits, *Dahomey, an Ancient West African Kingdom* (Evanston, Il: Northwestern U. Press, 1967).

own tools, pottery and the various ornaments they wore, and lived in isolation. Men wore penis sheaths as protection, of which there were several styles. According to Enzo de Chetelat, the most popular model was made of a long, dried, tubular reed of a special cultivated gourd. Others were finely woven cylindrical small baskets ornamented with bird feathers. Their head gear was decorated with bright feathers. Women wore a bunch of fresh leaves in front and back held by a G-string—their only 'clothes,' as they also did in north west Guinea, in Central Nigeria and in the former colony of the Ubangi-Chari.

The variety of ornaments worn by both sexes was extraordinary; ear, lip and nostril plugs made of ivory, bird quills, wood and brass, for example. The women and some men wore locally made quartz plugs through their lower lips. The plug was changed for a large one when the hole of the lip became too wide. The most usual personal object carried by a Somba warrior was a whip, like a small cat-o'-nine-tails' with several thongs of leather, each lash having at the end several fixed rings of metal. These whips were used as defense and in duals among rival Somba men.

All this had disappeared when we were there, but some homes remained a unique example of native architecture. We visited a family compound built of red earth and looking like a little château. It consisted of seven two-story circular huts with conical thatched roofs. The small yards were separated by tall walls in the same material.

The Sombas we saw and talked to were quite shy. They wore shorts or pants, mostly clothing distributed by relief organizations. Some women still wore loincloths. Ornaments and decorations no longer could be seen and the Sombas now leave their noses and lips alone. They were gradually being converted to Catholicism or Islam, mostly to the latter.

Perhaps the most interesting visit we made from an historical point of view was that to Ouidah,[32] a small port east of Cotonou close to the Togo border. Ouidah had had an infamous and cruel past as the greatest slave-trading center on the African west coast. On arriving at Ouidah from the interior slaves were housed in a long thatched shed fenced with palisades of sharpened stakes, each manacled to an iron chain. Once a day they were fed from a cauldron of millet gruel. The Portuguese, British and French had trading posts where the coastal merchants could exchange slaves for goods such as guns, powder, glass beads and cotton goods. The slaves were shipped to Brazil, the Caribbean and the United States. Many went to Haiti, bringing with them the voodoo religion and the cult of the ancestors which their descendants still practiced, with which I am very familiar as a result of my long stays in Haiti.

32 Pronounced WE dah.

In the 19th century, Ouidah included six or seven free towns, three governed respectively by the French, the Portuguese and the British, each having built forts for the needs of the slave trade. The towns were overseen by the Viceroy of Ouidah. All commerce, whether in slave trade or palm oil, was controlled by the *chacha*, the principal agent of the King for any transaction.

The kings of Dahomey were fully engaged in the slave trade along with the Europeans, and many Africans of lesser standing participated in it. The Europeans did not catch the slaves themselves. They only bought them. As a result the blame for this dark period of history should be focused equally on those who sold the slaves and on those who bought them. African scholars have argued that African rulers had no other channel for trade and did not know about the cruel fate reserved for the slaves during their voyages and later on the sugar and cotton plantations. The Kings of Dahomey simply claimed that they were trading their "conquered enemies." Their tradition held that captured prisoners belonged to no one. They were kinless. Since an individual had no meaning outside of the tribe he could either be absorbed by the conquering tribe, replacing Dahomeans killed in the wars, or sold to the foreign slave trade. The European forts that enabled this trade had long disappeared when we were there. For a long time the Portuguese maintained a governor with a few Portuguese guards. The house of the Governor was still there as were some old cannons and a small cemetery containing the tombs of former Portuguese governors. In 1961 the Government of Dahomey seized the Portuguese enclave in Ouidah and expelled the Governor.

A fascinating aspect of our visit to Ouidah was the story of the Brazilian population, which had been of capital importance in the development of Dahomey. In the nineteenth century many Dahomean freed slaves returned to Ouidah from Brazil. They wanted to come back and live in the land of their ancestors. In 1845 they began to arrive, already converted to Catholicism by the Jesuits. Soon they were a well-organized group in both Ouidah and Porto Novo, and in Lagos, Nigeria, venerating their ancestors. They became farmers around Ouidah, and some even prospered as slave traders themselves. They remained on the coast and became the aristocrats. Fully integrated, toward the end of the nineteenth century they played an important cultural role, holding important administrative positions in the government and in elective offices. Their names were de Souza, da Silva, etc., names obviously of Portuguese origin. The French accorded them special protection. Their group expanded not only from returning Brazilians but included many Dahomeans who had never been slaves but joined them through marriage or by taking a Portuguese name. During my stay in Cotonou I worked with quite a number of civil servants with Portuguese names.

Ouidah has always been considered the country's intellectual center. The Brazilian community helped Dahomey become a remarkable reservoir of well-educated Africans who were employed all over the French Colonial Empire to occupy various administrative posts.

The Cult of Ancestors

It would have been a serious omission to start drafting a national development plan without having studied the country's history, its traditional structures and the people's beliefs. The past explains the present and, to some extent, the future and, in many ways, determines how fast a country can progress on the road to development. Two aspects have dominated the life of the Dahomean people in the past: the cult of ancestors and the impact of French colonization.

Perhaps more than in any other West African country, the social system in Bénin is based on an ancestor cult and a communal kinship structure. The society is made up of clans or tribes united by blood. These clans have the same ancestor. In them the individual does not exist. It is the clan, past and present which counts, as the living and the dead together form the Dahomean society.[33] According to a Dahomean ethnologist, the ancestor stands between the people and the gods they worship, the latter personifying the forces of the Universe which the people fear as they often threaten them with destruction.[34] Transported by the slaves this cult is the origin of *voudun* (voodoo) in Haiti and other Caribbean islands and in Brazil.

In Bénin mystic ceremonies still take place in the countryside, dances and music accompanying a wealth of oral traditions transmitted from generation to generation. These ceremonies involve the phenomena of nature: the earth, the sun and the waters. In this mysterious world the ancestor rules as an absolute monarch over the destiny of the living. He passes judgments on his descendants and their misdeeds and this may even involve a death sentence.[35]

All clan members must know the home of the clan founder and where offerings to him in special ceremonies will take place. The notion of nation is less important to them than the place where their ancestor was born.

Dahomeans believe ancestors rest in the Valley of the Dead. Their souls, however, continue their terrestrial life, suffering from cold, hunger and thirst. Strangely, in their kingdom, "their dead walk backward, speak through the nose, sit

---

33 Dor Ronan, *Dahomey, Between Tradition and Modernism* (Ithaca, NY: Cornell University, 1975).
34 Abdon Tidjani, *Présence Africaine*, (Paris, 1951).
35 Melville Herkovits, *Dahomey, an Ancient West African Kingdom* (Evanston, Il: Northwestern U. Press, 1967).

on an upside down stool and call the night the day. In the evening their souls come back to earth and keep company with the living. Anticipating their visit, as soon as darkness comes, no one sweeps in front of the hut or throws water in the yard without shouting *Ago* (watch out). So that the dead may find something to eat during their night visits, one must never empty the sauce in a pot or wash dishes before daylight. The soul, having left its flesh, takes a new power; it knows, sees and hears everything." [36]

Shortly after we settled in Cotonou I was invited by a Dahomean to an ancestral ceremony in Ouidah which included several hundred descendants. They came from as far away as Lome, Togo and Lagos, Nigeria. Because they were so numerous it was held at a soccer field not far from the ancestral home. At one end of the field was a place for an orchestra and dancers. There were also men with funeral drums, gongs and rattles. During the ceremony a goat was sacrificed to honor the returning ancestors, represented by young men in beautiful costumes. The ceremony began at two o'clock in the afternoon and continued until after dark.

When we arrived the spirits of the ancestors were being invoked. The name of each ancestor was called, his deeds recounted and his praise sung. Then a dance started, the dancers clad in rich garb of velvet and brocades. A young man representing the most important ancestor was seated under a large umbrella on a high stool, holding a scepter. From time to time other young men in fine garments danced a kind of trot. I was told by my friend that one of the dancers, who wore a chief's cap and was garbed in white, represented Dambala, one of the *voudun* gods. At the end of the field we saw a file being formed, headed by an ancestor. He and his entourage started walking around the field to meet his descendants so they could talk to him, seek his advice or tell him their troubles. Sometimes the ancestor would chastise them for some misdeed they had committed. I understood that a similar ceremony took place every year. As we were heading home my friend told me that some of the people around the field surely believed that the return of the ancestors was no symbolic ceremony but the real thing.

The Impact of French Colonization

In all government offices and all over Cotonou, French is spoken by almost everyone who is part of the economic life. The Portuguese were the first Europeans to land on the West African coast at the end of the 15th century. They started the slave trade in Ouidah in 1530. Colonization of Dahomey by the French came much later and was gradual. It began with the arrival of French traders and missionaries on the coast

---

36 Olympe Bhely-Quenum, *Au pays des Fons* (Paris: Presence Africaine, 1965), 66.

and the signing of a treaty with Dahomean King Glebe in 1882 giving the French the right to establish a colony in Cotonou and a protectorate over Porto Novo. The Act of Berlin in 1885 confirmed these rights, but King Glebe and later King Behanzin refused to recognize the rights of the French over Cotonou. Both kings went to war but lost. In 1893 the French occupied the kingdom of Abomey and exiled Behanzin to the island of Martinique. The French took over the entire country including other small kingdoms and the land of the Sombas to the north.

At the beginning of their conquest they preserved the traditional structures of the kingdoms and were accepted by the people, who had suffered so much at the cruel hands of Behanzin. A new king, Azoli Agbo was appointed, but he also was later sent into exile. The French divided the country into administrative units called *cantons*, each headed by a French administrator, set aside the traditional system of administration and replaced it with a policy of assimilation, i.e. of direct rule. This led to conflicts with the village chiefs and in the 1930s forced the French to restore the traditional Kingdoms.

The most important consequence of French colonization was the separation of the elites from the popular masses. In all of Africa, French policy was to progressively create a local elite with whom colonial administrators could closely cooperate. To this end they set up "advisory councils of native notables," chosen among the chiefs. Later the councilors were elected by the people. Candidates to the councils had to be thirty years old and speak fluent French. Some chiefs were given jobs in the French Colonial Administration and were used as agents for the collection of the head tax, a major cause of opposition to the French presence in Dahomey. Because they had to collect taxes the traditional chiefs lost much of their influence as leaders of their own people.

The gap between the elite and the masses grew larger as a result of the French policy on education. Public schools were opened to recruit the sons of the Kings and of the chiefs and teach them French and French culture. Later they would be offered positions in the colonial administration. In all schools, public or Catholic or Protestant missionary schools, the language of instruction was French only.

The French also established village schools for the masses, teaching the children to read and write in French as well as practical work in the fields. In the towns and cities instruction was given in home economics, hygiene, etc. These schools employed native teachers trained in *écoles normales* (normal schools). On returning to their villages these native teachers served as examples to their people of what French civilization could do for them.[37] In 1912 Ponty, the Governor of Dahomey

---

37 *Journal Officiel du Dahomey*, (July 1914).

could declare that the education of these elites had served to make our influence accepted and facilitated our role in civilizing the people.

More schools were created in the towns than in the rural areas, as many of the peasants refused to send their children to school claiming they needed them in farming. Thus in 1934, despite the considerable efforts of the French to advance education, only about 7 percent of all school-age children attended school in the countryside. But the level of instruction was fairly good and was rated higher than in the other French West African colonies. Many young Dahomeans obtained a satisfactory school education and were recruited for the colonial service. These were sent to Dakar or to France for higher education, and soon there was a surplus of well-trained people. As they could not all find jobs in Dahomey they were used by the French in clerical and administrative positions all over the French Empire in Africa, a remarkable achievement which lasted until independence of the new African nations in 1960, when they were replaced by nationals. But then they had to return to Dahomey, and increased the ranks of the unemployed, creating a serious situation for the country.

The political structure of Dahomey greatly changed after World War II. During the Presidency of General Charles de Gaulle, the French Colonial Empire under the French Union was united with the mother country. The colonial territories were then given wide autonomy as a prelude to independence. Each African country was able to send elected representatives to the French National Assembly in Paris. Because of its small size Dahomey was entitled to one representative. Local Assemblies of elected councilors were also created. Those elected were the educated Dahomeans who had studied in France and the traditional chiefs played practically no role in these elections. Until 1950 regional and tribal factors had played little part in the post-war elections but after that they came to assume enormous importance. As winds of independence began to blow, candidates identified themselves with the traditional kingdoms of Abomey or Porto Novo, or with the North and their ethnic groups, mainly the Fons, the Gouns and the Baribas. When France granted independence to its colonies in 1960, too many political parties were organized in Dahomey, copying the French political system, creating as a result an extremely unstable political situation.

After the war, no outstanding Dahomean leader emerged. At independence it became a unitary state with separate executive, legislative and judiciary powers and universal suffrage, a copy of the French parliamentary system. As a result, the traditional chiefs were abolished and, for a while, it was thought that all traditional structures had been destroyed. But they managed to survive. The newly-elected representatives realized they needed the chiefs, particularly for collecting taxes, and soon a parallel system of authority was founded.[38]

The division between the elite and the masses became even more apparent when France gave scholarships to many young Dahomeans to study in French universities. Estranged from their traditional backgrounds, many lived like Europeans. When they returned to their country, they were not anxious to participate directly in the lives of their people, discarding the values of their own civilization and the countryside. They turned to France for help. Dahomey remained poor and insecure. They did little on their own, counting mainly on French financial and technical support, which was always offered generously. This went on until the '70s.

Political instability continued. The national constitution was changed several times. New political parties were formed. All this led to two *coups d'état* by the military in 1963 and 1969. Each time the President was forced to resign and new elections were called, revealing ferocious regional competition and destabilizing the nation. Among the candidates for the Presidency were Apithy from the south, Abonia Degbe from the center and Maga from the north, along with Zinzou, who was attached to no specific region. As no valid majority was obtained, the elections had to be canceled, creating acute political crises.

The Military Takeover

In the hope of restoring stability, a curious compromise was reached. A Presidential Council was formed called the Dahomean "triumvirate" under which the presidency would rotate every two years among the three former presidents who represented the three most important regions.

The "triumvirate" experiment did not work, principally because the three leaders did not cooperate as they had agreed they would. Instability and political agitation continued which led to a number of military mutinies and student strikes which were severely repressed. Six men were sentenced to death but the death sentences were left pending, while others were sentenced to prison for life.

Finally, in October 1972, the three leaders of the Presidential Council were eliminated by a military coup led by Major Mathieu Kerekou, the future President. After seizing the Presidential Palace practically without resistance, he announced on the radio that the Army had taken over the Government since "the authority of the State had disappeared everywhere."

The coup was the work of a small group of socialist-minded young army officers

---

38 Jacques Lombaire, *Autorités traditionnelles et pouvoirs européens en Afrique noire* (Paris: A. Colin, 1967).

who wanted to bring radical changes to the political and economic structure of Dahomey. They were hardly prepared for the job of running a nation. One of their first acts was to rename the country Bénin, the old name for the region.

Shortly after my arrival it became evident that they wanted first to detach themselves from French influence and the neo-colonialism which had characterized the period following independence. Other signs appeared. Diplomatic relations with Nationalist China were terminated and the People's Republic of China and North Korea were invited to open embassies in Cotonou.

Although the government was to be leftist, it was still not clear at that stage what exact ideology they would espouse. Were they going to be only ardent nationalists like many other Third World countries in Africa, or would they opt for anti-imperialism or go much further down the road of Socialism?

An Exercise in Planning

I will not put my readers through the lengthy phases of preparing a national development plan, even though I found it exciting in a country like Bénin. I simply wish to explain how we went about it and, for those interested in development, to give an idea of the country's natural and human resources and the public investment programs which were to be undertaken as first priorities.

During our first months in Cotonou, nearly two years after the coup, our team gathered the data needed for drafting the Plan. It was certainly not an easy period for such work. Planning is an organized conscious and continuous effort requiring the cooperation of many people, to determine the best means of reaching development objectives carefully selected in the national interest. This collective effort is preceded by a technical phase—the drafting of a Plan—on which we were working with the Government economists. We had to consult with the technical ministries on the sectional aspects of the Plan, then discuss our recommendations with a number of commissions—which we helped create—representing the various national interests. The Plan, once drafted, had to gain final approval from the highest authorities in the State. We hoped to complete our work in one year.

What we found first was that some of the technical ministries, Agriculture in particular, were jealous of the status and prerogatives recently given to the Ministry of Planning, which was rightly attached to the Presidency. Some officers in these ministries did not seem particularly anxious to fully cooperate with us. In the first place they did not have all the information at their disposal that was needed to draft the plan. So we organized various meetings and workshops with them and suggested ways of collecting the data. Gradually we had enough information to do some useful work, in particular to determine the priorities of national development based on existing natural and human resources and the projects already in progress.

We also had various meetings with the agencies of the Western donor nations since they contributed the lion's share of the investments needed to finance the development programs. The most important were France, the European Common Market Fund (FED), West Germany and the United States. But with the political orientation taken by Bénin, the future of foreign aid became somewhat uncertain and none of the donor government agencies could be precise about the amounts of future contributions.

The base of the Bénin economy is agriculture and its potential is substantial and varied. We had to concentrate our study on that sector. There are five natural regions in Bénin: the coastal area called *la Lagune*, about 2 to 5 kilometers wide, which is excellent for coconut cultivation; the north of that zone, where corn, peanut, citrus and palm oil are cultivated; the central plateau, where cotton and rice, benefiting from heavy rains, can be grown advantageously; the northwest, the Alacora, which receives the most rain, where rice, yams, sorghum and millet thrive; and the northeast, the Niger Plain, where cotton is the main crop.

In the south, we determined, clearly better yields had to be obtained for palm oil, the export crop, and aid for food crops had to be maximized, rice cultivation increased, corn exports increased to Nigeria where a considerable market existed.

There were climatic limitations for agricultural production in the south, near the coast, which received much less rain than neighboring countries such as Togo, located at a similar latitude. As a result Bénin has smaller coffee and cocoa crops and lower yields for palm oil than neighboring countries. Cotton in the Bon Borghore in the center was, however, a dynamic element of the economy, and with palm oil represented the major exports. Corn, cassava and rice were excellent crops for domestic use and also for export. Cattle raising and fishing were also important. Both, and especially corn, could grow significantly if the tse-tse fly problem could be controlled. Considerable efforts were already being made to combat endemic diseases afflicting cattle. There was also a program to develop the forestry resources.

One of the main requirements for agricultural development was to train the extension workers and restructure the rural development programs. The government of Mathieu Kerekou was particularly interested in developing village cooperatives, and much had to be done to train people in elementary management, supervised credit and literacy.

The mining potential of the country was very limited, except perhaps for phosphates, which hold some promise since fairly important phosphate deposits were being exported from Togo not far from the Bénin border. Finally, oil deposits had been discovered just off shore, but had not yet been exploited when we were there. It was expected, however, that production would be small, nothing like that of Nigeria. The prospects for industrialization were limited, but included cement and sugar production. With cotton a significant domestic product, the local textile industry could be expanded if foreign investors were interested.

We had no doubt that one of the greatest efforts of the Government was to concentrate on improving human resources through education and training. In 1971 the population was estimated at 2.7 million. A census organized by the United Nations was in progress. On the basis of available statistics, with a population growth rate estimated at about 2.8 percent, Bénin would double its population by the end of the century. Forty-five percent of the people were less than 15 years of age, a large burden on the economy. The average life expectancy was only 37 years, but was twice as high in the cities as in the rural areas. Literacy was only 11 percent. These figures gave an idea of the effort ahead but the situation was similar to other least-developed countries in Africa. However, some progress had been made. The number of children in primary education had doubled in ten years and secondary education had eight times more students in 1974 than at independence in 1960. In our view, the greatest efforts should be made in technical training.

As well, there was great need for serious improvement in the health sector, including the construction of hospitals and the training of personnel. Much had to be done in youth development, and this effort was to be helped in particular by the World Bank, newly interested in social development, which was willing to finance well-structured rural development programs involving youth and women. ILO, another UN agency, was helping the government in manpower planning and training. Our team believed that special public works programs could be organized on a fairly large scale to fight unemployment in the towns and underemployment in the rural zones, and we were supporting projects to be undertaken with food assistance from the World Food Program (WFP) and bilateral agencies for community work including conservation, irrigation, digging wells, grain storage, maintenance of roads from farm to market, schools, clinics, rural markets, youth centers and the like.

But finally, the most crucial problem in implementing the development plan was the precarious financial situation of Bénin, which lacked the savings needed to satisfactorily finance a public investment program. External assistance was therefore needed on a large scale.

As pointed out, the French, the European community, the Federal Republic of

Germany, the U.S. (including assistance given by U.S. Peace Corps Volunteers) and other Western countries had so far been the major donors through loans and grants for major development projects.

Now Bénin, in changing its political orientation, strangely enough seemed to count on the help of Communist China and North Korea, an assistance which turned out to be very limited. Before I left it included only technical assistance in rice cultivation from the Chinese and the promise of a match factory from the North Koreans. Yet help from these two countries seemed to be preferred even to that of the USSR, which had contributed only a small amount of assistance in the form of equipment. The Russian Ambassador, whom I met at an official reception, told me with a smile that some of his offers had not so far been accepted.

Another aspect of great concern to us was the preparation of the national budget, which was the prerogative of the Minister of Finance. He was supposed to include sufficient funds for the Government's share in the development program, including funds for current expenses such as local personnel, transportation and maintenance not financed by foreign aid. This was essential for the operation of the projects we were putting forward as, obviously, we did not want to draft a plan which could not be adequately financed in all respects, so we had to put considerable pressure on the Minister so he would agree on the absolute necessity to budget these items.

Bénin Becomes Marxist-Leninist

Despite all of Bénin's difficulties, our work was proceeding fairly well when, one day in October 1974, we were told in confidence by our Dahomean colleagues that a two-week high level seminar would take place at the Presidential Palace. More than 200 senior civil servants had been summoned to attend and listen to the orientation President Kerekou wanted to give to the nation. We had also learned through another indiscretion that a few officials from the braintrust of Guinean President Sekou-Touré had come earlier from Conakry to advise Kerekou and his entourage.[39] Neither the United Nations nor foreign embassies were invited to observe the seminar at the Palace, which was being kept very hush-hush.

Since our team had been invited to help prepare the national development plan, we felt we should at least have been asked to attend the meetings and the fact that we were not participating was very disquieting. The meeting was extended first two weeks, then six weeks, during which we lost the collaboration of our counterparts, who were required to spend their entire days at the Palace.

---

39 Guinea was the only French colony which after World War II did not want to join de Gaulle's French Union, and became a Marxist economy.

Finally, the result of these long discussions became known. On November 30, 1974, on the second anniversary of the Revolution, President Mathieu Kerekou and his entire government went to Abomey, the traditional capital. There, with great fanfare, the President spoke to the nation, declaring Bénin had chosen to become Marxist-Leninist and that its future development would follow the scientific doctrine, i.e. Communism. He wanted to make the Dahomean people the master of their own destiny, finish with foreign domination, stop economic exploitation and cultural alienation. Further, he said he wanted to destroy regional tribalism, eradicate corruption and strengthen the authority of the State. We listened to the speech on the radio in Cotonou, which announced a complete restructuring of agriculture in favor of small farmers without defining it, and for industry a revision of the investment code in favor of the Dahomean people, which meant the nationalization of various enterprises.

The ambience in Cotonou changed almost overnight. The Government lost no time in taking drastic action. It immediately nationalized banking and other credit institutions, insurance, cable and radio companies, and foreign firms transporting and storing petroleum products.

The Government became more dictatorial and suspicious of all who seemed to oppose its new policies, particularly the civil servants. The three Dahomean economists on our team, falling into that category, were suddenly transferred to other functions in the Ministry of the Interior, leaving us without local assistance. The Director-General of the Ministry of Planning, the principal officer with whom we worked daily, and through whom we had been able to arrange all our contacts with other units of the Government, disappeared from his office one morning at the beginning of 1975. He had been arrested and thrown into prison, accused of being the friend of a senior army officer who had allegedly taken part in an unsuccessful coup against the Government two or three years earlier. As mentioned, he held our esteem and was our greatest supporter in Bénin. Thanks to him we had made relative progress in preparing the plan. He had a wife and three children. We rarely heard about him from anyone at the Ministry after his arrest and I learned he was still in prison several years after I left Bénin.

The work of our team, of course, had to be completely re-evaluated. I discussed our problems with the UNDP Resident Representative in Cotonou and wrote confidential reports to UN Headquarters in New York. Since the UN gives technical assistance to all its members, irrespective of their political orientation, we would have to cope with the new situation and draft a Plan corresponding to the new objectives. Despite the political change the major western donors continued to assist

Bénin, although at a reduced level. It was doubtful that the help the Government had requested from Communist China and North Korea would come through in the quantities needed to make a difference.[40]

Personally, of course, I did not believe in Marxism-Leninism and thought the new orientation of the economy was going to be disastrous for the Dahomean nation. What our team had been preparing until then was not a plan for a centrally-focused Marxist-Leninist economy. It was only an "Indicative Plan," not a "Controlling Plan," which President Kerekou seemed to want to establish in accordance with his Abomey Declaration.

There was a great difference between the kind of economy we had in mind for Bénin and that toward which Mathieu Kerekou wanted to orient his country. Our plan was to reflect expectations, intentions, aspirations if you wish, but not the binding commitment of a Marxist-Leninist government. In other words, it was to be a guide for the government, its purpose being to establish a coherent public sector program and a sound economic policy, nothing more.

In contrast, plans made by Communist countries are documents of authorization; they tell each industrial and agricultural sector of the economy what it must produce and how much it must invest. In my view it would be ridiculous to prepare and try to apply such a plan in a country like Bénin with any chance of success.

As an American citizen I was no longer the kind of economist needed to head the team. I decided therefore to leave Bénin at the end of my one-year contract, which was rapidly approaching, turning down the UN invitation to continue in my position. Incidentally, finding a candidate to replace me took some time, and the economist who arrived several months later to head the team, a Belgian, found that he, too, could not work with a disorganized government and decided to leave three months after taking up his duties. Someone from Eastern Europe was finally recruited for the job.

Before I left Bénin, the team decided to submit to the government an interim plan, something which would show, first, to the UN in New York that we had made as much progress as we could in fulfilling our assignment and, second, to prevent the possibility of some unfriendly government official claiming that we had not done our job if no report had been submitted at that stage.

In February, 1975, I submitted to the Government an *Avant-Projet*, a provisional macro-economic plan related only to the global aspects of the economy, leaving sectional and regional planning for later. The work was sufficient to define the

---

40 Before I left it included technical assistance in rice cultivation from the Chinese and a match factory from the North Koreans.

objectives, priorities, strategies and policies for development based on the Abomey Declaration. It also included the means needed for the execution of a plan and financing. This provisional work, although imperfect, would enable the making of final decisions regarding the list of concrete development projects to be retained under the Plan, at a later stage when the data concerning the sectors would become available.

During the last weeks of my stay the atmosphere in Cotonou grew less friendly. Social contacts between Dahomeans and foreigners became rare. Civil servants had been instructed not to accept personal invitations to foreign homes. It was only at large embassy receptions, on flag days or similar celebrations, that we would meet a few of them. This was a pity because Dahomeans are a very cordial, smiling people with whom it would have been easy to continue pleasant and interesting relations.

In those days one had to be very careful of what one said, as one never knew how a conversation would be reported. The Chief Medical Officer of the General Hospital of Cotonou, a competent and well-known Frenchman, had devoted many years to the improvement of health in Bénin to the detriment of his own career as dean of the faculty of medicine at the University of Marseille. He had apparently voiced some mild criticism of government policies at a dinner party and had taken a French information officer from Paris in a small plane to photograph some section of Bénin, with no ulterior motive. Denounced as an opponent of the regime, he was put under house arrest for several weeks. It was only under French Government pressure that he was able to leave the country. He was undoubtedly among the valuable foreigners who should have been kept on in Cotonou, since he headed the only large hospital in the country. There was no one to replace him immediately.

Relations between the Government and the French Embassy had remained tense ever since a mob had burned the French Cultural and Information Center in Cotonou just before I arrived, but France did not want to break diplomatic relations. American relations with the Government were not at their best, either. Discussions of a U.S. technical assistance and aid program had bogged down and, after the takeover, American Ambassador Jim Engle told me even he had difficulty in making appointments at the Foreign Office. Because of this he had time on his hands to visit and stay a few days with Peace Corps volunteers assigned to various parts of the country. A number of them were doing excellent work drilling wells and training people in community development. For unknown reasons these visits appeared strange to the Government. The Ambassador told me he was summoned to the Ministry of Foreign Affairs and brought before a kangaroo court to explain himself. That was enough. Shortly after this ridiculous and undignified incident he left the country, never to return to Cotonou.

At this point I developed some health problems which necessitated my going to Paris for treatment. From Pairs I returned to UN Headquarters in New York, and shortly after, I retired. A few months later, I made my way to Haiti for the last episode of my overseas work—with the USAID of the State Department.

An Experiment Fails

I never thought that Bénin would be able to adjust to a Marxist-Leninist regime. The Republic of the Congo, west of Zaïre on the other side of the Congo River, is a small former French colony which also opted for Marxism-Leninism and its situation was as bad as that of Bénin. No African nation turning to scientific socialism has fared well. On the contrary, despite Bénin's desire under the new regime to change the education system, to modernize agriculture, to help the small peasants—which were good points in its programs—little progress if any has been achieved. Under the rigid rules of socialism, the centralization of decisions, the lack of funds, knowledge and good management, no rural development programs anywhere can be successful. I felt also that the nationalization of some industries would lead to disaster. All the state enterprises created after the revolution suffered deeply from mismanagement and lack of funds, and have failed. Progress in a nation depends on freedom and free enterprise. It has been proven all over the world that voluntary participation of the people is needed to achieve durable success.

In the 1980s Bénin's economic situation remained precarious. The growth rate in agricultural production was lower than in the '70s except in 1984-85, when ideal weather conditions had prevailed. The dislocation of the industries, in underutilization of production capacity and the difficulties of access to international and regional markets, deeply affected business. Stagnation continued in the transportation services sector. The management of the nationalized banks left much to be desired. According to UN reports, the slowdown in the economy created a substantial decrease in state revenues and a forced reduction of the budget, as well as difficulties in servicing the public and high deficits in the balance of payments. The experiment in Marxism-Leninism has proved a fiasco.

The deterioration of the economy would have been even more rapid without Western foreign assistance which, fortunately for the Dahomean people, continued to be available, although at a considerably reduced rate. President Kerekou was forced to make several trips to Paris to try to obtain more help to rescue his economy, and a consortium of donor countries met in the French capital on several occasions under UNDP sponsorship to keep aid and technical assistance at a level which would enable the country to survive.

* * *

In 1991 an important change occurred. Bénin cast aside its one-party system, and in March voters took part in the country's first free presidential election in three decades. Mathieu Kerekou, the head of the People's Revolutionary Party, which had brought Marxism-Leninism to Bénin, was soundly defeated in a runoff election. Prime Minister Nicethore Soglo, French-trained and a former World Bank executive director, won handily over the completely discredited and rigid Communist orthodoxy from which Kerekou himself had gradually retreated in recent years. Once again the forces of freedom had won, as had been happening widely throughout the world.

Helping the Third World: An Overview

Helping the Third World: An Overview

In 1975, at the end of my mission to Bénin, I retired. Fifteen years of field work and six long-term missions to the Third World taught me a number of lessons about the relationship between developed and developing countries:

- Now that the Cold War is over, the UN member states should concentrate on the relationship between the industrial countries and the least developed countries of the world, focusing on the reduction of the frightful economic gap that separates them. Assuring underdeveloped countries a better distribution of the world's resources can be done without impoverishing the people of industrial countries and must be done to bring the world to stability and peace.

- We must first address ourselves to the basics of people's lives, such as peasant farming, roads from farm to market, small irrigation projects, tree planting, cooperatives, teacher training, building schools and clinics, and other projects at the community level handled by the people themselves, developing their self-reliance and initiative. In Africa particularly, food production for the domestic market must have the highest priority.

- Teaching self-reliance and popular participation—especially to women—in community and regional development projects, building the infrastructure of the new nations, decentralizing authority, reforming public administration, and especially promoting free enterprise, are the basic to progress and should be top national priorities in all countries. The UNDP continues to promote such projects, and I would like to see even more projects at the grass root level. We must help create more "people to people" projects. Fortunately, in the last two decades we have seen such organizations as UNDP, the World Bank and the Regional Development Banks increase their financing of such projects. N. Diaye, a Senegalese who heads the African Development Bank, believes that ideas are more important than resources. He sees his bank taking the lead in shaping development rather than merely bankrolling it. [42]It is also a good sign that these international institutions are no longer financing projects such as huge dams and other costly undertakings for countries which

do not yet have sufficient management capabilities, trained personnel and adequate maintenance funds. We must avoid grandiose development schemes for which the Third World is rarely prepared.
- As I have emphasized in various parts of this book, education is the key to all development. Training human resources should be a significant aspect of all foreign aid programs. All UN and Specialized Agencies should emphasize these projects, and the U.S. should rejoin UNESCO and permit this Specialized Agency to increase its valuable contribution to world education.
- A large part of foreign aid and other bilateral aid has been military aid. This aid should be reduced drastically in favor of greater economic and humanitarian social assistance to countries in dire need of it. The UN should develop strategies for penalizing merchants or governments which sell arms to developing countries, especially small arms and portable missiles which aggravate local conflicts, create refugee problems and inflict chaos and misery on millions of people.
- So that aid can be more effective, donors should continue to press for accelerated fiscal and administrative reforms in recipient countries.
- I also believe that it is vital that assistance be tied to greater efforts to enforce human rights in recipient countries, forcing the governments to allow their people to progress toward democracy.

* * *

Three of my six missions were in Africa and another was in another African country in the Caribbean—Haiti. I have witnessed under-development, civil wars, bloodshed, corruption and bad governments. I also saw famine, the insufficiency of domestic food production and, now, the grisly specter of AIDS which spreading through Africa at an alarming rate. Yet I see no reason to be a prophet of doom. There is hope for Africa. Slowly, across the continent, governments are beginning to realize that they must do something about high food prices, low incentives to farmers, effective reduction of government deficits and effective administrative reforms. Many countries are beginning to return to private enterprise those industries and services which had been nationalized. Further, they are increasing their investments in education.

A recent United Nations/World Bank study reports encouraging signs that developing countries which have adopted key reforms are reaping improved economic results. Further, there is progress in human rights, accommodating dissent and decentralization of decision-making, especially in Nigeria and in Zimbabwe. In South Africa, dialogues between opposing forces continue to seek a solution for apartheid. Many obstacles remain, but African nations, on the whole, are beginning to take responsibility for their own development and for carrying out their own nation-building.

It is in the interest of the U.S. to pursue vigorously those UN goals which correspond to those of the United States: a democratic ideal, the value of a pluralistic society and the dynamics of free enterprise.

PART V

AT THE DAWN OF A NEW WORLD ORDER

PART V

AT THE DAWN OF A NEW WORLD ORDER

The most basic division of the world today is not between Communists and non-Communists, between blacks and whites, between rich and poor, or even between young and old. It is between those who see only the interests of a limited group and those who are capable of seeing the interests of the broader community of mankind as a whole.

Richard Gardner
Professor of International Law
Columbia University

A Seminar at Middlebury College

A few years ago, even though retired in Vermont, I still wanted to explain to American youth what the UN was all about. In 1984 Middlebury College, an outstanding New England liberal arts college, asked me to give a seminar during the Winter Term. The subject was *The United Nations in World Politics Today*.

This new experience gave me a great deal of satisfaction. I lectured daily for six weeks to Political Science students, and public lectures in the series opened to all the students and the townspeople. The College publicized the seminars widely; posters blanketed the campus.

I invited a number of UN guest lecturers, who, as a group, comprised a miniature United Nations; each lecture was packed. The topics ranged from the famous Pugwash Movement—which started in 1955 with the Manifesto issued by Bertrand Russell and Albert Einstein calling on all scientists of the world to join together in urging governments to renounce war rather than follow a course that could put an end to the human race,[1]—to anecdotes about the various conflict areas in the Middle East and the Congo, to the political, economic and social problems of Africa, to why the U.S. had withdrawn from UNESCO, to UN recruitment and the International Civil Service. Discussion was wide-ranging and animated.

---

[1] The first Pugwash Conference took place in Pugwash, Nova Scotia, Canada, and 30 such conferences in all in 75 countries throughout the world drew some 2000 scientists, including a number of Nobel Laureates.

During those January days the temperature plunged to -20°F, and some of the lecturers had come unprepared for the frigid weather. I loaned them a few extra pieces of warm clothing, Natalie prepared steak dinners, most stayed overnight in our guest room, and the seminar went on. It was conducted on a shoestring—the lecturers received no fee or stipend, but were reimbursed for their airfare.

The students enjoyed their discussions with men who had had direct experience in the various UN programs. They developed keen interest in the crisis the UN was going through and what should be its future.

I explained to them what the UN costs each American in dollars and cents today. Forty-five years ago the U.S. contributed almost half of the UN budget—exactly 48 percent—but now its share was only 25 percent. Our share of the total expenses, approximately $1 billion, represents about $4 a year for each American, less than the price of one dessert in a nice restaurant, or a little more than the purchase of two Sunday *New York Times* at Lyons' Place in Middlebury. And some Americans still want to reduce our burden. The students could not believe this, and were surprised also that, although the U.S. contribution to the UN system as a whole is the highest in absolute terms, it ranks only 16th among all the nations of the world on a per capita basis.

I found that the students' questions to be those an enlightened public would have asked. First they readily understood that since no member state gives up its sovereignty by joining the UN and that the UN can act only when its member states decide that it should, UN powers are very limited. They concluded that UN achievements and failures were only a reflection of the collective work of its members and therefore were the responsibility of the main actors, the member states.[2] The students were most disappointed that it was the lack of political will to work together that crippled the organization. Some wondered whether the question of national sovereignty should be restudied with a view to giving more power to the UN itself in certain areas such as maintaining peace.

When we came to discuss how UN and Specialized Agencies' actions affect our lives in an interdependent world, few students were aware that some of the public services they enjoy as part of the routines of daily life are UN-based. For example, without the Postal Union, the International Telecommunications Union and the International Civil Aviation Organization—all parts of the UN System—valuable and necessary international regulations would not exist. Indeed, we would not be able to fly safely all over the world without the international standards established

---

2 Lord Caradon, a former British ambassador to the UN, once observed that there was nothing wrong with the UN but its members.

and verified by ICAO. Orderly trade in materials and in manufactured products would also be impossible without such coordinated and documented international UN trade arrangements as the General Agreement on Tariffs and Trade (GATT) and, for commodity agreements, the United Nations Conference on Trade and Development (UNCTAD).

We spent considerable time pondering the fact that the present international economic system is in disarray and that the gap between the rich and the poor countries is wider than ever. The students could see the disastrous long-term effects this situation might produce for the whole world, should nothing be done to close the gap. They were keen on protecting the human environment. They probed for ways to meet our energy needs without destroying the fragile web of life. They wanted to know whether the UN had solutions. I explained that the multilateral approach in our interdependent world appears the best way to tackle these global problems, and the world is gradually becoming convinced that this is the only solution for the future. Yet today only 15 percent of aid and assistance is multilateral.

The students worked hard during the session and were extremely motivated. They understood fully that the UN can realize its potential only if the member states have the political will to use it more extensively. Among quite a few excellent final papers on the nature of the United Nations, two were outstanding. Both student authors were admitted that year to the Graduate School of International Affairs at Columbia University.

The seminar gave the UN its day at Middlebury College and generated numerous interviews on Vermont ETV, the regional PBS station carried throughout the state and into the province of Quebec. By all accounts the seminar had been a success.

1988-1991: Three Years to Remember

The situation in the UN did not improve in the mid-'80s. The organization has sunk deeper and deeper into a huge financial crisis. The bloodbaths of the Iran-Iraq conflict continued, and took the lives of millions of youths, despite UN efforts to bring about a cease-fire. "No negotiating process could curb a war in which the egos and the mutual hatred of two leaders were decisive factors," wrote Brian Urquhart in his memoirs. Olaf Palme, the former Prime Minister of Sweden was appointed representative of the Secretary-General to try to negotiate a cease-fire between the Ayatollah Khomeini and Saddam Hussein, but the two leaders would not listen to his views. His assassination in Stockholm, while he was walking home from a movie with his wife, remained mysterious. It was an outrageous act and a great loss for the international community: Palme was the third Swedish diplomat to give his life in the service of the UN in pursuit of peace.

In 1988, however, the UN's fortunes seemed to turn around, despite the terrible financial situation caused by non-payment of the assessment in arrears for many member states, including, shockingly, the United States. That year the UN regained some prestige because of the Secretary-General's successful activity on several diplomatic fronts. This opened new possibilities for similar actions by the UN and proved that multilateralism is capable of achieving results.

Securing of a peaceful solution in Afghanistan came about when the Geneva Accords were signed in April 1988 under the auspices of the Secretary-General, and were co-guaranteed by the U.S. and the USSR after several years of hard mediation. That year a cease-fire was reached in the eight-year Iran-Iraq war, and the independence of Namibia drew near to hand, enabling the Secretariat to ready itself to supervise general elections the next year in the territory and to assist in the task of nation-building. A negotiated settlement of all aspects of the Cyprus problem was in view. Dialogues were to be initiated in Cambodia and in Western Sahara. All this was expected to bring about important operations for the UN in the months to come, provided, of course, that the necessary funds for all these new activities could be found.

The future of the UN grew brighter with the improvement in international relations at the global level between the two superpowers. In August 1987, as I started these memoirs, I wrote in the foreword, "A day will come when the superpowers will become convinced that the UN can be used in their own interest, and to a much greater extent than today. This may happen sooner than one thinks." A few years later there can be little doubt that this point was being reached, as the two superpowers' trust of each other continued to grow from 1988 to 1990.

With the meetings between Ronald Reagan and Mikhail Gorbachev the superpowers began a process of arms limitation. They signed an INF treaty and sincerely engaged in the control of long-range nuclear weapons and in the reduction of conventional forces. The threat of global war and the extinction of mankind was no longer on everyone's minds. We could breathe: we knew that no one can win a nuclear war, although the fear of nuclear weapons proliferation still existed.

In his speech at the UN on December 8, 1988, Gorbachev asked for what amounted to a new world and the saving of our civilization. He offered unilateral troop cutbacks and said, "We feel that member states must review their attitude toward the United Nations, this unique instrument without which world politics would be inconceivable today." He strongly supported UN Peacekeeping operations and said the Organization should be able to assist its members in coping with the daunting challenge of our times and should work to humanize their relations. The Soviet leader's words presented not only a great challenge in Soviet-American relations, but an invitation to create a new international community. They suggested such an immense transformation in the way the Soviet Union usually conducted its foreign policy that one could wonder if, in view of the deteriorating internal situation in the USSR, Gorbachev would be able to achieve such change. Some asked whether the speech was shrewd Soviet propaganda at a time when the United States had clearly decreased its support to the UN.

Much greater change was to occur in 1989 and 1990 in the relationships of the two superpowers. An accelerated pace of negotiations and consultations took place during that span. Both sides promised a new world order.

Then, on August 2 1990, the world faced a new challenge when Saddam Hussein, the megalomaniac dictator President of Iraq, invaded Kuwait. The UN Security Council, by a thirteen-to-two vote, asked Iraq to withdraw immediately and unconditionally from Kuwait in an unprecedented group of 12 resolutions that drew the full support of four of the five permanent members. China abstained. In applying Article 42 of the Charter, one of the 12 resolutions called for full economic sanctions against Iraq, and another (Resolution 678) authorized the use of force. An international military coalition was dispatched to Saudi Arabia at that country's request, on the initiative of the United States. The force included 500,000 military men and women from 28 countries, 90 percent of them from the United States, equipped with the most modern weapons.

War broke out on January 16, 1991, one day after the withdrawal deadline set by the Security Council. Saddam Hussein had still refused to withdraw.

While still hoping that war could be avoided, President Bush addressed the UN General Assembly on October 2, 1990. On the support his country owes the United Nations, he stated:

> We must show that the United Nations is the place to build international support and consensus to deter and defeat aggression and to meet the other challenges we face: the threat to the environment, terrorism, managing the debt burden, fighting the scourge of international drug trafficking and the vast problem of refugees and peacekeeping around the world.

It struck me that the speech seemed to put an end to the ambivalence which the United States had displayed vis-a-vis the United Nations for more than a decade and that a green light had been given by the President so the U.S. could again be a leader in the strengthening and greater use of the United Nations.

But before the UN can be in position to fully work for the promised New World

Order, stability in the Middle East will have to be restored after the Gulf War and a new balance of power in the region established. The conflict between Arabs and Jews will have to be brought to an end to include settling the future of the Palestinian people, hopefully through a protracted and arduous Middle East Conference to find a formula for peace and stability in this tumultuous area, started through the tremendous mediation efforts of the United States in 1992. The UN must find a way to deal meaningfully with the wave of "ethnic cleansing" which has popped up in the former Yugoslavia and with smaller conflicts around the world—all most difficult endeavors, requiring the will of the Security Council and member states and the necessary funds.

The UN of Tomorrow

In the 1990 speech to the General Assembly in which he promised to work for a New World Order, President Bush clearly articulated a new role for the United Nations. This resulted from the moral stand taken by the U.S. against aggression and Bush's own belief in the role the U.S. should play in leading the world toward permanent peace. But his vision of a new role for the UN was also due in no uncertain part to the repeated pressure and concrete suggestions individuals and associations in the United States had put forward for several years on how to change the attitude of the Federal Administration in regard to the world body so it could again, in the U.S. national interest, play the determinant role set out for it in the UN Charter.

Considerable work was done in the '80s by various U.S. non-government organizations—among them the World Federalists, the League of Women Voters and the United Nations-USA Association. These groups proposed a new agenda for the world organization to the Bush Administration as it was taking office, stressing that the management of many of our problems is virtually impossible by a single nation or on a bilateral basis and that the multilateral approach of the UN is needed to solve them. I carefully followed their work and applauded their initiatives.

In New Canaan, Connecticut, on October 24, 1989, I participated in the 44th United Nations Day anniversary celebration, sponsored by the municipality and the UN Study Group.[3] The keynote speaker, Richard Gardner, a Professor of International Law at Columbia University, former Assistant Secretary of State in Washington and a champion of the multilateral approach to development, spoke of American attitudes in international relations. He said that we should blend power politics with multilateral action. He said we must be, at the same time, nationalists and internationalists, because we must recognize the interdependency of our world

---

3 New Canaan has always shown unusual support for the world organization.

and can no longer afford to be insular.

> We should reclaim our leadership in the UN and restore our traditional support for the United Nations Development Program as the main institution in the world for technical assistance and pre-investment activities. This support declined by one-third in real terms during recent years. The United States should be willing to resume our membership in UNESCO under its new management.

He also advocated a greater role for the International Atomic Energy Agency (IAEA), a UN Specialized Agency located in Vienna, which was created in 1953 on the recommendation of President Eisenhower as part of his "Atoms for Peace" program. The Agency demonstrated valuable leadership in giving warning and international technical assistance during the Chernobyl disaster. Later it did an exceptional job of destroying nuclear installations of Saddam Hussein after the Gulf War. No doubt the Agency could provide increased assistance in similar future disasters and help make nuclear installations safer all over the world.

Various other UN agencies also should be strengthened because of the remarkable work they are already doing which could be expanded to solve more of the threatening problems facing the world. Regarding drug control, the UN already has put forward important proposals, including a treaty for the apprehension and extradition of drug criminals, and measures to deal with crop substitution and drug prevention. The World Health Organization has tackled the AIDS problem globally and could become a major force in combating this terrible disease.

A decline in the birthrate is a critical element in solving the overall problems of the developing countries and the world as a whole. The role of the United Nations Fund for Population Activities (UNFPA), which has contributed excellent work toward this end, should be enhanced. World population, now five billion, will reach eight billion at the beginning of the next century even, if Third World families limit their size to two children. It could reach 12 to 15 billion by the end of the millennium if nothing is done to control its growth rate—now estimated at three births a second. Each hour brings 11,000 more mouths to feed—more than 95 million a year.[4] Yet global food production per capita is declining. This is particularly alarming in many developing countries, where population grows at an explosive rate. Many such countries have committed themselves to reducing their birthrate through family planning programs assisted by the UN. The international community should help the financing of many of these programs through a greater use of the UN Population Fund and other agencies such as the World Bank, and through non-governmental

---

4 Paul and Anne Ehrlich, *The Population Explosion* (New York: Simon & Schuster, 1990).

organizations like Planned Parenthood, Oxfam and Care.

Another foreboding prospect is the exodus of the farm population to the cities, the mushrooming of ghettos populated by the unemployed, and the projected burgeoning of the capital cities of certain developing countries to such gigantic proportions that they become unmanageable. A metropolis like Mexico City, for example, now hosts close to 20 million people and may reach 40 million by the end of the 21st century. International organizations are studying these problems and are beginning to advise local governments. They could carry out specific programs in the inner cities if funds were made available.

In the field of human rights, the UN has contributed a Universal Declaration and Covenants which are major achievements. UN debates over the years, however, have reflected regrettable double standards: in the past Israel and Chile were regularly denounced for violating human rights, but never the Soviet Union, East European countries or, until recently, Iran. This has all changed. The UN is beginning to send observers of human rights violations to a number of countries in crisis such as El Salvador, Nicaragua and Haiti, as well as teams to supervise elections.

Most importantly, the UN can play a considerably greater role in preserving and managing the global system against ozone depletion, acid rain, global warming, ocean pollution, disposal of nuclear waste, quality of ground water, etc. which all call for action better addressed at the multilateral level.

As the problems of global warming, air and water pollution, acid rain—the steady deterioration of our global environment—become more serious, greater scope should be given to the United Nations Environment Program to help solve them; the problem is global and can be solved only by a multilateral approach outlined in a new UN Agenda for Sustainable Development, based on the recommendations of the UN Conference on Environment and Development (UNCED) held in Rio de Janerio in June, 1992.

The task is urgent. The release of carbon dioxide into the atmosphere has increased by 20 percent since 1850. If nothing is done to change this trend, temperatures may rise by between 2.5°F and 10°F in the next fifty years. The culprits are synthetic chemicals such as CFCs (chlorofluorocarbons). This will require control programs not only in the industrialized countries producing these chemicals but also in many developing countries as they increasingly industrialize. Again the way to solve these problems is mostly multilateral.

Is the UN capable of undertaking all these tasks? Yes. A restructured United Nations, with appropriate funding, can tackle many of them in close coordination with bilateral efforts. Carlos Vegega points out in the letter quoted in Part III that a "reservoir of knowledge, expertise and dedication ... is available in the system. The importance of this resevoir of resources should be emphasized, especially when it appears that a decision has been taken, at the political level, to revitalize the Organization." A new world order depends on the political will of UN members to start and finance new UN programs, granting them sovereignty so that their execution is not hampered by political misunderstanding and bickering.

Outstanding progress by the international community was shown recently in repulsing Iraq's aggression against Kuwait by proclaiming a right to intervene and then actually intervening in countries which violate the rights of minorities and practice ethnic cleansing. We must also applaud recent proposals to create an international tribunal to listen to the claims of attacked minorities and condemn leaders accused of genocide and other crimes against humanity. This new institution will complement the work of the International Court of Justice, which adjudicates claims between governments.

In my view the most important part of the UN agenda is the creation of a versatile permanent UN military force, well equipped with brigades ready to act at any time, which could intervene and prevent aggression between neighboring states, or stop violence, civil disturbances and ethnic conflicts before they degenerate into full-scale wars.

The Role of the People

People also can help maintain peace on this Earth. I am convinced we need both the efforts of our political leaders and strong popular support. If the people want to overcome the forces opposed to peace they must work for it. One UN Secretary-General wrote that "the charter of the United Nations specifically talks of people and not governments. If leaders are unable to draw the all-important political conclusions, it will have to be the people who do so. More clearly than ever before, the people, regardless of frontiers, will have to make it patently clear that they do not want preparations for war, but designs for peace."[5] In 1959, President Eisenhower expressed that same view: "I like to believe that people in the long run are going to do more to promote peace than Governments. I think the people want peace so much that, one of these days, Governments had better get out of the way and let them have it."[6]

---

5 Kurt Waldheim, *In the Eye of the Storm* (Bethesda, Md.: Alder & Alder, 1986), 265.
6 Benjamin B. Ferencz and Ken Keys, Jr., *Planethood* (Loveline Books, Coos Bay, Oregon, 1991), 137.

To obtain this popular contribution, public opinion must be mobilized and organized along democratic lines. First the people will have to be educated for peace rather than for war. This will require a new set of school programs for children all over the world, giving them a "global" education.

Churches since the end of World War II have assumed an important role in denouncing the arms race. Many spiritual leaders have recognized that the arms race is primarily a moral and spiritual issue that must concern us all. Evangelist Billy Graham has expressed his conviction that political answers alone will not suffice, and that it is now time for us to urge the world to turn to spiritual solutions as well. Pope John-Paul II agreed, saying that humanity must make a moral about-face if we want to survive. He held that the earth belongs to us all, and we must cherish it in peace and in true brotherhood. In a speech before the UN General Assembly, October 4, 1965, Pope Paul VI echoed the idea by declaring that the progress of humanity must be measured not only by the progress of technology which shows man's uniqueness with regard to nature, but also, and chiefly, by the primacy given to spiritual values and by the progress of moral life. His Holiness Dalai Lama acknowledged the enormity of the task when he noted that, although attempting to bring about world peace through the transformation of individuals is difficult, it is the only way.[7]

As we know, non-governmental organizations all over the world, but particularly in the United States, are doing a great deal for peace, each in its own field studying the problem of peace, to bring people together across borders and to start concrete projects which will help the world's poor. I believe they should participate in the decision-making of the UN where often they bring more expertise than may be found among the delegates attending intergovernmental meetings.

Each concerned citizen also has a role to play. What that role may be will depend on the individual's interests and capabilities. Dr. Benjamin Ferencz suggests that some may be able to express an opinion in private, others may cast a vote, write a letter, sign a petition, write a book. Some may lead or join a march, run for peace, make a speech, teach a class or make a cash contribution to the worthy cause. Each person has an obligation to maintain peace today for future generations and to take such non-violent measures toward that end as may be within his or her power.[8]

To involve the people in the study of the peace process, a United Nations Peace University opened in Tokyo in 1975. A University for Peace, created by a UN Resolution, was also established in Costa Rica in 1983. Ferencz, an author-professor

---

7 H.H. The Dalai Lama, *A Human Approach to World Peace* (Boston: Wisdom Publications, 1989).
8 Ferencz, Benjamin, *A Common Sense Guide to World Peace* (Dobbs Ferry, NY: Oceana, 1985).

of International Law and former U.S. Prosecutor at the Nuremberg Trials, has proposed the creation of a Permanent Council for Peace, made up of independent and highly respected world personalities. This Council, backed by an educated and organized public, could speak with a powerful voice for public opinion to the governments of the world and serve as a mediator in helping conflicting parties resolve their differences by peaceful means. It has been proved that, properly applied on governments, the pressure of world opinion can have an irresistible effect on peace. The recent demise of Communism brought about by the peoples of Eastern Europe dramatically demonstrates it.

All these actions directed toward change at the national level prove that the people can take an active stand in favor of world peace if they want to. They can force governments to reduce their armaments. In this, much remains to be done. The military expenditures of the two superpowers until recently were between $700 and $800 billion per year, compared to between $1 and $2 billion for the UN: the world could do wonders if only a fraction of these sums were turned to peace and development.

Strong objections by people all over the world should force governments and private arms merchants to stop supplying weapons to the developing nations. Such an embargo would be the greatest imaginable step in preventing local wars, returning stability to many corners of the world.

The public has only one enemy: its sense of helplessness. Dr. Scott Peck, MD, said in one of his best- selling books, "Ultimately all that is required for peace is that we overcome our lethargy and resistance to change."[9] Lord Mountbatten, weary of our apathy, once wondered how we can stand by and do nothing to prevent the destruction of our world.

Global Education

Peace, and progress toward a stable and prosperous world, depend on a proper global education for all children of the world. School programs should include lessons which will teach them the realities of our world today. They are beginning to know more about the problem of maintaining peace and protecting the environment, but knowing more about the world organization and what its Specialized Agencies do can teach the children a great deal about how to solve current and future world problems. Most of what they have been taught in history concerns wars. It is time to talk to them more about how the world can live in peace. They should know

---

9 Peck, Scott M. *The Different Drum: Community- Making and Peace* (New York: Simon and Schuster, 1987), 263.

much more about geography, a subject in which the ignorance of American children—and adults—is appalling. (In a survey just before the onset of the Persian Gulf War, 75 percent of the adults surveyed could not locate the Gulf on a map.) The children should be taught more about the peoples of the world, their differences in beliefs and religions so that they will learn tolerance. As an anonymous proverb says: "As long as you cannot forgive the next man for being different, you are still far from the path of wisdom".

Ted Turner, head of the Turner Broadcasting System, is President of the new movement called the For a Better World Society, of which I am a founding contributor, whose purpose is to make television movies and videos that promote peace and the protection of the environment. Widely distributed, these films have already played a distinct role in educating the public on the problems of peace, the environment and development—a welcome change from the cheap violence, crime and war which dominate American TV. Addressing representatives of non-governmental organizations at UN Headquarters, Turner suggested that children should be taught one common international language as a second language to facilitate international cooperation and student exchanges. He reasoned that a common language would enable them to discuss world issues together and exchange new ideas and resolutions on peace and thereby accelerate the process of establishing world peace.

Interestingly enough, countries whose children routinely speak several languages, such as the Netherlands and Scandinavian countries, make, per capita, the greatest financial contributions to international cooperation in the UN development programs. Their young men and women, knowing foreign languages, are better equipped to accept other cultures, to show understanding of the problems of the world's poor, and to want to help them.[10]

I strongly believe that the introduction of global education is among the greatest reforms we can bring to educational systems throughout the world. UNESCO, UNICEF and concerned non-governmental organizations are already proposing new curricula to that effect. Recently the UNESCO Associated Schools Project in Education for International Cooperation and Peace, comprising secondary schools and teacher-training institutions in different parts of the world, was extended to include primary schools. The project teaches the approaches which are appropriate and applicable to any class at the primary level for the purpose of promoting

---

[10] Turner said that he had instructed his news services to try not to use the word foreign in describing events, but rather to substitute the word international. On this planet, Turner said, "we're not foreigners, we are neighbors." *UN Secretariat News*, 1990.

international understanding. Robert Muller, recipient of the 1989 UNESCO Prize for Peace Education, created the Robert Muller Elementary School in Texas, an experimental school in global education which should be a model for many such schools in the future. Many more schools should follow those experiments and go on to develop models of their own.

Is World Government the Future?

> *The United Nations is an important and useful institution provided the peoples and governments of the world realize that it is merely a transitional system toward a final goal, which is the establishment of a supranational authority vested with sufficient legislative and executive powers to keep the peace.*
>
> Albert Einstein

In 1946, as I was returning from the war, I was impressed by a widely read book entitled *The Anatomy of Peace*, which called for a democratic reorganization of human society. According to Emery Reves, wars always start between groups which exercise unrestricted power—tribes, dynasties, churches, cities, nations. Wars between these social units cease the moment sovereign power is transferred from them to a larger unit. Reves argued that the problem of peace is the problem of sovereignty. At a very early stage of human society, we discovered that—before we could live together as a family, tribe or nation—an elder, a chief, or a king had to impose certain restraints upon natural aggressions. In the 18th century a great change occurred. The principle that the law-making authority should be the people themselves was recognized, leading to the creation of the American and French republics and to the parliamentary systems of England and many other countries.[11]

By tracing the history of our institutions Reves showed that in the modern age the completely independent state is obsolete. He insisted that local affairs could be handled by local governments, and national affairs by national governments, but the regulation of international affairs and the maintenance of peace require a form of world government. *The Anatomy of Peace* reflects the position of the World Federalists who say the UN is too weak to govern; it has no powers and has not been able to stop wars. We still live under a war system. There is no enforcement for World Court decisions. What is needed to enforce peace, according to the World Federalists, is a World Democratic Republic providing for an international Congress to pass laws, an International Court to apply the laws and an Executive Branch to enforce them through a "United Nations of the World."

---

11 Emery Reves, *Anatomy of Peace* (New York: Harper Brothers, 1945).

They further observe that Americans achieved a nationhood through the Constitution of the United States of America which leaves all powers in the hands of individual states except those involving other states or nations. The Founding Fathers designed a government for the United States which left each nation-state (the thirteen separate states) in control of almost all decisions that affected its own citizens. They kept at the state level their own legislatures minimizing the risk of interstate conflict. In the United States, disagreements between states are settled legally—not lethally as in much of today's world. Because of the wise checks and balances that limit the power of Congress, the Supreme Court and the Executive Branch, no dictator can seize control of the Government of the United States. They conclude that this should also apply to a World Government.

Is it naive to think along those lines? There is no doubt that this is the answer to world peace, the distant goal to reach. The democratic concept of sovereignty means the transfer of sovereign rights from one man to all men, the people, i.e., the community. In our system today community means nations, a base which has become too narrow in the interdependent world in which we live. Nationalism tends to divide our world into small independent groups. The World Federalists see this as an insurmountable obstacle to free industrial programs, individual liberty, and social security.

Carl Van Duren in *The Great Rehearsal*[12] explains that in 1787 the problem was how the American people could learn to think nationally, not locally. Today the problem is how the people can learn to think globally.[13] How can those who call the vision of world government naive and impractical, not be impressed and (I hope) convinced by such notables as George Washington, Ulysses Grant, Theodore Roosevelt, Albert Einstein, Bertrand Russell, Winston Churchill, Dwight Eisenhower, Douglas MacArthur, Golda Meir, John Kennedy, Norman Cousins and many others? Because of their authority as world leaders and thinkers, I have thought it important to reproduce some of their better-known quotations in an appendix to this book.

At the Mid-Atlantic Conference on United Nations Reform and Restructure held at Villanova University in November 1978, Norman Cousins, Adjunct Professor of Medicine at the University of Southern California and a man who campaigned tirelessly for such humanitarian causes as world government, disarmament and peace, said that we must understand that the nation-state, though it is the highest

---

12 Carl Van Duren, *The Great Rehearsal* (Westport, Ct.: Greenwood, 1987).
13 Today a popular environmental-movement bumper sticker in Vermont encourages people to "Think globally, act locally."

Dawn of a New Era 349

achievement of man to date, can no longer accomplish its historic purpose unless it becomes part of a system of structured world interdependence. Cousins looked forward to a time when the human race will become truly civilized—when we at last have an institution to represent the human species as a whole. That is what the United Nations is all about. Cousins wanted to reform the United Nations so that it could properly represent the human species by providing a rule of law to which all nations must conform.

At the same meeting, Robert Muller, former United Nations Assistant Secretary-General, echoed those thoughts when he said that he would predict that, save for a nuclear holocaust or accident, the UN and its functional agencies and programs are the most powerful force for peace humanity has ever created, and will progressively become the global brain, nervous system, heart and soul of a human species transcending and evolving into an entirely new, global period of civilization.

Personally, I believe World Government will come. We will not see it in our day and at this stage nobody knows when the people of the world will be ready for it. We must, however, hope. It will require a complete change of the mentality of people and better education. We must remember that the creation of the United States of America was facilitated greatly by the Revolutionary War, the desire to go forward and the fact that English was the common language of the land. In Europe, while the idea of political and economic union has made tremendous progress in the last decade, culminating with the Maastricht Treaty not yet fully ratified by all European Parliaments, the people of many nations, speaking different languages, are still unsure whether they want to become citizens of a politically united Europe, as they stay closely attached to their own cultures. This will undoubtedly slow up the process of integration. We must never lose hope, and we must work hard toward a greater world integration every step of the way for a system encompassing preventive diplomacy, crisis management, peace keeping and peace enforcement, thereby "filling the gap between the real and ideal world."[15] The movement for more multilateral action through the UN is slowly progressing, but nationalism is still extremely strong. People are only now beginning to realize the truth in the words of Robert McNamara, Secretary of Defense in the Kennedy Administration and former President of the World Bank, who argued that if we want to survive, we must allow some of our sovereignty to be transferred to an international institution.[16]

Perhaps one of our greatest achievements in recent years has been for the UN to begin to enforce the principle that the world community has the right to intervene

---

15 Robert McNamara, *To Unite Our Strength* (Lanham: University Press of America, 1993), Preface.
16 Ibid.

through humanitarian action and military enforcement in countries at war, as in Bosnia and Somalia, to defend the interests of local populations who are being annihilated, as in the case of ethnic cleansing. In my view, this is not yet good enough, but we are working in a very important new aspect of international relations.

Progress toward a better distribution of wealth and a prosperous united world representing a true New World Order can only be attained step by step. While we are still far from world government, we must first focus on these four essential issues that work in that direction:

- maintaining peace and security through permanent collective security;
- significantly reducing the gap between the haves and the have nots, which would be financed in large measure by the conversion of most military assistance to developmental assistance;
- solving the global problems threatening survival of our planet;
- opening greater access to world trade for the developing countries, coupled with a reduction of their debts and an increase in direct foreign investment.

Epilogue

Epilogue

In the 1850s my grandfather was conscripted and gave seven years of his life to the French Army participating in Napoleon III's campaigns in Italy. In 1912 my father died at age 28; had he lived he likely would have fought and perhaps died in the bloody trenches of the First Great War. I fought in two armies in the Second World War, hoping it would be the last, but since then more than one hundred regional wars have broken out in various parts of the world. Yet, in 1993, there is renewed hope that a new drive for peace among all nations may banish war through a new and reformed United Nations.

I believe in the human spirit. I believe we can achieve peace on Earth, but only if we exercise the will to create the conditions that nurture peace.

I have been blessed. Born a citizen of the United States and reared a Frenchman, I was given the chance to share the culture of two of the world's greatest democracies. Further, I had the great privilege of raising a wonderful family in a country that encourages us to grow according to our desires. Even further, I had the extraordinary privilege of working for years in the United Nations.

At the UN, I enjoyed the honor of acquiring an inside view of the problems affecting world peace and world development on a globe so full of contradictions, and to work for these two great causes so closely linked. I wish I had been able to do more; looking back over the path of my life I see myself as just a small drop in the tumultuous flow of the river which carries mankind to its destiny. I remain full of hope for the future. My contribution has been modest, but I believe my life and that of my colleagues and their multitude of experiences can serve younger generations, not only those who want to go into international service, but all young men and women.

In closing these memoirs, my mind returns to the day I stood at the gate of the United Nations on the East River, ready to enter its new Headquarters, thinking of my buddies in the Fourth Armored Division who did not come home from the war. Thanks to the UN, the risk of another world war is now minimal.

A strengthened United Nations is our best instrument to deter aggression and to take the people of the world to a better life. It remains our only hope. Even in our violent and often war-torn world, where ignorance and misery exist in so many areas, mankind is progressing day by day. We must remain optimistic.

Appendices

APPENDIX I

The UN System: United Nations Organs, Specialized Agencies and Special Programs

The United Nations comprises six principal organs:
- the General Assembly;
- the Security Council;
- the Economic and Social Council;
- the Trusteeship Council;
- the International Court of Justice;
- the Secretariat.

All are based at UN headquarters in New York, except for the Court, which is located at The Hague.

Related by agreement to the United Nations and working in close cooperation with it are 17 UN Specialized Agencies:
- the International Labor Organization (ILO);
- the Food and Agriculture Organization (FAO);
- the World Health Organization (WHO);
- the United Nations Educational, Scientific and Cultural Organization (UNESCO);
- the International Board for Reconstruction and Development (IBRD);
- the International Developmental Association (IDA);
- the International Finance Corporation (IFC);
- the International Monetary Fund (IMF);
- the International Civil Aviation Organization (ICAO);
- the Universal Postal Union (UPU);
- the International Telecommunication Union (ITU);
- the World Meteorological Organization (WMO);
- the International Maritime Organization (IMO);
- the General Agreement on Tariffs and Trade (GATT);
- the World Intellectual Property Organization (WIPO);
- the International Fund for Agricultural Development (IFAD);
- the World Tourism Organization (WTO).

These specialized agencies, together with the United Nations and the Special Programs, Councils and Funds, which the General Assembly sets up to implement its decisions, comprise the United Nations "System," which has grown considerably since 1946.

The 14 Special Programs are:

- the United Nations Center for Human Settlements (Habitat);
- the United Nations Development Program (UNDP);
- the United Nations Children's Fund (UNICEF);
- the World Food Program;
- the United Nations Fund for Population Activities (UNFPA);
- the UN Conference on Trade and Development (UNCTAD);
- the United Nations Program for Drug Abuse Control (UNDAC);
- the United Nations Environment Program (UNEF);
- the United Nations Disaster Relief Coordinator (UNDRC);
- the United Nations High Commission for Refugees (UNHCR);
- the United Nations Industrial Development Organization (UNIDO);
- the United Nations Institute for Training and Research (UNITAR);
- the United Nations Relief Works Agency (UNRWA);
- the United Nations Volunteers (UNV).

Appendix II

Highlights of UN History

1945: June 26, the Charter of the United Nations is signed in San Francisco.
1946: January, the General Assembly meets for the first time in London.
1947: The Assembly adopts a plan that would, at the end of the British Mandate in Palestine in 1948, partition it into an Arab State and a Jewish State with Jerusalem under UN administration.
1948 The Universal Declaration of Human Rights is adopted.
1950 The Security Council calls on member states to help the southern part of Korea repel invasion from the north.
1953: Armistice in Korea results from initiatives made at the UN.
1956: War in the Middle East over the Suez Canal is ended with the deployment of a UN peacekeeping force in the Sinai.
1957: In the wake of Sputnik, the General Assembly takes up the peaceful uses of outer space.
1959: The General Assembly adopts the Declaration of the Rights of the Child.
1960: The General Assembly assumes a much more active role in the process of decolonization.
1961: Acknowledging that economic and social development in the poorer countries is basic to the achievement of international peace and security, the General Assembly declares the 1960s the UN Development Decade.
1962: The Secretary-General plays a key role in resolving U.S. Soviet confrontation over the issue of nuclear missiles in Cuba.
1964: UN Conference on Trade and Development declares trade a "primary instrument of development."
1965: Technical assistance activities get a big boost with the merger of the Expanded Program (1949) and the Special Fund (1959) to form the UN Development Program as the major channel of funding for the specialized agencies in the UN system.
1967: After war erupts again in the Middle East, the Security Council adopts Resolution 242, which calls for withdrawal of forces from occupied territories and recognizes the right of all States in the area to security. It becomes a widely accepted basis for a settlement of the Middle East problem.
1971: The International Court of Justice, in an advisory opinion requested by the

Security Council, declares the continued presence of South Africa in Namibia "illegal."
1972: The UN Environment Conference meets in Stockholm and adopts a historic declaration on the need for new principles to govern human activities in order to safeguard the natural world.
1973: Another war in the middle East ends with new UN peacekeeping forces in the Sinai and the Golan Heights.
1974: The Assembly calls for a New International Economic Order as a stable basis for interdependent world economy.
1975: World Conference of the International Women's Year convenes in Mexico City and adopts the Declaration on Equality of Women and Their Contribution to Development and Peace.
1977: The Security Council makes the arms embargo against South Africa mandatory.
1979: The General Assembly adopts the Convention on the Elimination of Discrimination Against Women.
1980: As the result of an international campaign coordinated by the World Health Organization, smallpox is totally eradicated from the world.
1982: The Conference convened by the Assembly adopts what could be the most significant legal instrument of the century, the wide-ranging Convention on the Law of the Sea.
1984: The General Assembly adopts the Convention Against Torture.
1985: The Office for Emergency Operations, created by the Secretary-General, spearheads a massive famine relief effort in Africa.
1987: The UN Environment Program obtains international agreement and signature of a world convention on the protection of the ozonosphere.
1988: The UN helps to cause the withdrawal of Soviet troops from Afghanistan.
1989: The UN establishes a special trust fund to enable even poor nations to bring disputes before the World Court.
1990: The Security Council, in an unprecedented and unanimous enforcement of the rule of law, imposes an escalating series of economic sanctions against Iraq for its August invasion of Kuwait.
1990: The UN helps to bring independence to Namibia and to move South Africa away from its inhumane support of apartheid.
1990: The International Law commission and the UN Legal Committee resumes consideration of an International Criminal Court to deal with drug trafficking and other international crimes.

APPENDIX III

THE PROMOTION OF PEACE: FAMOUS QUOTES

There is only one thing stronger than all the armies of the world and that is an idea whose time has come.

Victor Hugo

* * *

The primary cause of all disorders lies in the different state governments and in the tenacity of that power which pervades the whole world of their systems.

President George Washington

* * *

I am convinced that the Great Framer of the World will so develop it that it becomes one nation, so that armies and navies are no longer necessary. . . . I believe at some future day, the nations of the earth will agree upon some sort of congress which will take cognizance of international questions of difficulty and whose decisions will be as binding as the decisions of our Supreme Court are on us.

President Ulysses S. Grant

* * *

You cannot erect a peace system on a basis of the coercion of governments by governments, because that is trying to build a peace system on the foundation of war. The only basis for a peace system is a pooling of sovereignty for supernational purposes, that is the creation of a common nationhood, above but entirely separate from the diverse local nationhoods."

Philip Henry Kerr
Marquis of Lothian
Burge Memorial Lecture, 1935

* * *

Abolition of war is no longer an ethical question to be pondered solely by learned philosophers and ecclesiastics, but a hard core one for the decision of the masses whose survival is the issue. Many will tell you with mockery and ridicule that the abolition of war can only be a dream . . . . But we must go on or we will go under! We must have new thoughts, new ideas, new concepts. We must break out of the straitjacket of the past. We must have sufficient imagination and courage to translate the universal wish for peace—which is rapidly becoming a universal necessity—into actuality.

General Douglas MacArthur

* * *

I have long believed the only way that peace can be achieved is through World Government.

Prime Minister Jawaharlal Nehru of India

* * *

Internationalism does not mean the end of individual nations. Orchestras don't mean the end of violins.

Prime Minister Golda Meir of Israel

* * *

The federal idea, which our Founding Fathers applied in their historical act of political creation in the eighteenth century, can be applied in this twentieth century in the larger context of the world of free nations—if we will but match our forefathers in courage and vision.

Nelson A. Rockefeller
The Future of Federalism
Harvard University Press

* * *

We must create world-wide law and law enforcement as we outlaw world-wide war and weapons.

President John F. Kennedy

* * *

It is high time for humanity to accept and work out the full consequences of the total global and interdependent nature of our planetary home and of our species. Our survival and further progress will depend largely on the advent of proper global education in all countries of the world.

Robert Muller
Former UN Assistant Secretary-General

* * *

Index

A
Abomey, Bénin 309
Abrams, Lt. Col. Creighton 99
Acheson, Dean 35
Adu, Amishadai 236
Afghanistan 338
Aglion, Raoul 112
al Krim, Abed 176
Alphand, Hervé 29, 55, 59
Amboselli Game Park, Kenya 237
American Export Line 52
Amin, Idi 249, 253
André, Antonio 211
Anstee, Joan 169
Aristide, Jean-Bertrand 228
Avranches, France 86

B
Baker, Samuel 247
Barbot, Clément 207
Barka, Madhi Ben 179
Barnea, Jospeh 133
Bartholdi, Frédérick-Auguste 7
Batchelor, Owen 278
bauxite 287
Bazin, Rene 18
Beaucourt, France 6, 15, 50
Behoteguy, Scott 106
Belfort, France 21
Bellegrade, Dantes 219
Bénin 305
..Brazilians in 312
..Chinese assistance 321
..cult of the ancestors 313
..Development Plan 305, 318, 323
..impact of French colonization 314
..Marxism-Leninism adopted 321
..military takeover, 1972 317
..North Korean assistance 321
..Western assistance 325
Bennett, Michèle (Mrs. Jean-Claude
..Duvalier) 227
Berbers 188
Bermuda 44
Bernadotte, Count Folk 141
Besançon, France 15
Bishop Burton 66
Bleyfus, George 5
Bleyfus, Lucien 8
Block, Ed 74
Blum, Léon 33
Bosch, Juan 208
Bourguiba, Habib 174
Bowers, John 185
Bradley, General Omar 3, 92
Broadway, England 77
Bunche, Ralph 132
Burgos, Spain 21
Bush, George 339

C
Camp Ritchie, Maryland 74-75
Cape Haitian 59
Cauvin, Pierre 307
Chalmers, René 208
Chidzero, Bernard 236
Chile 117
Church House, England 113
Churchill, Winston 233
Cohen, Myer 155
Cordier, Andrew 132
Corley-Smith, Gerald 223
Cotonou, Bénin 306
Cousins, Norman 348
Creole 202
Cyprus
..citrus crop 267
..crisis, 1964 262
..food survey 272
..peacekeeping operation, 1964 261, 273
..population, 1960 262
..raid on Kokkina 269
..Turkish invasion, 1974 273
..Zurich-London Agreements, 1959 263

D
Dar-es-Salaam, Tanganyika 251
Dasle, France 3, 6-8, 10-11, 15
de Breuvery, Emmanuel 133
de Chetelat, Enzo 308
de Gaulle, Charles 48, 57
de Tocqueville, Alexis 173
Dietrich, Marlene 98

Dinesen, Isak 244
Draper, William, III 156
Dumbarton Oaks 85
Dunkirk, France 44
Duvalier, Dr. François (Papa Doc) 202, ..204
Duvalier, Jean-Claude (Baby Doc) 209, ..224, 227

E
Einstein, Albert 348
Eisenhower, Dwight 92, 343, 348
Enghien-les-Bains, France 10
Enosis 263
Entebbe, Uganda 234
Estimé, Dumarsais 204
Etchats, Raymond 118
European Parliament 18

F
Faine, Simone Olive (Mrs. François ..Duvalier) 205, 225
Falaise Gap, France 91
Faraj, Fouad 180
Ferencz, Dr. Benjamin 344
Fez, Morocco 192
Fobes, John 160
Folsom, Bob 67, 224
Foote, Sir Hugh 237
Fort Custer, Missouri 72
France
  ..*Action Française* 32
  ..*Confédération Générale du Travail* 33
  ..*Croix de Feu* 33
  ..*École des Hautes Études Commerciales* 20, 26, 41
  ..Free French 52
  ..*Front Populaire* 33
  ..*les Grandes Écoles* 26
  ..Ministry of Commerce and Industry 24
  ..Radical Socialists 32
  ..*Solidarité Française* 32
Franco, Francisco 23

G
Gallieni, General Joseph Simon 11
Gardner, Richard 340
Garreau-Dombasle, Maurice 56
Ghaddaffi, Mohamar 255-256
Giscard d'Estaing, Valery 163
Gorbachev, Mikhail 338

H
Hahn, Captain Maurice 83
Haiti 199
  ...American occupation (1915-1934) 203
  ...Richardot declared *persona non grata* 221
  ...sanctions against 229
  ...*Service Nationale des Endemies Majeures* ...... (SNE) 226
  ...*Tontons Macoute* 203, 219-220
  ...visit by Pope John Paul II 227
Haitian National Palace 203
Hammarskjöld, Dag 136-137, 141, 145
Hassan II (king of Morocco) 179
Heinl, Nancy 199
Heinl, Robert 199
Henry, Paul-Marc 155
Hessel, Stéphane 132
Hiss, Alger 111
Hoffman, Paul 155, 235
Hôpital Foch, Suresnes, France 44
Hotel Oloffson, Haiti 63, 213
Hussein, Saddam 339

I
Ibrahim, Abdallah Moulay 178
International Red Cross 269

J
Jackson, Sir Robert 156
Jamaica
  ...cockpit country 287
  ...election of 1972 294
  ...gun courts 291
  ...*Maroons* 287
  ...People's National Party (PNP) 295
  ...population, 1970 292
  ...racial mosaic 293
  ...Rastafarians 295
  ...Reggae music 296
  ...violence in 290
  ...youth development 281, 283-284, 290
  ...youth employment 280
Jamaican Labor Party (JLP) 295
Jebb, Gladwyn 113
Jumelle, Clément 206

K
Kampala, Uganda 235, 239
Katanga, Congo 144
Kater, Adrianus 181
Keenleyside, Hugh 153, 175
Kerekou, Mathieu 319, 326
Khrushchev, Nikita 144
Kingston, Jamaica 277
Korean Crisis, 1950 140
L
La Guardia Airport 36
La Guardia, Fiorello 35
La Haye-du-Puits, France 80-81
Labarthe Family 30
Labarthe, Émile 30
  .. *Comité Parlementaire du Commerce* 31
Lacour-Gayet, Robert 55
LaGuardia, Fiorello 43
Lake Albert, Uganda 247
Lake Success, New York 115
Lake Victoria, Uganda 246
Lalla Mimouna, Morocco 185
Laval, Pierre 48
Lawrence, Vin 278
League of Nations 33
Leclerc, General Phillipe 90, 103
Leopoldville, Congo 145
Lewis, Stephen 149
Lie, Trygve 111, 136
Lisbon, Portugal 52
Lyautey, Marshal Louis 177
M
MacMillan, Harold 31
Makarios, Archbishop of Cyprus 264
Makerere College, Uganda 237, 243
Manley, Michael 295-296, 298-299, 301
Marrakesh, Morocco 189
Matthews, Freeman 51
McCarthy, Joseph 132
McCarthy, Mary 5
McLean, Peter 253
McNamara, Robert 349
Middle East
  .. Palestine Crisis, 1947-1948 140
  .. Suez Canal War, 1956 141

Middlebury College, Middlebury,
  .. Vermont 335
Moffitt, George 65
Monnet, Jean 42
Mont St-Michel, France 88
Montbéliard, France 5
Montgomery, Field Marshall Bernard 97
Moore, O. Earnest 224
Morgan Bank 55
Morocco 173, 175
  .. *douar* 182
  .. *fellah* 182
  .. *jemaa* 183
  .. Operation Ploughing 186
  .. *Promotion Nationale* 186
Moselle River 99
Mountbatten, Lord Louis 345
Moynihan, Daniel Patrick 147
Muller, Robert 16, 133, 152, 349
Murchison Falls, Uganda 247, 249
Murphy, Bob 51
Museveni, Yoseri 257
Mutesa II 240
N
Nairobi, Kenya 234
Nancy, France 15
Narasimhan, C.V. 151
National Broadcasting Company 70
Ndola, Northern Rhodesia 145
Nedzelnedsky, Lt. Oleg 90
New Canaan, Ct. 125
New International Economic Order
  .. (NIEO) 161
New World Information and
  .. Communication Order 160
Nice, France 17
Nicosia, Cyprus 267
O
Obote, Milton 242, 256
Olivier, Marcel 34
Ouidah, Bénin 311
Owen, David 113, 131, 199, 235
P
Pagny-sur-Moselle, France 99
Palestine Crisis, 1947-1948 140
Palme, Olaf 337

Patterson, P.J. 300
Patton, General George S. 87, 90-91, 97
Peck, Dr. Scott 345
Penchayats 174
Perez de Cuellar, Xavier 149
Pétain, Marshal Henri-Phillipe 14, 47, 57
Peugeot 6
Piccard, Professor Auguste 23
Plaza, Galo 267
Pleven, René 59
Pope John-Paul II 344
Pope Paul VI 344
Port Royal, Jamaica 288
Port-au-Prince, Haiti 61
Prebisch, Raul 121
préparation militaire supérieure 41
Prince Saddrudin Aga Khan 158
Pusta, Karel 74, 84
R
Rabat, Morocco 175
Ramadan 193
Rateau, Captain 101
Reagan, Ronald 338
Rennes, France 88
Reynaud, Paul 48
Richardson, Elliot 164
Rockefeller Foundation 68
Roosevelt, Franklin Delano 54
Rukidi, George, III (King of Toro) 245
Rusk, Dean 166
Santa Cruz, Hernan 117
Santander, Spain 22
Santiago, Chile 117
Sarajevo, Bosnia 9
Sarrebourg, France 103
Schmidgall, Frank 181
seabed resources 163-164
Seaga, Edward 295, 299-300
Second World Conference on Environment and Development, Brazil, ..1992 159, 342
Selassie, Haile 295
Sheehan, Bill 81
Shirer, William 25
Singer, Hans 131

Soglo, Nicethore 326
Speke, John 245
Spence School, New York 6
SS Excalibur 54
SS Exochorda 42
SS Normandie 34
SS Queen Mary 76
St-Domingue 200
St-Lo, France 80
Standard Fruit and Steamship Co. 57
Stars and Stripes (newspaper) 85, 87
Ste-Mère-l'Église, France 79
Strasbourg, France 17, 103-104
Swahili 238, 240
Szper, Andrew 74
T
Tante Amélie 4
Télédiol 213
Thant, U 136, 138
The Comedians (novel) 214
Théart, André 225
Third World 167, 169
Thurston, Raymond 222
Thymayya, General Kodendera 266
Tillon, Charles 89
Tshombe, Moise 143
Tucker, Natalie 37
Turtle Bay, New York 123
U
U.S.
...Board of Economic Warfare 72
...Caribbean Basin Initiative (CBI) 301
...Office of Foreign Liquidation 105
...State Department 105
U.S. Army
...4th Armored Division 77, 87
...General Purchasing Agent 104
Uganda
...Christianity in 241
...Islam in 241
...Israeli assistance to 242
...*Kabakas* 239
...Kingdom of Buganda 233
...National Resistance Movement 257
UNESCO, U.S. withdraws from 160

United Nations 111
.. assistance to Haiti 210
.. Children's Fund (UNICEF) 211
.. Conference on the Environment,
......Stockholm, Sweden, 1972 152
.. Conference on Trade and Development
......(UNCTAD) 122
.. Congo Operations, 1960-1961 141-142
.. Development Programs (UNDP)
......150-151, 153, 203
.. Economic and Social Council (ECOSOC)
......113, 125
.. Economic Commission for Europe (ECE)
......114
.. Economic Commission for Latin America
......(ECLA) 117, 120
.. Education, Social and Cultural
......Organization (UNESCO) 159-160
.. Emergency Force, Middle East, 1956 141
.. Environment Program 342
.. Expanded Program for Technical
......Assistance (TAA) 153
.. Food and Agriculture Organization (FAO)
......123
.. Force in Cyprus (UNFICYP) 265
.. Fund for Population Activities (UNFPA)
......341
.. General Assembly 126, 140
.. Headquarters 124
.. International Atomic Energy Agency
......(IAEA) 341
.. International Labor Organization (ILO)
......123, 277
.. Military Committee 140
.. oath of allegiance 128
.. Peace University, Japan 344
.. peacekeeping operations 274
.. recruitment of the international staff 130
.. Second Committee of the Assembly 125
.. Secretariat 127
.. Security Council 139, 339
.. Special Committee on Palestine 140
.. Technical Assistance Program 235
.. UNDP Resident Representative 218
.. University for Peace, Costa Rica 344

.. World Food Program 211
.. World Health Organization (WHO) 341
University of Paris Law School 27
Urquhart, Sir Brian 113, 133

V
Valeur, Robert 56
Van Duren, Carl 348
Vannes, France 88
Varin, Roger 22, 38
Vegega, Carlos S. 129, 343
Verdun, France 9
Vichy Government 49
Vincent, Vince 81
Von Runstedt, General 103
Voodoo 202, 215
Vosges mountains, France 10

W
Waldheim, Kurt 136
Walters, Vernon 157
Whalen, Grover 35
Wilkie, Wendell L. 54
World Bank 320
World Court 165, 347
world government 347
World War I
.. Battle of the Marne 10
.. Battle of Verdun 14
.. Trench War 11
World War II 72
.. Bastille Day 84
.. fighting in the hedgerows 80, 82
.. French Army, 2nd Armored Division 90,
......103
.. French Resistance in Brittany 89
.. liberation of Paris 93
.. Operation Cobra 86
.. Operation Market Garden 97
.. *Service de Santé Militaire* 46
.. U.S. Military Intelligence in England 77
.. Utah Beach 78
World's Fair, New York, 1939 34
Wynter, Hector 279

Y
Youssef, Mohammed Ben 180

Z
Zanzibar 240, 251

Middlebury, Vermont 1992

About the Author

Jean Bleyfus-Richardot was born in New York City, but was raised and educated in France. He holds degrees in law and economics from the University of Paris.

He served in the French and American Armies in World War II. Before the war he worked for the French Government in Paris and after the war, with U.S. State Department in Washington D.C.

Most of his career was with the United Nations Secretariat in New York and in a variety of senior assignments in the developing world.

Now retired Mr. Richardot and his wife, Natalie live in New Canaan, Connecticut and Middlebury, Vermont.